Action Cinema Since 2000

Action Cinema Since 2000

**Edited by
Chris Holmlund, Lisa Purse,
and Yvonne Tasker**

THE BRITISH FILM INSTITUTE
Bloomsbury Publishing Plc
50 Bedford Square, London, WC1B 3DP, UK
1385 Broadway, New York, NY 10018, USA
29 Earlsfort Terrace, Dublin 2, Ireland

BLOOMSBURY is a trademark of Bloomsbury Publishing Plc

First published in Great Britain 2024 by Bloomsbury
on behalf of the
British Film Institute
21 Stephen Street, London W1T 1LN
www.bfi.org.uk

The BFI is the lead organization for film in the UK and the distributor of Lottery funds for film. Our mission is to ensure that film is central to our cultural life, in particular by supporting and nurturing the next generation of filmmakers and audiences. We serve a public role which covers the cultural, creative and economic aspects of film in the UK.

Cover design by Louise Dugdale
Cover image: *Everything Everywhere All At Once*, 2022,
Courtesy Everett Collection/Mary Evans

A catalogue record for this book is available from the British Library.

A catalog record for this book is available from the Library of Congress.

ISBN: HB: 978-1-8390-2278-4
PB: 978-1-8390-2277-7
ePDF: 978-1-8390-2280-7
eBook: 978-1-8390-2279-1

Typeset by RefineCatch Limited, Bungay, Suffolk
Printed and bound in India

To find out more about our authors and books visit www.bloomsbury.com and sign up for our newsletters.

Contents

Illustrations

Contributors

Cynthia Baron is a Professor in the Department of Theatre and Film and the doctoral American Culture Studies Program at Bowling Green State University. She is the author of *Modern Acting* (2016) and *Denzel Washington* (2015), co-author of *Acting Indie* (2020), *Appetites and Anxieties* (2014), and *Reframing Screen Performance* (2008), and co-editor of *Intersecting Aesthetics* (2023) and *More Than a Method* (2004). She is the editor of the *Journal of Film and Video*, *The Projector: A Journal of Film, Media, and Culture*, and the Palgrave Studies in Screen Industries and Performance Series. She is working on a book about representation and creative labor.

Mary Beltrán is an Associate Professor of Radio-Television-Film and a faculty affiliate of Mexican American & Latina/o Studies and Women's and Gender Studies at the University of Texas at Austin. She is the author of *Latina/o Stars in U.S. Eyes: The Making and Meanings of Film and TV Stardom* (2009) and *Latino TV: A History* (2022), and co-editor of *Mixed Race Hollywood* (2008).

Lisa Coulthard is Professor of Cinema and Media Studies in the Department of Theatre and Film at the University of British Columbia. She has published extensively on film violence, film sound, and film philosophy. She currently holds a Social Science and Humanities Research Council of Canada (SSHRC) Insight Grant studying the fight scene in cinema and a SSHRC Insight Development Grant on Digital Dark Tourism. She is currently working on monographs on the fight scene in cinema and on sound and violence.

Hye Seung Chung is Professor of Film and Media Studies at Colorado State University. She is the author of *Hollywood Asian: Philip Ahn and the Politics of Cross-Ethnic Performance* (2006), *Kim Ki-duk* (2012), and *Hollywood Diplomacy: Film Regulation, Foreign Relations, and East Asian Representations* (2020). She is also the co-author (with David Scott Diffrient) of *Movie Migrations: Transnational Genre Flows and South Korean Cinema* (2015) and *Movie Minorities: Transnational Rights Advocacy and South Korean Cinema* (2021).

David Scott Diffrient is Professor of Film and Media Studies in the Department of Communication Studies at Colorado State University. He is the co-editor of *Screwball Television* (2010) and *East Asian Film Remakes* (2023) as well as the author of *M*A*S*H* (2008), *Omnibus Films* (2014), and *Comic Drunks, Crazy Cults, and Lovable Monsters* (2022). Along with Hye Seung Chung, he is the coauthor of *Movie Migrations: Transnational Genre Flows and South Korean Cinema* (2015) and *Movie Minorities: Transnational Rights Advocacy and South Korean Cinema* (2021).

Glen Donnar is a Senior Lecturer at RMIT University, Melbourne, Australia. He has published diversely on stardom and celebrity, and on popular cultural and screen representations of men and masculinity. He is the author of *Troubling Masculinities: Terror, Gender, and Monstrous Others in American Film Post-9/11* (2020), and co-editor of *Asian Celebrity and Digital Media* (2023). His research has also been featured in *Media International Australia*, *Celebrity Studies*, *Journal of Popular Culture* and *Senses of Cinema*. He is completing a book on *Ageing Masculinity in Hollywood Action Film* (Bloomsbury).

Scott Higgins is Charles W. Fries Professor, Director of the Wesleyan College of Film and the Moving Image, and Curator of Wesleyan's Reid Cinema Archives. His books include *Harnessing the Technicolor Rainbow* (2007), *Arnheim for Film and Media Studies* (2011) and *Matinee Melodrama: Playing with Formula in the Sound Serial* (2016). He is currently at work on a study of Vincente Minnelli titled *How it Feels when the Universe Reels.*

Chris Holmlund is Professor Emerita of Cinema Studies, Gender/Sexuality/Women's Studies, and French at the University of Tennessee-Knoxville. Her books include (as author) *Female Trouble* (2017) and *Impossible Bodies* (2002), (as editor or co-editor) *The Ultimate Stallone Reader* (2014), *American Cinema of the 1990s* (2008), *Contemporary American Independent Film* (2004), and *Between the Sheets, In the Streets: Queer, Lesbian, Gay Documentary* (1997). Her most recent articles explore transnational vs. regional understandings of genre (*Transnational Screens*, 12.2), Swedish actors in action (*Journal of Scandinavian Cinema*, 10.3), and transgender elders (*Jump Cut*, 59).

Gina Marchetti serves as Chair of the Department of Humanities and Media Studies at Pratt Institute in Brooklyn, New York. Her books include *Romance and the "Yellow Peril": Race, Sex and Discursive Strategies in Hollywood Fiction* (1993), *From Tian'anmen to Times Square: Transnational China and the Chinese Diaspora on Global Screens* (2006), *The Chinese Diaspora on American Screens: Race, Sex, and Cinema* (2012), *Andrew Lau and Alan Mak's* Infernal Affairs*: The Trilogy* (2007), and *Citing China: Politics, Postmodernism, and World Cinema*

(2018). Her research and teaching interests encompass critical and cultural theory, world cinema, Asian and Asian American women filmmakers, and depictions of China and the Chinese diaspora on global screens.

Charlie Michael is Assistant Professor of Film Studies at Georgia Gwinnett College outside Atlanta. He is the author of *French Blockbusters: Cultural Politics of a Transnational Cinema* (2019) and the co-editor of the *Directory of World Cinema: France* (2013). His work has also appeared in journals such as *SubStance, Transnational Screens and The Velvet Light Trap*. He is currently working on two new projects—a co-edited volume on overlooked and underestimated French directors called *The Other French New Wave* and a monograph on *Spider-Man: Into the Spiderverse*.

Lisa Purse is Professor of Film at the University of Reading, UK. She has published widely on action cinema and action aesthetics, digital visual effects, questions of representation in genre cinema, and representations of war and conflict. Her books include (as author) *Contemporary Action Cinema* (2013) and *Digital Imaging in Popular Cinema* (2013), and (as co-editor) *Disappearing War: Interdisciplinary Perspectives on Cinema and Erasure in the Post-9/11 World* (2017) and *Mediating War and Identity: Figures of Transgression in 20th- and 21st-Century War Representation* (2020).

Krupa Shandilya is Associate Professor of Sexuality, Women's, and Gender Studies at Amherst College, with an affiliate appointment in English. She is the author of the monograph *Intimate Relations: Social Reform and the Late Nineteenth Century South Asian Novel* (2017) and has also translated Urdu poetry and prose. Her scholarly interests include South Asian and postcolonial literature, Bombay cinema, women's fiction, and feminist theory.

Lindsay Steenberg is Reader / Associate Professor in Film Studies at Oxford Brookes University where she is chair of the Equality, Diversity, and Inclusion Research Network. She has published numerous articles on violence in the media and the crime and action genres. She is the author of *Forensic Science in Contemporary American Popular Culture: Gender, Crime, and Science* (2017) and *Are You Not Entertained? Mapping the Gladiator in Visual Culture* (2020). She is currently working on a monograph on the fight scene with Lisa Coulthard at the University of British Columbia.

Lauren Steimer is an Associate Professor of Media Arts and Film and Media Studies and Director of the Film and Media Studies Program at the University of South Carolina. Her book, *Experts in Action: Transnational Hong Kong-style Stunt Work and Performance* (2021), traces a distinct, embodied history of transnational exchange by identifying and defining unique forms of expert performance common to contemporary globalized action film and television genres. She is the leading academic expert on the history of film, television, and live stuntwork.

Yvonne Tasker is Professor of Media and Communication at the University of Leeds, UK. She has written extensively on popular cinema. Her books include *Spectacular Bodies* (1993), *Working Girls* (1998), *Action and Adventure Cinema* (editor, 2004), *Soldiers' Stories: Military Women in Cinema and Television since WWII* (2011) and *The Hollywood Action and Adventure Film* (2015). Together with Diane Negra she has edited *Interrogating Postfeminism* (2007), and *Gendering the Recession*. She is currently working on a monograph *Jill Craigie: Film and Feminism in Post-war Britain* (co-authored with Sadie Wearing).

Acknowledgments

Many people deserve thanks for helping us bring *Action Cinema Since 2000* to fruition. Sincere gratitude to the Leverhulme Trust's Visiting Professor Scheme, the University of Reading's Department of Film, Theatre & Television and Heritage & Creativity Research Theme, and the University of Leeds for their financial support of Chris Holmlund's UK research visit and the action conference we organized at Reading in 2019. This anthology is shaped, in part, by the animated discussions and debates that took place there. Participants and attendees brought differing areas of expertise. From a host of countries—India, Sweden, France, Canada, Hong Kong, Australia, the US, and UK—they made the conference an energizing, thought-provoking experience. Several of these essays originated in conference presentations; a few contributions were invited subsequently. Scott Higgins, Scott Diffrient, Gina Marchetti, Lisa Coulthard, Lindsay Steenberg, Lauren Steimer, Lisa Purse, Yvonne Tasker, and Chris Holmlund shared their work-in-progress at various Society for Cinema and Media Studies (SCMS) conferences later. The ongoing discussions in and beyond the conference, and the feedback we have received in various venues—from our students and colleagues as well as at other conferences—have helped us hone our essays.

Thanks to the Bloomsbury production team for helping us turn our action observations into print and online offerings. Thanks especially to Veidehi Hans, our assistant editor, for her support and guidance. Thanks, too, to Bloomsbury RefineCatch's Merv Honeywood. Rachel Hall's assistance as we compiled this collection has been invaluable, as has the work of our copy editor, Mark Fisher.

On a personal note, each of us thanks our families—chosen and biological—for *their* encouragement and enthusiasm. We trust you know who you are; a comprehensive list would be long. This said, Chris would single out Christine Geraghty, Kathleen McHugh, and Diane Waldman for special acknowledgment; Lisa can't help but mention her "action kids," Mia and Hannah, and also thanks Faye Woods; and Yvonne would like to acknowledge Diane Negra.

Most of all, profound thanks to every one of our contributors for their patience, diligence, and insights. It has been a real joy to work with you. We have learned a lot, and we have had fun doing so. Last and not least—we thank each other. We each value the others' long investments in film and queer/trans/cis feminism, within the academy and in the world. Working together has been a blast, an action dream come true.

Introduction: Action as Mode

Chris Holmlund, Lisa Purse, and Yvonne Tasker

Action Cinema Since 2000: From Genre to Mode

This book explores action cinema since 2000. Here and in the essays that follow we expand upon José Arroyo's speculative 2000 description of big budget, popular, US (i.e., Hollywood) films as an "action/spectacle mode." For us and our contributors, it is not enough to say that "contemporary action/spectacle is less easily associated with genre" than were "the gangster film, westerns, action/ adventure" (vii). Thinking of action as mode is now *more* helpful than thinking of it as genre.

Action as mode frames a certain manner of filmmaking and viewing that exceeds—without eclipsing—genre. For good reason internet databases like the IMDb (the Internet Movie Database) and the free, online, open-content encyclopedia Wikipedia today categorize films by multiple genres, rarely by a single genre. That global streaming services like Netflix and Amazon Prime rely on algorithms to track and guide our viewing preferences similarly expands yet dilutes what is marketed and received as "action," further rendering it a mode rather than a genre.[1] The COVID pandemic has only exacerbated existing trends incorporating or foregrounding streaming. As Kate Fortmueller writes, "many of the pandemic pivots were in fact preestablished twenty-first-century distribution and exhibition practices" (2021: 5).

This volume focuses on the twenty-first century to engage more fully with recent developments in action film. We use the year 2000 as a convenient way to demarcate a period that merits further study. Despite well-documented socio-political shifts, economic changes, and contested public discourse around media representations, there have been comparatively few comprehensive academic appraisals of action films, particularly of those made after 2010. As a result, much of the work here considers action films released between 2010 and 2019, with some chapters looking forward beyond that, others looking backwards to action history.

The Scope of Action

So, what, exactly, is at stake in our naming and claiming of action as a mode? The switch in terminology represents more than merely the substitution of time-worn academic jargon for what was previously dominant industrial terminology, at least in the US and Europe. We prefer "mode" because it allows us to broaden our understanding of diverse—occasionally surprising—aesthetic and generic combinations, production practices, and economic investments, of varying geopolitical import.

Several issues nonetheless arise from our proposal that action be regarded as a mode, instead of—as has often been the case—as a genre with relatively fixed narrative, aesthetic, and institutional dimensions, where temporal and geographical delineations are taken for granted, as if eternal and omnipresent. Consider the diversity and sheer extent of action in cinema. The range of action is apparent in its multiple roots in chase, melodramatic, Western, gangster, jungle-adventure, fantasy, swashbuckler, science-fiction, war/combat, spy/caper, thriller, rape/revenge, disaster, and blaxploitation films. As this list—itself partial and skewing Anglophone—underlines, action exceeds genre though having a relationship to it, drawing on conventions, types, and markers developed within numerous cycles, series, subgenres, and genres.

Contemporary action is equally catholic with respect to its narrative, visual, and audial source material: its purview spreads across multiple settings and spaces with no single defining landscape as "home." It encompasses Hindi masala films, Mexploitation movies, Japanese Yakuza films, and more. Like comedy, melodrama, and romance, action's expansiveness complicates categorization. This is sometimes acknowledged through hybridized designators: action-comedy, say, or action-horror. Thus, although action is regularly spoken of as a stand-alone genre, at other times it is merely assumed to be part of the offer: Western, war, thriller are all terms that *imply* a strong action element. Action can be brutal and realist in its violence—e.g., *Easy Money* (*Snabba Cash*, Daniel Espinosa, 2010 [Sweden]), *Raging Fire* (Benny Chan, 2021 [Hong Kong]), and parts of *RRR* (*Rise Roar Revolt*, S.S. Rajamouli, 2022 [India]). Or it can be comic—e.g., *The Heat* (Paul Feig, 2013 [USA]), *OSS 117: Lost in Rio* (*OSS 177—Rio ne répond plus*, Michel Hazanavicius, 2009 [France]), and *Mirageman* (Ernesto Díaz Espinoza, 2007 [Chile]). Or it can slant toward fantasy—e.g., *Along with the Gods: The Two Worlds* (*Sin gwa hamkke*, Kim Yong-hwa, 2017) [South Korea]), other parts of *RRR*, and, yes, even *Ratatouille* (Brad Bird, Jan Pinkava, 2007 [USA]). Or it can engage with the epic—e.g., *Atanarjuat: The Fast Runner*

(Zacharias Kunuk, 2001 [Canada]). Or it can crazily combine many of the above—e.g., *Polite Society* (Nida Manzoor, 2023 [UK]).

The diversity of action thus has much to do with its ubiquity, notably in the use of action sequences, both in non-Western and Western action films and in films not labeled first and foremost "action." Despite this diversity, scholarship has, as is all too often the case, tended to concentrate on Anglophone films. The generic scaffold of action invariably takes mainstream Hollywood cinema as its reference point. Studies of national and regional action cinemas remain exceptions.

We want to highlight how genre as a concept tends to involve a canon, one that does as much to limit as to enhance understanding. Many pertinent films fall out of the established canonical core: they are deemed to "not quite" fit. Anglophone action scholarship has, additionally, tended to emphasize bigger budget US action films. As scholars working on action over several decades, we cannot help but notice that those films deemed "not quite" action often tend to originate outside Hollywood and its systems, that they may prominently feature women and non-white (or non-Caucasian-passing) performers, that they may encompass animation as well as live-action, and that they may be low-budget "knock-offs," adaptations, or elaborations. Some play theaters around the world, simultaneously or later appearing on television, in DVD and Blu-ray format, and/or available for streaming. Others go straight to DVD or are produced exclusively for streaming sites.

Made for only $200, the shoddily earnest *Who Killed Captain Alex?* (Nabwana I.G.G., 2010 [Uganda]) boasts its fans thanks to the internet. Made for roughly $8,000,000, the inventive schoolboy remake of the first Rambo film, *First Blood* (Ted Koetcheff, 1982), *Son of Rambow* (Garth Jennings, 2012 [UK]) enjoyed a successful if limited theatrical release and netted a BAFTA nomination. Low-budget US indie action films enjoy mixed fortunes: vigilante film *Lila & Eve* (Charles Stone III, 2015 [USA]) managed to recoup only $179,000 of its reported $4.9 million budget at the box office, despite starring established US stars Jennifer Lopez and Viola Davis and despite adhering to "tried and true" rape/revenge generic conventions.

Today many national and regional industries are known for action films, witness the transnational/international success of Hindi, Tamil, Telugu, Malayalam, South Korean, Hong Kong, and Japanese action films, and—among others—Thai, Brazilian, Chinese, Indonesian, Filipino, South African, French, Italian, and Colombian action-related titles. Hollywood studios are not automatically the most influential or the most popular action producers. Necessarily, framing action as a mode that operates expansively requires increased attention to the regional, even local, variations arising within assorted generic and sub-generic traditions. The "transnational," after all, is not inescapably synonymous with the "global": differences in production, distribution, and reception continue to obtain. We deem it essential to recognize the importance of carefully defined geopolitical and historical contexts.

Two examples suggest the complex balance of questions we envision in discussions of action as mode rather than genre:

Mulan (Niki Caro, 2020)

Based on a beloved Chinese folktale, Disney's $200 million live-action remake of its own successful animated film (Tony Bancroft and Barry Cook, 1998) seemed guaranteed to be globally successful. Its heroine, Mulan (Liu Yifei), is attractive and engaging, a strong Disney girl. Disguised as a man, she bravely takes her aging father's place, fighting valiantly against invaders and a wicked witch (Gong Li) (see Figure 0.1). Yet the film was poorly received everywhere, in good part due to its unusual dual release pattern. With theaters in the US, UK, France, and elsewhere shuttered due to Covid in 2020, Disney released a streamed version of *Mulan* on its pay-for-video-on-demand (PVOD) service, Disney+, but sent actual prints to the open theaters of Eastern European and Asian countries, the UAE, New Zealand, Russia, Hong Kong, Taiwan, and China. Upshot? *Mulan* grossed a bare $70 million "worldwide" in theaters—the lowest box office ever of any Disney live-action remake.[2]

A corresponding problem is that especially when seen on smaller screens, *Mulan* is rather lifeless. It was, after all, shot for the big screen. Competently directed by New Zealand's Niki Caro, mixing action, adventure, and drama with fantasy, *Mulan* features not only the charming newcomer Yifei and her male love interest (Yoson An) but also star supporting players (Donnie Yen, Jet Li, Gong Li), sumptuous costume design, and beautiful scenery.[3] Anglophone critics were often lukewarm, among them *Vanity Fair*'s Richard Lawson, *Vox*'s Aja Romano, the *New York Times*'s Manohla Dargis, and the London *Observer*'s Oliver Jones. Lawson (2020) called the film "inert," "a plodding bore"; Romano (2020) said it

Figure 0.1 Mulan (Liu Yifei) is confronted by the witch who knows her secret, Xianniang (Gong Li) in *Mulan* (© Walt Disney Pictures, 2020. All Rights Reserved).

was "superficial and perfunctory"; Dargis (2020) described it as a "less-than-buoyant epic"; Jones (2020) argued it will "leave many filmgoers . . . feeling like they've lost something important and essential." Online comments from viewers evinced a similar indifference.[4]

A third reason for *Mulan*'s poor reception and dismal box office, however, was the production's obliviousness to hot-button political issues, even though, as Fortmueller notes, "Disney aims for political neutrality as a means to cater to all audiences. . . ." She signals, however, that "this is increasingly difficult to achieve in the contemporary global political landscape" (2021: 65). Pro-democracy activists in Hong Kong, Taiwan, and Thailand called for a boycott because Liu Yifei supported the oppressive actions of the Hong Kong police. Western and Asian viewers objected to some of the film's locations: certain scenes take place in Xinjiang, where the Chinese government has imprisoned over one million Muslim Uyghurs to worldwide condemnation. Chinese media outlets failed to cover the film; earlier they had criticized Liu for giving up her Chinese citizenship to become American. China's 1.4 billion viewers preferred the Chinese-produced "main-melody" patriotic war film, *The Eight Hundred* (Guan Hu, 2020).

Saloum (Jean Luc Herbulot, 2021)

A moody action-horror-revenge-thriller, *Saloum* is Congolese director Herbulot's second feature. Intended for both transnational and domestic release, it combines local and regional elements with internationally recognized genre conventions. Shot in the tradition-laden, picturesque Sine-Saloum delta of southern Senegal, billed as "un southern," the film pays homage to spaghetti Westerns at the same time as it adds folkloric and Mexploitation hints, action tropes, and swarm *cum* creature feature design. Professional actors Yann Gaël, Roger Sallah, and Mentor Ba play a trio of swashbuckling mercenaries. Their plane is forced to land; they find lodging at a local guesthouse with a menacingly jovial owner. Another guest, a beautiful deaf-mute (Evelyne Ily Juhen) who has heard of their legendary exploits ("stories about heroes travel faster than bullets"), befriends them (see Figure 0.2). The quartet will soon encounter challenges beyond their imagining. The soundtrack by Reksider is memorable: sometimes droning, sometimes pulsating, always unnerving, a mix of African drums, flutes, and electronica with choral touches.

Local actors and area inhabitants appear as fishermen, poachers, villagers, and mangrove farmers, though only the unconvincing CGI effects and the frequent reliance on offscreen commentary betray the film's miniscule cost. A Senegalese production that received support from France's Fonds Image de la Francophonie, *Saloum* was completed for a bare 250 million CFA francs (approximately $370,000 USD) (FAAPA 2022). Premiered at the 2022 Toronto International Film Festival (TIFF), it screened at numerous festivals. In Africa it has

Figure 0.2 Under attack from unknown forces, deaf-mute Awa (Evelyne Ily Juhen) and mercenary leader Chaka (Yann Gaël) debate whether Awa will join their escape plan in *Saloum* (© Lacmé Studios, 2021. All Rights Reserved.).

been shown in seventeen countries. In the US, Canada, UK, and Ireland, at the time of this writing it can only be streamed through Shudder, a pay-for-play service known for thriller-horror-supernatural product. Critical coverage was comparatively sparse if consistently favorable, praising the original narrative and applauding the costuming, cinematography, art direction, and sound. *Playlist*'s review at TIFF set the tone for the reviews that followed: Andrew Crump (2021) trumpeted the "adrenalizing ride" that *Saloum* offers thanks to its "kinetic style, peppered by muscular camerawork . . . and fast cuts."

As is the case for many action hybrids, and especially for those produced beyond Anglophone borders, *Saloum*'s reliance on and play with genre is key to its transnational success. Its mix is familiar: horror relies on thrills as well as fright; action incorporates chills as well as excitement. But *Saloum* also includes, and occasionally re-positions, Senegalese, West African, and pan-African figures, facts, and folklore. One character cites Burkinabé Marxist revolutionary Thomas Sankara; another mentions Senegalese poet-president Léopold Senghor. A crucial sub-plot involves abused child soldiers. The narrative opens as the three antiheroes mop up after a bloody 2003 coup in Guinea-Bissau; in actuality, that coup was bloodless. The entire story revolves around Bainouk king Gana Sira Bana's curse of the people of Casamance in southern Senegal; the Saloum delta is part of Casamance. In subtitled translation, West African polyvocality is reduced to English—or French—monolingualism. Western specialists may savor the low-budget potpourri, but motivated Western fans must identify these and other ingredients using web searches.[5]

These two examples demonstrate how critical it is to nuance our approach to action: recognizing the specificities of each film and the conditions of its creation matter as much as identifying the wider industrial and cultural shifts of which it might be a part. This is necessary precisely because of the scope of contemporary action: its motley generic origins, complexly hybrid nature, heterogeneous scales and budgets, various national and regional origins, and differing reception. Yet the character of action—its common elements and chief attributes—is likewise crucial.

The Character of Action

Detractors of action films often underscore action's characteristics in their critiques, alleging an excess they find most pointed (and most redundant) in action sequences, and a supposedly corresponding paucity of narrative. This devaluing bears the vestiges of earlier eras' distinctions between "high-" and "low-" culture, with sensational narratives marginalized in cinematic canons, past and present. Scott Higgins (2008, 2016), Ben Singer (2004), and others link early action-adventure films and film serials to melodrama. Their framing usefully sees action spectacle not as "distinct from narrative," but rather as "part and parcel of a kind of narrative construction that favors sensational situations" (Higgins 2008: 82). We too recognize action's connection to melodrama, but we do not view contemporary action as simply a subset of melodrama. Instead, we find that today's action, *like* melodrama, "*shape[s]* the operation of generic worlds" through "aesthetic articulation." We believe, moreover, that action does so differently than melodrama does, even though, like melodrama, it too is "genre-generating" (Gledhill and Williams 2018: 5, emphasis added).

The action sequence links the many kinds of films that, we have argued, can be grouped under the action film umbrella. The *ways* that action tells stories are as, if not more, decisive as *what* those stories are. We find, in the action sequence, motion (punctuated by stillness and stasis) and rhythm: of the camera, of lighting, of voices, music, and sound. We additionally find a choice and delineation of physical bodies, and we admire the energetic movements of these bodies in the frame and as part of the soundscape. We appreciate, with Martine Beugnet, the emphasis on "the more sensual and experimental facets of the medium" (2007: 9), and the circulation and recombination of visual and aural tropes that draw on familiarity while promising novelty.

Digital technologies of sound and image have intensified these elements, offering visualizations of bodies, impacts, and environments, and digitally engineered sounds—music, sound effects, dialogue, spatialized forms of scoring—to extend the action sequence's scale, pace, movement, and duration. Alongside these overt transformations and expansions, a pro-filmic dimension persists, proposing the existence of a non-digital staging and performance. It is tempting to read the persistence of this profilmic aspect only in terms of twenty-first century nostalgia for the pre-digital, yet these profilmic features can offer differentiation within the marketplace.[6] Low-budget action films have regularly emphasized the labor of their action bodies through reference to real-world notions of physical effort, force, and impact.

Action sequences offer audiences densely affective fantasies of physical empowerment as movement towards spatial mastery. The affective turn in film studies, which moved beyond ocular-centrism to a broader conception of cinema's "sensuous address" (Sobchack 2004), was prompted in part by the mid-1990s discovery of so-called "mirror neurons" in the part of the brain responsible for controlling movement, the premotor cortex. These mirror neurons respond similarly whether someone is watching an action or performing the action themselves.[7]

Power is most often conveyed through expansive physical and vehicular endeavor. The audience registers what it is like to extend one's body in these ways through the "staging [of] a somatic experience of space," as Eileen Rositzka puts it (2018: 3). Velocity—the acceleration and prolongation of movement within and beyond the frame—counts for much. Watching, listening, we abandon logic for sensation, soaking in colors, bursts, and blasts, sensing rhythm, savoring speed. Action narratives, visuals, and sounds rouse, disturb, and incite viewers, in Jennifer Barker's words, "cut[ting] us loose from our moorings altogether for minutes at a time only to return us safely to them at the end, leaving us exhilarated, exhausted, and shaken" (2009: 107).[8]

The sensory force—the "ways," the "how"—of contemporary action has received less critical attention than the corporeal appeal of musicals or melodramas. Those scholars who have written on action—we include some of our own previous work—have mostly focused on the "what," i.e., on the kinds of stories told, drawing on traditional categories of literary analysis: plot, story, character, setting, theme. But the affective dimensions that elude analysis and/or attract ire are central to action cinemas.

Affects are anchored in the bodies of action heroes, be they human, robot, beast, or other. Action films deploy a range of stylistic strategies, performance skills, and technological tools, but always in the service of sustained attention to the physically rigorous challenges a given hero's body must endure and overcome to succeed. With some exceptions, Anglophone action films have historically offered the straight, white, cis-gender male as the archetypal action body, in contrast, for example, to East Asian action traditions that include skilled swordswomen and female martial artists as principal protagonists. Studies of casting and the roles played by heroes (including antiheroes), villains, supporting, and incidental characters have given rise to discussions of representation, both within and beyond the academy. Debates have raged around whether images matter, how, and for whom, and over what constitutes a positive, negative, realistic, or unrealistic image. Stereotypes—to a lesser extent social types—receive attention, including via marketing research and reception studies.

Privileging the sensory dimensions of action cinemas brings questions of representation and their real-world consequences into sharp relief. Vicariously experiencing densely affective fantasies of physical empowerment through screen bodies that do not reflect your own body has social effects well beyond the movie theatre. Your body is "trained" to feel and "moved" to conclude that you cannot, may not, must not take up space in particular ways in the world. The question of who can or may hold power resonates beyond any antagonisms portrayed on screen, and this helps explain why some action films become flashpoints for controversy while others fuel activist aspirations.

Action stars are necessarily part of such conversations. The relationship of individual star bodies to characters has been studied, and the extra-textual movements of stars—more rarely those of supporting actors—across national boundaries of production and reception have been documented. The movements of actors as characters within film narratives, i.e., their performances, especially those that go beyond branded physical markers such as Tom Cruise's grin or Sylvester Stallone's rumble have, however, been examined less frequently.[9] Bringing the detail and nuance of an actor's performance into sharper relief allows us to analyze the circumstances in which that performance emerges within the fictional world and against the backdrop of broader socio-cultural, economic, and production contexts.

Cynthia Baron notes that some action performances in English-language films—those of Denzel Washington, for example—are "bizarrely stressed," offering "hyperbolic shifts in expressivity" in between sonically charged, visually electrifying explosions (2015: 105, 104). Similarly exaggerated swings structure the performances of Ram Charan and N.T. Rama Rao Jr., the opposed action heroes in the Telugu-language action epic *RRR*: they move from grimacing, sweating, roaring physical action, to delicate elaborations of comedic moments or understated expressions of suppressed emotions.

Most national and regional action cinemas include empowered poses. Stock Western examples include standing tall, hands planted on hips, elbows out, legs akimbo to suggest readiness and resolve, power, and potential, à la Errol Flynn's Robin Hood. Other actors also direct audience responses using stance, posture, gestures, and facial expressions. Such shorthand is seemingly ubiquitous: comic books, video games, cinema, and social media employ similar techniques.

The whirling, twirling, pounding, slashing performances that so transfix, agitate, and galvanize us nonetheless come largely thanks to the practiced precision of unsung stunt artists, not stars.[10] Stunt teams supply stunt visualization of action sequences ("stuntvis")—edited footage of what the main fight beats will look like, including camera placement and movement—that provide a visual reference for directors, producers, visual effects teams, and other production and post-production departments. Their painstaking work is technically masked and legally hidden. As they, too, move across national boundaries of production and reception, moreover, local action aesthetics evolve.

Many contemporary action bodies are digital. With bigger budget films especially, digital visual effects generate masses and body doubles, sculpt performance overtly or covertly, and modify star, supporting, and bit part bodies through de-aging, bulking up, slimming down, and the like. Digital sound design intensifies the audience's appreciation of scale, momentum, and impact.

In varying combinations, such elements help make actors' and stunt workers' performances of violence seem believable, authentic, and realistic, or improbable and fantastic. What is conceptualized as credible or "authentic"—or unlikely, even implausible—varies over time, within media formats, according to viewing practices and conditions. Digital manipulations may even be viewed as barriers to action's own claims to verisimilitude. Anxieties about digital effects are, after all, grounded in longstanding concerns about the relationship of acting to technological change and cinematic illusionism.[11]

Many—though not all—action films engage with geopolitical anxieties in fictionalized forms. Many enlist socio-cultural concerns. By so doing they provide imaginary spaces for audiences "to work through those social contradictions that [their] culture needs to come to grips with" but cannot (Marchetti 1989: 187). They allow us to "solve" dilemmas—even if only within the realm of fantasy and usually on the level of individual endeavor rather than collective change.

Action's way of telling stories does lend itself to specific themes. These can be and are interpreted in various ways. Oft repeated, the emphasis on movement or transit speaks variously to rootlessness, migration, and modernity. Freedom and movement are pitted against constriction and restraint within narratives, by characters, and through the design and enactment of action set pieces, making action ethically elastic and hence more widely influential. As a mode, it is eminently adaptable because—to again cite Gledhill, if now with a decided emphasis on the body in action—"any body can be victim or oppressor" (2018: xxii). The questions around power and powerlessness that action films articulate may be posed in relation to a specific community, a region, a nation, even to the world. Or they may be delimited to individuals, structured as growth and maturation, or depicted as resilience and endurance. Knowing how to suffer well may be as essential as succeeding wildly.

Despite such variety there are absences in today's Anglophone action cinema—and relatedly scholarship—that we find striking. Few films even mention LGBTQ+ lives, despite the resonance of action tropes and performers for some queer audiences. Even as action cinemas have been valuable to Black stars in the West and for South and East Asian representation more broadly, issues of racism or structural inequalities around race are rarely addressed. A few male stars continue to thrive as they age, netting lead and supporting roles the world over, but the physical impact of their aging is buried or disguised thanks to narrative twists and visual dodges. Female action stars are rarely given the chance to age. When they are afforded the opportunity, they are portrayed as pathetic, comic, or horrifying. Physical transformations, violence, and injury are common, but disability is less commonly referenced. Stereotypes are routinely reproduced, less often questioned.

The 2000s do, however, at times take more progressive paths, offering new action narratives and new action bodies. At the same time, developments in local and regional financing, local and regional attitudes to cultural influence, and governmental policies on film production, tax relief, distribution, and censorship continue to change how action film circulates, and how it speaks—to multiple audiences.

Everything, Everywhere, All at Once

The modestly budgeted *Everything Everywhere All at Once* (Dan Kwan and Daniel Scheinert, 2022) centers on a Chinese immigrant family in the US. Starring martial arts comedienne Michelle Yeoh, it became a sleeper hit for independent production and distribution studio A24, winning seven Academy Awards: Best Picture, Best Actress, Best Director, Best Supporting Actor, Best Supporting Actress, Best Editing, and Best Original Screenplay.[12] No prior Oscars ceremony had celebrated so much East Asian talent at once. Unsurprisingly, then, *Everything Everywhere* has become a locus for debates around Asian and Asian American screen representation.

Everything Everywhere showcases action and comedy but begins in the economically and emotionally stressed every day. Yeoh plays Evelyn, co-owner of a struggling laundromat, with her ineffectual husband Waymond (Ke Huy Quan). She argues with her disaffected daughter Joy (Stephanie Hsu), tries to win her father (James Hong)'s approval, and organizes a Chinese New Year celebration for laundromat customers. Throughout the film she attempts to resolve a dispute with an Internal Revenue Service (IRS) officer named Deirdre Beaubeirdre (Jamie Lee Curtis). At the IRS office, Evelyn is unexpectedly recruited by a Waymond from another universe into a battle to save the world from Jobu Tupaki (Stephanie Hsu again) and her mystical bagel—a kind of existential black hole capable of destroying all universes.

Everything Everywhere goes to dizzying lengths as it winks at how Marvel deploys the multiverse to expand and market its cinematic universe. To overcome Tupaki and her henchmen and women, Evelyn must jump between universes, acquiring the skills she possesses in other—often more successful—lives: as a martial arts expert, a famous actress, a sidelined chef, a pizza street sign holder, an opera singer, a dominatrix, even a rock. Humor is found in the particularities of some of these lives and the ways they start to bleed into each other, producing surprising juxtapositions: from the outsize wobbly hat of the pizza sign holder to the racoon who teaches Evelyn's competitor chef how to cook, to the purposefully silly activities that must be performed to universe-jump or download skills—chewing someone else's gum, inserting a butt plug, telling someone unexpected you love them.

The film's multiverse settings establish a heterogeneous play with a range of cultural reference points within and beyond action cinema, from Michelle Yeoh's Hong Kong action back catalogue and Jackie Chan's movies to *The Matrix* (Lana Wachowski and Lilly Wachowski, 1999), *Planet of the Apes* (Franklin J. Schaffner, 1968), *Kung Fu Hustle* (*Kung Fu*, Stephen Chow, 2004), *2001: A Space Odyssey* (Stanley Kubrick, 1968), *Terminator 2: Judgment Day* (James Cameron, 1991), and *When Harry Met Sally* (Rob Reiner, 1989) to Michel Gondry and Wong Kar-wai.[13]

The reach outwards to audiences' extra-textual awareness of the main actors' career paths functions not just as fan service, but also as a reflection on the marginalization of actors of East Asian heritage. As Justin Chang (2023) notes in a (sometimes ambivalent) reflection on the film's implications for screen representation,

> The dearth of Asian American stories is something the movie, with its dizzying panoply of Evelyns, implicitly critiques; it's why Yeoh and Quan, two superb talents who've never had the Hollywood careers they've deserved, are so poignantly cast as a married couple trying to figure out where their lives went astray.

Each universe manifests itself as a different genre, with a different color palette. Like a videogame or escape room, skills become "treasures" or "power-ups" to acquire after a clue is acted upon, a correct route identified, or a problem solved. The intensively hybrid mix of action styles and a comedic tone is cut together by editor Paul Rogers, typically at breakneck speed, as if a music video or YouTube or TikTok mash-up. Action sequences play out across constrained areas—office cubicles, supply cupboards, corridors. Quotidian objects like computer keyboards, tables, or mops become weapons or defensive tools, à la Jackie Chan films.

In this way, the film's ludic dimensions invite audiences to conceive of heroism in terms of versatility and creativity. No small part of the film's humor—or its pleasure for fans of her martial arts and action work—comes in scenes where Michelle Yeoh performs a lack of physical confidence or must "download" skills from an Evelyn in another universe. Yeoh's star action body, and audience awareness of her real-world skills in dance, stunt-work, and martial arts performance, haunt laundromat-Evelyn. Her star action body "guarantees" the film's theme of human potential—Yeoh will become her fighting self soon! It also highlights the multiverse's potential to empower "little" people and thereby affect change. Yeoh embraces this ethos in the way she embodies workaday-Evelyn. In grey wig and dowdy costuming, she offers a delicately wrought performance: her ordinary-Evelyn is harried, unfulfilled, dismissive, nit-picking, and rather unlikeable. The contrast with the hybrid, ever-evolving, multiverse-powered Evelyns is dramatized primarily through nimble pivots to physical action, in fast-paced martial arts action sequences.

There is little digital intervention in the action sequences, as befits a film referencing various eras of East Asian martial arts cinema. The cast trained with wushu world champion Li Jing; she cameos as Evelyn's Pai Mai master in one universe. Brian and Andy Le's fight choreography was extensively pre-visualized and rehearsed with cast and stunt performers; the brothers appear in key office fights. Although in marketing parlance Yeoh and Quan do "most of their own stunts," Andy Le stunt-doubles for Quan, and Kiera O'Connor stunt-doubles for Yeoh. Action moments deploy archetypal wushu fight beats via "wire-fu" techniques in homage to 1970s and 1980s Chinese and Hong Kong martial arts movies.[14] As the Le brothers explain, these are combined with flips, twists, and spins taken from contemporary breakdancing and martial arts "tricking."[15]

Yeoh and co-stars Quan and Curtis provide contrasts between their universe iterations using physical and emotional performances that turn on a dime, often mid-scene. Quan worked with movement and dialogue coaches to distinguish rapid switches for Waymond; Jamie Lee Curtis additionally deployed improvisation techniques. Yeoh offers a masterclass in modulation as she distinguishes the various Evelyns—tightening her jaw and shoulder muscles, altering her gait, varying her gestures.

The effect of all of this is sensorially overwhelming. A core tenet of action is playfully evoked but refused: the redemption of the hero through violence. There are many stand-offs, but the tension repeatedly wanes because violence and antagonism are always met with empathy and kindness. Evelyn wins over Tupaki's helpers in the final battle by answering their deepest desires. As her antagonists sink into their reveries, she tries to prevent Tupaki/Joy from throwing herself into the vortex of the mystical bagel. The film supplies the conventional face-off between action hero and villain—they fight, they trade quips—and then denies it: the fight ends with a hug. Together, Evelyn, Waymond, and her father pull Tupaki/Joy back from the brink of the bagel's nihilistic whirlpool into the warmth of intergenerational reconciliation (see Figure 0.3).

The resolution brings action melodrama, with its patterning of discrete sensational situations and reversals of fortune, together with family melodrama and its focus on "generational and gender conflict" (Gledhill 1987: 9).[16] The lived experiences of Chinese immigrants is signaled through colloquialisms ("Big Nose" is a common nickname for white people), but especially through the constant slippage of language between English, Cantonese, and Mandarin.

Figure 0.3 Evelyn (Michelle Yeoh) only succeeds in pulling Joy/Jobu Tupaki (Stephanie Hsu) back from the annihilation of the mystical spinning bagel when her father (James Hong) and husband (Ke Huy Quan) join her in *Everything Everywhere All At Once* (© A24/AGBO/Ley Line Entertainment/Year of the Rat, 2022. All Rights Reserved.).

Yet strains are evident: in the tired environment, in Evelyn and Waymond's lost dreams, in Deirdre's patronizing and hectoring. Abandonment and leave-taking repeat across generations and through universes. To overcome the internal and external pressures on herself and her family, Evelyn must believe in herself, upskill, and fight, *and* she must hone her capacity for empathy, her openness to emotion.

In interviews and awards acceptance speeches Michelle Yeoh emphasized the film's challenge to Hollywood ageism and sexism, suggesting that the narrative communicates that "every woman deserves the chance to be a superhero." *Everything Everywhere* does indeed promote inclusivity: its action bodies are of many shapes and sizes. The inclusiveness extends to a purposeful queering of families: Joy is in a lesbian relationship; Evelyn and Deirdre are too, in another universe; there are references to sex toys and BDSM; and chef Chad (Harry Shum Jr.) is in love with a puppet raccoon named Raccacoonie (voiced by an uncredited Randy Newman). Yet there are limits, even in the multiverse. Accomplished actor James Hong is sadly under-utilized. His character is confined to a wheelchair for much of the film and given little to do. The emphatic nature of Evelyn's return to Joy and Waymond—"Don't call me Evelyn, I'm your mother!"— reveals that a profoundly conventional conception of gender and family subtends the film's progressive messages.

Conclusion

Action cinema of the twenty-first century continues to engage with and reflect socio-political, geopolitical, creative, and industrial developments. It continues to function as a site of commerce, exchange, experimentation, and activism, and to shore up local, regional, and national identities. It continues to offer fantasies of empowerment that say much about how power is understood in diverse contexts. Our conceptualization of action may well seem "everything everywhere, all at once" yet, as we have insisted, close analyses—of the industries, impacts, and affects of action cinemas are indispensable. What counts as "action" lies in the eyes, ears, and innards of those who look and listen. Action as a mode is, admittedly—and as is true of other media modes—conditioned by convention, restricted by race, ethnicity, and age, delimited by discipline, narrowed by nationality, and jinxed by gender. But because action has become a mode, it is at least not additionally constrained by canon.

Nor is 2000 a clear cut-off point, for us or our contributors. Anglophone industries have, since the 1990s, increasingly relied on transnational funding, distribution, audiences, and downstream venues for their profits. Indian, South Korean, Chinese, French, Japanese, and other producers have also reached out to transnational and diasporic funders and viewers. Since 2000 new, phenomenally popular, action genres have emerged—the People's Republic of China's main-melody action films are but one example. New generic blends have become prominent. Streaming services have assumed global as well as regional or national importance.

Whether or not *Everything Everywhere All at Once* will be as noteworthy or revelatory two, ten, or twenty years from now is, in the final analysis, unimportant. It may well not be the next *Matrix* or the next *Crouching Tiger, Hidden Dragon* (Ang Lee, 2000). It may not change the scope and character of future action. We *would* be thrilled if it were to break new representational and employment ground, given Hollywood's notoriously bad track record of utilizing and rewarding women, older people, and/or sexual, racial, and ethnic minorities as directors, as cast members and on crews. This anthology represents our collective continuation of these investigations across the frequently challenging, dependably invigorating, if occasionally tawdry, even tedious multiverse that is action.

Notes

1 Algorithms weigh content threads, and the dates, times, and numbers of minutes someone watches, considering the predilections of broader communities while localizing these by country, language, and cultural context. Although mathematically based, algorithms are not "neutral": they consider and thereby reinforce societal categorizations and hierarchies, be they gendered, sexual, racial, ethnic, generational, and/or religious. Streaming services thus expand genre, even as they—in part—rely on and reinforce genre. They go further than did earlier industries and critical appraisals in introducing and marketing "new" genres, subgenres, and cycles.

2 See Box Office Mojo, "*Mulan*" and Fortmueller (2021: 59–64).

3 Caro was already well known for *Whale Rider* (2002) and *The Zookeeper's Wife* (2017).

4 The poem, "The Ballad of Mulan," on which *Mulan* is based is known by every Chinese child. Likely written down in the fifth century, it concludes with Mulan returning home to her family, not with Mulan getting married: "We . . . never suspected that Mulan was a woman! / Most people tell the gender of a rabbit by its movement: / The male runs quickly, while the female often keeps her eyes shut. / But when the two rabbits run side by side, / Can you really discern whether I am a *he* or a *she*?" https://mulanbook.com/pages/northern-wei/ballad-of-mulan.

5   See for example Chatterjee (2022).

6   For example, *The Woman King* (Gina Prince-Bythewood, 2022) seeks to differentiate itself from the ubiquitous Marvel and DC cinematic universes by using a lot of profilmic stunt performance, and restrained use of DVFX mostly for image cleanup (e.g., removing stunt mats, sky replacement for continuity, adding fire, blood, dust, and brief uses of digital body doubles for verisimilitude). The rebooted Daniel Craig James Bond in *Casino Royale* (Martin Campbell, 2006) announces its shift from the ostentatiously computer-generated ice hotel / invisible car sequences of Pierce Brosnan's final Bond film, *Die Another Day* (Lee Tamahori, 2002), with a brutal close quarters hand-to-hand fight realized entirely through stunt performance alongside shots of the actors.

7   On mirror neurons see Rizzolatti et al. (1996), and Cisek and Kalaska (2004).

8   Our relationship may be grounded in mimesis and reciprocity but, Barker admits, we cannot copy certain camera movements—or, we would add, imitate certain sounds—regardless of whether these are digitally enhanced. While we may to some degree mimic tracking shots, whip pans, and canted angles in our own motion we cannot replicate Steadicam flows or supersonic flips. A "constant dialectic of attraction and repulsion, likeness and similarity . . . invitation and rejection . . . envelopment and estrangement" thus underpins action's allure (2009: 90).

9   But see McDonald (2013, especially 201–12) and Holmlund (2014).

10   See further Steimer (2021).

11   See further Bode (2017).

12   A24 is known for films that play with genre, take up issues of representation, and offer "meme"-able taglines.

13   See further *Everything Everywhere* DVD directors' commentary.

14   Waymond's "fanny pack" fight scene draws on the wushu rope dart technique seen in films like *Shaolin Temple* (Hsin-Yen Chang, 1982). Deirdre's flying kick echoes *The 36th Chamber of Shaolin* (Liu Chia-Liang, 1978), *Crouching Tiger, Hidden Dragon* (Ang Lee, 2000), and other films. Stunt coordinator Timothy Eulich worked with the Le brothers on the wire-fu elements.

15   Tricking is a freestyle discipline, which combines techniques from gymnastics, wushu, capoeira and taekwondo. It often circulates online via TikTok or YouTube. Geaghan-Breiner (2022).

16   See Bitney (2022) on the family business dimension of family melodrama.

Works Cited

Arroyo, José (2000), "Introduction," in José. Arroyo (ed.), *Action/Spectacle Cinema*, vii–xiv, London: BFI Publishing.

Barker, Jennifer M. (2009), *The Tactile Eye: Touch and the Cinematic Experience*, Berkeley: University of California Press.

Baron, Cynthia (2015), *Denzel Washington*, London: BFI.

Beugnet, Martine (2007), *Cinema and Sensation: French Film and the Art of Transgression*, Edinburgh: Edinburgh University Press.

Bitney, Joseph (2022), "Rethinking the family melodrama: Thomas Elsaesser, *Mildred Pierce* and the business of family," *Screen*, 63 (3) (Autumn): 327–45.

Bode, Lisa (2017), *Making Believe: Screen Performance and Special Effects in Popular Cinema*, New Brunswick, NJ: Rutgers University Press.

Box Office Mojo (n.d.), "*Mulan.*" Available online: https://www.boxofficemojo.com/title/tt4566758/ (accessed 30 September 2022).

Chang, Justin (2023), "The Oscars' best picture might seem radical. But it's as traditional as they come," *Los Angeles Times*, 12 March. Available online: https://www.latimes.com/entertainment-arts/awards/story/2023-03-12/oscars-2023-everything-everywhere-all-at-once-best-picture (accessed 20 March 2023).

Chatterjee, Pramit (2022), "*Saloum* Ending, Explained: What Is Chaka's Connection to Omar? What Has Omar Done to Sine-Saloum?" *Digital Mafia Talkies*, 8 September. Available online: https://dmtalkies.com/saloum-ending-explained-2022-horror-thriller-film-jean-luc-herbulot/ (accessed 18 October 2022).

Cisek, Paul and John F. Kalaska (2004), "Neural Correlates of Mental Rehearsal in Dorsal Premotor Cortex," *Nature*, 431: 993–6.

Crump, Andrew (2021), "*Saloum* Is a Kinetic, Genre-Bending Revenge Story," *The Playlist*, 17 September. Available online: https://theplaylist.net/saloum-genre-flick-revenge-story-tiff-review-20210917/ (accessed 17 October 2022).

Dargis, Manohla (2020), "Mulan Review: A Flower Booms in Adversity (and Kicks Butt)," *New York Times*, 30 September. Available online: https://www.nytimes.com/2020/09/03/movies/mulan-disney-review.html (accessed 1 October 2022).

FAAPA (Fédération Atlantique des Agences de Presse Africaines) (2022), "Le film 'Saloum,' de Jean Luc Herbulot, un mélange de thriller et de carte postale du Sine-Saloum," 5 August. Available online: http://www.faapa.info/blog/le-film-saloum-de-jean-luc-herbulot-un-melange-de-thriller-et-de-carte-postale-du-sine-saloum/ (accessed 14 October 2022).

Fortmueller, Kate (2021), *Hollywood Shutdown: Production, Distribution, and Exhibition in the Time of COVID*, Austin: University of Texas Press.

Geaghan-Breiner, Meredith (2022), "How The Kung Fu Scenes Were Shot in Everything Everywhere All at Once," *Insider Art*. Available online: https://www.youtube.com/watch?v=psWUuuoYMy8 (accessed 1 April 2023).

Gledhill, Christine (1987), "The Melodramatic Field: An Investigation," in Christine Gledhill, (ed.), *Home Is Where the Heart Is*, 5–39, London: BFI.

Gledhill, Christine (2018), "Prologue: The Reach of Melodrama," in Christine Gledhill and Linda Williams (eds), *Melodrama Unbound: Across History, Media, and National Cultures*, ix–xxvi, New York: Columbia University Press.

Gledhill, Christine and Linda Williams (2018), "Introduction," in Christine Gledhill and Linda Williams (eds), *Melodrama Unbound: Across History, Media, and National Cultures*, 1–14, New York: Columbia University Press.

Higgins, Scott (2008), "Suspenseful Situations: Melodramatic Narrative and the Contemporary Action Film," *Cinema Journal*, 47 (2): 74–96.

Higgins, Scott (2016), *Matinee Melodrama: Playing with Formula in the Sound Serial*, New Brunswick, NJ: Rutgers University Press.

Holmlund, Chris, ed. (2014), *The Ultimate Stallone Reader: Sylvester Stallone as Star, Icon, Auteur*, Bristol: Wallflower Press/New York: Columbia University Press.

Jones, Oliver (2020), "*Mulan* Is a High-Gloss Commercial for State Power," *Observer*, 3 September. Available online: https://observer.com/2020/09/mulan-film-review-liu-yifei-niki-caro-disney/ (accessed 30 September 2022).

Lawson, Richard (2020), "Disney's New *Mulan* Is a Dull Reflection of the Original," 3 September. Available online: https://www.vanityfair.com/hollywood/2020/09/review-disneys-new-mulan-is-a-dull-reflection-of-the-original (accessed 30 September 2022).

McDonald, Paul (2013), *Hollywood Stardom*, Malden, MA: Wiley-Blackwell.

Marchetti, Gina (1989), "Action Adventure as Ideology," in Ian Angus and Sut Jhally (eds.), *Cultural Politics in Contemporary America*, 382–97, New York: Routledge.

Rizzolatti, Giacomo, Luciano Fadiga, Vittorio Gallese and Leonardo Fogassi (1996), "Mental Representations of Motor Acts," *Cognitive Brain Research*, 3 (2) (March): 131–41.

Romano, Aja (2020), "Disney's new Mulan: Pack up, go home, you're through," *Vox*, 3 September. Available online: https://www.vox.com/culture/21419366/disney-new-mulan-review-2020-live-action-remake (accessed 30 September 2022).

Rositzka, Eileen (2018), *Cinematic Corpographies: Re-Mapping the War Film Through the Body*, Berlin: Freie Universität Berlin.

Singer, Ben (2004), "'Child of Commerce! Bastard of Art?': Early Film Melodrama," in Yvonne Tasker (ed.) *Action and Adventure Cinema*, 52–70, London: Routledge.

Sobchack, Vivian (2004), *Carnal Thoughts: Embodiment and Moving Image Culture*, Oakland, CA: University of California Press.

Steimer, Lauren (2021), *Experts in Action: Transnational Hong Kong-Style Stunt Work and Performance*, Durham, NC: Duke University Press.

"The Ballad of Mulan," trans. in *Mulanbook*. Available online: https://mulanbook.com/pages/northern-wei/ballad-of-mulan (accessed 1 October 2022).

Chapter 1

Accounting for Action: Racial Discourse and Chronologies of Genre

Yvonne Tasker

Writing on the Black gangster film in 1993, Mark A. Reid observes that: "In general, little attention has been given to the filmic representation of race in film genre criticism" (2012: 558). Although studies such as Adilifu Nama's *Black Spaces: Imagining Race in Science Fiction Film* (2008) have placed race front and center within a discussion of genre, Reid's characterization still holds. Moreover, while some chronologies of US action cinema regard classic Western and gangster films as antecedents of modern forms of action, the significance and longevity of Black Westerns or gangster films feature less often. In turn, while the formative significance of Black action film of the 1970s on Hollywood is sometimes acknowledged, the influence of Hong Kong action has typically been understated or omitted. Such repeated neglect underlines and intersects with Reid's wider point about the exclusion of discussions of race and representation in writings on genre.

As argued in the introduction to this book, action can be usefully characterized as a mode of filmmaking, one that crosses and incorporates multiple genres, series, and cycles. In the conceptualization of modern action as all-action—a cinema in which, as James Kendrick puts it, "Action is not a characteristic, but *the* characteristic" (2019: 2)—the extensiveness of US action in its historical dimensions has been downplayed. As a result, chronologies and film histories account for action in specific, partial, ways. This chapter reflects on the implications of these absences and omissions for an analysis of race and action cinema.

Black action film emerges from the wider moment of Blaxploitation and is most often debated in that context. This seems to support Novotny Lawrence's contention that the term Blaxploitation itself is reductive since "it fails to assign individual films to their respective genres" (2008: 20): in other words, it risks replicating a history of exclusion within scholarship. Presenting case studies to demonstrate how "the addition of blackness expands the detective, horror, gangster, and cop action genres" (2008: 25), the latter exemplified by *Cleopatra Jones* (Jack Starrett, 1973), Lawrence highlights the importance of genre designators and the work that they do. Yvonne D. Sims also reflects on the risks of separating Black action from the development of US action in general. Commenting on the cultural impact of Sigourney Weaver's portrayal of Ripley in the 1979 film *Alien* (Ridley Scott), Sims argues for recognition that: "her celebrated character was made possible by the action heroine in blaxploitation movies. It was African American actresses who redefined the way women were depicted on the screen in the genre of movies commonly referred to as 'blaxploitation'" (2006: 9).

The thriving space of superhero cinema also sees absences in accounting for action. While I (2019), along with others, have pointed to the commercial success of *X-Men* (Bryan Singer, 2000), there are other points of origin involved in harnessing the commercial possibilities of comic-book material. Two years before the release of *X-Men*, *Blade* (Stephen Norrington, 1998) had generated $131 million worldwide, demonstrating the commercial appeal of this mode of filmmaking. As Blade, Wesley Snipes exemplifies the kinetic, mobile action hero. Jonathan Gayles critiques the gender politics of the *Blade* trilogy but emphasizes the action mobility of the central character: "Blade is completely kinetic as he leaps, slices, kicks and punches his way through the film" (2012: 286). Nama also finds the film evocative in terms of movement: "By using time-lapse photography, *Blade* created an eerie sense of movement and space that conveyed a sense of the uncanny and a cityscape populated by vampires" (2011: 139). A dark action horror film that adapted the Marvel Comics character, *Blade* acknowledged not only its comic-book origins, horror and action conventions, but also martial arts and Blaxploitation cinema (at its height when the Blade character debuted in Marvel Comics in 1973). Though it generated two successful sequels, in production and aesthetic terms *Blade* cannot be bracketed with the much-discussed Marvel franchise that commences with *Iron Man* (Jon Favreau) in 2008, not least since the film's visceral violence and horror elements earned an 18 rating in the UK and an R rating in the United States.[1] The post-2008 Marvel cycle would aim for a light-hearted tone and a broadly conceived family audience; it would not showcase a black superhero until *Black Panther* (Ryan Coogler, 2018).

In *Spectacular Bodies* I argued that "formulations of race, constructions of blackness in particular, are central to the American action cinema" (1993: 35) and yet, as per Reid's contention more broadly, foundational scholarship on action as a genre has less often foregrounded questions of race. If discourses of race are central to US action but not as often to classic scholarship on it, what does this tell us about how action has been conceptualized? As I will explore in this chapter, much excellent scholarship engaged with questions of race focuses on action performance and stereotyping as much as (or more than) with questions of genre.

This chapter aims to position action since 2000 in an historical frame, elaborating some of the ways in which US action has been conceptualized by earlier scholars. My concern with the chronology of US action cinema is intimately bound up with how that chronology has been narrated and understood. Might a more expansive understanding of action better recognize the significance of race and ethnicity? I am concerned here not only with scholarly writing and with historicizing action but also with aesthetic dimensions of action and with questions of representation.

The chapter is organized into three sections. The first looks at early critical accounts of action, highlighting foundational essays on the Western, the gangster film, and noting the attention paid to those Hong Kong martial arts movies starring Bruce Lee that played in the US. The second moves on to Black action cinema, examining critical responses that engage most often with performance and stereotype. The final section addresses the presence of Black women in action in earlier decades, before turning to analysis of a recent film, *The Old Guard* (Gina Prince-Bythewood, 2020), which works to delineate a heroic Black woman as action protagonist (Figure 1.1). *The Old Guard* exemplifies the range of contemporary action: there are overtones of horror, fantasy, and romance. With a gay male couple also in the central group, it is also markedly more inclusive than most action films are.

Figure 1.1 While early action scholarship has paid less attention to the role of Black women in action, filmmakers such as Gina Prince-Bythewood have explicitly sought to articulate Black female heroism in action cinema. Here US Marine Nile Freeman (Kiki Layne) reflects on her position in the team of immortal warriors in *The Old Guard* (© Netflix, 2020. All Rights Reserved).

Critical Accounts of Action: Myth and Movement

Revisiting key early writings can be instructive in thinking both about how action is critically constituted, and the ways that discourses of race do and do not figure in that construction. I survey here some foundational essays on the Western and the gangster film, both genres that subsequent critics have taken to be formative for action as it is understood today. During the 1950s Robert Warshow, in the US, and André Bazin, in France, both take the Western to be fundamental to American cinema, contrasting it to the gangster film; both in turn regard speed and movement as central features of the films they discuss. Writing in the late 1960s and early 1970s, Colin McArthur discusses only the gangster film. He concentrates on iconography and characterizes the gangster film as a site of violence associated with the city while speculating on the gangster's symbolic and ideological significance. Also writing in the 1970s, Stuart M. Kaminsky explores Hong Kong action films, which had become popular in the US.

In his influential 1950s writings, Bazin makes clear that what matters to him about the Western is its ability to function on a mythic level. He writes: "It is easy to say that because the cinema is movement the Western is cinema *par excellence*. It is true that galloping horses and fights are its usual ingredients. But in that case the Western would simply be one variety of adventure story" (2005: 141). Here he seeks to distinguish between the adventure story's narrative kinetic elements—the chase, the quest—and the Western's kinetic elements; he prefers thematic complexity. The value judgment he makes is clear when he writes of "the continuous movement of the characters, carried to a pitch of frenzy" (2005: 141). For Bazin, ". . . the Western must be *something else again* than its form. Galloping horses, fights, strong and brave men in a wildly austere landscape could not add up to a definition of the genre nor encompass its charms" (2005: 142, emphasis added).

While the noisy, violent, dynamic qualities so redolent of action today are prominent in Bazin's reflections, in analyzing them he appeals instead to myth—or even art—*in spite of* rather than *because of* familiar elements having to do with energetic movement. He would write in 1946 that *Scarface* (Howard Hawks, 1932) was both the epitome of the gangster film and utterly unique. While the film "sketched in the dramatic rhetoric of the genre," Bazin finds "this tradition of submachine gun bursts, bullet-riddled bodies, and screeching brakes . . . the least interesting, precisely because it had no trouble establishing itself and can now be found everywhere" (1997: 111). It is not the kinetic qualities that distinguish *Scarface*, but its treatment of a moral and/or social scenario. However, it is in the thematic significance and emotive power of these kinetic qualities that action scholarship, in contrast, has tended to locate Bazin's "something else again."

Ideas of spatial mastery are charged and complex in distinct ways when considered alongside the prominence of racial discourses in US action; both the contested character of public space and the political charge of Black visibility come to the fore. Warshow and Bazin find in the Western and in gangster films a profound engagement with ideas of America. Bazin describes the Western as a genre that involves but transcends motion to function as core American myth. Discourses of race and ethnicity are also evident in earlier work on the Western and gangster film as national myth. In "The Western: Or the American Film *Par Excellence*" Bazin makes explicit the racial (and racist) framings and hierarchies of both the Western film and scholarship on it. He foregrounds landscape as fundamental to what he regards as the moral and mythical significance of the Western:

> These immense stretches of prairie, of deserts, of rocks to which the little wooden town clings precariously (a primitive amoeba of a civilization), are exposed to all manner of possible things. The Indian, who lived in this world, [note Bazin's use of the past tense] was incapable of imposing on it man's order. He mastered it only by identifying himself with its pagan savagery. The white Christian on the contrary is truly the conqueror of a new world. The grass sprouts where his horse has passed.
>
> 2005: 145

Bazin owns the character of the Western hero in explicit ethnic and racist terms and develops his argument with reference to setting, type, and a racialized opposition between nature and culture. In the same breath as he valorizes a lifegiving "white Christian," he frames the Western in terms of "an inevitable and necessary contradiction" which stems from the lack of "moral difference between the outlaw and the man who operates within the law" (2005: 146). His analysis indicates how resonant an imagery of the outsider hero is, while his reverie on the whiteness of the hero underlines the exclusionary character of much US action.

In his 1954 essay "Movie Chronicle: The Westerner," Warshow writes that the values of the Western can be expressed "in the image of a single man with a gun on his thigh. The gun tells us that he lives in a world of violence, and even that he 'believes in violence'" (1964: 105). He thus encapsulates the Western in terms of its iconography of violence and its gendered hero. Warshow does not address questions of race and representation and yet they work to complicate the imagery he evokes, as does the character of the society in which the hero's potential violence is imagined. Warshow also writes that the gangster "is the 'no' to that great American 'yes' which is stamped so big over our official culture and yet has so little to do with the way we really feel about our lives" (1964: 90).

In this vein, scholars have long held that popular films articulate issues of national identity. In a much-cited quotation McArthur postulates that: "The

Western and the gangster film have a special relationship to American society . . . it could be said that they represent America talking to itself about, in the case of the Western, its agrarian past, and in the case of the gangster film/thriller, its urban, technological present" (1972: 18). McArthur's observation is telling with respect to the subsequent conceptualization of US action as a type of filmmaking in which racial and national(ist) tropes are prominent. To what extent, we can ask, do the action elements (as we think of them now) of the Western and gangster film contribute to the conversation about America that McArthur sees being staged through cinema? To what extent does race, whether the racial and ethnic diversity of the United States or the racist hierarchies of its social, political, and cultural institutions, form part of that conversation? Within discourses of the nation and of the people, how are differences and inequalities acknowledged and/or repressed and how do these silences register in cinema and scholarship on action? The expressive mobility of heroic figures, and the centrality of violence to action cinema, are surely key sites for thinking about these questions.

Warshow also characterizes the gangster in kinetic terms: while the gangster is for him a man "without culture," nonetheless "he is graceful, moving like a dancer among the crowded dangers of the city" (1964: 89–90). This evocation of the gangster as dancer calls to mind comparisons between action and the musical, whether in terms of an emphasis on choreography and physicality, the timing of punctuating action sequences or the significance of the soundtrack. Musical rhythms and sonic tempos more broadly are vital to action cinema. This is not a recent connection or comparison. Indeed, both the connections between action and the musical and the extent to which they function to foreground race, are highlighted in Kaminsky's essay "Kung Fu Film as Ghetto Myth." Here he couples Bruce Lee as a figure in flight and Fred Astaire, suggesting that both are involved with "films of performance" (1974a: 129). An image of Astaire in yellowface from the Limehouse Blues number of *Ziegfeld Follies* (Lemuel Ayers et al., 1945) points to the musical's sustained association with racial impersonation and appropriation.

Agility, respect, and movement through space with violence and grace are at stake in different ways in many of the accounts of action discussed here. Warshow contrasts the gangster's "unceasing, nervous activity" (1964: 89) with the Western hero's "repose" (1964: 91), referring to repeated images of the hero at ease within a landscape that is a site of action. McArthur highlights the characteristics of stars: "Men such as [James] Cagney, [Edward G.] Robinson and [Humphrey] Bogart seem to gather within themselves the qualities of the genres they appear in so that the violence, suffering and *angst* of the films is restated in their faces, physical presence, movement and speech" (1972: 24, original emphasis). Contrasting Lee to Astaire, Kaminsky highlights kineticism, foregrounding graceful violence even while it operates beyond, or outside class-bound rules. Elsewhere Kaminsky notes a fundamental connection between dance and the gangster film. He recalls that both George Raft and Cagney "were professional dancers before becoming movie gangsters," adding that the figuring of the "dancer as criminal" facilitates "a nervous, graceful sense of movement, or hyper-vitality" (1974b: 20).

Foundational writing on the Western and gangster film tends to conceive of movement within the frame as a kinetic element bound up with ideas of freedom and the nation and with destruction. Writing of what he calls the post-war "superwestern"—meaning both technological innovations such as widescreen and an increasing self-reflexivity—Bazin perceives a new interest in US history. Evaluating revisionist Westerns according to an ideologically loaded chronology, he describes "the beginning of [the] political rehabilitation of the Indian" in *Fort Apache* (John Ford, 1948), (2005: 151). Warshow too detects a change in Westerns, a "deeper seriousness" expressed nicely in spatial terms: "Once it has been discovered that the true theme of the Western movie is not the freedom and expansiveness of frontier life, but its limitations, its material bareness, the pressures of obligation, then even the landscape itself ceases to be quite the arena of free movement it once was, cutting down more than it exaggerates the stature of the horseman who rides across it" (1964: 96–7). But restrictions on movement are both culturally and historically bound up with histories of race and class, with patterns of immigration and with migration North as well as West, for instance. Kaminsky discerns this effectively, pointing to the class associations of the Kung Fu hero and the popularity of these films with urban Black audiences in the US during the 1970s.

Writings on action couple questions of heroism and genre with national mythology. The movement of the Western hero through wilderness, and the rhythms associated with the gangster's transit through urban space, also speak in multiple ways to ideas about gender and race. Important early genre scholarship thus leads to, and is resonant for, our thinking about race and action cinema more broadly.

Black Action Film, Discourses of Race, and US Action Cinema

Given the centrality of the Western as well as of gangster/crime films in articulating an idea of America, it is unsurprising that Black performers and producers have engaged so fully, creatively, and oftentimes profitably with these forms, indeed with action more broadly. Action emerged as an increasingly distinct mode of filmmaking in late 1960s Hollywood; by this point it had already begun to give greater space and prominence to Black male performers, notably sports stars. Paula J. Massood points to "the increasing appeal of the more powerful characters played by a rising cadre of black sports-heroes-turned-actors, like Jim Brown and Fred Williamson" (2003: 82).[2]

Amy Abugo Ongiri also notes the importance of star athletes as part of her account of spectacular Blackness. Emphasizing the physicality and attractiveness of the athletic body, she writes: "Blaxploitation as a genre was primarily focused on beautiful Black phallocentric masculinity as epitomized by many of the genre's major stars—Jim Kelly, Jim Brown, Fred Williamson—who were former athletes" (2009: 173–4). The 1970s film career of martial artist turned actor Jim Kelly (who co-starred with Bruce Lee and John Saxon in *Enter the Dragon* [Robert Clouse, 1973]) also points to New Hollywood's awareness/appropriation of Hong Kong action. Gladstone L. Yearwood writes of Brown and Williamson: "These macho men were skillful perpetrators of action; their violence seemed to be historically justified by the oppression of blacks in society. But their sensational racial wars only fed the coffers of the film industry" (1982: 48). Scholarship has continued to explore such tensions around the political and cultural value of Black action cinema. For Reid, *Sweet Sweetback's Baadasssss Song* (1971) director Melvin Van Peebles created "a new black hero to attract a young black audience," drawing "from both white popular culture and black mythology and folklore" (1993: 77).[3]

For good reason scholarship on Black film and on race and representation has foregrounded questions of characterization and stereotype as much as, indeed rather more than, genre. Hollywood cinema's marginalization of Black stars and performers into stereotypical and minor roles is a feature of decades of film production. Donald Bogle's influential account of Black stardom in US film traces recurring stereotypes, considering these alongside what Black actors did with these types, often giving performances that circumvented their reductive character in ways that Black audiences appreciated. Bogle also comments on the use of athletes turned actors and studies tropes that emphasize power and violence. Under the subheading "Buckmania" he describes early 1970s films as "heady male action fantasies, with tenacious buck protagonists performing deeds of derring-do while self-righteously giving lip service to the idea of political commitment" (2010: 241). He sees "shades of the old Buck" in his account of Wesley Snipes's intense and forceful action roles, though he stresses the subtlety Snipes's performance in *New Jack City* (Mario Van Peebles, 1991). His response echoes Warshow's elaboration of the gangster: "Throughout he is vibrantly alive, a kinetic mass of movement and energy ready to strike at any moment" (2010: 408).

A concern with stereotypes thus emerges from the ways in which Black performers have been associated with and showcased in action genres: while action has been an important space for Black actors in US cinema, they have usually been cast as sidekicks or buddies who are loyal to suffering white heroes. Both scholars and actors have remarked, moreover, on the frequent dislocation of Black characters from communities of color and on the failure to satisfactorily develop story arcs for Black action stars. Some critics explore the complex politics attendant on the commercial potential of young Black audiences. Action elements—violence and movement through urban space—are recurrent themes, and while clearly connected to a mythology of gender and nation that positions Black characters as heroic, many writers are more concerned with the ways in which such films trivialize or commercialize Black experience and expectation. For example, contrasting *Sweet Sweetback's Baadasssss Song* with *Shaft* (Gordon Parks, 1971), Reid discerns a troubling masquerade in the latter: "like doll makers who painted Barbie's face brown, MGM merely created black-skinned replicas of the white heroes of action films" (1993: 84). *Shaft*, and by extension studio-produced Black action films more broadly, represent for Reid a contextless, acritical articulation of blackness.

Ed Guerrero's reading of Eddie Murphy's action comedies, which consolidated Murphy's position as one of the highest-earning stars in Hollywood during the 1980s, suggests they successfully manage similar ideological tensions. While race is the "source of energy and tension" in Murphy's action films, ultimately the challenge is, for Guerrero, the "one-dimensional blackness," with Murphy's characters both contesting their exclusion and yet being utterly isolated and "contained by a white environment" (1993: 132). The same is true of stars such as Will Smith in 1990s action films. The fantasy framing of films such as *Independence Day* (Roland Emmerich, 1996) and *I, Robot* (Alex Proyas, 2004) addresses race only obliquely and racism barely at all.

For Reid, Black action was the result of industrial, political, and creative factors in the early 1970s. Black action film proved, "Despite . . . flaws . . . to be a popular genre which focused on black themes and provided opportunities for blacks in the American film industry" (1988: 34). However, the legacy and impact of both Blaxploitation and Black action more generally is broader than this might suggest. Guerrero briefly explores questions of legacy, Black stardom, and celebrity. Rather than thinking of Blaxploitation as "a dead genre," he argues we "should view [it] more as discursive cultural compost" since it "fed the rise of today's black celebrity culture, from hip hop, gangsta rap, to star status black filmmakers and actors . . ." (2009: 90–91). Guerrero, Reid, and Yearwood focus their accounts on Black male stars (Bogle also discusses female stars). Their scholarship productively explores the articulation of race and action heroism across decades, highlighting connections and patterns of influence that continue to register within and beyond cinema.

Black Women in Action: Critical Perspectives and Stars in Ensemble Action

While Black scholars in particular have highlighted the complexities and ambiguities of Black male stars in action, scholarship in general has less often focused on Black female stars. Not only are women of color frequently marginalized onscreen, but they are also side-lined in much action scholarship, as studies of women in Black action—and of Black women in action in general—make clear. Mia Mask (2009) and Sims (2006) analyze performers, stardom, and types as key sites of interpretation and meaning. Stephane Dunn (2008) explores the legacy of Blaxploitation now by looking squarely at female rap artists, suggesting an accounting that brings Black women to the fore.

In this context it is instructive to reflect on how scholarship has conceptualized and named action, and to look at who gets to take action (and what kind of action) on screen. To this end, I offer a brief commentary on two films that feature Black female stars in action then turn to *The Old Guard* as a recent ensemble action film. While both *Fatal Beauty* (Tom Holland, 1987) and *Set It Off* (F. Gary Gray, 1996) have been analyzed in relation to stars and genre, as well as larger contexts of race and representation, neither features prominently in scholarship on action. That omission, I want to suggest, speaks to the sort of accounts of (and accounting for) action that have come to predominate. Kara Keeling describes *Set It Off* as innovating and transforming the conventions it employs to the extent that reviewers found it difficult to locate the film "into their existing generic categories" (2003: 36). That sense of not quite fitting categories is in part why such films have not been central to action scholarship. They are further marginalized by the omissions and racist assumptions of the earlier critical accounts that many regard as lynchpins for today's action films.

In part since the film was not a commercial success, *Fatal Beauty*—which stars Whoopi Goldberg as narcotics cop Rita Rizzoli—tends to be considered relatively briefly and with a focus on Goldberg's career, as well as within the larger context of women in crime films. Linda Mizejewski, for example, reflects on how much *Fatal Beauty* has in common with other "investigating women scenarios" (2004: 4), her analysis firmly located in genre and again referring to types—the "action-style woman as investigator or cop" (2004: 118). In *Spectacular Bodies* I argue that Rizzoli's capacity for action is both celebrated and contained (1993: 33–4). The film appears more often in reflections on casting, stereotype, and Goldberg's stardom than in work on action or genre. Lisa Pertillar Brevard emphasizes Goldberg's limited choice of parts despite her media prominence, observing that in her role as Rizzoli, she "intentionally strikes a necessary balance between farce and fierceness" (2012: 41). Frankie Y. Bailey describes Goldberg's character as "taunted and teased" by male detectives, suggesting that race functions as "an inescapable, though never mentioned, subtext to her contentious exchanges with her colleagues" (2009: 88). While regarding *Fatal Beauty* as "mediocre" and doing little to develop the star's portfolio, Mask usefully highlights the importance of (grotesque) comedy to both Goldberg's stand-up and film performances. Mask underlines the disruptive function of comedy, suggesting that readings of Goldberg's films need to take account of "the generic conventions of comedy and the instability of identity within the genre" (2009: 108). Following

Figure 1.2 Whoopi Goldberg—here seen in undercover clothing—performs disruptive unruliness in her tough cop persona as Rita Rizzoli in *Fatal Beauty* (1987).

this line of argument, Rizzoli's flamboyant unruliness—evident in, for example, visual gags over undercover garb, but also in a passionate determination to track down lethal drugs—can be framed in relation to the space of action comedy more broadly (Figure 1.2).

Set It Off is an action film in the gangster tradition. Four women are led by circumstance—poverty and discrimination, loss and grief—into crime. Having had their loot stolen, the four attempt one last bank robbery, but all are killed except for Stony (Jada Pinkett). Three of the film's four stars—Vivica A. Fox, Queen Latifah and Pinkett—have subsequently had strong associations with action roles (including film and television). Despite its use of heist, chase, fight, and other conventions, *Set It Off*, like *Fatal Beauty*, is relatively rarely included within discussions of action. Kimberly Springer situates *Set It Off* in relation to images of violence, invoking the stereotypical figure of the Sapphire.[4] Contrasting it to the differently framed violence at the heart of *Waiting to Exhale* (Forest Whitaker, 1995), Springer underlines the class discourses and importance of aspiration underpinning Stony's survival when her three co-conspirators are violently killed. Only Keeling frames *Set It Off* as action, locating it both in relation to what she terms the "ghetto action cycle" and (like Springer) films such as *Waiting to Exhale* which "consolidate a 'black middle class' market" (2003: 36).

In contrast to *Fatal Beauty* and *Set It Off*, the Netflix film *The Old Guard* (2020) *was* widely received as action. Prince-Bythewood speaks of her enthusiasm for Greg Rucka's screenplay—adapted from his graphic novel—with its "bad-ass" women warriors and the presence of "a young Black female hero, which we never see and absolutely need to see" (2020). The film features a group of immortal warriors/mercenaries who originate from different periods in history and different parts of the world. Led by the oldest among them, Andy (Charlize Theron), the group initially consists of Booker (Matthias Schoenaerts), who discovered his immortality during the Napoleonic wars, and lovers Nicky (Luca Marinelli) and Joe (Marwan Kenzari), who met during the Crusades. War is thus explicitly a crucible for these warriors. The newest member of the group, Nile Freeman (Kiki Layne), is also a soldier. A US marine, her "death" while serving in Afghanistan is followed by an inexplicable recovery. Although sharing a martial identity—their intimacy and connection underlined by shared dreams/ nightmares—members of the group deploy weapons and elements associated with different fighting styles. Combat and images of the team's repeated deaths and reanimations are central to the film's aesthetic. Violence is at times graceful, as in the balletic duel between Nile and Andy on the plane, at times grotesque, notably in the wounds that the group suffer (and recover) from.

The immortality of the members of the "Old Guard" is central both to the film's narrative and its visual construction. Fantasy, supernatural, and horror elements are at work alongside and intertwined with the war and the spy film, highlighting digital surveillance as a facet of modern life. Immortality renders the group outsiders who are subject to persecution and potential exploitation. They are isolated from society, losing friends and family through the passage of time. The narrative possibility that each death may be final is less of an immediate risk than discovery and capture.

Andy's demeanor is world-weary, even despairing. She is exhausted not only by a life of violence, loss, and death but also by the difficulty of doing good, of making a difference. The film's opening sequence pictures the team shot and seemingly dead, having been lured into a basement; these images are complemented by Andy's reflection in voiceover that she has "been here before, over and over again," that she is "just so tired of it." Centuries earlier, we learn, Andy and her sister immortal Quynh (Veronica Ngo) were accused of witchcraft. The latter's fate, entombed in an iron maiden underwater, haunts the others, confirming their outsider status. Newcomer Nile is part of this connection: able to sense each other's pain, the Old Guard are linked by/in exclusion. Such bonding of the military group as apart from society speaks to long-established war film tropes (Figure 1.3).

Prince-Bythewood emphasized in interviews her ambitions for *The Old Guard*. She wanted to showcase Black women on screen and to move towards inclusivity more broadly, notably by preserving the queer relationship between Joe and Nicky from the graphic novel. She was enthusiastic about now working in action. Prince-Bythewood (2021) also commented on her excitement in being able to "disrupt" action by linking action and romance. While action has long operated in and through homosocial logics, the depiction of the film's gay couple

Figure 1.3 Reprising war movie tropes, Andy (Charlize Theron) and Nile (Kiki Layne) overcome tensions to fight as a team in the climactic battle of *The Old Guard* (© Netflix, 2020. All Rights Reserved).

is hugely significant. Alongside that relationship, the film depicts Andy and Quynh's time together through conventions that suggest a lesbian comradeship. The depiction of the pair's condemnation for witchcraft speaks to the persecution of women (queer women, women of color) as outside patriarchal power structures.[5] Yet if *The Old Guard* disrupts action, it nonetheless employs recognizable action conventions. The outsider figure with capacity for violence is a potent site of meaning, redolent for harnessing action narratives to a sense of social anger if less often critique.

The Old Guard's action unfolds across several countries, features multiple fight sequences, shows extraordinary heroes in scenarios of peril, and provides an atmospheric soundtrack which underscores both the dramatic and the action sequences. Freedom to move through space and grace in violence are prominent. The choreography depicts the team's movement within urban, rural, and military spaces: the team travels on foot, by car, train, and plane. Members fight in cramped rather than open spaces (the latter are reserved for flashbacks). The violent confrontation prefigured in the opening shots is contained in a basement; later the scene will be replayed through a video screen, a gamified commodity. Just as Cleo (Queen Latifah)'s death is seen as horrific television spectacle in *Set It Off*, the recording of the team's death and revival in *The Old Guard* cues the audience to the existence of malevolent social forces: Steven Merrick's (Harry Melling) cruel, greedy pharmaceutical corporation seeks to monetize the group's physiology.

United by a martial identity, the film firmly suggests that Andy will transfer power to Nile, a young Black woman who is, as Stina Novak and Corina Wieser-Cox suggest, aligned with "modernity" and "fluidity" (2022: 79). While multi-racial action films are frequently organized in hierarchical manner, replicating structures that position whites as leading characters, *The Old Guard* works against these conventions. The film's warriors are different ages, ethnicities, and nationalities. Nile's alliance with ex-CIA man Copley (Chiwetel Ejiofor)—initially Merrick's ally—and her determined assault on the corporate headquarters where her comrades are held captive, mark her as a figure able to navigate spaces of modernity, and in particular the complexities of a world dominated by data. The film's final image—following a coda that reintroduces Quynh and tracks the group through historical imagery—is of Nile's image caught on surveillance in Merrick's building, gun in hand and ready for action. That image is then erased, presumably by Copley who has been tasked with covering the group's digital tracks.

The tense relationship between Nile and Andy is at the dramatic center of *The Old Guard*. They shift from tutelage and conflict (hand-to-hand fights in the desert and aboard a cargo plane), to alignment (they shoot together), then in a reversal Nile defends a newly vulnerable Andy. The film thus plays with and rewrites war movie conventions whereby characters of color are repeatedly sacrificed. Moreover, rather than the older more experienced warrior dying once they have passed on their wisdom, *The Old Guard* has Andy survive even as Nile takes charge.

Conclusion

I have sought in this chapter to foreground the place of Black women in action cinema, and to underline how our accounting for action needs to take notice of both filmmaking conventions and the significance of stars, types, and stereotypes. The range and scope of post-2000 action cinema, and its multiple roots, means that our accounts of it are typically—perhaps inevitably— partial, highlighting some dimensions and downplaying others. In this context, I have explored significant absences regarding race in some of the foundational genre studies relied on by action scholars. Extrapolating from these absences we can ask useful questions about the conventions that have shaped action cinema. While Black women have long been a presence in action, it is telling that films in which they are protagonists—examples from several decades are mentioned here—are marginalized within histories of action. But these histories help to define the object of study. Moving past an idea of Hollywood action as the terrain of whiteness involves understanding the range of predecessors available, and the fluidity/adaptability of the myths that are so central to action cinema. Doing so can enable productive analyses of the role of Black women in recent—and quite different—action films such as *Lila and Eve* (Charles Stone III, 2015), *Proud Mary* (Babak Najafi, 2018), *The Woman King* (Gina Prince-Bythewood, 2022) and *Black Panther: Wakanda Forever* (Ryan Coogler, 2022).

Since action tropes foreground physicality in ways that risk falling into reductive stereotyping, both performers and filmmakers are involved in negotiation with the action image. This chapter has contrasted the absences of foundational genre scholarship with the rich work on Black action and Black action stars as entailing negotiations with—and at times resistance to—persistent racial stereotypes and limiting roles. Such analyses prompt consideration of both how much ideas about race need to be centralized in analyses of action, and the importance of including female roles and stars in this discussion.

Notes

1 With the exception of *Deadpool* (Tim Miller, 2016)—in any case adjacent rather than central—the films in the Marvel Cinematic Universe are all rated PG-13 in the US.

2 A New Hollywood iteration of the war film, *The Dirty Dozen* (Robert Aldrich, 1967) provided football star Brown with his first role in an ensemble film, showcasing his athleticism and forging an association with action roles. Released during the Vietnam War, *The Dirty Dozen* is set in World War II, a period in which the US military remained segregated. As Richard Slotkin notes, the film acknowledges yet sidesteps its depiction of an inclusive unit: "The excuse for his presence is that this is a special unit, recruited from condemned prisoners for a suicide mission" (2001: 490).

3 Reid describes Van Peebles's use of conventions from Westerns in which "heroes tended to be social outcasts, inarticulate, single males who are placed in violent situations" (1993: 77). He refers specifically to *Hang 'Em High* (Ted Post, 1968), which features a violent revenge plot and is tonally appropriate to his reading of Black action as rejecting political cultures of non-violence.

4 For Dunn the Sapphire image designates a "bitchy and deceptive black female" (2008: 115), a type which she sees intersecting with the sexualized imagery of the Jezebel figure. Springer sees the Sapphire type as devaluing women; while the Sapphire "is not afraid to be loud and to speak her mind" (2001: 176), the Sapphire is castigated for her limited independence.

5 Novak and Wieser-Cox (2022) discuss in detail the film's use of queer coding and its rejection of tropes by which queer characters are killed off in action texts.

Works Cited

Bailey, Frankie Y. (2009), "Screening Stereotypes: African American Women in Hollywood Films" in Drew Humphries (ed.), *Women, Violence, and the Media: Readings in Feminist Criminology*, 75–98, Boston: Northeastern University Press.

Bazin, André (1997), "The Crisis of French Cinema or *Scarface* and the Gangster Film," in Bert Cardullo (ed.), *Bazin At Work: Major Essays and Reviews from the Forties and Fifties*, trans. Alain Piette and Bert Cardullo, 135–7, New York: Routledge.

Bazin, André (2005), *What Is Cinema?*, vol. 2, trans. Hugh Gray, Berkeley: University of California Press.

Bogle, Donald (2010), *Toms, Coons, Mulattoes, Mammies, and Bucks: An Interpretive History of Blacks in American Films* (4th edn), New York: Continuum.

Brevard, Lisa Pertillar (2012), *Whoopi Goldberg on Stage and Screen*, Jefferson, NC: McFarland.

Dunn, Stephane (2008), *"Baad Bitches" & Sassy Supermamas: Black Power Action Films*, Urbana: Illinois University Press.

Gayles, Jonathan (2012), "Black Macho and the Myth of the Superwoman Redux: Masculinity and Misogyny in Blade," *The Journal of Popular Culture*, 45 (2): 284–300.

Guerrero, Ed (1993), *Framing Blackness: The African American Image in Film*, Philadelphia: Temple University Press.

Guerrero, Ed (2009), "The So-Called Fall of Blaxploitation," *Velvet Light Trap*, 64: 90–1.

Kaminsky, Stuart M. (1974a), "Kung Fu Film as Ghetto Myth," *Journal of Popular Film and Television*, 3 (2): 129–38.

Kaminsky, Stuart M. (1974b) *American Film Genres: Approaches to a Critical Theory of Popular Film*, Dayton, OH: Pflaum Publishing.

Keeling, Kara (2003), "'Ghetto Heaven': *Set It Off* and the Valorization of Black Lesbian Butch-Femme Sociality," *The Black Scholar: Journal of Black Studies and Research*, 33 (1): 33–46.

Kendrick, James (2019), "A Genre of Its Own: From Westerns, to Vigilantes, to Pure Action," in James Kendrick (ed.), *A Companion to the Action Film*, 35–54, Hoboken, NJ: John Wiley & Sons.

Lawrence, Novotny (2008), *Blaxploitation Films of the 1970s: Blackness and Genre*, New York: Routledge.

Mask, Mia (2009) *Divas on Screen: Black Women in American Film*, Chicago: Illinois University Press.

Massood, Paula J. (2003), *Black City Cinema: African American Urban Experiences in Film*, Philadelphia: Temple University Press.

McArthur, Colin (1972), *Underworld USA*, London: Secker & Warburg.

Mizejewski, Linda (2004), *Hardboiled and High Heeled: The Woman Detective in Popular Culture*, New York: Routledge.

Nama, Adilifu (2008), *Black Spaces: Imagining Race in Science Fiction Film*, Austin: University of Texas Press.

Nama, Adilifu (2011), *Super Black: American Pop Culture and Black Superheroes*, Austin: University of Texas Press.

Novak, Stina and Wieser-Cox, Corina (2022), "'This Is the World We Made': Queer Metaphor, Neo-Colonial Militarization, and Scientific Ethics in *The Old Guard* (2020)," *gender forum*, 82: 75–97.

Ongiri, Amy Abugo (2009), *Spectacular Blackness: The Cultural Politics of the Black Power Movement and the Search for a Black Aesthetic*, Charlottesville: University of Virginia Press.

Prince-Bythewood, Gina (2020), "*The Old Guard* Director Gina Prince-Bythewood on Casting Kiki Layne," *Variety*, 11 July. Available online: https://variety.com/2020/film/news/the-old-guard-director-gina-prince-bythewood-on-casting-kiki-layne-1234703876/ (accessed 1 August 2022).

Prince-Bythewood, Gina (2021), "*The Old Guard* Director Gina Prince-Bythewood on Shooting Love Scenes and Action Sequences," *Variety*, 14 July. Available online: https://variety.com/2020/scene/news/the-old-guard-gina-prince-bythewood-charlize-theron-kiki-layne-1234706426/ (accessed 1 August 2022).

Reid, Mark A. (1988), "The Black Action Film: The End of the Patiently Enduring Black Hero," *Film History*, 2 (1): 23–36.

Reid, Mark A. (1993), *Redefining Black Film*, Berkeley: University of California Press.

Reid, Mark A. (2012), "The Black Gangster Film," in Barry Keith Grant (ed.), *Film Genre Reader IV*, 558–75, Austin: University of Texas Press.

Sims, Yvonne D. (2006) *Women of Blaxploitation: How the Black Action Film Heroine Changed American Popular Culture*, Jefferson, NC: McFarland.

Slotkin, Richard (2001), "Unit Pride: Ethnic Platoons and the Myths of American Nationality," *American Literary History*, 13 (3): 469–98.

Springer, Kimberly (2001), "Waiting to Set It Off: African American Women and the Sapphire Fixation," in Martha McCaughey and Neal King (eds), *Reel Knockouts: Violent Women in the Movies*, 172–99, Austin: University of Texas Press.

Tasker, Yvonne (1993), *Spectacular Bodies: Gender, Genre and the Action Cinema*, London: Routledge.

Tasker, Yvonne (2019), "X-Men/Action Men: Performing Masculinities in Superhero and Science-Fiction Cinema," in James Kendrick (ed.), *A Companion to the Action Film*, 381–97, Hoboken, NJ: John Wiley & Sons.

Warshow, Robert (1964), *The Immediate Experience: Movies, Comics, Theatre, and Other Aspects of Popular Culture*, New York: Anchor Books.

Yearwood, Gladstone L. (1982), "The Hero in Black Film: An Analysis of the Film Industry and Problems in Black Cinema," *Wide Angle*, 15 (2): 42–50.

Chapter 2

Dirt Research: Contemporary Stunt Work in Action

Lauren Steimer

When sketching the boundaries of a national production context, it is best to start with your feet on the ground, treading the well-worn paths of the raw materials necessary to support an industry. "Dirt research," as pioneered by Harold Innis (2007), requires site-specific observation and an ethnographic approach to the "staples" that define any individual economy. The practice of dirt research unearths the material circumstances of media production. In the case of action cinema and television, this method rematerializes the seemingly impossible bodies and preternatural feats of on-screen action. The function of this approach is to ground action spectacle in labor practices and to reorient action media studies in its approaches toward directors, stars, and performance. For example, dirt research into stunt industries around the world reveals the differences between location-specific patterns of access to employment (certification systems vs. nepotistic hiring practices), the creation of coalition-building units (craft unions vs. smaller groups, clubs, and networks), and categories of on-site work practices (flexible vs. rigid considerations of job duties).

Stunt workers all over the world find jobs in live-performance combat theater, in films, and on television. The means by which they find that work is distinct from the evaluation processes employed in their local environments. These stunt workers are hired either because they have achieved certification from an accrediting body or because they are known within the local stunt community to have the required skills to perform the dangerous task at hand. Regardless of which of the above pathways helps them to secure work, the predominant factor worldwide that contributes to consistent employment is the strength and depth of a stunt worker's network. Those networks are generally androcentric, nepotistic, and lack large-scale racial and ethnic diversity.

There has been a sea change in transnational action design since *The Matrix* (Lana and Lilly Wachowski) was released in 1999. The transition from European and American boxing traditions to Asian martial arts-style fight work on screen and the new dependency on wire-rig-heavy productions, with integration of computer-generated components, has meant that stunt performers working in major production hubs have had to adjust their training and specialize in new disciplines to secure employment. In this new era of on-screen action spectacle design, stunt workers are simultaneously more protected than they have ever been by safety equipment, more commonly ensconced in wire rigs in front of green screens, and more radically endangered by the effects of the dwindling stunt job market.

This chapter asserts that the visual economy of contemporary action is defined by the raw materials provided by the precarious and often invisible labor of stunt workers: choreographed fights, wirework, body burns, car crashes, and explosions. To speak with precision about these tactics, the conditions of their production, and the people who produce them, action scholars may venture forth into the field and explore action spectacle creation in-situ. Dirt research on action can garner more precise knowledge of the working conditions of action spectacle production, the industrial structures limiting the career growth of women and racial minorities in each setting, and the lived relationship to the transnational flow of action style across borders. The goals of our ethnographic projects can be to better contextualize the people, non-human animals, objects, and environments of action spectacle production. This methodological shift requires detailed analyses of genre, sub-genre, and cycle, as well as style, narrative, meaning-production, affect, gendered performance, racialized address, and spectatorship. It does not negate earlier traditions of action scholarship. This approach retains the key concerns of action film studies, yet it also reorients the discipline with a new set of skills designed to facilitate more nuanced approaches to these mainstays of action analysis, by grounding them in the conditions of action production.

There is no globally consistent labor system via which stunt work is evaluated and procured, but two patterns of access to employment operate in major media production hubs—a certification system and informal nepotistic craft networks. In the United Kingdom, Australia, New Zealand, and the Republic of Ireland, prospective stunt workers train in various disciplines (e.g., martial arts, climbing, diving, horse riding, precision driving) and are tested to achieve certification to work in the industry as provisional, professional, or expert members. These regimented systems are generally designed to mimic the UK standard certification process and are designed to help young stunt performers consistently find work in a manner that eliminates the nepotistic hiring structures more common to US stunt communities, while ensuring specific safety standards are met. Stunt work cultures around the world tend to follow systems akin to either the UK certification system or the US approach. In the US system, stunt workers and coordinators form units with selective entry processes. These teams help to promote the careers of members and the exclusive acceptance processes limit the access of under-trained performers to ensure safety on set. South Africa, India, and Hong Kong follow more laissez-faire organizational frameworks. Both the UK and US systems are in theory designed to ensure safety on set by selecting only the most well-trained stunt performers for long term work in the industry. The UK framework does so by regimented testing and certification. The US stunt labor market attempts to maintain safe working conditions via a stunt person's reputation within the community. In practice, both systems tend to exclude women and racial minorities, such that the practices of "wigging" (putting a wig on a stunt man to double an actress) and "paint downs"/"black ups" (covering the face and visible appendages of a white stunt worker in pitch black makeup to double a Black/Māori actor or actress) still occur in many national production climates, including *all* of those mentioned above. These practices are less common in the USA and UK than they were in decades past, but that is not due to either of the evaluative frameworks for employment in those industries. Rather, it is more directly an effect of pushback from organized collectives of stuntwomen and stunt workers of color.

Because stunt networking practices have historically excluded under-represented minorities, workers who are members of minority communities like Thulani Ndlovu, Dee Bryant, Olivia Summers, and Angela Meryl have formed their own organizations and schools to promote visibility in their own stunt communities. Thulani Ndlovu started the Dimensional Stunt School to train Black stuntmen and stuntwomen in South Africa in 2002, "where white stunt actors capable of bungee jumping off a bridge, disarming a knife-wielding attacker or being set on fire outnumber Blacks 7 to 1" (Goering 2004). The school aims to provide employable, trained, and safe Black stunt workers to an industry more prone to paint downs than any other. Tired of hearing about wig downs and paint downs—common because so few white stunt coordinators knew of any skilled Black, Latina, and Indian American female precision car and motorcycle drivers—Dee Bryant, Olivia Summers, and Angela Meryl formed the Association of Women Drivers in 2020. They wanted to ensure that trained minority stuntwomen did not lose out on opportunities due to flaws in Hollywood organizational frameworks for stunt labor. They also wanted to enable stunt workers to respond, proactively, to the stunt industry's discriminatory hiring practices. These contemporary attempts to correct inequities in stunt industries have historical precedents in the 1960s in the US. The Stuntmen's Association of Motion Pictures formed in 1961 in Hollywood in a successful attempt to help qualified white stuntmen and stunt coordinators find work in the industry. Women and racial minorities, excluded from this organization, faced difficulties infiltrating Hollywood. The Stuntwomen's Association of Motion Pictures and the Black Stuntmen's Association (which also allowed women to join) were formed in 1967 to mitigate the problems faced by minoritized stunt workers effectively blocked from gainful employment due to the dominance of the Stuntmen's Association (Figure 2.1). The fight for equal access

Figure 2.1 Black Stuntmen's Association members circa 1967. Courtesy of Nonie L. Robinson.

to work for women, racial minorities, and disabled stunt workers is a persistent obstacle in many major global production hubs.

To approach action from the perspective of precarious labor requires a radical turn away from the star or the action auteur as the primary focus of scholarly investigations and a methodological shift away from representational analysis of seemingly singular personalities. Stunt workers are commonly effaced by the production process and made ever more invisible by scholarly emphasis on the representational attributes of stars, who very often take credit for the labor of their stunt doubles. This chapter demonstrates that scholars concerned to address action labor can adjust our approaches so as not to participate in this double erasure. In what follows, I sketch the parameters of the dirt research paradigm, reorient action film and media studies away from directors and stars and toward stunt workers, and outline some of the revelations uncovered by this approach.

Innis: Dirt Research

Canadian economic historian and media theorist Harold Innis pioneered the form of fieldwork he referred to as "dirt research" in the 1920s. Like many of us, Innis conducted research at libraries and archives but found the access provided by these outlets to his main objects of analysis fundamentally incomplete. He began to take research trips in which he traveled by canoe to map out eighteenth and nineteenth century routes for the fur trade in Canada. The dirt research method is a form of infrastructural ethnography designed to account for human and non-human labor, the environmental conditions of production and distribution, as well as commonly used objects and mechanisms necessary to these processes. As Karen Stanbridge argues: "It was ethnography extreme" (2014: 389). Innis's process included furious notetaking, extensive interviews, and personal sketches. His method accounted for geology, geography, weather conditions, and the availability of the resources (human, non-human, and otherwise) necessary to the production of a staple commodity within an industry. As Charles R. Acland explains, "[b]y 'dirt' research, Innis meant a form of witnessing and experiencing the sites, routes, venues, and operations of industrial production, refinement, and transport. To do this, he travelled extraordinary distances through remote regions, doing so by rail, boat, and canoe." Acland explains that '"dirt' research was not conventional ethnographic writing, but rather a form of attentiveness to the minute and localized aspects" of every stage of production and distribution processes (2014: 8). Innis's attention to the intricacies of production and distribution chains mirrors Richard Schechner's call for scholars to be attentive to the entirety of the performance process and not simply the singular instance of the body on stage or screen, which is simply one step in this chain of events that comprise a performance (1985: 19). Schechner's reframing of the act of performance as not a singular event but part of a sequence that begins with training and early knowledge formation in bodily disciplines indicates pathways for dirt research in action. Studying the raw materials that comprise action spectacle involves tracing the entire performance sequence—from the individual stunt worker's training to the profilmic performance, and finally to the visible on-screen event (e.g., a fight, a fall, an explosion).

Contemporary action, if understood as a genre, is a fundamentally promiscuous one, as Yvonne Tasker points out: "most contemporary or post-classical action films are indeed more or less hybrids, drawing on and combining generic plots, settings and character types from sources including science-fiction, the western, horror, the epic, war films, crime cinema and thrillers, disaster movies, swordplay and martial arts, even comedy" (2004: 4). Action as *genre* operates as a useful shorthand for both industry and audiences. James Kendrick says, even more broadly, that the action genre (he uses the word "genre") is "difficult to define in absolute terms" because it "can be set anywhere and at any time, feature almost any plot, and utilize virtually any character type," and "overlaps to varying degrees with numerous other genres." Nonetheless he also distinguishes the *contemporary* action genre. For him it contains "a core set of characteristics: spectacular physical action; a narrative emphasis on fights, chases, and explosions; and a combination of state-of-the-art special effects and stunt work. In today's action films, physical action is central, frequent, intense, and increasingly divorced from the laws of physics. Action is not a characteristic, but *the* characteristic" (2019: 3, 2). While physical action may be the defining characteristic of modern action, spectacular corporeal displays in the form of fights, falls, and explosions were and remain common to many genres dating from the 1910s. In its current incarnation, action may simply just have more of these moments of "physical action" than other generic incarnations. That might lead us to believe that stunt workers most often find work on action films. This is decidedly not the case. Indeed, studying where, how, and why stunt workers ply their skills provides new insight into the structure of action labor on set.

Staples of Action: Stunt Workers

For stunt workers, "action" represents the possibility of paid employment across a much wider range of genres than typically covered by action scholars. Work in action is, moreover, not medium-specific, or even specific to media: laborers and practices flow across film, television, video game, and live-performance traditions and they transcend/ignore national boundaries. Most stunt workers cobble together paychecks from gig work on films and television shows that audiences and industries alike consider as outside any "pure" action genre. Increasingly, due to the content boom in television series, much of their work is in television rather than for film. Meanwhile the early career stunt workers who find the most consistent work do so in live-performance venues like scripted medieval jousting tournaments as dinner theater, stunt shows at theme parks, and touring arena superhero shows. Stunt workers are hired to deliver "physical action" as safely as possible, without endangering the actors. The degree to which stunt workers are consistently needed to fall, fight, or be lit on fire for a production underlines the diverse range of production settings in which action design is showcased.

Although physical action is a necessary and expected element of the action genre, it is consistently present across genre and media forms. This revelation might encourage scholars to shift our approach to historicizing action. Action performance—with stunt workers as one test case—is not confined to a single medium, a singular genre; it crosses national borders, can be found in different centuries, and/or is specific to the dawn of film (Christine Gledhill and Linda Williams use both temporal conceptualizations in *Melodrama Unbound*). In fact, Gledhill and Williams's argument that in "mainstream cinema and much television, the central aesthetic is melodrama, not something called "classical cinema," is equally as true of action cinema and television when viewed through the historical lens of stunt labor (2018: 2).

Following Gledhill and Williams, a labor-forward approach to action performance simultaneously makes clear and "unbinds" the historical connections and transitions in spectacular physical performance in all action-infused genres including chase films, travel films, swashbucklers, westerns, slapstick comedies, science fiction films, horror films, driving films, epics, war films, disaster movies, musicals, and many more. The rise and fall of all these genres, sub-genres, and cycles, and the shifts in style and form of physical action on screen are often due to how the available stunt labor has been trained, whether on film and television productions or through work with touring rodeo shows, wild west shows, Turkic and Cossack horse trick performances, circus acts, music hall/vaudeville acts, gymnastics team shows, martial arts tournaments, and precision driving competitions. The raw material for much physical action production is the body of the stunt worker.

Staples of Action Economies: Action Stars vs. Bodies Without Names

While the star's body is certainly a raw material for action production as well, this body, and our emphasis on it, commonly obscures the skilled work of the expert performer. The stunt worker becomes a body with no name. Focus on the action star's body as signifier of various (sometimes competing) meanings remains productive, but one should take care not to duplicate the erasure of the identity of the stunt worker that is perpetuated by the technologies of stardom. Action analysis has the capacity to deconstruct the corporeal amalgam of skilled expert performer and posturing actor. A major shift in action star studies is required: the body of the star is not singular. This acknowledgment extends beyond consideration of stunt doubles to the entire team participating in the construction of the star: costume designers, makeup artists, prop creators, dialogue coaches, and many more.

Some action stars may not excel at delivering dialogue or be able to perform certain emotional registers convincingly, as Chris Holmlund explains of Sylvester Stallone's propensity for "monosyllables" or "grunts" (2014: 3). Nevertheless, they are experts at making audiences and even scholars believe that they do most or even all their own stunts. Though much effort is spent on publicity material, interviews, and behind-the-scenes featurettes showcasing stars doing their own stunts, as a rule, they do not. This information is not revealed to audiences or the press, and all efforts are made to erase the work of the stunt double. Stunt doubles, in turn, do not reveal the truth of the production process on the record, though it is widely known inside the industry that stars do not perform stunts. Stunt workers keep this secret, knowing that to do otherwise would severely impact their chances of future employment. Action stars are generally very good at two things: mimicking the movements of stunt doubles for match shots and lying about this process in interviews. For example, an anonymous South African stunt performer pointed out that one of the most famous Hollywood action actresses who often claims to "do her own stunts" in high-prestige action films, not only did not do her own stunts, but was absent and "difficult" to work with for much of the film's production (Capazorio 2014). In these instances, an actor's face can be performance captured onto their stunt double. This process of erasure is not simply a Hollywood phenomenon; Indian stuntman Javid Gauri explains that "we don't even get a credit. . . . In a scene, when the character takes off their helmet and shows their face to the audience, the hero [star] gets all the glory and we feel bad" (quoted in "The Stuntmen of Bollywood" 2019). The practice of stars taking credit for the work of their stunt doubles is not new, nor is it necessarily nation specific. There are outliers such as the Hong Kong media production context, but many star systems all over the world, including India, the United States, and the United Kingdom (among many others) have relied on a similar technology of stardom for decades. The erasure of stunt workers serves many purposes, but the primary function is to suture the star to their character and in doing so to make the actor come across as invincible, daring, and exceptional.

The conflation of star and action is an effective marketing practice, which can make action spectacles more engaging for audiences because of the star's seeming commitment to their craft. To reveal the truth of the action production process is to divorce the action star from their character and to position them as vulnerable, fearful, and average compared to their stunt double. This deceptive discourse has continued because the action star's persona is predicated on this distinction—to wit: unlike stars from other genres, action stars are committed to delivering an authentic physical performance regardless of the precarity of the scenario. Any representational analysis of the action star should assert the high caliber of acting that is involved in the spectacle of action production and in the promotion of the spectacle of action production. Scholars have the power to name the labor of the stunt worker.

Staples of Action Economies: Action Directors vs. Action Designers

Films and television episodes may require directors to advise actors and showrunners to set the narrative arc of a production, but that does not make these above-the-line workers the primary staples of action production. Much like action stars, directors and showrunners often misrepresent their contributions to action production. Like those stars who are billed and known as "action stars," certain filmmakers market themselves as "action directors." Such a moniker can help a director get consistent work in the action genre. Some directors and showrunners also speak about their work with an air of machismo, which cements the public and industry perceptions of these figures as linked to and capable of crafting complex action spectacles. Historically, film and media studies scholars have described a collection of these directors as action "auteurs," suggesting that they were responsible for all creative decisions. In most cases scholarly misconceptions that directors (and showrunners) craft action spectacles were conditioned by belief that these media professionals frame their artistic impact honestly and by an understanding reinforced by a lack of ethnographic on- and off-set research. While there *are* many small independent action productions in which the director or cinematographer may have more input into the action design, this is not the case for the majority of productions. It is possible to shift the focus of action film scholarship away from the supposedly overwhelming influence some directors have and recognize how much below-the-line professionals add.

Action design is not commonly in the purview of above-the-line personnel. Directors may make some editing choices or provide the action coordinator with suggestions, but overall, "action directors" are not heavily involved in action creation. Work generally falls to the action or stunt coordinator, fight coordinator, the second unit director, and the stunt crew, and it is increasingly referred to as "action design." The practice of creating a previs video for fight scenes, i.e., a video rendering that includes choreography, cinematography, precise editing, and suggestions for special effects, has become such a standard part of action design work in the last ten years that every ambitious stunt worker must master not simply martial arts or gymnastics, but also Adobe Premiere and camera work.

As part of the action design process, the stunt coordinator, fight coordinator, second unit director, and stunt crew will choreograph the performance, suggest the camera's placement and edits, train the actors for simple movements, and study the actors' comportment to match them more closely for insert shots. Lisa Purse describes the presentational strategies of action design as:

> a slowing or quickening of editing pace, or of movement within the frame; a significant change of scale or of the spatial relations between objects; the explicit display of special effects that register as out of the ordinary. In both what is shown and how it is shown, then, spectacle's novelty is relational, depending for its impact on marking itself out from its context. These differentiating strategies inform spectacle's capacity to trigger a range of intense responses, from shock and surprise to wonder and exhilaration.
>
> 2011: 28

A dirt research approach borrowing Purse's formulation of spectatorial address can unearth a more detailed production history, linking the training history of the fight coordinator and the stunt team members to the affective goals of editing, framing, and the execution of specific moves or styles. Though the current push toward analytical study of the work of below-the-line laborers has shed light on the working conditions and cultures of production environments, dirt research adds a more detailed understanding of training histories and communities of stunting practice *per se*. While production studies approaches often look to the labor environment of a film, television program, or individual television episode, as a form of ethnography dirt research is concerned with longer circuits of production and skill acquisition. For example: *Buffy the Vampire Slayer* (1997–2003) showrunner Joss Whedon told *Buffy* stunt coordinator Jeff Pruitt that Whedon did not want Hong Kong-style action design for the show (Pruitt and Crawford 2017). Whedon made this declaration because the coordinator had worked on the *Mighty Morphin Power Rangers* (1993–1996) television show and Whedon was worried about *Buffy* using a similar aesthetic, unaware that the action design for *Power Rangers* was not the dominant aesthetic for Hong Kong-style action work or that the series was a Japanese–US

Figure 2.2 Sophia Crawford (doubling for Sarah Michelle Gellar as Buffy) behind the scenes in "The Wish" episode of *Buffy the Vampire Slayer* (© Jeff Pruitt, "BUFFY s3," YouTube, 2013. All Rights Reserved).

co-production. Pruitt, the stunt coordinator, and Buffy stunt double Sophia Crawford were both trained in Hong Kong and, as such, *Buffy the Vampire Slayer* was dominated by vampires bouncing into frame off mini trampolines and multi-beat martial arts fight sequences (Figure 2.2). Joss Whedon did not know the defining components of Hong Kong-style action, nor did he have any substantive input on the action design work (Pruitt and Crawford 2017). He is not the exception to this rule.

Barring examples like small Ugandan productions akin to *Who Killed Captain Alex?* (Nabwana I.G.G., 2010), most of the people credited as action directors by scholars have not been greatly involved with action direction.[1] A dirt research approach to action as mode does not eliminate the possibility of scholarship on action "auteurs," it simply reorients our focus to the collaborative process of the action design team—a movement away from the singular artist and toward the creative assemblage. Moreover, analyses of creative practice that are better attuned to the collaborative nature of production are more prone to reveal and elaborate upon the important roles played by women and minorities, whether above- or below-the-line. They have been under-represented in both scholarly literature and popular accounts of media industries.

Viva la Revolución: Action Studies Unbound and Transnational[2]

Consider the revolutionary potential of approaches to action in relation to the lived experiences of the laborers. Their corporeal skills are the primary staples of transnational action economies: stunt workers, stunt coordinators, and fight coordinators. Stunt workers can act as doubles for stars or actors or provide background action as unnamed assailants. Stunt coordinators are usually long-standing members of their local stunt community, having worked consistently in the industry for a decade or longer. Stunt coordinators oversee hiring the stunt team and organizing high falls, fire burns, and car crashes. The role of fight coordinator is of more recent provenance. This position became more common in the last two decades. The function of this crew member is to choreograph combat sequences between the stunt performers and to help to train the actors for their comparatively minor roles in these segments.

Appreciating the efforts of stunt workers and coordinators allows us to circumvent the problematic gendered and racialized erasures caused by previous attempts to reduce action as a "mode" to big budgets and high concept films, a process that Chris Holmlund rightly calls out (2005: 97). Our new labor-focused approach incorporates a wider range of media forms, national settings, and eras, in films that require the work of stuntwomen and stunt workers of color.

Additionally, positioning the body of the stunt worker as a raw material frees at least some of us from chair-bound research, allowing forays behind and beyond the film screen. From the perspective of stunt labor, there is no distinction between action work in film, television, video games, commercials, and live performance. The stunts required for visual media and live shows are fundamentally the same, but what distinguishes the style, safety, and equity of employment in each venue the world over are three regulatory mechanisms: unions, insurance policies, and hiring practices.

For Sylvia Martin, the key difference between Hollywood and Hong Kong production frameworks is unionization:

> [F]or over 80 years, Hollywood has had strong unions shaping the conditions of much of the media labor, due in large part to their ability to collectively bargain (although there is a growing abundance of nonunion labor). In contrast, Hong Kong's entertainment industry has a long history of weak unions and guilds, particularly for below-the-line workers, and this has been exacerbated by the lack of a collective bargaining law in the territory's history and the strong influence of pro-business investors who can easily replace activist crew members.
>
> 2017: 42–3

The division between unionized and non-unionized stunt labor plays out as a distinction between rigid job functions and flexible work environments (respectively) in the words of Martin's research subjects. In Martin's recounting, stunt laborers in Hong Kong frequently malign the lack of creative freedom in Hollywood productions. A dialectic between creative "flexibility" and a regimented and restricted production culture is also reflected in the more precarious and cutting-edge action design produced by Hong Kong stunt teams in comparison to the safer, if more comfortably derivative action design common to many Hollywood stunt cultures. The exchange is one of creative freedom for the security of safety procedures and insurance coverage. The safety structures of stunt production in the Hollywood milieu are bolstered by union presence and rigid insurance protocols. These procedures and labor structures are less common in stunt production frameworks outside of the United States and the United Kingdom. For example, in India, too, stunt workers lack strong unions or insurance protection and are regularly asked to perform without safety controls, as Al Jazeera reports:

> Sometimes, stunt work can be a matter of life and death. Accidents are common, and some are fatal. Balaji Raghav's brother Uday jumped to his death in an incident at a lake outside Bengaluru in 2016. Uday and another stuntman had to jump 60 feet (18 meters) from a helicopter into the lake, but

instead of a spectacular action scene, the camera recorded the two men drowning.

"The Stuntmen of Bollywood" 2019

As this example suggests, countries and individual productions lacking union presence and insurance protections are more likely to endanger the lives of their stunt workers for the sake of an impressive shot of a body on fire, falling from a helicopter, hanging from a building, or falling from a great height. It is worth noting, however, that the work of individual stunt performers most often garners public attention via news reports like the one quoted above. The stunt worker becomes visible and knowable through tragedy. Trade periodicals and popular press reports most commonly name individual stunt workers and shed light upon their creative practice in relation to "accidents." The framing of such events rarely places blame on individual productions or studios. After several Indian stunt people were injured, the South Indian Cine Stunt Directors and Stunt Artistes Union drafted a set of safety standards, but their union lacks the power to command stunt insurance policies, and as such, even minor injuries can be career-ending due to the medical costs (Naig 2020). While there are procedures to minimize accidents on set, the less structured and regulated the work culture, the more expendable the stunt worker is in any given production.

Let's Get Dirty: Sweat Research in Action

When left to ponder the basic materials of action cinema many scholars turn to much of Tasker's 1993 field-defining work on the centrality of the spectacular body in action. If one approaches action's spectacular bodies from the perspective of dirt research, one will arrive at a new understanding of the mechanisms by which such bodies become spectacular and narratively important. The spectacular body of today's action film star is an amalgam of the work of that star and their stunt double, along with a team of additional stunt workers, stunt and fight coordinators, personal trainers, and a coalition of other creative laborers. As the spectacular body is so often central to the expressive register of action, it seems logical to begin our dirt research in action with the sites of stunt craft training and performance. To do this, some of us need to extend our research beyond the traditional settings of libraries and archives and head into the field, visiting live performance venues and training academies (Figure 2.3). Supplementing traditional research with a more hands-on approach will make it possible to: 1) trace the origins of on-screen action to the pre-production process; 2) better grasp the physicality of action design;

Figure 2.3 The author is set on fire during her dirt research trip to the Irish Stunt School. © Lauren Steimer.

and 3) gain more detailed insight into the transnational exchange of technique and practice.

Contemporary film and television stunt work traces its lineage to a thrilling collection of live performance traditions and venues around the world, including but not limited to the circus, carnivals, rodeos, and Chinese operas. As noted above, fight work has been a mainstay of both traditional and illegitimate theater for hundreds of years. The landscape for action design is constantly changing. Significantly, Innis created dirt research to operate, according to Liam Cole Young, in the ablative tense: "[t]o think in the ablative, a grammatical case not present in English, is to think in motion, to observe patterns, relations, and dynamic change" (2017: 229). The ablative case is defined by a movement away from something, a separation. In dirt research on action, the scholar both moves transnationally and/or translocally from action locale to locale and tracks the patterns between these spaces and cultures in their own scholarship. To best map the transitions in transnational action design, some academics and reporters need to visit martial arts academies, tricking gymnasiums, circuses, rodeos, jousting competitions, Peking Opera houses, parkour championships, horse riding schools, animal training facilities, tactical weapons training ranges, and stunt training gyms, just as often and intensely as we frequent the libraries and archives. Action media studies research practices are expansive: from reading, watching films, and taking notes, to personal interviews with stunt performers, fight coordinators, second unit directors, stars, and the entire below-the-line labor team as its members intersect with and participate in the craft of action design. The close study of physical on-screen action is an ablative methodology requiring constant adaptation, language, and skill acquisition. This type of research is attentive to stunt craft terminology, martial arts styles, and precision driving routines. Beyond the more typical research skills common to film studies, this approach incorporates kinesthetic drawing, photographic documentation, and detailed descriptions of the tactility of wire work and weapon play. For action scholars to achieve greater corporeal proximity to our research we may wish to cultivate new forms of body-knowledge.

Dirt research into action reveals distinctions in how stunt labor is organized, the degree to which resources and safety are intertwined, and the flow of craft tactics from one national setting to another. Stunt workers in both unionized and non-unionized labor systems congeal into clusters. Stunt teams and schools form around veteran stunt workers, who have often worked as stunt or fight coordinators. These organizations are either highly selective, with members being chosen by senior team members based on their performance on set, because of their success in national sporting competitions, or because they frequent gyms and dojos common to stunt communities. In the latter, novice stunt workers are admitted to a school or enroll in individual classes and the senior members who run the program train the younger generation and help the most exceptional students to find work in the local industry. The open structure of the vetting processes at these academies can lead to a more diverse labor pool, as women and racial minorities are selected in much smaller numbers by the highly selective organizations.

In national media milieus without union protection or insurance provision, makeshift safety equipment is frequently used. The most ubiquitous object in any stunt team arsenal the world over is the cardboard box. Cardboard boxes are used as protection for high falls and as a staging mechanism to plan fight sequences and stunts. In US and UK frameworks, these objects were later replaced with airbags and crash pads, but in settings lacking budget or union regulations, cardboard boxes are the default safety equipment used by stunt workers on all sets. The cardboard box is an ever-present staple of the stunt industry due to the way stunting skills, historically, have been shared between countries. With the post-Fordist studio production model more widespread and international co-productions becoming more common from the 1960s to the present, individual stunt workers often find work on productions with crews of mixed national origin. According to stunt team lore, the cardboard box was originally used by US or possibly French stuntmen as a cushion for falls. Boxes were easily and cheaply available regardless of national context, so local stuntmen in Eastern Europe, Asia, and Oceania adopted the practice once they witnessed foreign stunt workers use them on set. The same trajectory can be sketched for a technology as modern as the previs video, a process whereby stunt teams shoot a low budget version of a fight or stunt in advance as a proof of concept or as a blueprint for the production team. This tactic was frequently employed for elaborate Hong Kong fight sequences in the 1990s and became standard practice in Hollywood stunt communities after US stuntmen working in Australia on *The Matrix* witnessed the Hong Kong stunt team shoot previs videos. From the US the practice moved to the United Kingdom and to New Zealand, where local stunt workers observed its use on *The Chronicles of Narnia: The Lion, the Witch and the Wardrobe* (Andrew Adamson, 2005). The circulation of action practices and technologies does not, however, always follow a straight line. The use of previs stunt videos evolved in Asia much more quickly thanks to proximity to the Hong Kong production market and the rise in international co-productions.

Dirt research in action mandates interaction with pre-screen and live action labor, which though it requires greater familiarity with martial arts styles and intersecting bodily disciplines like dance, gymnastics, trick riding, and precision driving, also calls for active engagement in stunt craft work and pedagogy. This method requires on-site observation, personal interviews, and (at times) active participation, to get sweaty, to jump and to fall, to put on protective equipment, to play with swords and to wield stunt craft weapons. The field researcher must "get dirty," i.e., must conduct research on stunt teams and action/fight coordinators to learn how action design is planned and organized. From this vantage point, it is easier to examine transnational stunt craft networks—to better understand how practices and fighting styles traverse global screens. Lastly, dirt research makes it possible to teach action media analysis in the ablative tense—moving our students away from previous notions of the spectacular body of the action star as a singular object and toward a new conceptual paradigm of collaborative and always shifting spectacular action labor. When we consider the raw materials of action cinema, we push for a vast and all-encompassing labor-forward approach that looks not only at the work and training histories of stunt performers, but also that of production design team members, people working in the costume department, designers and managers in the property department, and composers, music supervisors, and the sound design team. The action film has collective labor contexts and histories above and below-the-line that have been ignored. They are waiting to be unearthed.

Notes

1 Low-budget productions often do not have funding for an action designer and directors may be more involved in the process.

2 In the introduction to *Melodrama Unbound: Across History, Media, and National Cultures*, Christine Gledhill and Linda Williams unbind melodrama "from many critical misconceptions" to demonstrate that the primary aesthetic of film and television, globally considered, is melodrama (2018: 2). This chapter does not make a relative

claim that action is the central aesthetic of all film and television, nor that action can be easily removed from historical or geopolitical contexts. Rather, this piece borrows from Gledhill and Williams the process of unbinding itself. Action is unbound from the constraints of a single genre, media form, and from the limitations of media forms themselves. Using labor as a focal point, action is unbound from previous critical misconceptions of action as a simple genre for simple audiences. This act of unbinding reveals that action as a mode across and beyond media is as sophisticated as the labor of its production is arduous.

Works Cited

Acland, Charles R. (2014), "Dirt Research for Media Industries," *Media Industries Journal*, 1 (1): 1–5.

Capazorio, Bianca (2014), "Risk and Reward for SA Film Stunt Workers," *Sunday Times* (South Africa), 13 July. Available online: https://www.timeslive.co.za/sunday-times/lifestyle/2014-07-13-risk-and-reward-for-sa-film-stunt-workers/ (accessed 15 August 2020).

Gledhill, Christine and Linda Williams (eds) (2018), *Melodrama Unbound: Across History, Media, and National Cultures*, New York: Columbia University Press.

Goering, Laurie (2004), "Casting Call: South African Stunt People," *Los Angeles Times*, 20 August. Available online: https://www.latimes.com/archives/la-xpm-2004-aug-20-et-goering20-story.html (accessed 12 August 2020).

Holmlund, Chris (2005), "Wham! Bam! Pam! Pam Grier as Hot Action Babe and Cool Action Mama," *Quarterly Review of Film and Video*, 22 (2): 97–112.

Holmlund, Chris (2014), "Introduction: Presenting Stallone/Stallone Presents," in Chris Holmlund (ed.), *The Ultimate Stallone Reader: Sylvester Stallone as Star, Icon, Auteur*, 1–26, New York: Columbia University Press.

Innis, Harold A. (2007), *Empire and Communications*, Toronto: Dundurn Press.

Kendrick, James (2019), "Introduction: The Action Film: 'Over Familiar and Understudied,'" in James Kendrick (ed.), *A Companion to the Action Film*, 1–8, Hoboken, NJ: Wiley-Blackwell.

Martin, Sylvia J. (2017), *Haunted: An Ethnography of the Hollywood and Hong Kong Media Industries*, New York: Oxford University Press.

Naig, Udhav (2020), "Safety in the Dream Factory: 'Indian 2' Shoot Tragedy Gives a Wake-up Call to Tamil Film Industry," *The Hindu*, 8 March. Available online: https://www.thehindu.com/news/national/tamil-nadu/safety-in-the-dream-factory/article31012504.ece (accessed 8 June 2020).

Pruitt, Jeff and Sophia Crawford (2017), "Buffy Stunts," [Conference Panel], WhedonCon, Los Angeles, 20 May.

Purse, Lisa (2011), *Contemporary Action Cinema*, Edinburgh: Edinburgh University Press.

Schechner, Richard (1985), *Between Theater and Anthropology.* Philadelphia: University of Pennsylvania Press.

Stanbridge, Karen (2014), "How to Commit Canadian Sociology, or 'What Would Innis Do?'," *Canadian Review of Sociology/Revue canadienne de sociologie*, 51 (4): 381–94.

Tasker, Yvonne (1993), *Spectacular Bodies: Gender, Genre and the Action Cinema*, London: Routledge.

Tasker, Yvonne (2004), "Introduction: Action and Adventure Cinema," in Yvonne Tasker (ed.), *Action and Adventure Cinema*, 1–14, London: Routledge.

"The Stuntmen of Bollywood" (2019), *Al Jazeera*, 26 September, Available online: https://www.aljazeera.com/programmes/101east/2019/09/stuntmen-bollywood-190926105116068.html (accessed 10 June 2020)

Young, Liam Cole (2017), "Innis's Infrastructure: Dirt, Beavers, and Documents in Material Media Theory," *Cultural Politics*, 13 (2): 227–49.

Chapter 3

Big and Loud: The Sonic Aesthetics of the Fight Scene in Digital Action Cinema

Lindsay Steenberg and Lisa Coulthard

Big, Loud, Noisy: The Action Film as a Sonic Cinema of Attractions

Criticizing the "movie-as-Theme-Park" phenomenon of Hollywood action cinema in the 1990s, Larry Gross decries the "Big Loud Action Movie" for its aesthetic hyperbole (2000 [1995]: 3). Although his article does not focus on sound, the use of "loud" as a disparaging designation highlights the fact that action films have been and continue to be thought of as noisy, sonically chaotic, and sometimes dangerously high-volume cinematic objects. Such commonplace rhetoric obscures the nuance and complexity of the soundscapes of action cinema. It also fails to consider the significant attractions of action cinema's spectacular soundscapes.

Interrogating the complexities and pleasures of "big loud" action cinema, this chapter focuses on the Hollywood blockbuster fight sequence, arguably one of the biggest, loudest scene types in the genre. We contend that sound is not only crucial to the fight scene's appeal but is key to its construction as an identifiable set piece. The fight scene is set apart from the narrative through its architecture, kineticism, and spectacle; it is also set apart through sound and music. By defining spatial boundaries, mapping the violent confrontations of bodies in motion, and drawing the viewer in through propulsive and immersive effects, sound in the fight scene is a defining cornerstone of bigger budget action's impact. "Impact aesthetics" (King 2000) have become synonymous with action cinema, a pairing that we contend is easily and productively transferred to a sonic register.

To analyze action's sonic impact aesthetics, we draw from a dataset of post-millennial fight sequences from some of the loudest, longest running, and most financially lucrative Hollywood action franchises. The restriction to post-millennial fights is significant because of the development of digital surround sound technologies, which allow for dense soundscapes that amplify volume and intensify sonic effects. Incorporating sonic visualization, production studies, sound and music studies, critical reviews, media paratexts, and close analysis, we zero in on the human-scaled fight scene, arguing that as a set piece it is largely framed and realized via distinct spatial chronotopes that work in concert with sound.[1]

The fights we focus on are most accurately labeled as "hand to hand" rather than unarmed, as they prioritize contact between bodies—striking, blocking, grappling—as well as the use of found objects as weapons. Physical fight scenes are instructive because they rely on the yoking of violent impact and spectacle with sonically charged affect, using propulsive beats, loud high- and low-frequency effects, and loud booms of bodily contact. More than just being loud, fight scenes have potential to be acoustically assaultive and haptically charged.

After establishing the slippery connotations of loudness and the concept of sonic impact aesthetics, we focus on two contrasting sonic chronotopes as case studies: fights set in loud or quiet spaces.[2] Specifically, we analyze fights staged inside the expansive and loud public performance locale of the opera house and those fought in the quiet, liminal space of the public bathroom. The qualities of these spaces transform the ways combatants fight one another and shape the sonic character and impact of the scene. They further illustrate the nuanced and meticulous nature of many fight scenes' sound designs. Too often, we argue, these are oversimplified and overlooked as merely big and loud.

Defining Loudness in the Post-Dolby Fight Scene

Loud is an imprecise term: for instance, loudness can be volume but also unpleasant brashness or enjoyable thudding viscerality. It can describe the clamor of machine, crowd, or pyrotechnic noise, or simply indicate that music and effects are louder than dialogue. Even volume—a relatively precise term—is a complicated category. Screenings at cinemas are different from home viewings. Each can be further broken down: by the architecture, speaker placement, technological sophistication of the setup and space; by the quality and format of the film being viewed; by the hearing capacity, sensitivity, and age of the listener; by the number and placement of the audio-viewers. Furthermore, this does not even begin to consider the listening variations of earbuds or headphones.

These variances have become heightened in an age of digital surround or post-Dolby sound (the era following the popularization of Dolby Digital in the 1990s). Digital surround sound makes room for sound effects to come to the foreground and allows for greater immersion, higher volume, more robust low frequency effects, and more intricate soundscapes. The post-Dolby fight sequence layers sound to direct attention, guide audience response, intensify suspense, and highlight emotional stakes. Sound in the fight scene encourages spectatorial affect through thundering amplification, energizing or sedating rhythms (heartbeat sounds escalating tension for instance), sonically jolting "stabs," and the hapticity of low or high frequencies. Focusing on sound effects and Foley in particular, Michel Chion articulated what he saw as the potential for digital surround sound to make the materiality of bodies and things more present and weighty. In a pre-digital era, noise on the soundtrack was interference, something to be eliminated. With technological advances that eradicate interference, noise has now become an important entity, offering texture, materiality, and a more sensory-focused cinema. It is not incidental that Chion tied action cinema to this digital sonic shift:

> Recent American productions like John McTiernan's *Die Hard* [1988], Steven Spielberg's *Indiana Jones and the Last Crusade* [1989], or James Cameron's *The Abyss* [1989] have also added to this renewal of the senses in film through the playful extravagance of their plots. In these movies matter—glass, fire, metal, water, tar—resists, surges, lives, explodes in infinite variations, with an eloquence in which we can recognize the invigorating influence of sound on the overall vocabulary of modern-day film language.
>
> 1994 [1991]: 155

He goes on to note that these films point to a return of an epic quality in cinema, "making its appearance in many films in the form of at least one fabulous sequence. Think of the Dantesque escape of the heroes, in thunder and rain, in Andrey Konchalovskiy's *Tango and Cash* [1989], which is otherwise a pretty bad film" (Chion 1994 [1991]: 155). Chion is not alone in noting this shift. For instance, Jeff Smith outlines the key ingredients of this post-Dolby style: "increased volume, low frequency effects, expanded frequency range, the spatialization of sound, the 'hyperdetail' of contemporary Foley work, and the use of nondiegetic sound effects as stylistic punctuation" (2013: 338). Echoing Chion's claims for Dolby's "sensorial capacities" (2009 [2003]: 133), Smith notes "Dolby's ability to enhance the visceral experience of cinema" (2013: 337). As both highlight, action cinema is an ideal home for the amplification and elaboration of these capacities and tendencies. The claims for digital sound's impacts on style are not limited to the theatrical experience, but are built into sound design, including home and mobile exhibition.

A Violent Sensory Cinema: Loudness in the Fight Sequence

To Chion's list of glass, fire, and metal, we add the human body in our focus on the hand-to-hand physical fight scene. For us, the body is the center point of action cinema's sonic impact aesthetic. The fight is a fundamental feature of big budget Hollywood cinema, from the shaky desperation of the bathroom knife fight in *The Bourne Ultimatum* (Paul Greengrass, 2007), to the hyperreal authenticity of the stairwell fight in *Atomic Blonde* (David Leitch, 2017), to the elaborately staged operatic sequence in *Quantum of Solace* (Marc Forster, 2008), to the spotlit brutalism of the final boxing match in *Creed* (Ryan Coogler, 2015). On the one hand, these fight scenes offer a performance of realism and authenticity that stresses physical violence; on the other, they offer a digitized unreality that transforms violence into pure fantasy. The hand-to-hand fight sequence is a paradoxical object that illustrates the central ambivalences of digital corporeality and, as such, it is a crucial site for interrogating contemporary sonic impact aesthetics.

For the spectacle-focused syntax of the fight scene, the capacities of post-Dolby surround sound highlight the corporeal, affect-driven, and energizing pulse of engaging action cinema. Sometimes dismissively referred to as "chaos cinema" (Stork 2013), the impacts, collisions, and kinetics of contemporary action have sonic import and texture. They also have affective weight: impact in this framework has a multiplicity of meanings that are beyond the merely assaultive or chaotic. Sonic impact aesthetics are characterized by complexity, enveloping immersion, affectively charged viscerality, and energizing dynamism. Within this framework, loudness is not merely the average or peak decibel level of the soundscape of a film's theatrical exhibition or sound mix/design. To describe a film as loud is to confirm its nature as an impactful cinematic spectacle, to recognize its sonic complexity, and to appreciate how sound works through dynamism to communicate and augment the fight scenes' qualities of urgency, kineticism, and haptic intensity.

Yet complexity (i.e., multiple interwoven tracks) does not necessarily make for noise or even loudness in the era of digital sound design. Not only can extremely quiet, exceedingly subtle sound effects take hundreds of tracks to create, but the packed and loud soundscape is not always indecipherable noise. As Mark Kerins comments when analyzing the extended freeway chase scene of *Terminator 2: Judgment Day* (James Cameron, 1991), although it is impossible for the average listener to identify the multitude of sounds individually, the upshot is not sonic chaos but rather a clear communication of "intense movement, speed, and action" (2010: 69). To take Michael Bay's *Transformers* (2007) as an illustrative example of a wider trend in digital action sound design: a single moment in the mix of this film can contain anywhere from 100 to 1000 tracks, something inconceivable with pre-digital sound technologies. *Transformers*'s sound mixer Greg Russell comments on the astonishing number of tracks his team required, "Altogether, with all pre-dubs and outboard gear, I was out to 256 tracks on the console, which was pretty much a full load" (Isaza 2010). Likewise, Bay recalls that the destruction of Chicago scene had 30,000 fades and caused a computer crash, testifying to the importance he puts on sound design in the construction of his signature collision-centered aesthetics (Giardina 2011).

However even very loud action soundtracks like that of *Transformers* are as much about dynamism as magnitude. As *Transformers*'s sound designer Erik Aadahl says: "When I first read the script, I remember thinking how huge it seemed. But I hoped that there could be more to the soundtrack than just 'big and loud' Bay-hem" (Isaza 2010). According to Aadahl, the sound team worked carefully to create robot personalities through sound, and this sonic characterization was not always focused on the big or obnoxious. He recalls,

> Our goal was to play the opposite of "big." . . . To get tiny, quiet, and intimate. To make the audience lean in, not get pushed back. For me, the scene plays like a symphony of little sounds. . . . It's a funny psycho-acoustic phenomenon, that "small" sounds can be manipulated to sound bigger than "big" sounds. In sound design we often find the "macro" in the "micro".
>
> Isaza 2010

In the same article, Aadahl also describes the importance of dynamism and contrast in the action sequence soundtrack. Rather than extended sequences of pure loudness, the goal instead is to differentiate and demarcate, to provide loudness through contrast not merely through volume or noise: "Quiet scenes help cleanse the sonic palate. . . . Dynamics are the key to both storytelling and sound" (ibid). For sound editors like Aadahl, the small details are important as each character is paired with a specific sound that is distinct in terms of timbre and frequency, and each weapon effect has layers and nuance. Each loud, explosive moment is positioned carefully to take full advantage of sound dynamism to stress magnitude, momentum, and weight.

Even when dynamic, however, the roller coaster ride of Bay-hem suggests the extent to which many set pieces in digital action cinema attempt to move beyond human stakes and scale. Their loudness may be built through mechanization and fueled by speed, for instance the robots of the *Transformers* series (2007–) and the car chases of the *Fast and Furious* franchise (2001–). Such sonic mechanization speaks to the wider sensation-driven conventions of the post-Dolby action sequence and includes large-scale military battles and explosions as well. However, the human body is the focalizing element distinguishing the fight scene from the action set piece. Even when chases or battles create sensational set pieces, they are frequently punctuated by physical combat of some form. Often the fighting is intercut with chases, countdowns, or threats to innocents, or there is a culminating epic fight between key characters.

Mission: Impossible—Fallout's (Christopher McQuarrie, 2018) final set piece is illustrative in this regard as it cross-cuts between several action scenes but remains rooted to the closer range fights between protagonists and antagonists.

It is densely scored and takes approximately twelve and half minutes of the film's runtime. Viewers of the *Mission: Impossible* franchise (1996–) have come to expect an intense combination of astonishing landscapes, Ethan Hunt's (Tom Cruise) acrobatic/climbing skills, urgent deadlines and countdowns, women/civilians in peril, high speed chases, and martial arts showdowns. *Fallout*'s climax intercuts several of these elements: a helicopter chase, a fight between Hunt and August Walker (Henry Cavill) on a clifftop, a scene of hand-to-hand combat as Benji Dunn (Simon Pegg) and Ilse Faust (Rebecca Ferguson) face Solomon Lane (Sean Harris). There is also a tense countdown as Luther Stickle (Ving Rhames) tries to disarm the bomb that would destroy a village and kill Ethan's ex-wife (Michelle Monaghan). Linking all these tense moments, the soundscape fuses mechanical sounds (in this case helicopters) with music and sound effects. As supervising sound editor James Mather notes, the two-minute helicopter chase scene was a sonic challenge: because of all the percussive sounds (helicopter motors, guns, strikes) it was hard to create sonic differentiation and dynamism, both of which are needed for a sense of momentum for the relatively lengthy scene (Figure 3.1). To generate energy and anticipation, the sound team worked with the Shepard Tone, an auditory illusion whereby a tone seems to continually rise or fall. Developed by Roger Shepard, it consists of overlapping notes played one octave apart. Because of the sense of rising or falling without any resolution or any real movement, the tone creates anxiety and suspense. As Mather notes, "we wanted to get our helicopter sounds, engine whines, and stress and twisting metal sounds to be part of this Shepard's Tone movement," which had to be achieved by adding tonality to the percussive sounds of gunshots and blade flaps. It also involved distinguishing the helicopter sounds through effects and pitch bending so Hunt's helicopter sounded more like a jet and Walker's sounded

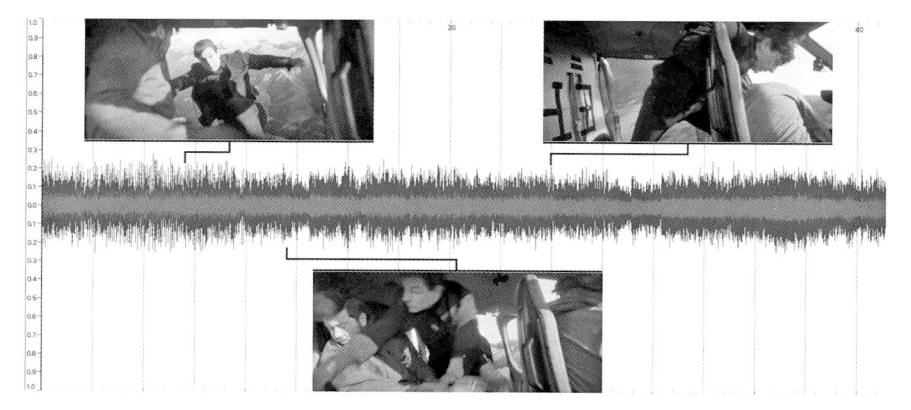

Figure 3.1 The final multi-layered fight sequence in *Mission Impossible: Fallout* (© Paramount Pictures, 2018. All Rights Reserved) is sonically dense and complex in order to create dynamism and momentum (authors' sonic visualization).

more "blade heavy." Working with composer Lorne Balfe, the sound team attempted to ensure that music and effects took turns: "This way the chase would always have momentum, whether it was the music pushing it or the sound design" (Mather in Andersen 2018).

These comments are illustrative of the sound editor's challenges when approaching an action fight scene: how to maintain energy, dynamism, anticipation, suspense, and a sense of movement without turning the soundtrack into a constant, indistinguishable wall of noise? They also point to the subtlety and precision of sounds that might be dismissed as mere noise (the whir of helicopter blades for instance). The shifts from loud to quiet, enclosed area to wide open landscape, musicality to machinic whirs work in concert with modulations of tone and pitch. Sound makes the action clear and energizing and creates suspense, tying the crosscuts together into a single spectacular action sequence.

From Loud to Quiet: The Sonic Architecture of the Spectacular Fight Scene

As the *Fallout* scene indicates, space and architecture are crucial elements in building an effective soundscape: the move from the openness and altitude of the clifftop fight to the quieter ticking tension of disarming a bomb is key to creating a sonic dynamism that shifts from quiet to loud and back again. *Fallout*'s multivalent intricacy is illustrative of wider post-Dolby trends that prompt us to consider the ways sound works to frame fight scenes within architectural locales. In the section that follows, we zero in on two distinct audio-visual fight categories determined by their sonic architecture: the loud fight in the public performance venue, i.e., arenas, theaters, nightclubs, and the quiet fight in semi-private liminal settings, i.e., public bathrooms, elevators, and rented hotel rooms. Focusing on the opera fight and the bathroom fight, respectively, we argue that the quiet category is often objectively just as loud (contains as many spikes in volume) as its loud counterpart. However, the pattern of dynamics is distinct: moments of silence make spikes of sounds more startling. Although our process of sonic visualization has its limitations, a sense of dynamism and complexity is clearly visible in Figures 3.1–3.3, which show schematics of volume, frequency, and rhythm.

These two categories are further delineated by their use of iconic sounds associated with either loud or quiet moments (e.g., labored breathing as quiet and gunfire as loud; classical music as quiet and rock music as loud). Quiet scenes tend to intersperse loud spikes of sound (a single gunshot, an unexpected

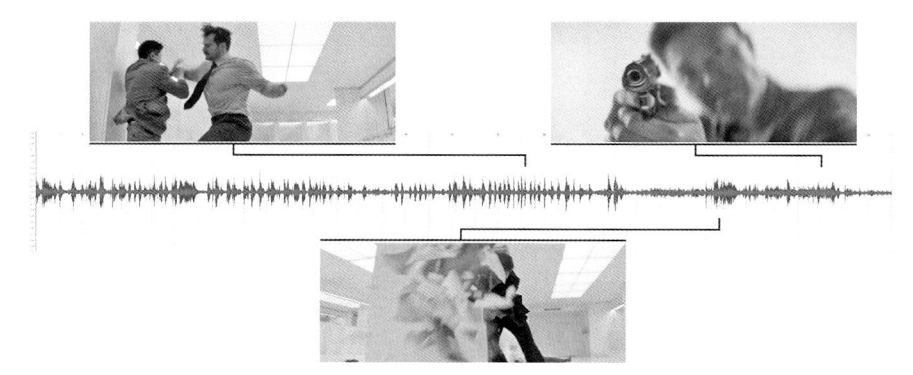

Figure 3.2 The 'quiet' fight that unfolds in the public bathrooms in *Mission Impossible: Fallout* (© Paramount, 2018. All Rights Reserved) contrasts moments of relative silence with jarring spikes in sound (authors' sonic visualization).

punch, the smash of glass breaking) with relative silence. This is visible in the sonic visualization of the bathroom fight in *Fallout* where empty sites are punctuated by strikes, smashes, and vocalizations. *Fallout*'s final and loudest fight scene, on the other hand, presents an unbroken, dense strata of sound and music. Thus, loudness may describe the relative difference or similarity between the mountains and valleys of sound, with a louder landscape having less differentiation and greater density of sound.

In an article interrogating race and the key chronotopes of the film noir, Julian Murphet (1998), drawing on Vivian Sobchack, argues that noir locations can be usefully placed in three functional categories: public, domestic, and liminal. While the loud set pieces of action are often found in large public places, contrapuntal examples can be found in transitional areas like bathrooms, hotel rooms, stairwells, kitchens, elevators, and hallways. Like the noir anti-hero who is seen in shabby urban alcoves, action heroes like Jason Bourne and James Bond often fight in rundown hotels. Yet they are equally comfortable fighting in luxury suites and expensive restrooms in high end hotels, such as the iconic Burj Khalifa in *Mission: Impossible—Ghost Protocol* (Brad Bird, 2011) and the Continental, the hotel of choice for assassins in all the *John Wick* films (Chad Stahelski, 2014–). The design of the fight sequences, in tandem with fight choreography and cinematography, transforms their fights into elaborate set pieces.

Many of the loudest fights in our dataset take place in large-scale venues designed to hold crowds: nightclubs, theaters, opera houses, sports stadiums, and combat arenas. These spaces enhance audio-visual spectacle and highlight the fight sequence as a performative event. Key examples include the fight at the Red Circle nightclub in *John Wick* (Chad Stahelski, 2014),[3] the final boxing match in *Creed*, and the battles during opera performances in *Quantum of Solace* and *Mission: Impossible—Rogue Nation* (Christopher McQuarrie, 2015). A continuum of taste positions some of these locales as "low culture" venues (i.e., the fight/ sports arena) and others as "high culture" sites (i.e., the opera house). The glitzy nightclub falls somewhere in between. Despite this spectrum, every fight scene is produced and recorded as a multi-level sonic set piece. Each is staged as a disruptive intervention into, for example, the dance club or the opera house. (Martial arts tournaments and boxing matches are exceptions: performances there revolve around fighting.)

What follows is a close analysis of the loud public space of the opera houses visited in *Rogue Nation* and *Quantum of Solace*, then a discussion of the quieter, claustrophobic public bathrooms in *Fallout* and *Casino Royale* (Martin Campbell, 2006). By focusing on two different ends of the volume spectrum, these sequences allow us to draw out the ways in which loudness and noise are relative, not absolute, categories. They also enable us to investigate the contrastive atmospheres that are key to the dynamism of sound effects and music: corporeal violence is as incompatible with the musical elegance and audience silence of opera as it is with the muted noise, anonymity, and implied etiquette of the upscale public washroom. Of course, contemporary action films attempt to maximize innovation by setting fights in unlikely or unexpected places. These spatial distinctions work sonically, using background music, noise, and relative quiet to intensify the sound of blows, hits, and punches.

The Opera Fight: *Rogue Nation* and *Quantum of Solace*

Fights in performance sites are characterized by backstage secrecy or subterfuge, in which the fighters, or their true motivations, are hidden from the venue's crowd. This echoes the fact that the hero belongs to a secret society, whether that is John Wick's assassin network, Hunt's Impossible Mission Force (IMF) or Bond's MI6. Battles in performance venues have a symbiotic relationship to diegetic music, which often registers the sequences' sound design. Additionally, sounds generated by the crowds onscreen form a kind of wave of noise that ebbs and flows with the movements, range, and speed of the fight choreography and in response to the patterns of the diegetic performance, whether that is a boxing match (*Creed*) or a violent operatic sequence (*Quantum of Solace*). The fights are rendered dramatic and "loud" through the filters of sound and music, which cut across the continuum of high and low culture.

To unpack this in more detail, we turn to the Bregenz open air theater fight in *Quantum of Solace* and the Vienna State Opera fight in *Rogue Nation*. The former features Giacomo Puccini's *Tosca*, the latter Puccini's *Turandot*. Like *John Wick's* multi-level fights in music venues (the concert in the Roman baths of Caracalla or the Red Circle nightclub), *Rogue Nation* and *Quantum of Solace* weave their chases, punch-ups, and orchestrated assassinations in and out of performances, in both cases here written by, arguably, the most cinematic of opera composers: Puccini.[4]

Rogue Nation's opera fight is the high point in a sequence that sees disgraced IMF agent Hunt leading an investigation into an assassination plot. This plot takes Dunn and Hunt, armed with sophisticated surveillance devices, and dressed undercover in tuxedos, to Vienna's opera house where they face off against multiple agents, including a hitman with a flute-shaped gun, another man disguised as a police officer, and the glamorously dressed sniper, Ilse Faust, who is hiding inside a moveable pagoda. While Dunn waits in an electronic control room, Hunt moves unchallenged through the labyrinthine backstage area. His pursuit of the flute-assassin takes him upwards, onto the rigging and gangways above the stage where he and the flautist scuffle in time with the *Turandot* music below (Figure 3.3).

The music of the opera swells, working as film score. It is perfectly paired with the action of Hunt's fight and, later, with Dunn's grapple with another of the assassins. Over the powerful music of the well-known *Nessun Dorma* aria, smaller noises are audible: the rip of a curtain, the click of a gun being assembled, the metallic clanking of the gangway rigging, the thwacks of blows, exhalations, and grunts. The juxtaposition of sound effects and Puccini's music reinforces the immediacy and stakes of the backstage fight.

While so-called classical music is conventionally associated with intellectual or contemplative quiet, it is sometimes used as contrastive accompaniment to stylize the hyper-violent fight sequence. Contrastive music prompts listener attention through unexpected pairings that clash with the emotional valences of the key figures or actions in a scene. Case in point: *John Wick: Chapter 3—Parabellum*

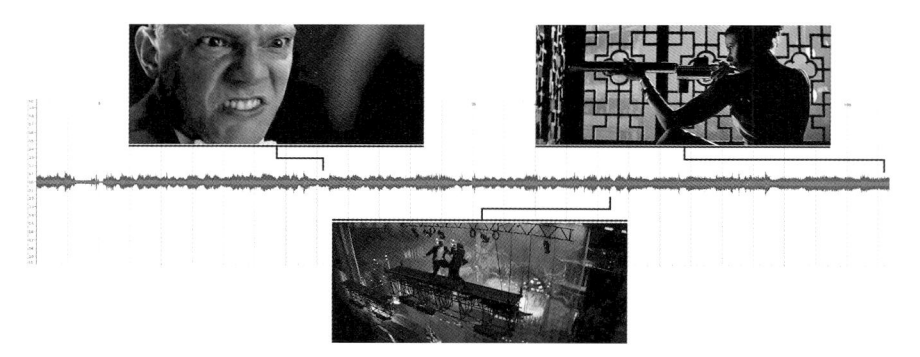

Figure 3.3 The violence of this fight sequence in *Mission Impossible: Rogue Nation* (© Paramount, 2015. All Rights Reserved) is significantly timed to the music of Puccini's *Turandot* (authors' sonic visualization).

(Chad Stahelski, 2019) uses Antonio Vivaldi's "Winter" to accompany the shootout at the Continental hotel, integrating gunshots with the score as percussive elements.

When accompanying scenes of violence, opera's musical elegance, polished composition, and high cultural cachet can be a prominent instance of contrastive scoring. In some cases, however, the emotional valences of the music are aligned rather than contrastive with the onscreen action. *Quantum of Solace* and *Rogue Nation* rely on popular perceptions of the Puccini operas as hyper-emotional. Both films thereby yoke emotion to violent action. Nonetheless the sequences have distinctly different emotional valences because the heroes are characterized and played differently: Daniel Craig is a taciturn and brutal James Bond, Tom Cruise a playful and acrobatic Ethan Hunt. Although they obviously hear the music, Bond and Hunt do not truly listen and remain emotionally removed: the opera performances function as echoes of their physical struggles rather than as moments of psychological interiority. The violence of *Tosca* especially resonates with the fight sequence happening backstage, but it is distanced from the emotions of the fighter-protagonist.[5]

The operatic performances in *Quantum* and *Rogue Nation* signal sonic and architectural set pieces that frame the fights. They are also critical to the narrative. In a nod to *The Man Who Knew Too Much* (Alfred Hitchcock, 1956), the camera of *Rogue Nation* lingers on the sheet music as Ilse Faust follows along, an ominous red circle signaling the exact moment of attack. Music is weaponized: it is both a script for murder and literally a weapon: the flute is used as a gun. The instructions on the music: *poco allarg.* (a slight slowing down) to start, played *a tempo* (in time) for the decisive attack and then *affrettando* (picking up speed) are echoed in the rhythm of the backstage fights, confirming the complex choreography of the interconnected sequences on stage (with the opera), in the rigging (with Hunt), in the pagoda (with Faust), and in the control room (with Dunn). In *Quantum*, Bond observes a nefarious deal organized by the shadowy Spectre via an earpiece. The device doubles (or rather, trebles) the process of listening on screen as the spectator hears the opera, the whispered Spectre plot, and the score of the film.

As Bond chases the assassins into the hallway, music and other sounds drop out completely. As he moves through the theater's restaurant/bar and kitchen, the music from *Tosca* takes over, maintaining a unified volume as the scene cross-cuts between performance space and bar (Figure 3.4). The music of *Tosca* dominates the sounds of the fight until distinct gunshots can be heard punctuating Puccini's music. The rapid intercutting of the stabbing in the theatrical performance with a high-octane chase and gunfire sequence decenters Bond as the agent of action, an effect stressed through sound. We do not hear Bond's voice or breathing, only crowd noises, gunfire, and the objects he bangs into. Instead, the operatic performers are emphasized: we hear their yells, gasps, and

Figure 3.4 The performers in *Tosca* dominate the soundtrack during the opera fight sequence in *Quantum of Solace* (© MGM, 2008. All Rights Reserved; authors' sonic visualization).

breath. The music mutes Bond's violence while highlighting the operatic brutality being performed on stage.[6]

These opera fights are part of a larger category of fight scenes in musical venues, a tradition firmly established in earlier action films and escalated in more recent films (in terms of complexity of staging, musicality, and choreography). The nightclub and concert fights in the *John Wick* series have clear rhythmic patterns determined by the techno/dance music and timed to the sound of gunshots and strikes. In contrast, the opera fights in both *Quantum* and *Rogue Nation* are densely scored (with music playing over the entire sequence) with smaller or quieter sounds spiking noticeably on the sonic visualizer (see Figures 3.3 and 3.4). They become focal points: the clang of boots on backstage gangways, the turning of pages of sheet music, a dramatic exhalation of breath, etc. This produces the psycho-acoustic effect mentioned by *Transformers* sound designer Aadahl, wherein smaller sounds are manipulated to ring louder than big sounds like an operatic performance. What Aadahl terms a "symphony of little sounds" encourages the audience to draw closer here too (Isaza 2010). This more intimate sound design differentiates the opera fight from other fights set in large-scale performance venues.

The bountiful "symphony of little sounds" is part of the doubly staged and hypermediated Puccini operas themselves, amplified through diegetic audio-visual surveillance technology, such as the CCTV in *Rogue Nation* and the earpieces in *Quantum of Solace*. The emotional and spectacular impact of opera as a narrative art form provides prosthetic accompaniment to, or distanciated commentary on, the cinematic fight scenes. *Tosca* and *Turandot* can simultaneously operate as shorthand for a cosmopolitanism often associated with (cinematic representations of) opera attendance while also providing stories that can mirror, comment on, and offer emotional prompts for the fight scenes themselves. While such emotionality might remain impossible for Bond, as a character or brand, we would argue that the operatic stakes of the fight scene exploit the flatness of affect, or detachment, of heroic characters such as Bond, commenting on spectacle, performance, and even the excesses of the action set piece in general.

Both the opera fight and Puccini's diegetic operas themselves mobilize narrative dangers and violent spectacle. *Turandot* is the story of a series of riddles that must be solved if a suitor is to win the hand of Princess Turandot. Those who fail, die. *Tosca* is best described as a political thriller full of deception, revenge, betrayal, and torture. Opera's threats are rendered literal in *Rogue Nation,* where musical instruments become weapons and assassinations are timed to music. Hunt must use his martial arts skills and trademark climbing abilities to disarm assassins hiding in the opera set, keep privileged spectators safe, and navigate the complicated architecture of the opera house. Here *Turandot* becomes a roadmap to an elaborate backstage assassination plot that is as violent as the opera's onstage executions. In *Quantum of Solace*, *Tosca* largely serves as a backdrop for dangerous criminals making clandestine deals and the spies who are licensed to hunt and kill them.[7]

The opera fights of *Rogue Nation* and *Quantum of Solace* build their impact thanks to Puccini's music and the accompanying "symphony of little sounds." In resonant contrast, we now examine how "small sounds" are used in quieter semi-public areas such as public bathrooms. There we find fights that are often equally loud but oriented in significantly different ways.

The Bathroom Fight: *Fallout* and *Casino Royale*

The structures of the quiet fight sequence throw the big loud fights of mega-franchise films into relief, highlighting the spectacular dimension of the latter. Hotel rooms, bathrooms, and comparable venues are often associated with silence or solitude, but they are only semi-private. This adds a layer of urgency and, particularly in the case of public washrooms, heightens the sense of vulnerability. Public bathrooms demand decorum. Only certain noises are countenanced because random strangers may enter, interrupt, overhear, or interfere. Sonically, moreover, the public bathroom allows for naturally occurring variance. External sounds and/or music from the outside can bleed into the private space every time the door opens and a new patron arrives. Echoey acoustics stress resonance, add reverb, and amplify volume. The sound design of the bathroom fight emphasizes corporeal defenselessness. Bathrooms are places of taboo and abjection, a feature exploited by sequences such as the bathroom massacre in *Full Metal Jacket* (Stanley Kubrick, 1987) or, more recently, the sewage flood that engulfs the family home in *Parasite* (Bong Joon-ho, 2019). Even the sounds commonly associated with these areas are unsettling, repugnant.

A truly surprising number of fight scenes are set in bathrooms. To cite only five: *The Warriors* (Walter Hill, 1979) features bathroom set gang warfare. *The Raid 2* (Gareth Evans, 2014) situates a showdown in a bathroom stall. Harry Tasker (Arnold Schwarzenegger) fights terrorists in the bathroom of the Bonaventure Hotel in *True Lies* (James Cameron, 1994). Isaiah Bone (Michael Jai White) proves his fighting abilities in a prison bathroom in *Blood and Bone* (Ben Ramsey, 2009). Jason Bourne (Matt Damon) ends his frenetic Moroccan chase over a toilet in *The Bourne Ultimatum.* Common elements are high-frequency sounds of breaking glass or porcelain (from mirrors, sinks, and toilets), the gushing and flushing of water, and the echoing reverberations of vocalizations and gunfire. Musical scoring tends to be diegetic and spatially removed, which makes it more muted than in other locations. The music has a nuanced relationship to the violence: it fades in and out when doors open, or subtly rises in the mix when fights occur.

We take *Fallout*'s extended bathroom fight as our first illustration. Like the backstage fight, the bathroom brawl takes place in a hidden space, in this case the large men's washroom of a nightclub (The Grand Palais) in Paris. The bathroom is illuminated by bright flat lighting and is framed by white walls, sinks, and mirrors; the muted sound of the dance floor's music is the only musical accompaniment. The fighters are IMF's Hunt, partnered with CIA Agent August Walker, against an enemy operative posing as the illegal arms dealer, Lark (Liang Yang). The fight moves from an open sink area into the cramped interior of a toilet stall (filmed in an overhead shot) where the three combatants must fight at extremely close range. Bodies and sounds bounce off the walls of the stall, adding to the desperate intimacy of the blows. All three characters are equally matched and exceptionally skilled martial artists.[8]

The music is diegetically motivated and often, but not uniformly, muted. It comes from the dancefloor and fades and rises in the mix, depending on spatial perspective but also according to the rhythms of the fight. When Walker stands to fight after being knocked down, the pulsing bass (like a heartbeat) of Death in Vegas's "The Consequences of Love" comes forward in the mix. After Walker falls the music continues to increase in volume, with the bass beats amplifying as "Lark" points his gun at Hunt. It decreases in volume with the shot from Ilse Faust's gun, then rises slightly with the shot/counter shot editing between Hunt and Faust. The musical dynamism is highlighted by staccato fight sounds, with individual quieter noises (e.g., the rustle of clothing) causing a sound spike equal to much louder noises (e.g., gunfire and glass smashing are no louder than punches). Hits with fists are relatively equal in sound levels to the fake Lark's bashes with a metal pipe, a phenomenon that reinforces our insistence that the human body itself provides sonic anchoring for the violent scale of the fight scene. The sonic visualization here clearly demarcates moments of relative silence, against which sounds stand out in sharp contrast (see Figure 3.2). Hits, impacts, and blocks are crisp and defined, designed to highlight the combatants' skills and—behind the scenes—those of the stunt performers. The fight between Walker, Hunt, and "Lark" abruptly ends when "Lark" is shot by MI6 agent Faust. Significantly, her gunshot is quieter than the punches traded earlier, but registers its impact in the shocked silence and stillness that follows.

A similar bathroom fight reboots the Bond franchise in the opening sequence of *Casino Royale*. However, as the sonic visualization reveals, the Bond bathroom fight is louder, more sonically dense, and scored with non-diegetic music. Three flashbacks to this fight are intercut with Bond's conversation with a corrupt operative in his office, demonstrating once again the dramatic use of silence to frame violence. Smashes of sinks, vocalizations, and music abruptly interrupt the office quiet. The final click of Bond's gun (even with its silencer) spikes louder than the dense soundscape of the bathroom shots. This is the significant moment when Bond's "00" status is confirmed because of the successful assassination. The sequence then cuts back to the bathroom, as Bond's adversary (who had appeared dead) rises from the floor to aim his gun. Bond quickly turns around as his signature musical motif is accompanied by the franchise's iconic gun barrel point of view shot. It is not pushing the point too far to insist that this bathroom fight (with its abject associations and staccato sound design) re-launches the Bond brand with Craig as star as more visceral and brutal than the comic and self-referential films with Pierce Brosnan. Indeed, *Casino Royale*'s reinvigoration of the franchise proves that the bathroom fight can realize Chion's supposition regarding the potentialities of digital sound: sound adds weight and materiality to spectacle. Through sonic impact aesthetics neglected liminal spaces such as bathrooms perfectly demonstrate Chion's vision of a newly revivified epic quality of cinema.

Conclusion

We have argued that architectural spaces (e.g., bathrooms or opera houses) and their corresponding sound profiles provide the weightiness and "renewal of the senses" that Chion imagined (1994 [1991]: 155). This is manifested, first, through spatial associations: abjection, privacy, and vulnerability with public bathrooms;

and luxury, cosmopolitanism, and melodrama with opera houses. Weightiness and haptic impact are staged and realized through sounds and especially through the canny manipulation of sound mix dynamics tied to the violence visited by bodies on one another. The sound of a skilled fist against a muscular torso is as loud as a sniper shot; human heartbeats are audible over (and through) the throb of dance music. The spike of breaking glass that threatens to reveal clandestine combatants grappling in public toilets followed by a reduction in volume is engineered to draw the spectator/auditor in, then push them away. The complex musical layers of opera house sequences may both conceal and showcase backstage assassins. The sensational stories and sounds of opera augment the fights, though the fight sequences also rely on smaller, bodily focused noises: the thud of a punch, the rip of a curtain, the click of a gun. All, in *Rogue Nation*'s case, are literally timed to the music.

Fighting and violence are constructed sonically around spatial acoustics. What we are calling sonic impact aesthetics can helpfully begin to refute the notion that action cinema is simply "big and loud." Building on previous work (Coulthard and Steenberg 2022), we have begun theorizing loudness as a critical category that enmeshes violence with sound in ways that are considerably more dynamic, nuanced, narratively motivated, and affectively charged than has been previously acknowledged.

Acknowledgments

The authors would like to thank their research assistants: Ellie Berry, Jemma Dash, and Harrison Wade. Their contributions to the process of sonic visualization and to the analysis of the sequences themselves have provided a foundation for our analysis. This chapter is an outcome of a larger project funded by an Insight Grant from the Social Sciences and Humanities Research Council of Canada.

Notes

1 Bahktin defines a chronotope as a solidification of time and place: "Time, as it were, thickens, takes on flesh, becomes artistically visible; likewise, space becomes charged and responsive to the movements of time, plot and history" (Bahktin, cited in Bemong and Borghart 2010: 4). To this formulation we add the findings of subsequent works that draw on Bahktin's formulation, especially Murphet (1998).

2 We treat "loud" and "quiet" as oversimplified categories that require a critical deconstruction. We are interested in complexities associated with both terms. We do not view either merely as an indicator of volume.

3 See Coulthard and Steenberg (2022).

4 For further discussion on Puccini and his relationship to entertainment culture, see Wilson (2007).

5 This is unlike what happens in, for example, the staging of *Tosca* in *Milk* (Gus Van Sant, 2008), that Marcia J. Citron argues prefigures the protagonist's murder (2011: 317).

6 Citron argues that the techno-opera production in *Quantum* creates a sense of detachment. *Tosca*'s narrative violence and Puccini's populist music work within the Bond context to ensure that "the protagonist and arguably his brand remain aloof from opera's transformative qualities" (2011: 318).

7 In an amusing commentary, one of the audience members observes many of the undercover criminals leaving their seats. He whispers: "Well, *Tosca*'s not for everyone."

8 Liang Yang, who plays Hunt and Walker's opponent, the pseudo-Lark, is a martial artist, stunt performer, and choreographer. Although many stunt men and women worked on *Mission Impossible: Fallout*, no one is *credited* as doubling Tom Cruise. Two uncredited stuntmen are listed on IMDb as having doubled Henry Cavill.

Works Cited

Andersen, Asbjoern (2018), "How *Mission: Impossible-Fallout*'s Intense Sound Was Made—Exclusive Interview with James Mather," *A Sound Effect*, 9 August 2018. Available online: https://www.asoundeffect.com/mission-impossible-fallout-sound/ (accessed 19 October 2020).

Bemong, Nele and Pieter Borghart (2010), "Bahktin's Theory of the Literary Chronotope: Reflections, Applications, Perspectives," in Nele Bemong, Pieter Borghart, Michel De Dobbeleer, Kristoffel Demoen, Koen De Temmerman and Bart Keunen (eds), *Bahktin's Theory of the Literary Chronotope: Reflections, Applications, Perspectives*, 3–16, Gent: Academia Press.

Chion, Michel (1994 [1991]), *Audio-Vision: Sound on Screen*, trans. Claudia Gorbman, New York: Columbia University Press.

Chion, Michel (2009 [2003]), *Film, A Sound Art*, trans. Claudia Gorbman, New York: Columbia University Press.

Citron, Marcia J. (2011), "The Operatics of Detachment: *Tosca* in the James Bond Film *Quantum of Solace*," *19th-Century Music*, 34 (3): 316–40.

Coulthard, Lisa and Lindsay Steenberg (2022), "Red Circle of Revenge: Anatomy of the Fight Sequence in *John Wick*," in Stephen Myers Watt and Caitlin Grace Watt (eds), 41–62, *The Worlds of John Wick*, Bloomington: Indiana University Press.

Giardina, Carolyn (2011), "'Transformers' Director Michael Bay Weighs in on the Importance of Sound (Q&A)," *The Hollywood Reporter*, 2 December. Available online: https://www.hollywoodreporter.com/news/michael-bay-transformers-dark-of-the-moon-269204 (accessed 19 October 2020).

Gross, Larry (2000 [1995]), "Big and Loud: Action Movies and the *Die Hard* Trilogy," in José Arroyo (ed.), *Action/Spectacle Cinema*, 3–9, London: British Film Institute.

"How Martial Arts Master Liang Yang Taught Felicity Jones to Kick Ass in 'Rogue One'" (n.d.), *Men's Journal*. Available online: https://www.mensjournal.com/health-fitness/how-martial-arts-master-liang-yang-taught-felicity-jones-kick-ass-rogue-one/ (accessed 19 October 2020).

Isaza, Miguel (2010), "Erik Aadahl Special: The Sound Design of 'Transformers' [Exclusive Interview]," *Designing Sound*, 25 March. Available online: https://designingsound.org/2010/03/25/erik-aadahl-special-the-sound-design-of-transformers-exclusive-interview/ (accessed 18 October 2020).

Kerins, Mark (2010), *Beyond Dolby (Stereo): Cinema in the Digital Sound Age*, Bloomington: Indiana University Press.

King, Geoff (2000), *Spectacular Narratives. Hollywood in the Age of the Blockbuster*, London: I.B. Tauris Publishers.

Murphet, Julian (1998), "Film Noir and The Racial Unconscious," *Screen*, 39 (1): 22–35.

Smith, Jeff (2013), "The Sound of Intensified Continuity," in John Richardson, Claudia Gorbman, and Carol Vernallis (eds), *The Oxford Handbook of New Audiovisual Aesthetics*, 332–55, Oxford: Oxford University Press.

Stork, Matthias (2013), "Chaos Cinema: Assaultive Action Aesthetics," *Media Fields Journal*, 6 August. Available online: http://mediafieldsjournal.org/chaos-cinema/2013/8/6/chaos-cinema-assaultive-action-aesthetics.html (accessed 19 October 2021).

Wilson, Alexandra (2007), *The Puccini Problem: Opera, Nationalism, and Modernity*, Cambridge: Cambridge University Press.

Chapter 4
"French Touch" Action Cinema

Charlie Michael

In the delightfully implausible smash-and-grab robbery attempt that launches *Lost Bullet* (*Balle perdue*, Guillaume Pierret, 2020), Lino (Alban Lenoir) grips the steering wheel of an unassuming European hatchback. Rejecting pleas for sanity from his passenger, Quentin (Rod Paradot), he sends the car barreling down the sort of narrow urban alleyway it looks designed for navigating. Bursting through a storefront window, he loses control, plowing through several interior walls before landing—in a cascade of glass and cement—on an adjoining block (Figure 4.1). Sirens approach, but our impetuous driver-hero is trapped by possibly the worst-timed seatbelt malfunction ever. As Quentin retreats on foot, Lino resigns himself to certain capture.

Lino's Renault Clio is, as it were, more than just a car. Narratively, it has a role in the intrigue; our hero is a savant mechanic known for maximizing this type of vehicle. A special ops investigator (Ramzy Bedia) later springs his conditional prison release:

Figure 4.1 Lino's (Alban Lenoir) little Clio hatchback sits in an alley after its unexpected crash through walls in *Lost Bullet* (© Netflix, 2020. All Rights Reserved).

Lino will be tapped to help apprehend drug runners. Yet Quentin's incredulous response to their robbery scheme—"your car won't hold, Lino!"—gestures at other possible meanings. Even without knowledge of the venerable French manufacturer Renault, its iconic and omnipresent Clio, or the significance of larger American cars to French cinema's conception of modern cool—think *Lola* (Jacques Demy, 1961) or *A Man and a Woman* (*Un homme et une femme*, Claude Lelouch, 1966)—any viewer grasps that Lino's ride is unremarkable, and especially compared with the souped-up vehicles in other contemporary action films, most notably the French *Taxi* franchise, which features a similarly retrofitted vehicle as part of an immensely popular series of buddy comedies.[1] Lino's choice of transportation thus might read as a self-deprecating reference to an entire history of transatlantic, auto-vehicular differentiation, primed to highlight cinematic "little differences" along the lines of what *Pulp Fiction* (Quentin Tarantino, 1994) parodies by referencing the French phrase for a McDonald's cheeseburger.

Produced as a Netflix original from France, *Lost Bullet*'s compact construction, unassuming generic bearing, and sardonic flair for localized details typifies a growing recent line of action films issuing from France's media industries. Yet one might also question to what degree those who find *Lost Bullet* on their streaming queues even care about the film's origin story or cultural subtext. Do non-English dialogue, unfamiliar cast members, vaguely European backdrops and fleeting cultural references qualify this as a legitimately French cultural product? To what degree do such minute details make a dent in our broader historical account of globalized action cinema? What type of methodology, what sort of cultural specificity, and even what flavor of filmmaking practice would be required to better illuminate the significant and ongoing role of French-made action in a global landscape increasingly mediated by search algorithms and a vaguely construed sense of "Europeanness"?

In response to these questions, this chapter proposes a brief, transnational review of the industrial origins and stylistic features of recent French-produced action films. In so doing, it both outlines and advocates for what it calls a *centripetal* methodology for assessing emerging Franco-European transnational production cultures. That term is proposed here as a complement to other recent accounts of transnationalism in film and media, which are often primed to track a more *centrifugal*—i.e., outwardly oriented—sense of creative and economic energies that evade or transcend perceived national parameters of industry, circulation, or identity. In this sense, a centripetal approach would further highlight the obverse of what many transnational accounts often overlook—the strategic moves and creative concessions that localized practitioners make to facilitate, to make do with, and to work *within* a globalized generic repertoire. For action genres in France, this is a balancing act performed by a generation that hopes to reach international viewers, and to bear in mind those national and regional audiences who can read—even celebrate—the cunning ways their "own" films finesse the contours of a globalized popular idiom with localized particularity. Along these lines, Pierret and a growing cohort of recent Franco-European action filmmakers (Fred Cavayé, Eric Valette, Jean-Patrick Benes, Julien Leclercq, Frédéric Jardin, and others) make films that are sensitized to how the "little differences" in action cinema *do* matter. In a marketplace more known for Hollywood blockbusters and distinctly cultural products (e.g., Asian action genres), this generation of localized French talent finds a contingent identity via a self-effacing approach to the genre that highlights certain conventions—spatial articulation, physical exertion, sardonic humor—in ways that signal both the contradictions and the opportunities of a nascent enterprise.

Mixing Metaphors, Emerging Theories

So common are games of citational referentiality in popular cinema these days that they run the risk of being dismissed as callow commercialism. This is especially true in scholarship on French cinema, which traditionally tends to prize the industry's defiance of Hollywood (Buchsbaum 2017) and where the validation of popular forms remains rare, despite considerable recent inroads in economics (Creton 2012, 2020 [1994]) and popular genres (Gimello-Mesplomb 2012a, 2012b; Harrod 2015; Jullier 1997, 2002; Moine 2015). The recent French sociological literature suggests this dynamic is rapidly changing, perhaps most notably in Frédéric Martel's work of the 2000s, which broadly questions the embedded intellectual presuppositions about "mainstream" cultural products in a North American mode (2006, 2010). A recent study by Vincent Cicchelli and Sylvie Octobre (2018) adds qualitative heft to this view, challenging Pierre Bourdieu's now canonical 1979 study of taste and class by claiming that the intense circulation of global cultural products in France, particularly since the 1990s, calls for a reworking of the "hierarchy of cultural practices and aesthetic genres," especially for a millennial audience who navigates between foreign and national cultural products with a more "omnivorous" sensibility than ever before (2018: 6).

Commercial forms of entertainment routinely present similar methodological questions for theorists of transnational cinema. Building on earlier theories of national cinema, some recent accounts of the field advocate for approaches that highlight disempowered traditions more than commercial ones (Hjort 2010; Nagib 2020), while others favor a more mobile perspective that suspends value judgment long enough to give commercial filmmaking its due (Ezra and Rowden 2006; Shaw 2014). From an agnostic viewpoint, it appears that a properly "critical transnationalism" (Higbee and Lim 2010: 17–18) can recognize that all films are not created equal, validating the plurality of forms and reception, and acknowledging that "national" and "transnational" influences are often intertwined in ways that resemble what Thomas Elsaesser once likened to a "hall of mirrors" (2005: 47), because tracing influences always involves methodological caution about "comparing like with like" (Halle 2008: 27).

Despite different aesthetic value judgments, these theorists do tend to share a grounding, metaphorical assumption, compelled by the prepositional freedom to move away from national containers and to cut *across*, move *beyond* or circulate *outside* the presupposed limits of economies, geographies, and imaginaries in a methodological gesture outlined almost three decades ago by Arjun Appadurai (1996). Recent scholarship on French-made action genres often shares in this more-or-less *centrifugal* impulse, construing genre conventions as a function of how French-based artisans strategically access global distribution networks or manifest stylistic components that derive primarily from elsewhere (Gleich 2012; Vanderschelden 2007, 2009). Other recent work performs a similar account from a more inward-looking centripetal vantage point, highlighting the localized impact or relevance of global forms, and how they intertwine—stylistically, ideologically— with nationally construed traditions (Michael 2019; Pettersen 2012, 2023; Rappas 2016). The distinction here thus involves a constant balancing act between the two mutually inclusive, transformative tendencies involved in accommodating, adapting, and responding to the push to "go global," since the 1990s. This chapter aims to expand and give breadth to the second *centripetal* viewpoint of French action cinema, revealing the stylistic preoccupations of a genre that perhaps began with—but has since moved well beyond—EuropaCorp.

Whither "French Touch" Action?

Two production studios deserve distinction in the origin story of contemporary "French touch" action in its neo-Hollywood mode. The first one, StudioCanal, appeared in the mid-1990s as a production affiliate for Canal+, the "French HBO" created in the 1980s to anchor the Mitterrand administration's new conception of a deregulated French media industry. As Canal+ rode the rapid rise and fall of several ownership groups, it looked for a successful combination of strategies to compete with Hollywood, including founding a writing wing specifically for the production of "B films" (Canal+ Ecriture), flirting with foreign investment in Hollywood blockbusters, and mounting several of its own super-productions—of which *Brotherhood of the Wolf / Le Pacte des loups* (Christophe Gans, 2001) remains the most memorable. In more recent iterations, the studio found equilibrium as a producer of both nationally and transnationally targeted motion pictures like the action-comedy hybrid *Paddington* (Paul King, 2014) and its sequel (Paul King, 2017) (Meir 2018).

The second firm took a much narrower view. From the start, EuropaCorp cast its lot almost entirely with action—a genre which, to that point, had scant representation from national producers. Fresh off their international success with *The Fifth Element* (1997) and frustrated by the lack of vision at the venerable French major Gaumont, Luc Besson and his producer Pierre-Ange Le Pogam founded a "go it alone" outfit to back their next idea for a small French-language buddy comedy set in Marseille. The enormous domestic success of that film— the first of the now five-deep *Taxi* franchise—paved the way for numerous other French-language series, including the noted *parkour* film *District B-13* (*Banlieue 13*, Pierre Morel, 2004) and its sequel (Patrick Alessandrin, 2009) as well as English-language martial arts offerings like *Kiss of the Dragon* (Chris Nahon, 2001) and *Unleashed* (*Danny the Dog*) (Louis Leterrier, 2005) that imported Hong Kong action talent to Europe. Along the way, Besson and LePogam devised a plan to periodically pool resources to fund bigger-budget franchises that could compete with Hollywood. For nearly two decades, EuropaCorp successfully did this on a bi-annual basis, first with the *Transporter* and *Taken* franchises, which gave them mounting credibility with foreign distributors in North America and Asia, allowing them to avoid relying on local distributors like Pathé-Gaumont and state-run agencies like Unifrance (Maule 2008).[2] While several projects of the mid 2010s met with rousing box office—most notably *Lucy* (Luc Besson, 2014)—a series of subsequent disappointments including *Valérian* (Luc Besson, 2017) has since consigned the studio to receivership, and perhaps even an eventual Netflix buyout.

So far in the critical literature, the question of French-made action still orbits rather uneasily around Besson's influence. In the fall of 2017, for instance, a roundtable of critics at the *Forum des Images* explored the possible emergence of a distinctive, contemporary "French touch" action style. After a useful discussion of earlier examples—including several forgotten Jean-Paul Belmondo films of the 1970s—the discussion was sidetracked by a familiar, vexed debate about Besson ("La French Touch du cinéma d'action existe-t-il?" 2017).[3] The panelists' discomfort was not surprising, given the firm's releases have become by far the most visible action films to come from their domestic industry, and are usually lacking in identifiable cultural elements (Martin-Jones 2012). Lisa Purse conducts a sustained reading of the narrative and stylistic features of several EuropaCorp films, proposing that further investigations might still sharpen our understanding of how other Franco-European producers have sought an "internationalizing formula" of action (2011: 170–89). Building on my previous work (2005, 2019, 2020), the remaining pages of this chapter consider recent "French touch" action cinema beyond Besson, outlining a few of the repeated stylistic patterns across a diversity of recent productions from the Hexagon.

Mutable Locations

The most memorable scene from *Point Blank* (*A Bout Portant*, Fred Cavayé, 2010) features our hero, Sam (Gilles Lellouche), fleeing authorities through the hallways of the Paris Metro. In a flurry of handheld gray tones, Sam and the duo of police detectives who pursue him remain surprisingly center screen in almost every composition. The sequence flips rhythmically back and forth between them as they traverse the identifiable, physical obstacles of a big city locale (obstructive ticket turnstiles; precarious train platforms; crowded escalators). Periodically, we also crosscut to Captain Vogel (Moussa Maaskri), who berates his charges via walkie talkie, demanding updates on their positioning on the subway map. These exchanges mark a confluence between the spatial details of the film's intrigue and its potential for multiple readable positions. For native Parisian viewers (or really anyone familiar with the Metro), the sequence rewards via authentic spatial detail. Moment by moment, Sam's whereabouts hew closely to the routes carried on nearly every metro stop wall in the city. Agents report back to Vogel ("*Opéra! Direction Balard!*") as cutaways and whip pans show surveillance monitors bearing miniature, grainy replicas of Sam as he dashes by surveillance cameras. According to Cavayé, the crew only got permits to shoot in the early morning, so had to herd hundreds of caffeinated extras to simulate the daily bustle at several Line 8 locations in turn (McCracken 2011). Despite this specificity, viewers unacquainted with Paris do not need a Metro map to make sense of the sequence. Instead, the detailed, geographical elements of the Metro space offer an extra dimension that—like Lino's car, the little Clio—brings a significant (but irreducible) quality to the film's range of meaning. A Parisian variation, then, on the momentarily legible but ultimately anonymized train stations in so many recent Hollywood action films, Cavayé's scenic articulation conveys a texture at once nondescript enough to travel and cultural enough to reward—but never require—a localized perspective.[4] At the same time, the sequence undoubtedly references, while hardly trying to, dozens of iconic appearances of a locale that populate a national cinema tradition—from New Wave-era classics like *Zazie in the Metro* (*Zazie dans le métro*, Louis Malle, 1960) or *Le Samouraï* (Jean-Pierre Melville, 1967) to reflexive references in *The Last Metro* (*Le dernier métro*, François Truffaut, 1980) or *Subway* (Luc Besson, 1985).

    This mutability of space and place on transnational action screens presents problems for even the most assiduous of recent attempts to define novelty. *Point Blank* is a well-appointed film, each shot thoughtfully curated, but none of its features appear particularly noteworthy on the surface. As David Bordwell (2002) suggests, the efficient plotting approach of numerous recent Hollywood films often goes hand in hand with what he terms "intensified continuity," which fittingly describes Cavayé's orchestration of ornamental options—variable shot scales, a continuously mobile camera, shorter average shot length (ASL)—that heighten visual stimuli without altering the spatio-temporal principles of scenic efficiency that have anchored a mainstream global industry for nearly a century now. At the same time, when we relax our insistent focus on technique as an explanatory element, the loosely construed "place-ness" of actual locations must also relate somehow to more abstract potential for meaning structures. Figuring somewhere on a continuum of global action's perpetual potential for real cultural content in its flux of locales, the signs of identifiable "place-ness" here lurk somewhere between what Meaghan Morris (2004) calls the "major" (star-driven, big-budget, special effects, mainstream audiences, multiplatform distribution) and "minor" circulation forms (low-budget, athlete-performers, cost-cutting aesthetic, niche audiences, direct-to-DVD) of global action. Morris uses Hong Kong films as her example, and her approach is helpful in understanding the ways today's omnivorous French directors can knowingly borrow from different traditions within the action genre, using that knowledge to position themselves within it. Without such ready access to the digitally enhanced, star-driven, ensemble casts of the *James Bond* or *Mission: Impossible* franchises, domestically oriented directors like Cavayé still benefit from a pool of athletic performers, which they can combine with the tried-and-true formulae of constructive editing, and an expanding group of independently run post-production outfits like Le Labo and StudioB. All these resources increasingly work together, facilitating a rise of action genres at other studios like Gaumont and Studio Orange, who have been especially motivated in the wake of EuropaCorp's launch of a state-of-the-art post-production suite in its "Hollywood style" *Cité du cinéma* (completed in 2012). In a table enumerating her two global modes of circulation, Morris describes how both traditions use city spaces as functional backdrops for action, but in ways that can be distinguished in terms of class context and the mobility of the characters within it. Major films, she claims, tend toward the globalized "non-spaces" of the modern city (hotels, resorts, airports, commercial centers) while their minor counterparts can only afford to stage fights in "any-place-whatevers" (busses, trains, factories, wharfs).

Morris is clear that she does not intend these two designations to be mutually exclusive, but rather evocative of a multifaceted tradition that moves freely between them. This is certainly true in the Gallic case today, as numerous recent French practitioners of these generic codes show a knowledge of how to play within the readable parameters of global action spaces, in the city and otherwise. In some cases, working in an omnivorous manner between traditions becomes a way to market authorial credibility to the press. In interviews, Cavayé repeatedly describes his approach to action as "something like a Claude Sautet film plus the Jason Bourne trilogy" (McCracken 2011). This nod to diverse reference points might seem pretentious if it were not also accurate. Sautet, known in France for a quotidian tonality more than any one mode of filmmaking, worked for over three decades in his home industry, endowing seventeen different films with instant middlebrow credibility. Perhaps anticipating a similar career path, Cavayé has recently moved on to other genres like drama and comedy, but he is still remembered for the unofficial trilogy of action thrillers he directed to begin his run: *Anything for Her* (*Pour Elle*, 2008), *Point Blank* (*A Bout Portant*, 2010) and *Mea Culpa* (2014). He claims stylistic inspiration for the two later films came while shooting the frantic final act of *Anything for Her*, the story of a high school teacher (Vincent Lindon) who plots to spring his wrongly convicted wife (Diane Kruger) out of jail and ends with a desperate prison break attempt. The second and third films instead frontload the build-up to just fifteen minutes, dispensing narrative pretense in favor of almost non-stop action. All recount the exploits of wrongly-accused, everyman patriarchs—Lindon saves his wife (*Anything for Her*); Lellouche saves his (*Point Blank*); the stars team up to save Lindon's wife and child (*Mea Culpa*). But what unites the three more than stars or thematic preoccupations is their mundane stylistic feel: a suspenseful, quotidian, social-realist style of cinematography, punctuated by spasmodic action scenes with quick editing and a roving, handheld camera. Amidst these, Cavayé inserts other fleeting moments of rooted, cultural experience, as in the dramatic climax of *Mea Culpa*, when a gunfight breaks out on a TGV (French bullet train), and our heroes must dive to avoid gunfire, weaving in and out of the narrow, geometric aisles as they take cover. Lest we think this could be "any train whatever," the puffing pneumatic doors—familiar to any EuroPass holder—suggest otherwise.

Other recent French-made action films exploit the implicit tension between the identifiable fabric of space and place yet take it in another direction entirely. Consider, for instance, the variance between Cavayé's entry and *Arès* (Jean-Patrick Benes, 2016), a largely overlooked recent dystopian sci fi just lately rescued from obscurity by Netflix. As José Arroyo notes, action-film milieux present problems for classification not only because of their relaxed relationship to spatial anchorage, but also because of the essential transportability of action as an ingredient across genres (2000: xii). Exploring the flipside of *Point Blank*'s fungible quotidian detail, Benes moves in the opposite direction on a low-budget aesthetic—spaces that are dystopic and fantastic, but no less mutable. At first blush, *Arès* offers a similar thematic appeal to *District B-13*, as it transports us to a near-future 2035 where Paris has devolved into a raucous capital of homeless masses who look to kick-boxing cage-matches to distract them from the exploitation of their corporate overlords. Reda (Ola Rapace), stage name Arès, is a fighter whose refusal to take a performance-enhancing drug forces him to confront a vast network of corruption, eventually making him fight once again—this time to defend the lives of his two young nieces. Visually conceived along the lines of *Blade Runner* (Ridley Scott, 1982), the film's chiaroscuro

lighting masks its overall lack of décor with a dark, unadorned look, apt for depicting downtrodden characters under a corrupt surveillance state. Previously recognizable only as a muscular bad guy in action films like *Skyfall* (Sam Mendes, 2012), the Swedish-born Rapace's stilted French contributes to the film's vaguely European bearing. When Reda fights, the staging of the matches resembles starkly lit UFC showdowns but shot in tight medium and close-up shots without the looping UFC crane views that show screaming fans. The film manages to steer around its financial shortcomings (a reported budget of just €5 million) by navigating repeatedly to a digitally modified, cloudy view of the Eiffel Tower, here outfitted with a ring of enormous video screens (Figure 4.2).

Simple in its conception, this single image returns to us multiple times in *Arès*, looming over numerous exterior shots and communicating the essential narrative information—the cage matches are televised, both for us and for the diegetic audience. Crucially, the impoverished multitude represented in *Arès*, shown frequently in the film via reaction shots as they watch the Tower screens from below, were actually not paid extras, but demonstrators in Ukraine, captured by the film crew during a brief trip to the real anti-government protests that occurred in Kyiv during February of 2014. As Benes reports, the film crew found there a real "city on the verge of revolution," where they were able to glean footage that they later combined digitally with Chinese skyscrapers—gathered during a separate trip to Shenzen and Shanghai—and iconic French monuments ("*Arès*: Secrets du tournage" 2016). Ironically, by flexing his knowledge of what Morris would call the "major" mode's non-space iconography, Benes performs a cost-cutting maneuver along the lines of the "minor" one, here augured by so many other factors—Reda's anti-hero, Rapace's on-screen anonymity and the bloody cage matches themselves.

Extreme Exertion

If one salient feature of recent French-based action films is their cost-cutting manipulation of space and place, it should not obscure a more proximate focus in nearly every shot of these films: human bodies. Popular cinema commonly compensates for its spatial fungibility by anchoring itself in the exertion of bodily performance (Holmlund 2002; Tasker 1993). Moreover, screen bodies take on a particular significance for young directors working in the context of what Tim Palmer calls the contemporary French film "ecosystem." French film has become known internationally for its fascination with the *cinéma du corps*—a strain of extreme art cinema that challenges conventional representations of the body through graphic violence, explicit sex, and an aggressive avant-garde aesthetics (2011: 57–95). Palmer emphasizes that *cinéma du corps* directors like Gaspard Noé and Catherine Breillat can also be understood as part of a community where a reservoir of exchange nourishes a culture of "applied cinephilia" that cuts across categories of practice conventionally thought separate—from film school graduates of *La Fémis* (the national film school) to technicians like Pierret, Cavayé, and Benes, who cut their teeth working in television or the commercial sector (2011: 95–151). Yet while these stylistic connections have been applied to horror (McCann 2013), they have yet to be mapped onto action genres.

Numerous contemporary French action films show an almost morbid fascination with extreme human exertion. In some cases, this feature dovetails with the aforementioned qualities of ambiguous space and place. Another recent overlooked gem, the crime thriller *State Affairs* (*Une affaire d'état*, Eric Valette, 2009), features a penultimate scene where police detective Nora (Rachida Brakni) chases Michel (Thierry Frémont), a mid-level hitman who holds the key to unraveling a crime spree linked to the government. Valette's parallel editing flits between these characters as they run and progressively injure themselves. (Michel nurses a gunshot wound, Nora is upended by a marauding bicyclist.) Though they are initially surrounded by undifferentiated urban space, their running surface gradually shifts to cobblestones, rendering their limping gaits even more labored as they meet with a steep incline. Though unknowing viewers would not recognize these as hallmarks of Montmartre, Valette soon doubles down on the sequence's topographical qualities. Both the visuals and the characters' pulmonary exertion accelerate as Michel reaches the incline to Sacré Coeur first, launching himself up the steps, gasping, pulling seemingly out of reach. Nora, meanwhile, struggles to find him, scanning the crowds ahead, glimpsing a dark form as it lurches up the stairs. Near the top, in a slightly longer shot, Michel stops, bending over as his chest heaves in distress. He vomits, then continues upward. Nora, her face bloodied, persists by choosing the option favored by most beleaguered tourists—the funicular streetcar that runs parallel to the staircase Michel has scaled.

Expertly distending the suspense along with the spatial specifics of a known locale, Valette makes us wait and watch as Nora tries to blend in with the crowd inside the ascending funicular car. The constructive manipulation of space rewards us here, but the suffering of these bodies is paramount. Michel stops running, donning his beanie and strolling into a crowd of craftspeople he must already know are clustered in front of the cathedral. Nora follows him, her breath returning, and Valette offers a bravura, point-of-view tracking shot, literally embodying her vision as she (and we) moves forward through the crowd. In a rhythmic contrast this shot interrupts the previously frantic pacing with a slice-of-life, *vérité* panorama of street artisans. Nora approaches a man from behind. A cutaway shows Michel brandishing a knife, but in a final reversal, he surrenders without a fight, as if relieved the labored chase is finally over.

Watching these films, it is hard not to be struck by the sheer exuberance of the performers and the duration of the scenes depicting their struggles. Mainstream crossover performers to the genre (Lellouche, Brakni, Lindon) are on record as having performed all but the most extreme of their own physical stunts in the films. Lellouche's shirt is so drenched with sweat in *Point Blank* that we wish he would remove his jacket before hurdling yet another turnstile. For his starring role in Valette's subsequent film *The Prey* (*La Proie*, 2011), former comedian Albert Dupontel—a director in his own right—showed a similarly almost "suicidal" commitment to stunt work (Desbrun 2011).

In many cases, the cost-cutting aesthetic in play here also brings about a striking return to the same enclosed spaces, over and over. Nearly all of *Sleepless Night* (*Nuit Blanche*, Frédéric Jardin, 2011), for instance, takes place inside a nightclub, as Vincent (Tomer Sisley) desperately pursues his son's kidnappers. In the process, he traverses the kitchen multiple times. This becomes a source of humor (by the end, all the employees know him, even helping him fool his assailants by substituting bags of flour for cocaine) and provides several scenes of abject, physical exhaustion. A central, prolonged confrontation between Vincent and Lacombe (Julien Boisselier) proves particularly drawn-out, recalling Hong Kong films by Jackie Chan and Sammo Hung: the two actors make use of nearly every surface and cooking implement within their grasp. Each performer is left gasping for breath, and we watch them tend their wounds in subsequent scenes.[5] Although the handheld slipperiness of the cinematography recalls *Bourne* directors like Doug Liman or Paul Greengrass, these are characters who deal with far more physical consequences than we ever see befall the superhuman Bourne (Matt Damon).

In some cases, the commitment to bodily spectacle even completely replaces recent French action cinema's concern for narrative comprehension. Historically, this tendency traces more generally to the industry's smaller-scale "off-Hollywood" methods of artisanal practice as a whole, but also to the ways that mode of production combines with a recent commitment to mounting credibly "globalized" action scenes. Again, EuropaCorp was the pathbreaker here. As former Besson screenwriter Robert Mark Kamen reports, the firm frequently saved money in its busy first decade of production by streamlining nearly every department other than stunts and visual effects. Scripts, rather than a combined product of writing teams or constant revision, came from a simple collaboration between Besson's fountainhead of "original ideas" and one-off efforts by himself or one of his appointed house scribes, who could stitch together the necessary premise for a film's other prerogatives: "big set pieces, practical action, martial arts [. . .] and very few computer-generated effects" (Goldstein 2009). This truncated narrative tendency continues unabated in more recent French-produced action films, in some cases bringing other stylistic options on the palette—like bodily spectacle—to the fore.

One of the most curious elements of *Lost Bullet*, for instance, is the perfunctory nature of the romance plot. Rather than simply getting pushed aside by the obsessions of a vengeful patriarch like Bryan Mills (Liam Neeson) in *Taken* (Pierre Morel, 2008), Lino's backstory with his old flame, Julia (Stéfi Celma), becomes central to both his motivations and the intrigue of the film. Despite this, their backstory is quite easy to miss—contained entirely in a brief close-up when Lino glimpses Julia's photo among a stack of other suspects. Though Lino visibly hesitates in the ensuing reaction shot, there is nothing to specify their relationship other than perhaps cringe-worthy "B-film" gender clichés (our alpha hero must be attractive to any woman this striking). This is even more strained later, as we have perhaps almost forgotten about their connection until Lino is framed for the murder of Charas (Ramzy Bedia) and must break out of prison. Julia re-emerges as the one member of the special ops team who remains uncompromised by a crooked mutiny. Former stuntman Pierret chooses to express what was probably their earlier romantic connection through physical conflict. A bloody Lino

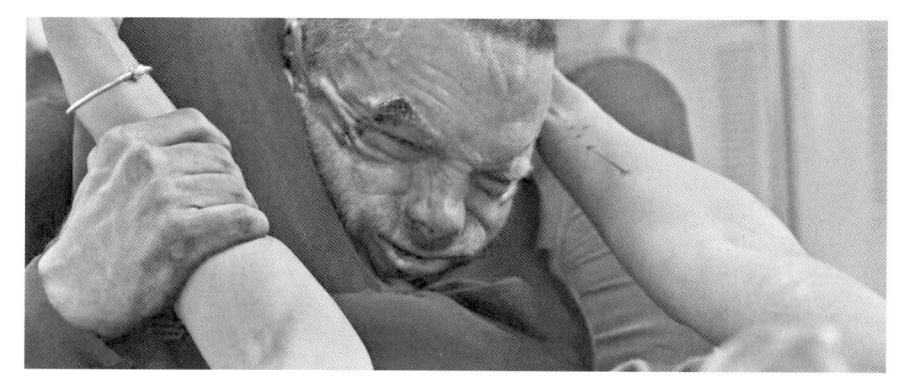

Figure 4.3 Lino (Alban Lenoir) struggles against a choke hold by Julia (Stéfi Celma) in *Lost Bullet* (© Netflix, 2020. All Rights Reserved).

confronts Julia, confesses he has no proof of his story, and embraces her. Moments later she knees him in the crotch and a struggle ensues, replacing what could have been a sex scene on a car with frantic, gasping violence that reaches an affect-laden *détente* when she clenches his neck between her thighs (Figure 4.3). The two (apparently former) lovers collapse in "post-coital" exhaustion. Lino and Julia may end *Lost Bullet* in the archetypical slots we equate with coupling in other action films—sympatico as if to fight together another day—yet there is never another hint of their bond.

Citational Humor

Contemporary French action films would be far less interesting if they were always serious. A third attribute that cuts across recent "French touch" films is a pervasive sense of self-deprecating humor—often about the relative absence of action scenes in French cinema, or the absurdity of finding them there. For there remains an abiding sense in this emerging regional action cinema—"made in France"—of an industry toiling in the shadow of many others, at once blessed with a palette that is globally quite infinite and nationally rather repressed.

This feature cross-pollinates with the two characteristics discussed above, namely spatial articulation and physical exertion. Valette's criminally underseen *The Prey* (*La Proie*, 2011) offers a succinct example. In yet another variation on the "wrong man" plot, convicted bank robber Franck Adrien (Albert Dupontel) breaks out of jail in a last-ditch effort to rescue his family from a bloodthirsty former cellmate (Stéphane Debac) who has been wrongly released before him. As Adrien traipses across the countryside, pursued by police, Valette's cinematography tracks his increasingly frantic runs across empty cornfields and through abandoned trainyards (a rural variation on what Morris might term "any space whatevers" (2004: 190)). Periodically, though, Adrien crosses paths with unsuspecting "regular" people, perhaps nowhere as memorably as when he jumps onto a moving regional train to evade police. From inside the silent cabin, several passengers look emphatically unmoved as Adrien peers down from above, struggling to open a window (Figure 4.4).

Humor here derives from a series of realizations. Initially, it stems from the passengers' apparent disinterest in a man peering at them, upside down, outside the window of a moving train. Next, however—emphasized by the duration of the shot—comes the recognition that this is in fact a French regional train. While this is a reasonable position for a man to occupy in an action film (like the one we are watching), the passengers' lack of recognition may therefore not be due to their preoccupation with cell phones or magazines, but rather to a culturally conditioned tendency to respect privacy, or perhaps also to their utter lack of familiarity with anything like an action hero showing up during a rural train ride. In

Figure 4.4 Passengers fail to notice Adrien (Albert Dupontel) during their train ride in *The Prey* (© StudioCanal International, 2011. All Rights Reserved).

either case, after a moment of awkward hesitation (for the train interloper)—and pluralistic readability (for the viewer)—Adrien forces open the window, sending the passengers fleeing while jolting us back into a more quotidian cause-and-effect sequence.

The point of disambiguating these interpretive options is not to say that they are terribly novel. Encounters between action heroes and "regular people" are a norm throughout action films globally. Think perhaps of the awkward explanation Peter Parker (Tobey Maguire) offers two awestruck middle schoolers after a back flip in traffic in *Spider-Man 2* (Sam Raimi, 2004): "You know, kids, eat your green vegetables!" Rather, the claim here is that *The Prey* is constructed to have a plural readability. Valette injects this scenic beat with a stab of playful irony, highlighting the gap between this film and those "other" action films—the more prominent global ones—where the prospect of "insane hyperbolic action that explodes into everyday life" is more familiar (Desbrun 2011). Bringing the trappings of "hyperbolic action" into collision with the sleepy rhythms of the mundane, he abruptly switches the frenzy off moments later. After he forces his way out of the window, the image track cuts to an exterior shot of Dupontel, who rolls off the train and, surprisingly, simply strolls away through a cornfield. Cut to the next scene.

The Prey is not a comedy—at least not for most of its run time—but moments like these offer a final possibility for describing the contours of an emerging identity of "French touch" action style. For while comedy is itself a generic construct, the possibility for parody of other conventions, for most theoretical models, only emerges once a set of conventions have been firmly established in context—what Thomas Schatz calls the "mannerist" stage of generic evolution (1981: 207). Without the added layer of a French domestic action tradition already in place, most of the gags in the recent breakout blockbuster hit *RAID Special Unit* (*RAID Dingue*, Dany Boon, 2016) would fall flat, as they assume the mundane cohabitation of global and local reference points, much as Boon's most famous hit—*Welcome to the Sticks* (*Bienvenue Chez les Ch'tis*, 2008)—parodies the regional distinctions within France by using a knowing irony about their actual close geographic proximity. On a similar note of absurd juxtaposition, the recent hit romantic comedy *Alibi.com* (Philippe Lacheau, 2017) features a protagonist obsessed with the cult action film *Bloodsport* (Newt Arnold, 1988). A jubilant pastiche that exaggerates Lacheau's cinéphile reverence and lampoons his distance from a foreign cultural product, *Alibi.com* offers a counterexample to the intense notes of a film like Valette's. For Geoffrey (played by Lacheau), the absurdist *coup de grâce* comes in a fever-dream sequence that splices his own stiff imitation with Van Damme's iconic roundhouse from *Bloodsport*'s final scene—in the process winning him the (even more) improbable affections of Flo (Elodie Fontan). Drawing on the expertise of EuropaCorp personnel, Lacheau and his team mount action scenes that credibly mimic globalized aesthetics to embrace their use in a (self-deprecating) French context. Notwithstanding their slapstick rom-com packaging, moments like these testify to the presence of action as a domestic ingredient, ready for use by today's omnivorous French directors.

Conclusion

If contemporary France has become an unexpected source of unflinching action cinema, that is a consequence of both strategic and creative responses to globalized popular culture. Bursting from film-loving imaginings and cultural knowingness, this inspired, often sardonic, oft-underestimated tradition deserves a fresh look. Collectively, these are movies that constitute an emerging group style, generating inspiration from the genre's kinetic possibilities, but also from its relative obscurity, even disrepute, in localized discourses of legitimacy. Notable for their compact construction, skillful editing, and spatial choreography, these films intermittently reference concrete spatial geography while deploying forms of corporeal grittiness and winking referentiality that evoke localized traditions. Far from erasing cultural difference, then, a *centripetal* view of French action genres highlights "little differences" as a locus for engagement with the stylistic dynamics of cultural exchange. While the precise coordinates of an emerging "aesthetic-cultural cosmopolitanism" (Cicchelli and Octobre 2018) in France must remain speculative for now, analyses like this one shed light on the ways recent films render themselves broadly readable to globalized audiences, all while signaling distinctions to those familiar with local contexts and traditions.

Given the kneejerk remake impulse of Hollywood studios, some critics may be less than sanguine about the value of these French-made films within the global action film industry. Still, "French touch" action's deft construction, its gritty corporeality, and its refreshingly playful outlook suggest a burgeoning pool of local talent ready to find global visibility. Such a prospect could be more likely as we look down the barrel of a global media industry shaped by COVID-19. As Netflix and its competitors exert new dominance, the reformulation of media uptake practices after lockdown culture also means national media industries must be re-constituted for a new set of existential challenges—and opportunities. Freed from the gauntlet of theatrical supply chains, streaming platforms seem poised to reconstitute the playing field, though it remains an open question how—or if—they will choose to amplify French and/or European success.[6] Though Besson's earnest attempt to build an independent, off-Hollywood mini-major studio might ultimately fail, EuropaCorp's legacy may be that it has provided the technical facilities and production culture needed to mount modern-looking action. Paris is now the home to trained technicians and performers who, like Pierret and Lenoir, stand revved and ready to chase the next *Lost Bullet*. Given the momentum of streaming providers on the European market, those opportunities look primed to continue for at least the near term (Lemercier 2020). Whatever the case may be, future changes will call for a mobile form of criticism—ready to retrace new forms of exchange beyond national containers, but also to validate the ingenuity of domestic industries that manage to regroup, rethink, and repurpose their talent base, channeling their inward potential outward and into an uncertain future.

Notes

1 Titles include *Taxi* (Gérard Pirès, 1998), *Taxi 2* (Gérard Krawczyk, 2000), *Taxi 3* (Gérard Krawczyk, 2003), *Taxi 4* (Gérard Krawczyk, 2007), and *Taxi 5* (Franck Gastambide, 2018).

2 Titles include *Taken* (Pierre Morel, 2008), *Taken 2* (Olivier Megaton, 2012), *Taken 3* (Olivier Megaton, 2015), *The Transporter* (Louis Leterrier and Corey Yuen, 2002), *The Transporter 2* (Louis Leterrier, 2005), *The Transporter 3* (Olivier Megaton, 2008), and *The Transporter Refueled* (Camille Delamarre, 2015).

3 The version of the anglicism "French touch" used here first circulated in music criticism circles of the 1990s as a way to describe the distinctive stylistic contributions of French-produced dance music that managed to define itself as identifiably French in sensibility despite lacking the cultural markers music of previous generations like the *chanson française*. See Julien (2002).

4 For instance, Nick Jones discusses the localized particularities of the Waterloo train station sequence in *The Bourne Ultimatum* (Greengrass, 2007) as instrumentalized for the purposes of a "cat-and mouse" game. See Jones (2015: 44–70).

5 The recent Netflix original, *The Wolf's Call* (*Le chant du loup*, Antonin Baudry, 2019), similarly acquaints the viewer with the interior layout of a submarine, depicting an underwater nuclear missile crisis primarily through handheld camera and claustrophobic close-up shots. A comparable huis clos unfurls in *The Nest* (*Nid de Guêpes*, Florent-Emilio Siri, 2002). There, nearly the entire scenario takes place in a single warehouse. A gang of small-time criminals is trapped together with French special forces transporting a dangerous foreign mob boss to trial. When heavily armed gangsters come to rescue their leader, the crooks must ally with the military officers. Copious amounts of gunfire ensue.

6 The three films analyzed in this chapter represent some of the contradictions inherent in the production and distribution of contemporary French action cinema today. Although categorized on the stack menus as Netflix "originals," *Lost Bullet* and *Arès* are exemplars of the types of international deals the streaming giant is currently pursuing. *Lost Bullet* is a film Netflix *commissioned*—so it had no theatrical distribution at all. *Arès*—like many other recent Gallic actioners—is a Netflix *acquisition*, which means it had a (meager) theatrical run in France when it was released in 2016 (just prior to the Netflix production commission boom in France). Released a few years earlier in 2010, *Point Blank* dates to the pre-Netflix phase in France. It did quite well nationally and enjoyed a modest North American and European run (and a subsequent US remake). The three films thus represent three of the options—Netflix commission, Netflix acquisition, and traditional theatrical distribution with eventual remake—available to contemporary action directors. See further Meir (2021) on streaming's impact on European media companies.

Works Cited

Appadurai, Arjun (1996), *Modernity at Large: Cultural Dimensions of Globalization*, Minneapolis: University of Minnesota Press.

Arroyo, José (2000), "Introduction," in José Arroyo (ed.), *Action/Spectacle Cinema: A Sight and Sound Reader*, vii–xv, London: British Film Institute.

"*Arès*: Secrets du tournage" (2016), *Allociné*, 23 November. Available online:https://www.allocine.fr/film/fichefilm_gen_cfilm=234386.html (accessed 24 April 2022).

Bordwell, David (2002), "Intensified Continuity: Visual Style in Contemporary American Film," *Film Quarterly*, 55 (3): 16–28.

Bourdieu, Pierre (1987 [1979]), *Distinction: A Social Critique of the Judgment of Taste*, trans. R. Nice, Cambridge, MA: Harvard University Press.

Buchsbaum, Jonathan (2017), *Exception Taken: How France Has Defied Hollywood's New World Order*, New York: Columbia University Press.

Cicchelli, Vincent and Sylvie Octobre (2018), *Aesthetico-Cultural Cosmopolitanism and French Youth: A Taste of the World*, London: Palgrave McMillan.

Creton, Laurent (2012), *L'Economie du cinéma en 50 fiches*, 3rd edn, Paris: Armand Collin.

Creton, Laurent (2020 [1994]), *Economie du cinéma: perspectives stratégiques*, 6th edn, Paris: Armand Colin.

Desbrun, Cécile (2011), "Interview d'Eric Valette pour La Proie," *Culturellement Votre*, 24 March. Available online: https://culturellementvotre.fr/2011/03/24/interviewdericvalettepourlaproie/ (accessed 11 December 2020).

Elsaesser, Thomas (2005), *European Cinema: Face to Face with Hollywood*, Amsterdam: Amsterdam University Press.

Ezra, Elizabeth and Terry Rowden, eds (2006), *Transnational Cinema: The Film Reader*, London: Routledge.

Gimello-Mesplomb, Frédéric, ed. (2012a), *Les cinéastes français à l'épreuve du cinéma fantastique*, Paris: L'Harmattan.

Gimello-Mesplomb, Frédéric (2012b), *L'invention d'un genre: Le cinéma fantastique français*, Paris: L'Harmattan.

Gleich, Joshua (2012), "Auteur, mogul, transporter: Luc Besson as 21st Century Zanuck," *New Review of Film and Television Studies*, 10 (2): 246–68.

Goldstein, Patrick (2009), "Screenwriter Kamen Is Taken with Director Besson," *Los Angeles Times*, 10 March.

Halle, Randall (2008), *German Film After Germany: Toward a Transnational Aesthetic*, Chicago: University of Chicago Press.

Harrod, Mary (2015), *From France with Love: Gender and Identity in French Romantic Comedy*, London: Bloomsbury.

Higbee, Will and Song-Hwee Lim (2010), "Concepts of Transnational Cinema: Toward a Critical Transnationalism in Film Studies," *Transnational Cinemas*, 1 (1): 7–21.

Hjort, Mette (2010), "On the Plurality of Cinematic Transnationalism," in Kathleen Newman and Nataŝa Ďurovičová (eds), *World Cinemas, Transnational Perspectives*, 12–33, London: Routledge.

Holmlund, Chris (2002), *Impossible Bodies: Femininity and Masculinity at the Movies*, London: Routledge.

Jones, Nick (2015), *Hollywood Action Films and Spatial Theory*, London: Routledge.

Julien, Olivier (2002), "La technologie de la French touch: Les Paul ou Pierre Schaeffer?" *Musurgia*, 9 (2): 71–84.

Jullier, Laurent (1997), *L'écran post-moderne: un cinéma d'allusion et de feu d'artifices*, Paris: L'Harmattan.

Jullier, Laurent (2002), *Qu'est-ce qu'un bon film?*, Paris: La Dispute.

"La French Touch du cinéma d'action existe-t-il?" (2017), Round table with François Barge-Prieur, Alex Masson (critic), Rafik Djoumi (critic), Emmanuelle Spadacenta (editor), 15 October. Available online: https://www.forumdesimages.fr/les-programmes/toutes-les-rencontres/table-ronde-french-action (accessed 10 December 2020).

Lemercier, Fabien (2020), "Netflix continues to splash the cash on French films," *Cineuropa*, 7 October. Available online: https://cineuropa.org/en/newsdetail/393435/ (accessed 11 December 2020).

Martel, Frédéric (2006), *De la culture en Amérique*, Paris: Flammarion.

Martel, Frédéric (2010), *Mainstream: Enquête sur cette culture qui plaît à tout le monde*, Paris: Flammarion.

Martin-Jones, David (2012), "*Colombiana*: Europa Corp and the Ambiguous Geopolitics of the Action Movie," *Senses of Cinema*, 62. Available online: https://www.sensesofcinema.com/2012/feature-articles/colombiana-europa-corp-and-the-ambiguous-geopolitics-of-the-action-movie/ (accessed 11 December 2020).

Maule, Rosanna (2008), *Beyond Auteurism: New Directions in Authorial Film Practices in France, Italy and Spain since the 1980s*, Chicago: Intellect.

McCann, Ben (2013), "Horror," in Tim Palmer and Charlie Michael (eds), *Directory of World Cinema: France*, 277–83, London: Intellect.

McCracken, Kristin (2011), "*Point Blank*: What Would You Do?" HuffPost, 31 July. Available online: https://www.huffpost.com/entry/point-blank-what-would-yo_b_913830 (accessed 10 December 2020).

Meir, Christopher (2018), *Mass Producing European Cinema: StudioCanal and Its Works*, London: Bloomsbury.

Meir, Christopher (2021), *European Conglomerates and the Contemporary European Audiovisual Industries: Transforming the Industrial Landscape Amid the Arrival of*

SVOD Platforms, a High-End Television Boom, and the COVID-19 Crisis. Report conducted for the European Commission. Available at https://www.researchgate.net/publication/353403529_European_Conglomerates_and_the_Contemporary_European_Audiovisual_Industries_Transforming_the_Industrial_Landscape_Amid_the_Arrival_of_SVOD_Platforms_a_High-End_Television_Boom_and_the_COVID-19_Crisis (accessed 22 November 2022).

Michael, Charlie (2005), "French National Cinema and the Martial Arts Blockbuster," *French Politics, Culture & Society*, 23 (3): 55–74.

Michael, Charlie (2019), *French Blockbusters: Cultural Politics of a Transnational Cinema*, Edinburgh: Edinburgh University Press.

Michael, Charlie (2020), "EuropaCorp and the Landscape of Contemporary French Action Cinema" in Ana Vinuela and Bruno Cailler (eds), *EuropaCorp, une majeure française? Cahiers de champs visuels*, 18–19: 201–26.

Moine, Raphaëlle (2015), *Les genres du cinéma*, 2nd edn, Paris: Armand Colin.

Morris, Meaghan (2004), "Transnational Imagination in Action Cinema: Hong Kong and the Making of a Global Popular Culture," *Inter-Asia Cultural Studies*, 5 (2): 181–99.

Nagib, Lucia (2020), *Realist Cinema as World Cinema: Non-cinema, Intermedial Passages, Total Cinema*, Amsterdam: Amsterdam University Press.

Palmer, Tim (2011), *Brutal Intimacy: Analyzing Contemporary French Cinema*, Middletown, CT: Wesleyan University Press.

Pettersen, David (2012), "American Genre Film in the French Banlieue: Luc Besson and Parkour," *Cinema Journal*, 53 (3): 26–51.

Pettersen, David (2023), *French B Movies: Suburban Spaces, Universalism and the Challenge of Hollywood*, Bloomington: Indiana University Press.

Purse, Lisa (2011), *Contemporary Action Cinema*, Edinburgh: Edinburgh University Press.

Rappas, Ipek A. Celik (2016), "The Urban Renovation of Marseille in Luc Besson's *Taxi* Series," *French Cultural Studies*, 27 (4): 385–97.

Schatz, Thomas (1981), *Hollywood Genres: Formulas, Filmmaking and the Studio System*, New York: McGraw Hill.

Shaw, Deborah (2014), "Deconstructing and Reconstructing Transnational Cinema," in Stephanie Dennison (ed.), *Contemporary Hispanic Cinema: Interrogating the Transnational in Spanish and Latin American Film*, 47–67, Woodbridge: Tamesis.

Tasker, Yvonne (1993), *Spectacular Bodies: Gender, Genre and the Action Cinema*, London: Routledge.

Vanderschelden, Isabelle (2007), "Strategies for a 'Transnational'/ French Popular Cinema," *Modern & Contemporary France*, 15 (1): 37–50.

Vanderschelden, Isabelle (2009), "Luc Besson's Ambition: EuropaCorp as a European Major for the 21st Century," *Studies in European Cinema*, 5 (2): 91–104.

Chapter 5

No Exit from "Hell Joseon": National Tragedy and Heroic Rescue in South Korean Action-Disaster Films

Hye Seung Chung and David Scott Diffrient

Decades of accumulated national tragedies and collective traumas in South Korea have contributed to the popularity of action cinema as an ostensibly "escapist" form of domestically produced entertainment. From the suppression of civil liberties, the violation of human rights, and the massacre of protesters under successive military dictatorships during the 1960s and 1980s, to the long list of infrastructural disasters (e.g., bridge collapses, building explosions, etc.) that make people question their country's safety standards in its rush for economic development, such traumatic events seem to call out for the comforting familiarity of crowd-pleasing genre productions in which mortal dangers are defused by narrative's end. However, far from being merely a diverting means to distract audiences from the crushing realities of life in a class-stratified society marked by increased unemployment, wealth inequality, and widespread distrust of government officials, contemporary blockbusters such as Kim Ji-hoon's *The Tower* (*Tawo*, 2012), Park Jung-woo's *Pandora* (2016), Ryoo Seung-wan's *Veteran* (*Beterang*, 2015), Kim Yong-hwa's *Along with the Gods: The Two Worlds* (*Sin gwa hamkke*, 2017), and Lee Byeong-heon's *Extreme Job* (*Geukan Jigeop*, 2019) put these and other public grievances in the spotlight.

Mainstream cultural producers' tendency to engage narratively, either directly or indirectly, with the sources of social malaise and political apathy affecting millions of Koreans has not been lost on commentators. For example, on August 3, 2016, the freelance film critic Min Yong-jun tweeted that director Kim Seong-hun's *Tunnel* (*Teoneol*, 2016) represents the "disaster" (*jaenan*) that is the Republic of Korea (ROK). In this compelling survival tale, a lone commuter remains trapped inside the titular structure for 35 days due to shoddy construction, bureaucratic inefficiency, and botched rescue efforts. Min's tweet, like so much of the critical discourse swirling around his country's cinematic output, epitomizes a sentiment that has come to be known as "Hell Joseon." That neologism equates Korea (formerly known as the Joseon Dynasty, before its 1910 Japanese annexation) with the kind of nightmarish existence or hopelessness associated with the darkest netherworlds of religious scriptures and fantasy texts. Hyperbolic though the sentiment might be, it is widely shared among the nation's youth and accurately reflects their generational angst and uncertainty about the future. According to a 2016 survey of 3,173 college students and corporate employees, 90 percent of respondents in their twenties and thirties said that they have adopted the damning rhetoric of "Hell Joseon" at various times in their young lives (Gu 2016).[1] The idea has often been invoked in response to the cutthroat competitiveness of the current job market and failures on the part of the ROK government.

The most high-profile of those failures is a catastrophe that occurred in the early spring of 2014. During the morning hours of April 16, the MV Sewol—a ferry packed with 476 passengers and crewmembers making its way to Jeju Island, a popular destination for family vacations and school trips—capsized due to overloading and the improper securing of cargo. A variety of poor decisions were made by the ship's captain, his mates, and the helmsmen, who were the first to be rescued when the government's patrol boat arrived. The captain was later sentenced to life in prison for murder. More than half of the survivors were rescued by private fishing boats. No attempt was made by government rescuers to enter the tilting ship. To the shock and dismay of many Koreans, the sinking of the Sewol ferry resulted in the deaths of 304 passengers, including 250 students from Danwon High School.

Significantly, the term "inaction" has been used frequently by bereaved family members, news reporters, and human rights organizations to characterize the crew members' negligence and the mishandling of coast guard rescue operations (Park 2017: 131). Not surprisingly, *action* cinema—a mode of spectacle-filled, effects-driven wish-fulfilment that pivots on scenes of heroic achievement in the face of hostile forces and seemingly insurmountable obstacles—has consequently emerged as a powerful way to compensate imaginatively for the government's dismal failures in recent years. In fact, the seemingly far-fetched scenarios at the heart of *Tunnel*, that same year's action-horror *Train to Busan* (*Busanhaeng*, Yeon Sang-ho, 2016), and the equally hybrid action-comedy mashup *Exit* (*Eksiteu*, Lee Sang-geun, 2019), have been directly compared to the Sewol disaster by several Korean critics.

This chapter examines these recent trends in South Korean action cinema, taking *Tunnel* and *Exit* as key texts through which to speculate on the perceived need, advanced by critics and upheld by filmmakers, to remedy the failings of elected leaders. Though one is an action drama and the other is an action comedy, the two films share similar premises and narrative trajectories, beginning with an unforeseen disaster (a tunnel collapse and an act of biochemical terrorism, respectively) that reveals inadequacies within organizations tasked with protecting the public. Slow, inefficient, or incompetent authorities force these films' characters to fend for themselves to survive. While the manner in which these isolated individuals manage to do so differs from film to film (e.g., rummaging in the dark through rubble in search of water and other basic necessities; jumping from rooftop to rooftop in order to flee plumes of toxic gas spreading throughout a skyscraper-filled city), a common thread is their shared focus on ordinary people racing against the clock, beating the odds, and becoming capable (if reluctant) action heroes in the process. Indeed, the films' protagonists—a car salesman and an unemployed rock-climbing enthusiast—become the type of hero modern-day Korean society sorely needs. Compensating for the *lack* of action that characterizes government responses to national tragedies and social problems, the *abundance* of that very thing in *Tunnel*, *Exit*, and other post-Sewol films is what brings action cinema to the forefront of the popular imagination, making escape from "Hell Joseon" an intoxicating possibility, if only within the realm of fiction.

Contextualizing Contemporary Korean Action Films

The 1997 Asian financial crisis had a ripple-effect on South Korea's motion picture industry, leading up to and following the production of several action films about organized crime. As part of a cycle of similarly themed motion pictures, each combining gangster film iconography and broadly comedic performances, such crowd-pleasing releases as Jo Jin-kyu's *My Wife Is a Gangster* (*Jopok manura*, 2001) and Jeong Heung-sun's *Marrying the Mafia* (*Gamunui yeonggwang*, 2002) responded to that crisis in seemingly counterintuitive ways, often parodying genre conventions and satirizing the deeply paternalistic messages of forerunners that mythologized "heroic, militant, or melancholy" male protagonists who, in the words of Michelle Cho, had been "corrupted by an underground cash economy that accompanies state-orchestrated, high-growth development" (2020: 49). The impulse to *de*mythologize gangster films runs parallel to a shift in the perception of men's status as their families' primary breadwinners. What had been a deeply ingrained ideological "norm" began to crumble as more "unemployed or bankrupt fathers found their usual role in society undermined" as a result of the national crisis (Martin-Jones 2007: 57). As class divisions became more pronounced in South Korea's "new postindustrial, globalizing economy" of the early 2000s, such films furthermore contributed to elevating "the 'soft' masculinity of the wealthy metrosexual over the physicality of the brawny, brainless gangster" (Cho 2020: 49). Yet, as Cho notes, the female body also became a figure of brute toughness and comedic abjection throughout those socially and economically tumultuous years (2020: 49). It was a period when South Korea's transformation into what scholars have referred to as a "neoliberal welfare state" exacerbated existing conflicts, further disenfranchised millions of low-wage workers, and widened the gap between the rich and the poor (Song 2009).

After the 1997 Asian financial crisis, the Kim Dae-jung-led South Korean government—on the back of a \$57 billion bailout loan from the International Monetary Fund (IMF)—implemented the economic restructuring, which had additional effects on action cinema. One of the initiatives was to grow the local entertainment industry through a combination of government-backed investment funds, private capital, and an export-oriented economy (i.e., the regional and global distribution of the country's cultural products in addition to electronics and other consumer goods). Because Kim's administration appreciated the "soft-power" potential of popular culture, locally produced motion pictures, and especially action films, as well as television series (or K-dramas), and musical acts were seen as useful means for putting South Korea on the international stage while helping it to regain its economic footing. Moreover, newly founded media conglomerates such as CJ Entertainment and Lotte Entertainment (benefiting from their parent companies' broad economic basis in the food and shopping industries) poured large amounts of capital into Chungmuro (a shorthand for South Korea's once self-contained film industry), modernizing its business through vertical and horizontal integration. Thus, at the turn of the twenty-first century, larger budgets enabled filmmakers within the conglomerated motion picture industry to invest more in production design, star-filled ensemble casts, computer-generated imagery (CGI), and other visual effects than at any time in the nation's history, through history itself remained a core facet of many films' box-office appeal.

A case in point is writer-director Kang Je-gyu's *Shiri* (*Swiri*, 1999), a Hollywood-style action blockbuster that, despite its emphasis on visual spectacle and dazzling effects, is rooted in distinctly Korean sentiments around national division and the endlessly deferred prospect of reunification. Featuring a group of secret intelligence agents from the South who attempt to foil a terrorist attack from the North, and chock-full of the semantic ingredients that most audiences around the world would associate with the action mode ("car chases, explosions, and gun fights") (Gilbert 2012), this Samsung-backed motion picture became a box-office sensation at the time of its theatrical release because it seamlessly fused elements associated with US and Hong Kong action movies, adding "indigenous South Korean content [related to] the national memory of loss" (Jung 2011: 6).[2] Within a few months of its theatrical release, *Shiri*'s success was surpassed by another action-filled blockbuster, the mystery-thriller *JSA: Joint Security Area*

(*Gongdonggyeongbi guyeok*, 2000), directed and co-written by Park Chan-wook. Like *Shiri*, *JSA* explores the ramifications of prolonged military confrontation and the legacy of the Korean War, throwing South Korean border guards and their North Korean counterparts together in moments of hostility and friendship across the Demilitarized Zone (DMZ).

Just as *Shiri* and *JSA* had done, in 2003/4 two more star-filled, spectacle-driven blockbusters—Kang Woo-suk's *Silmido* (2003) and Kang Je-gyu's *Tae Guk Gi: The Brotherhood of War* (*Taegeukgi hwinallimyeo*, 2004)—examined Korea's division and strained inter-Korean relations. Both garnered more than 11 million admissions, or roughly one quarter of the country's entire population at the time of these films' release. Though they imitate the genre conventions of Hollywood action films and crime thrillers, these commercial hits both "provide[d] an occasion or a site for audience and filmmaker alike to revisit and reconsider issues specific to Korea through cinematic means" (Choi 2010: 39).

2005 was a pivotal year in the annals of South Korean action cinema, a watershed moment when all of the abovementioned themes—gangland violence, national division, terrorist threats, tough women, and troubled masculinity—were operative in high-profile theatrical releases, among them Kim Jee-woon's neo-noir crime film *A Bittersweet Life* (*Dalkomhan insaeng*), Lee Myung-se's anachronistic period piece *Duelist* (*Hyeongsa*), Park Chan-wook's female-focused psychological thriller *Lady Vengeance* (*Chinjeolhan Geumja-ssi*), Park Kwang-hyun's cheerful Korean War film *Welcome to Dongmakgol* (*Welkeom tu dongmakgol*), and Ryoo Seung-wan's brutal boxing movie *Crying Fist* (*Jumeoki unda*). Particularly noteworthy—though frequently overlooked—is Kwak Kyung-taek's *Typhoon* (*Taepung*, 2005). A fusion of action and disaster genres that focuses on North Korean terrorists' efforts to wreak havoc on the peninsula, *Typhoon* not only harks back to *Shiri* but also anticipates subsequent theatrical releases about natural and manmade catastrophes like *The Tower*, *Tunnel*, and *Exit*.

Tellingly, a passage of dialogue in *Typhoon* foretells the kind of rhetorical maneuvers of late that make "hell" an especially apt metaphor for the neoliberal, post-recession condition of living in South Korea. It occurs when Sin (Jang Dong-gun), a North Korean refugee and the leader of a group of pirates plans to send uranium canisters into a typhoon, unleashing radioactive rain on millions of people (as revenge against the South Korean government, which rejected his family's defection request, leading to their massacre at the hands of North Korean border guards). He meets a Russian arms dealer in Vladivostok who harbors resentment towards his government's leaders due to their mismanagement of a public crisis. Shaking hands with Sin, the man grumbles that for him and his countrymen, "the Chernobyl accident was a tragedy we'll never forget." "If the stupid politicians didn't try to cover it up," he explains, "hundreds of young people wouldn't have died." Then, watching lab rats on a video monitor being exposed to deadly chemicals before being incinerated, the Russian operative sums up his and Sin's predicament, stating "all this is from hell." "The world is hell," the film's terrorist antihero responds, capping the scene with an expression that has become all-too-familiar among Koreans whose jaundiced attitude toward the never-ending "rat race" of a competitive, goal-oriented society is reflected in much of today's popular culture. The above scene points toward similarly worded passages of dialogue in more contemporary films that deal overtly with the existential quandaries associated with "Hell Joseon."

Why a Happy Ending? Rescue as National Imperative in *Tunnel*

When writer-director Kim Seong-hun first read So Jae-won's tragic novel *Tunnel* (written in 2000 but published in 2013 after being initially rejected by several major publishers), he had no intention of adapting it for the big screen, for he believed that doing so would be too painful an undertaking for himself and that the resulting film would be too bleak or harrowing for audiences to endure. The filmmaker changed his mind, however, after landing on the idea of creating a "more positive, uplifting protagonist" modeled after the heroes of Western survivalist tales, such as Daniel Defoe's *Robinson Crusoe* in the 1719 novel of the same name and Tom Hanks's character Chuck Noland in director Robert Zemeckis's 2000 production *Cast Away* (Kim 2016). In his hands, what had been an introspective disaster narrative (focusing on the trapped protagonist's self-reflection and the omniscient narrator's social criticism) was transformed into an exciting, crowd-pleasing film brimming with special effects and rapidly edited, race-against-the-clock action sequences.

In So Jae-won's novel, protagonist Jeong-su is a lonely worker in a nuclear plant in the countryside who becomes a passive disaster victim during a weekend commute to visit his family and celebrate his four-year-old daughter's birthday. In the film, the protagonist (Ha Jung-woo) is an automobile salesman who is more active and assertive from the opening scene. His lucky break comes when he scores a big deal with a rental-car company right before driving into a tunnel. He excitedly tells the buyer on the other end of the line that he will call right back, after exiting the tunnel, to sort out contract details. Midway through what becomes a doomed drive home, however, ominous thumping sounds precede the unthinkable: the structure's concrete walls give way and tumble down like ocean waves behind Jeong-su's car. Within seconds the ceiling of the tunnel splits and the screen goes black. When Jeong-su regains consciousness, covered in ash and debris, the first thing he reaches for is his cellular phone. To his relief, it is still working. Unlike his counterpart in the novel, who calls the insurance company and relies upon someone else to report his accident, the hero dials 119 (the Korean version of 911).

Integral to Jeong-su's transformation from passive disaster victim who commits suicide in despair (in So's novel) to active action hero who does not give up hope until he is finally rescued (in Kim's film) is the expansion of the spaces in which he is seen inside the tunnel, and the addition and delineation of other characters. In the novel, Jeong-su is trapped in the tunnel alone. In the film, he finds other living creatures and seeks to help them. On his third day inside the tunnel, searching for a way out, Jeong-su encounters a pug. The dog's owner is trapped on the other side of a narrow ventilation passage. Slowly but surely, Jeong-su crawls to the other side and meets the stray pet's owner, Mi-na (Nam Ji-hyun), a woman trapped in the driver's seat of her vehicle. Her car is stuck between concrete slabs. She is dehydrated. Jeong-su shares his bottled water with her and allows her to borrow his cellphone to call her mother (Figures 5.1 and 5.2).

During their short, heart-wrenching conversation, we learn that she is a new corporate recruit who was on her way to a job orientation. In his August 2016 interview with *Huffington Post Korea*, filmmaker Kim Seong-hun explained his motivations in creating this character. For him, Mi-na personifies the stress experienced by many young jobseekers. Though she has succeeded in landing a potentially lucrative job, she finds herself trapped "in an absurd place," one that showcases the narrow range of options available to would-be employees who sometimes find themselves figuratively "stuck" in the way that this character literally is (Kang 2016). Jeong-su promises Mi-na's mother on the phone that he will protect the young woman, but she soon passes away: she has been fatally pierced by a piece of steel rebar. His brief encounter with this weak and immobile

Figure 5.1 Jeong-su (Ha Jung-woo) discovers that he is not the only person trapped inside the collapsed tunnel, in one of the few relatively calm interludes of Kim Seong-hun's *Tunnel* (© Showbox, 2016. All Rights Reserved).

Figure 5.2 After sharing his water bottle with her, Jeong-su (Ha Jung-woo) allows Mi-na (Nam Ji-hyeon), a stranger trapped in the driver's seat of her vehicle, to make a final call to her mother on his cellphone in *Tunnel* (© Showbox, 2016. All Rights Reserved).

individual shows him to be the fitter of the two characters and, in accordance with action film conventions, all but guarantees his survival. Indeed, her death rekindles Jeong-su's will to live, especially now that he has inherited the dead woman's pet.

Another key change from the novel is the transposition of an unnamed expert on the outside (with whom the protagonist communicates via a cellular phone on low battery) to a somewhat comical and more vocal supporter. Now he is named Kim Dae-gyeong (Oh Dal-su) and is the captain of the Fire Department's rescue team. Early on, he risks his own life by driving into the tunnel from the opposite direction. He barely escapes death by reversing his jeep just before the entrance collapses. Later, feeling guilty because he advised the trapped man to do so, he goes so far as to drink his own urine. When Jeong-su's phone dies and the car radio becomes his only source for news from the outside world he hears a heartbreaking announcement that recovery operations will cease in order to protect rescue workers and to relaunch the delayed construction of another tunnel nearby. Yet he does not give up his fight for survival. Happily, his desperate non-stop honking of his vehicle's horn is picked up by a microphone that Dae-gyeong has accidentally dropped from an underground rescue capsule. This leads to his miraculous rescue minutes before the tunnel's scheduled demolition, presented through race-against-the-clock parallel editing between his claustrophobic space and the comparatively open space of his rescuer. Significantly, in So's novel, Jeong-su commits suicide by setting his car on fire. Two days later, his scorched vehicle is found; demolition of the tunnel has been completed. Learning the victim had been alive and that he took his own life after hearing a radio-broadcast message from his wife, who cannot imagine he is still alive, members of the public—or those whom the author refers to in the novel's subtitle as "we nameless killers"—launch a witch hunt against the bereaved and accuse her of murdering her husband for a cash reward from the construction company (So 2016). In a state of abject agony, Mi-jin takes her own life as well as that of her sleeping daughter.

Starkly different from the novel's downbeat conclusion, the film's happy ending is not only occasioned by action film conventions but also tied to the South Korean motion picture industry's financial exigencies. *Tunnel*'s distributor, Showbox, aimed to make the film a summer blockbuster. Its hefty price tag (by local moviemaking standards) was to be recouped many times over. With over 7 million admissions, *Tunnel* lived up to company expectations, ranking fourth in the list of 2016's highest grossing domestic releases. Familiar with the novel, not all cultural commentators have been satisfied with the film's concluding scenes, which struck many of them as being arbitrary and manipulative. For example, film critic Kim Gyeong-uk complains that the "process of transforming a horrific tragedy into a perfect happy ending" (in which the couple, now reunited, behave as if nothing has happened) dilutes the "original message" of the story, nudging it into the realm of fantasy. Like other cultural commentators, he draws a connection between that example of "absurd" wish-fulfilment and the "collective attempt to cure the trauma of the Sewol incident by rewriting the scene of rescue." Posing the question of whether a happy ending like this might function as a "defense mechanism," capable of defusing the volatile rhetoric surrounding actual tragic events and manmade disasters, Kim points his readers toward an allegorical reading of *Tunnel* that, fittingly, lies just below its surface—a subtext that can easily be lifted from its "subterranean level" to the "ground level" of text (2016).

Journalist Jo Yun-ho similarly describes watching *Tunnel* as a kind of "déjà vu" experience, one that immediately brings the Sewol tragedy to mind (Jo 2016). Director Kim's satirizing of the exploitative media frenzy, the incompetency of hypocritical politicians, and the cruelty of public attacks against the victim's family bears an eerie resemblance to the aftermath of the Sewol ferry disaster. As Jo points out, the female head of the Ministry of Public Safety and Security (Kim Hae-suk) recalls the former South Korean President Park Geun-hye. The minister visits the disaster site after Jeong-su has been rescued. He is waiting to be transported to a hospital via helicopter. She demands that a photo be taken of her with him. He is lying on a stretcher, his eyes covered for protection from the blinding light of the sun, incapacitated. He whispers a few words in Dae-gyeong's ear. The rescue captain turns to a group of inquisitive journalists to ventriloquize the survivor's message: "All of you assholes, fuck off." The man's crude language startles the Minister, stopping her in her tracks. Clueless, she asks her aide: "Who? Me? Why?"

Jo Yun-ho argues that the yellow jacket the character wears and her self-serving response are thinly veiled references to the former President. Park had waited seven hours after the Sewol ferry sank before making her first public appearance to address the matter, only to pose a naive question to a phalanx of flashing cameras: "Is it still so difficult to find survivors even if they have their life jackets on?" The National Assembly had impeached her on December 9, 2016. The Constitutional Court upheld the decision three months later.

According to Jo, a main difference between the Sewol tragedy and *Tunnel*'s story of survival is Dae-gyeong's *ungdap* ("response"). Even after Jeong-su's wife signs a consent paper that will cease rescue efforts and demolish the collapsed tunnel, the captain goes underground, alone, for one final check. He tells the underling who tries to stop him, "I told him to wait. Leaving him there is too cruel. I'll just check whether he is alive or not." Without such a responsible "response" on the part of Captain Kim, Jeong-su's final honks on the car horn for help would have remained undetected. *Tunnel* thereby becomes a powerful tale of compensation for—not merely a reflection of—the many failings that characterized the Sewol disaster. Watching *Tunnel*, Korean audiences can therefore revisit, if only allegorically, scenes of rescue and can metaphorically rewrite the traumatic history of the recent past. The film serves as a defense mechanism, a tool through which society might absolve itself of guilt and confront its government's inability to protect hundreds of innocent children on a school outing. In this sense, action films serve a purpose beyond merely entertaining the masses. Perhaps it is no surprise that rescue has become such an entrenched theme in contemporary Korean action films. Many, like *Tunnel*, reflect on failures occasioned by hypocritical politicians, profit-driven corporations, and complicit journalists while substituting responsible characters like Captain Kim who help ensure a happy outcome to disaster. Sadly, people like Kim were missing when the Sewol passengers drowned at sea.

Survivalist Masculinity and Youth Unemployment: The Ascendence of the Unemployed Hero in *Exit*

In recent years, several big-budget productions, including *Pandora* and Park Kwang-hyun's *Fabricated City* (*Jojakdoen dosi*, 2017), have featured young underdogs. Initially either unemployed or disgruntled with their dead-end jobs, they are vaulted into leadership roles once disaster strikes or a seemingly unsolvable crime occurs. *Pandora*'s protagonist Jae-hyeok (Kim Nam-gil) sees no future in working for a nuclear power plant and would rather sail to South America than waste his life at a nine-to-five job. *Fabricated City*'s lead, Kwon Yoo (Ji Chang-wook) once was a national taekwondo champion but now slacks off daily at an internet café. Both occupy a position between *baeksu* (a slang word meaning someone who is unemployed) and *God-su* (a neologism that suggests an individual's heightened sense of self-worth, regardless of employment or lack thereof). In 2014, when youth unemployment rose as high as 470,000 (10.9%), *God-su* began creeping into common parlance, thanks to its circulation via K-dramas, TV talk shows, and social media sites (Ko 2014).

Director Lee Sang-geun's comically infused action-disaster film *Exit* (a summer blockbuster hit that garnered 9 million admissions) deals head-on with this phenomenon, a rhetorical byproduct of "Hell Joseon." The film opens with a low-angle medium shot of a young man whose back is turned to the camera. Wearing a cut-off T-shirt, he flexes his muscles and stretches his arms and shoulders as part of a warm-up exercise set to fast rhythmic music. It is a simple yet significant opening image, one which recalls lean, muscular men in earlier action films and immediately foregrounds male physicality as the starting point for a story about heroic achievement. Initially a nameless body, this object of the camera's gaze is treated with the same fetishistic attention to detail as that which has traditionally codified women's corporeal presence onscreen, as well as that of the muscular male action hero. A montage shows the as-yet-unnamed protagonist performing push-ups, chin-ups, and other exercises in what appears to be an athlete's outdoor gym but is soon revealed to be a children's playground area. The tone is upbeat and humorous: three older ladies watch our hero from the comfort of a nearby bench, their stares at once blank yet fixed on his body. When one gives him a thumbs up, he bows awkwardly yet politely. A less-appreciative onlooker—a middle-aged woman drying peppers on the lawn—mutters disapprovingly, "He's here *again*."

Although her comment might not seem to be important, as the first spoken line of the film it points to the protagonist's dogged perseverance, his ability to follow through on a grueling regimen that, through sheer repetition, will serve him well later in the story. But the older woman's remark, intended as a putdown rather than as flattery, also suggests that the person we will come to know as Yong-nam (Jo Jung-suk) spends much of his afternoon hours not at work—where someone his age *should* be—but in a place reserved for juvenile play. A group of boys arrive and make their own dismissive remarks about Yong-nam from a distance. Armed with plastic water guns, the six kids cast disapproving looks at the man they call the "village idiot" swinging on the monkey bars. One is Yong-nam's nephew, Ji-ho (Kim Kang-hun). The scene concludes with the boy hurriedly walking away and denying any relation to the crazy "Iron Bar Man" calling out to him. The child's embarrassment is subsequently echoed by the humiliation that Yong-nam's aging parents and older sister feel, owing to his professional failures. The young man's earlier ambition has been replaced by boredom. As Yong-nam later admits to a distant relative who asks him: "What do you do all day?," besides his exercise routine, his day consists solely of eating, shitting, and sleeping. He is, in other words, the most inactive of action-film heroes.

The blue muscle shirt worn by Yong-nam in the first minutes of the film is printed with a Hawaiian logo of palm trees and the words "Another Day in Paradise," an ironic reminder of an imagined space of heavenly bliss, far removed from the "hell" of his current situation and indicative of the lofty position to which he aspires. Beginning with this scene, *Exit* exposes the considerable gap between the self-esteem of *God-su* and the societal perceptions of *baeksu*. Where once Yong-nam had been one of the best mountain climbers of his college club (years ago), in his late-twenties he can barely afford a haircut and idles away his afternoons in a playground occupied by older women and children. Yet this is the lowly foundation upon which his eventual success is erected. He overcomes not just one but several obstacles on his ascendent journey toward heroism in the face of national calamity. "Ascendence" is an apt way to describe this hero's journey: thanks to his playground training, which sustains his strength and mountain climber skills, the film has him scaling tall buildings and leaping across rooftops to escape a toxic gas unleashed by a bioterrorist. As the vaporous white chemical spreads like wildfire throughout Seoul, drifting up and forcing Yong-nam and his family upward as well, we are granted several high-angle aerial shots of the city, recalling several other contemporary South Korean action films (from Jang Hoon's *Secret Reunion* [*Uihyeongje*, 2010] to Lee Seong-Tae's *Derailed* [*Du namja*, 2016]).

The film invokes "Hell Joseon" in emphasizing how many disasters threaten Yong-nam and other young people. In another early scene he commiserates with a drinking buddy after receiving a text informing him of another job application's rejection: "The dream . . . is long gone. We're just useless excess." Then, seeing an earthquake warning flash on his cell phone, he mutters "I'm just glad that it's not here" before gulping down another drink. His friend, equally disaffected, responds, "You think you're safe? You're living inside a disaster. Earthquakes and tsunamis aren't the only disasters. Our lives are the very definition of disaster!"

In a later scene, as part of a 70th birthday party celebration for Yong-nam's mother, the extended family gather for a buffet in a large event hall ironically named Dream Garden (literally translated as "Cloud Garden"). His relatives plague him with uncomfortable questions. A female cousin expresses envy for his *God-su* lifestyle: "My dream is to live like you. How do I do that?" Importantly, during this scene, he encounters his old college crush and former mountain-climbing club member, Eui-ju (Im Yun-a). She is now the deputy manager of the event hall. To impress her, Yong-nam fibs about his current job status, telling her that he is a venture capitalist. Unbeknownst to him, Eui-ju telephones a mutual friend to confirm that he is who he says he is. She discovers his lie but says nothing to him yet.

Suddenly the light satirical tone of what looks to be a comedy about unemployment shifts into high gear as an action-disaster film, with shots of a lone bioterrorist intercut with the birthday party. The man bears a grudge against the chemical company where he used to work and now is releasing toxic gas from a diesel truck parked on a city street. The white vapors spread through the nighttime air like fog, poisoning pedestrians who fall to the ground, their mouths foaming and their screams of agony echoing between the high-rise buildings. A group of teenagers seeking shelter from the quickly spreading gas desperately knock on the locked doors of a convenience store to the horror of three shoppers, though the clerk only looks impassively at them from behind a glass partition. With no one to help them, the teens collapse on the sidewalk, writhing in pain. Further chaos ensues as choking drivers swerve down roads and cause traffic accidents. Some career into buildings; a gas station's pumps explode upon contact. A flaming vehicle hits a truck carrying gas canisters, sending them flying into the night sky like fireworks. When one canister crashes through the window of the room where Yong-nam and his family are wrapping up their festivities, the guests flee the scene in panic.

Another allegorical reference to Sewol is embedded in this sequence via the contrasting responses of Eui-ju and her verbally abusive boss Manager Gu (Kang Gi-yeong), the son of the event hall's owner. Facing a state of emergency in which she is called upon to act expeditiously but with level-headedness, Eui-ju prioritizes the safety of her guests and checks each room to ensure that everyone evacuates before taking refuge herself. Her manager, on the other hand, only thinks about his own survival and hides scarce resources such as gas masks from others. Yong-nam emerges as a natural-born leader of the stranded group. He begins to lead Eui-ju and his friends and family to the building's roof. Finding access blocked by a locked door, he puts his rock-climbing skills to use, jumping from one section of the building to another and then scaling down it to access and open a locked door from the other side. Thanks to Yong-nam's God-like daredevilry, the group finally makes its way to the roof and collectively draws the attention of a helicopter pilot by flashing their cell phones and using a karaoke sound amplifier.

When the rescue helicopter arrives, however, there is not enough space for everyone. Eui-ju volunteers to stay behind. Matching her selflessness and despite his parents' tearful pleas, Yong-ham remains with her. In contrast, Manager Gu hops into the helicopter's evacuation carrier before his guests can even board. The two young people wait with mounting desperation for another helicopter. As a chopper approaches, Yong-nam, now sobbing hysterically, directs Eui-ju's attention to a group of high-rise skyscrapers in the distance and declares that—once they are safe and the citywide threat has finally subsided—he will dedicate himself to landing a job in one of those buildings. The emotionally excessive moment tips over into humor: Eui-ju finally confronts him about his slacker tendencies and asks why he had lied to her about his unemployment. Before he can answer, however, the helicopter that had been heading toward them veers off to rescue a larger group of people on an adjacent building's rooftop. This temporarily

Figure 5.3 From a notably elevated position, Yong-nam (Jo Jung-su) and Eui-ju (Im Yun-a), the heroes of Lee Sang-geun's *Exit* (© CJ Entertainment, 2019. All Rights Reserved), spot a group of young girls and boys trapped inside a school classroom as toxic gas spreads throughout Seoul—one of this film's most overt references to the Sewol tragedy.

suspends Yong-nam and Eui-ju's anticipated rescue and gives writer-director Lee Sang-geun an excuse to ratchet up the tension with even more death-defying stunts and edge-of-your-seat action throughout the second half of *Exit*.

During its second half, the film makes its most obvious reference to the Sewol tragedy. Having made their way to another building's rooftop, greeted by the sound of another approaching helicopter, Yong-nam and Eui-ju spot a group of teenagers on the eighth floor of a building across the street. Young girls and boys are trapped inside a school classroom (Figure 5.3). They cry out for help through the open windows. Again Yong-nam and Eui-ju unselfishly and heroically defer their own rescue. Because they line up a group of mannequins to point toward the students, the helicopter, which had been coming for them, changes course. Once again, Yong-nam and Eui-ju put the lives of others before their own. For many Koreans, their sacrifice symbolically atones for the collective guilt experienced in the aftermath of governmental failure five years earlier. Not surprisingly, audiences also found Yong-nam's confrontation of his generation's socioeconomic dilemmas cathartic (Park 2019).

Conclusion

Tunnel and *Exit* allegorize the Sewol ferry disaster in various ways, shuttling between reflection and compensation and showcasing the heroic struggles of unconventional yet immensely relatable protagonists who embody the best, most laudable attributes of a society that has otherwise succumbed to the worst aspects of consumer capitalism over the past two decades. In *Tunnel*, the righteous head of the rescue refuses to give up on the man trapped inside the tunnel even after that man's own family does. In *Exit*, a more unlikely *baeksu* hero—the shame of his family and a failure in the eyes of a success-driven society—eventually saves the day and wins the girl thanks to survivalist skills deemed useless within the corporate job market. However, the "rescue" or "exit" that occurs with each film's denouement is temporary. Jeong-su and his wife are last seen driving across a suspension bridge—another potential site of disaster. Eui-ju joins Yong-nam as a *baeksu* after quitting her job in protest at Manager Gu's sexual harassment of her.

Although the death-defying action that occurs in *Tunnel*, *Exit*, and numerous other South Korean films offers a creative response to the government *inaction* that many politically committed citizens have protested in recent years, these inspiring narratives about the rugged individualism and steadfast struggles of lone heroes leave a bittersweet aftertaste. Notably, in Bong Joon-ho's *The Host* (*Gwoemul*, 2006), an action blockbuster that uses a flesh-eating mutant as a red herring to expose the failings of a dysfunctional South Korean society (a critique directed at the state emergency response system, the US military presence in Seoul, and news media), it takes the collective efforts of those who live on the margins (a homeless man, an unemployed former activist, a lazy snack shop owner, etc.) to ultimately kill the titular monster. Bong's satire affirms the power of what Nam Lee calls "horizontal solidarity" (2020: 140), a spreading out of heroic capability among the disenfranchised to achieve what the technology and war arsenals of both US and South Korean governments have failed to do. By contrast, *Tunnel* and *Exit* celebrate the rugged masculinity of individuals in overcoming a human-made crisis with survivalist skills and mental endurance. To those of us who believe that the only way to "save" a society hellbent on becoming a dominant force in global trade and neoliberal capitalism is to strengthen existing coalitions and work collectively toward a more just and equitable place to live, these films might not be the "solution" that they are purported to be.

Notes

1   The survey was jointly conducted by JobKorea and Albamon, two of the many employment service websites to take such results seriously.

2   *Shiri* was shown on nearly 600 screens across the country and garnered 5.8 million admissions (approximately one seventh of the nation's entire population).

Works Cited

Cho, Michelle (2020), "Popular Abjection and Gendered Embodiment in South Korean Film Comedy," in Maggie Hennefeld and Nicholas Sammond (eds), *Abjection*

Incorporated: Mediating the Politics of Pleasure and Violence, 43–64, Durham, NC: Duke University Press.

Choi, Jinhee (2010), *The South Korean Film Renaissance: Local Hitmakers, Global Provocateurs*, Middletown, CT: Wesleyan University Press.

Gilbert, Ammon (2012), "REEL ACTION: Killer Elite (2011)," *JoBlo*, 20 January. Available online: https://www.joblo.com/reel-action-killer-elite-2011-with-jason-statham-clive-owen-and-robert-de-niro/ (accessed 9 October 2021).

Gu, Hui-ryeong (2016), "90% of Both College Students and Corporate Employee Say 'Hell Joseon Is Correct,' ("Daehaksaengdo jikjangindo 90%ga 'heljoseon matda'")," *Joongang Daily* (*Joongang Ilbo*], 1 July. Available online: https://news.joins.com/article/20249142 (accessed 9 October 2021).

Jo, Yun-ho (2016), "One Thing That Was Present in *Tunnel* but Absent in the Sewol Ferry" ("*Teonel* eneun isseotjiman Sewolhoeneun eopseodeon hangaji"), *MediaToday* (*Midieo oneul*), 21 August. Available online: http://www.mediatoday.co.kr/news/articleView.html?idxno=131694 (accessed 9 October 2021).

Jung, Sun (2011), *Korean Masculinities and Transcultural Consumption: Yonsama, Rain, Oldboy, K-Pop Idols*, Hong Kong: Hong Kong University Press.

Kang, Byeong-jin (2016), "*Tunnel*'s Director Kim Seung-hun" ("*Teoneol* ui Kim Seong-hun gamdok"), *HuffingtonPost Korea*, 17 August. Available online: https://www.huffingtonpost.kr/news/articleView.html?idxno=34574 (accessed 9 October 2021).

Kim, Gyeong-uk (2016), "*Tunnel*, Actually Ha Jung-woo Is Dead" ("*Teoneol*, sasil Ha Jeong-u neun jugeotda"), *Pressian*, 22 September. Available online: https://m.pressian.com/m/pages/articles/141606?no=141606 (accessed 9 October 2021).

Ko, Dong-hwan (2014), "Unemployed 20s Cover Shame with Newly Coined Nickname 'God-su'," *Korea Times*, 4 April. Available online: https://www.koreatimes.co.kr/www/nation/2018/06/511_%20154764.html (accessed 6 May 2022).

Lee, Nam (2020), *The Films of Bong Joon Ho*, New Brunswick, NJ: Rutgers University Press.

Martin-Jones, David (2007), "Decompressing Modernity: South Korean Time Travel Narratives and the IMF Crisis," *Cinema Journal*, 46 (4): 45–67.

Min, Yong-jun (Kharismania) (2016), August 3 tweet, Twitter.

Park, Jin-hai (2019), "*EXIT* Tells of Hilarious Escape from City Engulfed by Toxic Gas," *Korea Times*, 28 June. Available online: https://www.koreatimes.co.kr/www/art/2020/02/689_271416.html (accessed 9 October 2021).

Park, K.S. (2017), "'Stay Still': Sewol, a Tale of Fatal Censorship, Fatal Paternalism," in Jae-Jung Suh and Mikyoung Kim (eds), *Challenges of Modernization and Governance in South Korea: The Sinking of the Sewol and Its Causes*, 121–42, New York: Palgrave Macmillan.

So, Jae-won (2016 [2013]), *Tunnel* (*Teoneol*), reprint edn, Seoul: Jakgawa bipyeong.

Song, Jesook (2009), *South Koreans in the Debt Crisis: The Creation of a Neoliberal Welfare Society*, Durham, NC: Duke University Press.

Chapter 6

Mesmerizing Outsiders: Washington, Mackie, and Performance in Action Cinema

Cynthia Baron

Released twenty years apart in different eras of the American entertainment industry, *Training Day* (Antoine Fuqua, 2001), starring Denzel Washington, and *Outside the Wire* (Mikael Håfström, 2021), starring Anthony Mackie, both depart from prevailing commercial norms by placing a captivating, well-armed Black male character center stage. Despite the many action films featuring Washington, Mackie, Will Smith, Vin Diesel, Dwayne Johnson, and other actors of color, in Hollywood the "ethnicity of the action hero still frequently 'defaults' to Anglo American" (Purse 2011: 114). Yet rather than frame *Training Day* and *Outside the Wire* as anomalies, the chapter's reparative approach recognizes the films' integral connections with African American expressive traditions and thus considers narratives about Black soldiers, lawbreakers, and sci-fi characters to illuminate the heroic dimensions of Washington and Mackie's outsider characters (Carrington 2016: 24; Reid 2005: 37–59).

Training Day takes place in contemporary Los Angeles while *Outside the Wire* is set in 2036 war-torn Ukraine, yet the films have parallel narratives. Speaking as a producer of *Outside the Wire*, Mackie explains that his movie is "100 percent *Training Day*" (Feldberg 2021). In both films, the audacious actions of the supremely capable main characters generate audience-engaging tension and keep multiple opponents off balance. Echoing tragedies that explore the dissipation of power, both narratives also eventually frame their provocative main characters as villainous threats the novice heroes are compelled to destroy. However, while the rookies ultimately assert their newfound agency, the films' charismatic antagonists complicate simple identification with the young male characters and the societies that their victories support.

Stylistically, the films' performances abide by "genre-specific rules" (deCordova 1991: 116), and *Training Day* reflects the influence of gangster films whereas

Outside the Wire draws on war film and science fiction conventions. Washington's bravura performance recalls the gutsy, flamboyant portrayals of memorable antagonists in gangster films. By comparison, Mackie delivers clever lines and displays momentary anger, but his intense, often restrained characterization shares common ground with stoic portrayals of war heroes and androids in science fiction narratives. *Training Day* pits seasoned Black cop Alonzo Harris (Washington) against his new rookie partner, white officer Jake Hoyt (Ethan Hawke), while the partner-opponents in *Outside the Wire* are super soldier Marine Captain Leo (Mackie) and Air Force Lieutenant Harp (Damson Idris), an entitled Black drone pilot sent to the war zone to gain field experience and support the high-risk mission of Captain Leo. In *Training Day*, Washington and Hawke are separated by race, age, and the contrast between Washington's leather-jacketed, imposing presence and Hawke's thinly clothed, wiry body. Yet the actors' embodiments of their characters' shared agility, toughness, and quick wittedness creates a bond between the cops. By comparison, in *Outside the Wire*, the partner-opponents are not markedly distinct from one another due to race, age, or physical size, but performances establish key contrasts between the soldiers. Mackie's Captain Leo is physically and emotionally attuned to everything in his surroundings whereas Idris creates a fish-out-of-water character ill-suited to handling the demands of combat or moral ambiguity.

Performances also contribute to the films' closing critiques of compliant "peace keepers" and unrestricted power. Reflecting the cynicism of gangster films, the final images of Hawke's slight build and weary stance convey the weakness of regular cops who are outmatched by the criminality that pervades the white power brokers they serve. Illustrating Jake's failure to dispel corruption, the scene shows Jake outside his dimly lit home as audiences hear a fabricated "official" report that Alonzo had been killed serving a high-risk warrant. The concluding scenes in *Outside the Wire* use Mackie's engaging performance to challenge the professed rationality of US military might as Leo (the non-human) persuasively lays claim to ethical action in the film's final philosophical standoff. Mackie's gravity in Leo's dying moments undercuts Idris's glib embodiment of the "good" Black soldier who defeats the "militant" Black soldier (McClancy 2019: 139); the closing images of Idris's ebullient walk toward the camera suggest that this "good" Black soldier ignores or fails to understand that he is a pawn used by the US military.

Black Expressive and Cinematic Traditions

Self-directed Black wrongdoers in a white society, Alonzo and Leo share common ground with Stagolee, a Black folklore figure who emerged in the late nineteenth century as Jim Crow legislation bolstered white supremacy and Black Americans experienced freedom as a condition that offered no protection under the law. Whereas "legitimate" whites especially saw the law as protecting their rights, emancipated people experienced it as a terrifying incursion on their freedom. In this context, a Black man "so bad that even the police steer clear of him" could appeal to Black Americans for whom the law was "both absent and your foe" (Munby 2011: 1, 136). Moving through the world without cowering at the threat law enforcers present, the Stagolee hero retains his figurative power to restore the "agency of death" to subordinated people, even if the victories are pyrrhic (Munby 2011: 181). Against the backdrop of contemporary America, the brazen confidence Washington and Mackie exude as they move through dangerous (physical and social) settings makes their characters appealing, even heroic. Bravely defiant in the face of annihilation, like Stagolee, their characters can be cultural heroes even though they imperil not just whites but also communities of color.

The threat that charismatic Stagolee figures pose to white regimes is suggested by early films that demonize racial and ethnic criminals who reject the rule of (white) law. *The Black Hand* (Wallace McCutcheon, 1906) presents "racial difference" as jeopardizing the social order in its story of New York police capturing unassimilated Italian gangsters who issue "black hand" extortion letters (Grieveson 2005: 13). Similarly, *The Regeneration* (Raoul Walsh, 1915), about a white gangster who reforms, includes imagery that associates blackness with crime (Grieveson 2005: 25–31). Later, films in the gangster genre would depict racialized outsiders in a more ambiguous light. Thus, the swaggering, self-determined Black man in *Training Day* evokes ethnic gangsters made famous in *Little Caesar* (Merlyn LeRoy, 1931), starring Edward G. Robinson, *Public Enemy* (William A. Wellman, 1931), with James Cagney, and *Scarface* (Howard Hawks, 1932), featuring Paul Muni. Led by consummate actors from New York's Lower East Side who convey a "powerful sense of street realism [in part through their] distinctive non-Anglo ethnic accents," these 1930s films belong to a multifaceted tradition of gangster and gangsta narratives that capture the ethos, physicality, and "language of those stuck on the wrong side of the ethno-racial divide" (Munby 2011: 168, 167).

Following two decades of rage-filled rap music and a wave of nihilistic Black gangsta films, *Training Day* was primed to depict the complexities of a Black Stagolee figure who could be both villain and hero. Moreover, Washington's Stagolee portrayal belongs to an expressive tradition that includes the urban dramas of Black filmmaker Oscar Micheaux, the gangster films of Black star Ralph Cooper, and popular Black crime fiction beginning with the novels of Rudolph Fisher. For example, despite Micheaux's emphasis on morality and racial uplift, in dramas such as his 1937 film *Underworld*, "the nightclub underworld [of gangsters comes] across as a space of vital black expression and creative energy" (Munby 2011: 62).[1] *Dark Manhattan* (Harry L. Fraser and Ralph Cooper, 1937) presents gambling and other "criminal" activities as belonging to an essential alternative economy for Black Americans denied participation in white business. Fisher's novels, *The Walls of Jericho* (1928) and *The Conjure Man Dies* (1932), vividly illuminate the logic of the Black urban poor's apposite "criminal" choices in the face of racism. Alonzo's transition from dutiful rookie cop to streetwise Stagolee figure is especially legible when considered in relation to Chester Himes's *Harlem Detective* series, which elucidates the "absurdity of being both black and detective" (Munby 2011: 105). As the nine novels published between 1957 and 1969 reveal, "classical" (white) detectives like Philip Marlowe and Nick Charles might sometimes experience "individual alienation," but Black detectives' outsider status is an entrenched social fact in white society (Munby 2011: 101).

Outside the Wire's depiction of a daring, armed Black man can also be placed in larger cultural traditions. In this futuristic narrative, Leo is not like the other soldiers, because he is a biotech android and the only Black soldier in his unit until Harp arrives. The sci-fi narrative's racial dimension brings it into the realm of Black speculative fiction and reveals that despite science fiction's historical overrepresentation of white authors, characters, and experiences, the genre is well suited to representing Black experiences, including those involving "technology, be it branding, forced sterilization [or tasers] brought to bear upon black bodies" (Dery 2008: 8). Leo's pivotal role in *Outside the Wire* builds on a range of Black sci-fi characters made famous by Avery Brooks, Wesley Snipes, and Will Smith in the 1990s (O'Brien 2017: 177–96; Nama 2011: 126–54). Brooks's portrayal of Captain/Commander Benjamin Sisko in *Star Trek: Deep Space Nine* (Paramount 1993–1999) has led sci-fi fans to rank Sisko as one of the top characters in the *Star Trek* cinematic universe. Snipes's starring role in the *Blade* trilogy (1998, 2002, 2004) fueled the rise of films featuring Marvel comic characters, and Smith became a major star due to his leading role in the successful sci-fi thriller *Independence Day* (Roland Emmerich, 1996).

Outside the Wire also continues the film tradition that overturns D.W. Griffith's racist depiction of a Black soldier in *The Birth of a Nation* (1915). In Griffith's film, the Yankee soldier in blackface, whose leering glances prompt a Southern belle to leap off a cliff, infamously presented "the dangers of arming a black man and clothing him in the authority of the state" (Reich 2016: 6). In sharp contrast, early African American filmmakers emphasized Black soldiers' contributions to the US. For example, *The Trooper of Troop K* (Harry A. Grant, 1917) featured a reenactment of brave 10th Cavalry "Buffalo Soldiers" in the 1916 Battle of Carrizal.[2] At midcentury, *The Negro Soldier* (Stuart Heisler, 1944), an Army documentary scripted by Black writer-director Carlton Moss, had influence beyond the separate cinema of Black independent film and prompted a "sea change" in mainstream depictions of Black men (Reich 2016: 3; Cripps 1993:

102–50). In subsequent years, Stan Shaw's brave and compassionate hero in *The Boys in Company C* (Sidney J. Furie, 1978) and Washington's servicemen who challenge commanding officers in *Glory* (Edward Zwick, 1989) and *Crimson Tide* (Tony Scott, 1995) represent a sampling of films that feature African American soldiers as honorable men whose actions contrast with the ethical limitations of their white officers.[3]

Following "the New Jim Crow" (Alexander 2012) social system in place since the US Vietnam War (1955–1975), America's increasing use of military vehicles and SWAT teams in communities of color, the US government's turn to torture, mercenaries, and drone warfare, and the racial reckoning in the summer of 2020, a militant Black soldier who challenges his superiors' collateral damage policies in *Outside the Wire* became a hero well suited to contemporary US action cinema. The film echoes the ethical questions raised in other contemporary films about Black soldiers. Like *Da 5 Bloods* (Spike Lee, 2020), *Red Tails* (Anthony Hemingway, 2012), *Miracle at St. Anna* (Spike Lee, 2008), and *The Manchurian Candidate* (Jonathan Demme, 2004), which features Washington and Mackie as members of the same ill-fated military unit, *Outside the Wire* illuminates white society's callous treatment of Black servicemen who have historically received high-casualty combat assignments. For those acquainted with Marvel character Isaiah Bradley, introduced in the comic *Truth: Red, White, and Black* (2003) and featured in *The Falcon and the Winter Soldier* (Disney+, 2021), Leo's prototype biotech status recalls Bradley's fate as a Black man subjected to super soldier experiments. Because Leo performs dangerous assignments behind enemy lines despite his superiors' distrust and disdain, *Outside the Wire* also dramatizes the "staggering sociopolitical contradictions experienced by real black servicemen fighting for freedom abroad but discriminated against at home" (Nama 2011: 117). Seen in relation to Black expressive traditions, Leo's plan to launch nuclear missiles against US cities makes him a monstrous threat to people of color, who are not responsible for America's endless wars, even as his character retains sympathy as another super soldier opposed to the social injustice for which (white) America is responsible.

Charismatic Outsiders in Disparate Eras

Like other action films, *Training Day* and *Outside the Wire* favor the "maverick or outsider figures over those who represent institutions or authority in a more straightforward way" (Tasker 2015: 93). Yet the two films complicate familiar patterns: the charismatic outsiders, Alonzo and Leo, are condemned for the brutality that has served their superiors, while the novices, Jake and Harp, engage in redemptive violence. In *Training Day*, both police officers fight criminals who pose a threat to (white) life and property, yet Alonzo dies discredited and alone, whereas Jake's trajectory of empowerment promises him a position within the halls of power. In *Outside the Wire*, both soldiers strive to save lives, but Leo is destroyed as an alien outsider, while Harp's violence, which remains under military control, wins commendation from white superiors. Once Alonzo and Leo's actions threaten the white-dominated system, the law enforcers become villains, and, as Black men, they are outsiders who are expendable in ways white maverick action heroes are not.

The characters' abject, isolated narrative position suggests that these roles would not interest major stars. However, as the precedent of Shakespeare's *Richard III* suggests, stage and screen villains constitute meaty roles because they challenge actors to "explore motivations, experiences, and reactions they would never have in real life" (Stuart 2019). Bad-guy roles can garner praise for performances by stars like John Travolta, because the portrayals and characters seem unpredictable. Charismatic portrayals of villains complicate audience allegiance, so that long after the heroes have won the day, the antagonists' perspectives remain compelling, as illustrated by Alan Rickman as Snape, starting with *Harry Potter and the Sorcerer's Stone* (Chris Columbus, 2001), Tom Hiddleston as Loki beginning with *Thor* (Kenneth Branagh, 2011), and Michael B. Jordan as Killmonger in *Black Panther* (Ryan Coogler, 2018).[4]

Training Day and *Outside the Wire* not only offered compelling roles for their lead actors, they did so in releases indicative of their industrial eras (Balio 2013; Fritz 2019). *Training Day* was produced when studios often relied on A-list actors alone to attract audiences. Marketed by mobilizing Washington's star power, *Training Day* topped the domestic box office in its opening week, continuing a string of commercially successful "Denzel Washington films." It was also Washington's only 2001 film, reflecting the era's view that stars must maintain their exclusivity (Baron 2015: 62–114). Twenty years later, the situation was different. Writing about *Outside the Wire*, one critic explains: "Anthony Mackie is a real-deal, raw-energy, slick-as-hell *movie* star. But in the year 2020, being a star means finding him everywhere: in theaters, on TV, and in the nebulous middle-ground of streaming" (Patches 2020; italics in original). In 2019, Mackie not only appeared in *Avengers: Endgame* (Anthony and Joe Russo), he also had leading roles in four films, *IO* (Jonathan Helpert), *Point Blank* (Joe Lynch), *Seberg* (Benedict Andrews), and *Synchronic* (Justin Benson and Aaron Moorhead), a leading role in an episode of *Black Mirror* (Channel 4, 2011–2014; Netflix, 2016–2023), and a supporting role in *Miss Bala* (Catherine Hardwicke). In 2020, he starred in *The Banker* (George Nolfi) and the second season of *Altered Carbon* (Netflix, 2018–2020). A star known worldwide as Sam Wilson/Falcon beginning with *Captain America: The Winter Soldier* (Anthony and Joe Russo, 2014), and as Captain America following *The Falcon and the Winter Soldier*, Mackie further proved himself as an actor in *Outside the Wire*.

Despite differences in the entertainment eras, Washington and Mackie came to their respective films with formal actor training (Fordham University for Washington, the Juilliard School for Mackie), select leading roles on Broadway, and twenty years of screen experience. Washington secured his initial co-starring role in *Carbon Copy* (Michael Schultz, 1981); Mackie's first leading roles were in Spike Lee's *She Hate Me* (2004) and *Sucker Free City* (2004). Their resumés included independent films such as *Mississippi Masala* (Mira Nair, 1991) for Washington and *Night Catches Us* (Tanya Hamilton, 2010) for Mackie. They had both been recognized for their war films: Washington received a Best Supporting Actor Oscar for *Glory* and Mackie had a leading role in *The Hurt Locker* (Kathryn Bigelow, 2008), which won the Oscar for Best Picture. They had also starred in bio pics, with Washington in *Malcolm X* (Spike Lee, 1992) and *The Hurricane* (Norman Jewison, 1999), and Mackie in *All the Way* (Jay Roach, 2016) and *The Banker*.

Fans' emotional investment in Falcon, the first Black superhero (introduced in 1969 and given Wakandan wings in 1974), had strengthened Mackie's association with heroic types. Thus, while Mackie had played drug dealers and militants, portraying a character willing to launch nuclear missiles at US cities represented a risky departure. Washington's associations with heroic characters also made embodying an unrepentant murderer a potentially perilous professional choice. *Training Day* productively overturns biracial buddy film tropes, but Alonzo also directly inverts the ideals of Malcolm X, taking advantage of Black Americans rather than striving to empower them. In *Outside the Wire*, Leo negates the "magical negro" narrative in which Black characters use their powers to help white protagonists, but as a Black man powerful and determined enough to destroy millions of lives to make his point, he is the nightmare version of Sam Wilson/Falcon.

Spectacular and Intimate Conflict in *Training Day*

Training Day mobilizes Black gangster film conventions to challenge the idea that the American Dream is within reach of anyone brave, smart, and resolute enough to seek it. Set in urban Los Angeles, the film features sustained physical and emotional conflict in a narrative marked by tension that starts high and never lets up. Alonzo initiates the day's ongoing battles, calling Jake's home early in the morning. On the phone, he flirts with Jake's wife and then throws the rookie further off balance by instructing him to meet at a diner (not the police station) and to wear street clothes (not his freshly pressed uniform). At the diner, Jake tries to establish himself as a viable candidate for Alonzo's unit and subsequent promotions, but Alonzo first toys with him, then crushes him into submission.

Laban Movement Analysis offers ways to describe the actors' micro-calibrations in *Training Day*'s close-contact battles. Laban terms highlight observable aspects of physical expression, as well as audible dimensions of vocal expression, so that connotations of movement, gesture, and facial or vocal expression become more legible. Laban analysis directs attention to the *impelling inner action* (the conscious or reactive impulse) externalized through the direction, speed or rhythm, degree of resistance, and degree of control in movements-gestures-expressions. Qualities in physical/vocal expression exist on four continua: *direct* to *flexible*; *sudden* to *sustained*; *strong* to *light*; and *bound* to *free-flowing*. (1) *Spatial aspects* involve the direction, place, and shape of movements-gestures-expressions; (2) *temporal aspects* entail speed and rhythm; (3) *weight* or *strength* reflect the resistance to gravity; and (4) *energy flow* involves the degree of control in movements-gestures-expressions.

Laban analysis also groups spatial, temporal, and weight/strength qualities into eight "efforts." Four are strong: *pressing* efforts are strong, direct, and sustained, while *thrusting* ones are strong, direct, and sudden; *wringing* efforts are strong, indirect, and sustained, whereas *slashing* ones are strong, indirect, and sudden. The other four efforts involve lightness: *gliding* efforts are light, direct, and sustained, while *dabbing* ones are light, direct, and sudden; *floating* efforts are light, indirect, and sustained, whereas *flicking* ones are light, indirect, and sudden (Baron and Carnicke 2008: 188–207; Baron 2010).

Initially developed for modern dance and later incorporated into acting-directing vocabularies, Laban terms facilitate studies of performance by complementing analyses that use script analysis concepts such as given circumstances, objectives, actions, and units of action. Dramatic tactics exist along a spectrum that includes threatening and inducing actions. To take charge, observe intently, conclude an event, demand a response, imply a hidden arsenal, attack (verbally or physically), or overpower (in literal or figurative ways) are threatening tactics. By comparison, inducing tactics aim for win-win situations and feature actions such as confirm (e.g., nodding), disarm (e.g., handshakes), lull, amuse, inspire, flatter, be frank, and seduce. Notably, all dramatic actions prompt a response from another character. They include actions such as soothe, tease, and warn, which might appear in non-battle scenes, along with actions such as bait, challenge, deflect, destroy, goad, hammer, knife, menace, nail, punish, repulse, shock, stalk, and taunt, which fuel conflicts of all types (Baron and Carnicke 2008: 208–31).

In *Training Day*, Alonzo and Jake's first direct skirmish takes place at the diner. In retrospect, the scene is significant because it illuminates the characters' respective ways of moving through the world and anticipates dynamics in the scenes with overt physical conflict. The actors' movements, gestures, and facial and vocal expressions establish the contrast between their characters. Washington's are direct, whereas Hawke's are flexible. The irregular rhythm of Washington's physical and vocal expression has a sudden quality, while Hawke's regular rhythm is more sustained. Washington's performance features strong movements, whereas the qualities in Hawke's body and voice are light. Washington is tightly bound, but Hawke uses free-flowing physicality to represent Jake.

These contrasts appear in the opening seconds of the scene. As Hawke blithely enters the diner, he uses a light and free-flowing gait. Washington is already in a secure position for the confrontation, his posture strong and bound. Sitting opposite one another, Washington maintains a lower, more guarded plane than Hawke, who squirms throughout the scene. Washington uses his hands, arms, and shoulders as a forceful, coordinated unit, whereas Hawke uses flimsy, isolated gestures. At times, Washington darts forward, almost lunging at Hawke, who glances from side to side as if looking for a way to escape. Transforming the booth into a bunker from which he fires direct shots, Washington sits motionless, before and after gestural and vocal jabs, to depict the veteran observing how the young man deals with his attacks.

The irregular tempo of Washington's movements reveals that Alonzo is determined to keep his challenger off balance. At one point, he snaps his newspaper taut; at another he quickly taps the pistols in his double shoulder holster together. He sometimes abruptly replaces a smooth flow of dialogue with sharp, minced words punched out at Jake/Hawke. He intermittently raises an eyebrow, drops into a whisper, or fixes Hawke in a cold stare. By comparison, Hawke's physical and vocal expression takes on increasingly sustained qualities. With a glazed look coming into his eyes, he puts longer and longer pauses between his words and phrases. Finally replacing nervous glances with open-eyed stares, he shows that Jake is stunned by the encounter.

The distinctive weight and resistance in each actor's physical and vocal expression convey the characters' contrasting temperaments, as well as Alonzo's success in reaching his objective (make the rookie subservient) and Jake's failure to impress his new boss. Washington's strong movements, which emerge from an inner reserve of energy and determination, establish Alonzo as someone who has learned to anticipate resistance to his objectives. His voice deep and full, Washington shows that Alonzo enjoys his authority. His strong movements, which fight against the downward pull of gravity, confirm the veteran's goal for the meeting; his increasingly strong movements show that Alonzo aims to control this rookie whose cooperation is essential to his plan to secure the million dollars he needs that day.

Subsequent scenes feature violence even in moments of intimate dramatic conflict. From the moment Alonzo and Jake meet, the film creates tension by

Figure 6.1 Early in *Training Day*, physical and dramatic action converge as Alonzo (Denzel Washington) suddenly escalates the threat he poses to his partner-opponent, Jake (Ethan Hawke) (© Warner Bros., 2001. All Rights Reserved).

keeping them constantly on the move in a story that takes place in one day. It also increases the pressure by putting Alonzo and Jake in confined spaces. One of the film's most searing dramatic and physical conflicts takes place when Washington and Hawke are in Alonzo's black Monte Carlo. Angered that Jake has not agreed to smoke some confiscated PCP-laced marijuana, Alonzo stops his car in the middle of an intersection and threatens to shoot Jake if he does not comply with his order (Figure 6.1).

The partner-opponents' battle of wills escalates again in the dimly lit house of Alonzo's drug-dealing Vietnam War buddy, Roger (Scott Glenn). After holding Roger at gunpoint while his undercover officers locate the cash-filled trunks Roger had hidden under his kitchen floor, Alonzo insists that Jake kill Roger. However, suddenly catching Alonzo off guard, Jake/Hawke snatches the shotgun Alonzo/Washington is holding and threatens to shoot Alonzo even if the other cops fire on him. During the standoff, Alonzo orders his men to drop their weapons and then persuades Jake to turn over the shotgun, mesmerizing him with praise and appeals to reason. Later, in the characters' final one-on-one standoff on a dark street in the south Los Angeles neighborhood where Alonzo keeps his mistress, young son, and cash reserves, Alonzo strives to maintain control, even though Jake finally has the upper hand (Figure 6.2). Here again, dramatic and physical conflict intertwine in this action film, which depends on the actors' distinctive performances.

During the film's first two acts, Washington uses advancing movements, gestures that expand into the space around him, and line readings marked by speed, pressure, and directness. As the narrative moves toward the third act, Hawke's performance begins to incorporate the strong, sudden, and direct qualities of Washington's portrayal. Following plot coincidences that facilitate the

Figure 6.2 A brazen Stagolee figure, defiant to the end, the veteran (Denzel Washington) dares the rookie (Ethan Hawke) to shoot him in the physically and dramatically brutal final sequence of *Training Day* (© Warner Bros., 2001. All Rights Reserved).

white hero's victory over the threatening Black man, Hawke increasingly incorporates direct pressing and thrusting movements, while Washington turns to wringing and slashing movements as his control wanes. Alonzo has been fighting all his life; whereas Roger came home from Vietnam and made millions as a drug dealer with insider protection, Alonzo worked under the thumb of powerful white men, playing the game but remaining the outsider. After a day of battling Jake, who is an obedient enforcer of the laws that protect white life and property, Alonzo's body is eventually animated only by the bullets that cause him to twist and lurch in disparate directions in the hail of fire from the Russian mobsters' guns.

Embodiments of Partner-Opponents in *Outside the Wire*

Outside the Wire recalls *Training Day* in depicting the desperate plans of a risk-taking officer foiled by a rookie determined to prove himself (right) to the veteran. In the film, Mackie's "career trajectories as a military service member (in *The Hurt Locker* and as Sam Wilson/Falcon in the Marvel Cinematic Universe) and a science fiction hero (*Altered Carbon* season 2, *Synchronic*)" come together (Hadidi 2021). Blending Black speculative fiction and cinematic representations of Black soldiers, *Outside the Wire* explicitly highlights the Black soldiers' social identities. Once Leo and Harp have left the other Marines to embark on their high-risk mission, Leo challenges Harp with questions: "Why would the US Pentagon pick my face to represent the United States Marines? Why wouldn't they make me a blond-haired, blue-eyed, varsity peckerwood?" Harp gives a flippant answer but in fact, for "a programmed warrior like Leo, being Black is part of his skillset as much as his identity" (Feldberg 2021). Being Black belongs to Leo's military expertise because, as someone who represents neutrality rather than American abuses abroad, he can gain people's trust and secure intelligence. Further, in contrast to Harp, Leo is fully aware that as a Black soldier tasked with assignments behind enemy lines, he exemplifies America's historical exploitation of Black soldiers.

Fulfilling the action hero's role, "a clearly-enjoying-himself Mackie with plenty of pithy one-liners and memorable insults" carries audiences through most of the film (Hadidi 2021). Critics noted that Mackie is "quick with a sardonic grin and a fiery temper" (Hadidi 2021) and "excels in a series of one-on-one fight scenes," including the "nice piece of combat" in Leo's belated battle with the villainous warlord (Ehrlich 2021). Mackie's charismatic performance is a counterpoint to Idris's off-balance, petulant portrayal of Harp. Throughout the film, Mackie's embodiment of Leo features physical and vocal expression that tends to be direct, strong, and bound, whereas Idris conveys Harp's novice status through lighter, more scattered, and more free-flowing physical/vocal expression, especially in early action scenes. The steady, deeper-pitched voice that Mackie uses to portray Leo contrasts with the higher-pitched, whining twang adopted by resonant-voiced British Nigerian Damson Idris, whose voice here often breaks as if Harp were a teenager. Both actors incorporate sudden qualities into their physical/vocal expression, yet Mackie's emerge as neat, often dabbing punctuations in an ongoing fluid and controlled flow, while Idris's arise jerkily and irregularly, as flicks. The distinctions between the veteran and the newbie are visible even in the actors' gaits: Mackie tends to lean forward as he moves smoothly with no wasted motion, while Idris walks upright, his arms sometimes swinging loosely at his sides.

The characters' first encounter evokes Alonzo and Jake's initial meeting. Yet Mackie's performance shows that Leo aims to establish his authority by dazzling rather than crushing the novice. As Leo assesses his recruit and whisks him into the battle zone, Mackie quickly switches between various threatening and inducing actions, at one moment observing Harp/Idris intently, at another being frank with Harp in a way that confirms the youth's intelligence. Gently taking charge by deflecting Harp's rigid, textbook comments with dismissive chuckles, Mackie delivers a verbal punch whenever the rookie exposes his naïve arrogance. Conveying both threat and allure, Mackie often has his arms folded across his chest, keeping Harp at a distance, yet his easy smile and smooth, reassuring voice welcome Harp into his world. The combination of Leo's changing dramatic actions, Mackie's continual movement, and the brisk pace, varied volume, and evolving rhythm of his vocal delivery cause Harp to be mesmerized by his new commanding officer. The rookie's grudging respect for Leo, which takes hold in the characters' twenty-minute opening encounter, becomes awestruck esteem

Figure 6.3 Leo (Anthony Mackie) removes his weapons as he essentially glides (using light, sustained, direct movement) toward the nervous rebels to defuse their standoff with the Marines in *Outside the Wire* (© Netflix, 2021. All Rights Reserved).

when Leo, Harp, and fellow Marines encounter rebels outside the base. The heavily armed US soldiers anxiously threaten a band of civilians "stealing" materials from a wrecked supply truck. Harp, shaking and wide-eyed, fumbles while trying to get into defensive formation. In contrast, Leo single-handedly disarms the townspeople through bravery, charm, and rule-breaking diplomacy (Figure 6.3).

Soon after, the warlord's men open fire on the rebels and the Marines. Leo acts decisively while Harp huddles and then flails about in fear. The qualities that infuse Mackie's and Idris's movements contrast sharply. Leo quickly and assuredly removes Harp from the skirmish, essentially carrying the floundering rookie away by the scruff of the neck. Later in the film, the disparity in the two soldiers' bravery and fighting abilities comes into full view during the extended battle with the warlord's fighters at the bank that has housed the nuclear missile launching device. Whereas Harp almost shoots a civilian and, for the most part, stays huddled with the citizens who have been held hostage, Leo gracefully and flamboyantly dispenses with enemies throughout the building and then secures the device after an acrobatic rooftop chase.

The observable qualities in the actors' physical and vocal expression are also essential to the partner-opponents' ongoing close-contact sparring scenes. To suit the tight framing and camera movement used at times in dialogue and action scenes, Mackie and Idris generate legible facial and vocal expressions that communicate the characters' emotions even when on screen for only a few seconds. In the close-ups, the actors often "do *more* than [they] would ever do in real life or on the stage" (Tucker 2003: 39) because their faces alone must communicate the character's temperament, immediate state-of-mind, and goal-driven behavior. For instance, after Leo rescues Harp following the battle at the bank, Mackie and Idris are locked in proximity as they drive to Leo's next destination. Here, Harp discovers that Leo intends to move beyond military authority. Fighting to rein in his rogue commanding officer, Harp/Idris shouts furiously at Leo/Mackie; in counterpoint, Leo remains coolheaded, ending the rookie's outburst with a decisive blow to his head. Contrasting performance details in this dialogue scene convey exposition, character revelation, and dynamic action. In the film's final battle sequence, facial expressions captured in tight shots again convey the partner-opponents' physical and emotional conflict. When Harp enters the nuclear missile launch space, Leo catches him off guard and they engage in close-contact fighting. Shots of Mackie's furrowed brow and the surprisingly gentle expression in his eyes convey Leo's compassion for the rookie. Notably, Leo does not kill Harp in their hand-to-hand combat but instead uses a choke hold to render Harp unconscious.

Leo's compassionate action allows Harp to renew the battle minutes later. Reflecting Harp's knowledge that there is a drone ready to fire on the site at his command, Idris moves purposefully (with strong, sustained, and direct qualities) as he aims and shoots Leo with armor-piercing fire. Lying disabled by Harp's attack, Leo's emotional speech quickly deflates the rookie's agency and clarifies that his own destruction had been key to his plan from the start. Mackie's reclining body and measured vocal expression recall images from both the war film genre and Black speculative fiction, presenting Leo as the heroic Black soldier who sacrifices himself and as the Black android that "willfully misuses" technology designed to do the white master's bidding (Dery 2008: 13). For a moment, Leo and Harp return to their mentor and trainee roles, with Idris wide-eyed and attentive as Mackie chokes out Leo's dying wish for an end to the US government programs that created him and the drones which Harp pilots in military operations that kill civilians. Yet Harp snaps back into being the "good" soldier, loyal to his master, the US government. Breaking the bond between the Black soldiers, Harp leaves Leo to be destroyed in a drone strike explosion. For Harp, stopping the "militant" Black soldier helps secure his place in white society. For the film's white officers, the drone strike halts the launch of a nuclear missile and saves the social order by destroying a Stagolee figure who refuses to cower to white authorities.

Intertwined Spectacular and Dramatic Conflict

Training Day and *Outside the Wire* feature nuanced performances that illuminate character and thematic complexity in scenes of dramatic as well as physical conflict. The two films show their young heroes "becoming powerful" but feature the outsiders who drive the narratives forward as the rookies react haphazardly

(Purse 2011: 33). Washington and Mackie embody their characters' charm, acuity, and decisiveness. The villains' heroic dimensions give them depth and complexity: Washington and Mackie employ an "empowered stance" as they approach confrontations, and their characters possess action hero "skill sets (combat, reconnaissance and field skills) and character traits (resilience, determination, assertiveness)" (Purse 2011: 66, 23). The villains' complex characterizations also arise from the presence of visible threats. In *Training Day*, the looming threat that Russian gangsters pose to Alonzo, together with the dismissiveness with which the powerbrokers in Los Angeles treat him, lend this villain a vulnerability that can elicit sympathy. In *Outside the Wire*, the Russian-backed warlord targets Leo early on, and his fighters represent ongoing threats to Leo. On the home front, Leo's commanding officer displays contempt for him from the outset and seems to relish the idea of destroying him with drone technology. These threats make the Black super soldier a sympathetic figure well into the film.

Training Day and *Outside the Wire* show that locking opponents together in physical proximity facilitates action-filled character interactions. While some action movies keep the hero and villain at a distance until late in the film, *Die Hard* (John McTiernan, 1988) illustrates the value of placing the opponents in close range—in this case, within a single location. *Training Day* and *Outside the Wire* escalate the tension created in films such as *Die Hard*: they make close contact a necessary part of the opponents' professional roles and emphasize chase elements that keep the characters constantly moving across a threatening landscape.

Training Day and *Outside the Wire* also demonstrate that spectacular and dramatic scenes can be strongly connected in narratives with relentless tension. The ongoing battles between the partner-opponents do not follow the "pattern of switching between action and release" (Tasker 2015: 90). They do not intersperse action sequences of conflict and challenge with dialogue scenes that offer rest and exposition, as happens in *I, Robot* (Alex Proyas, 2004), which illustrates the more familiar action-release pattern. Placed between high-energy chase and fight sequences, a quiet six-minute scene featuring Del Spooner reveals the experience that haunts him, and Will Smith's performance elicits sympathy for the hero when Smith's voice trembles and his eyes well up with tears as he talks about the girl who lost her life in the car accident that he survived. In contrast, action scenes in *Training Day* and *Outside the Wire* illuminate character just as dialogue scenes are infused with conflict, challenge, and action. The films' narratives parallel the structure in *The Hurt Locker*, which "deploys action sequences of varying pace that achieve different sorts of dramatic effect" (Tasker 2015: 17). In this film, violence or "the threat of violence is thematically central" to its various action scenes, which include "a prolonged gun battle in the desert" and "a drink-fuelled fistfight between comrades" (Tasker 2015: 17).

In *The Hurt Locker*, action is "not an interruption of cinematic story-telling, but part of it" (Tasker 2015: 17). *Training Day* and *Outside the Wire* indicate that the converse can be true as well: storytelling sequences can be filled with dynamic action. In these two films, dialogue scenes are not a respite from violence or the threat of it. The partner-opponents are bound together in ongoing physical and verbal contests as they hurtle across menacing terrains. There is no interruption in the action, because tension, threat, and conflict shape essentially every scene. The partner-opponents are strongly motivated to bend the other character to their viewpoint, causing threatening actions to be used even in dialogue scenes. Noting that mirror neurons in human brains cause the same physical and emotional responses "whether a person is watching an action or performing it," Lisa Purse highlights action cinema's capacity to "prompt involuntary physical responses" as viewers watch actors perform spectacular behavior (2011: 44, 43). For *Training Day* and *Outside the Wire* viewers, witnessing action scenes *and* ones in which characters/actors figuratively knife, crush, or destroy one another can generate embodied responses. The actors' performances in action and dialogue scenes differentiate the characters, illuminate their motivations, and contribute to the tension. The performers' behavior, whether spectacular or mundane, conveys their characters' goals, fears, and attitudes. The actors' embodied portrayals of conflict, chase, and challenge contribute to the films' illustration of action as a cinematic mode.

Conclusion

Exemplifying the richness of contemporary action cinema, *Training Day* and *Outside the Wire* mobilize the engaging outsider portrayals of Washington and Mackie at the height of their respective careers. Marshaling gangster, war film, and science fiction conventions, the films present audiences with charismatic central characters who complicate the distinction between villain and cultural hero. In so doing, Washington and Mackie's performances confound dominant society's unexamined equation between blackness and criminality. Yet the films also remain open to interpretations that reflect audiences' cultural perspectives, especially about if or how the central characters' racial identities matter. Seeing the films in ahistorical terms, some viewers might compare *Training Day* primarily to films such as *Narc* (Joe Carnahan, 2002), *The Departed* (Martin Scorsese, 2006), or *Rampart* (Oren Moverman, 2011), which feature ruthless white cops. They might see *Outside the Wire* as most closely related to *Robocop* (Paul Verhoeven, 1987), *Terminator 2: Judgement Day* (James Cameron, 1991), or *Chappie* (Neill Blomkamp, 2015), which all frame whiteness as the unmarked norm. Still, *Training Day* and *Outside the Wire* do illuminate historically specific lived experiences when seen in relation to Black expressive traditions. Moreover, as twenty-first century iterations of folk hero Stagolee and the cultural heroes in Black gangster films, Black speculative fiction, and Black war films, Washington's and Mackie's mesmerizing outsiders sustain cultural-aesthetic traditions in which depictions of bravura Black masculinity can be lawlessly entertaining *and* soberly critical of the status quo.

Notes

1 The film is based on an Edna Mae Baker short story, not the 1927 von Sternberg film.

2 Other early films include *Heroic Negro Soldiers of the World War* (William S. Smith, 1919), which documents Black soldiers' participation, and *Within Our Gates* (Oscar Micheaux, 1920), which presents military service as uplifting the race.

3 Black independent film *The Spook Who Sat by the Door* (Ivan Dixon, 1973), depicts Black militant soldiers in its story about a former CIA agent who launches a "paramilitary revolution against the U.S. government" (Reich 2016: 185). *Dead Presidents* (Albert and Allen Hughes, 1995) dramatizes a story recounted in Wallace Terry's book *Bloods: An Oral History of the Vietnam War by Black Veterans* (1984).

4 Washington received Best Actor nominations for *Malcolm X* and *The Hurricane* but finally won the Oscar for *Training Day*. *Outside the Wire* helped secure Mackie's A-list status; to compete with news that *The Falcon and the Winter Soldier* starring Anthony Mackie and Sebastian Stan was the "biggest premiere launch for an original [Disney+] series," Netflix lifted its standard secrecy to announce that its "Anthony Mackie film," *Outside the Wire*, was Netflix's "most-watched entertainment of the year [reaching] 66 million households in the first quarter" (Romano 2021).

Works Cited

Alexander, Michelle (2012), *The New Jim Crow: Mass Incarceration in the Age of Colorblindness*, New York: The New Press.

Balio, Tino (2013), *Hollywood in the New Millennium*, London: British Film Institute.

Baron, Cynthia (2010), "Film Noir: Gesture Under Pressure," in Christine Cornea (ed.), *Genre and Performance: Film and Television*, 18–37, Manchester: Manchester University Press.

Baron, Cynthia (2015), *Denzel Washington*, London: British Film Institute.

Baron, Cynthia and Sharon Marie Carnicke (2008), *Reframing Screen Performance*, Ann Arbor: University of Michigan Press.

Carrington, André M. (2016), *Speculative Blackness: The Future of Race in Science Fiction*, Minneapolis: University of Minnesota Press.

Cripps, Thomas (1993), *Making Movies Black: The Hollywood Message Movie from World War II to the Civil Rights Era*, New York: Oxford University Press.

deCordova, Richard (1991), "Genre and Performance: An Overview," in Jeremy G. Butler (ed.), *Star Texts: Image and Performance in Film and Television*, 115–24, Detroit, MI: Wayne State University Press.

Dery, Mark (2008), "Black to the Future: Afro-Futurism 1.0," in Marleen S. Barr (ed.), *Afro-Future Females: Black Writers Chart Science Fiction's Newest New Wave Trajectory*, 6–13, Columbus: The Ohio State University Press.

Ehrlich, David (2021), "'Outside the Wire' Review: Anthony Mackie Is an Android Soldier in Netflix's Silly Future 'Training Day,'" *IndieWire*, 15 January. Available online: https://www.indiewire.com/2021/01/outside-the-wire-review-netflix-1234609669/ (accessed 31 July 2021).

Feldberg, Isaac (2021), "Anthony Mackie Is the Leading Man We Need," *Inverse*, 4 February. Available online: https://www.inverse.com/entertainment/anthony-mackie-interview (accessed 31 July 2021).

Fritz, Ben (2019), *The Big Picture: The Fight for the Future of Movies*, New York: First Mariner Books.

Grieveson, Lee (2005), "Gangsters and Governance in the Silent Era," in Lee Grieveson, Esther Sonnet, and Peter Stanfield (eds), *Mob Culture: Hidden Histories of the American Gangster Film*, 13–40, New Brunswick, NJ: Rutgers University Press.

Hadidi, Roxana (2021), "The Android Action of Netflix's Outside the Wire Raises Big Questions, Then Drops Them," *Polygon.com*, 15 January. Available online: https://www.polygon.com/2021/1/15/22234007/outside-the-wire-review (accessed 31 July 2021).

McClancy, Kathleen (2019), "Black Skin, White Faces: *Dead Presidents* and the African-American Vietnam Veteran," in Clémentine Tholas, Janis L. Goldie, and Karen A. Ritzenhoff (eds), *New Perspectives on the War Film*, 131–58, Cham, Switzerland: Palgrave Macmillan.

Munby, Jonathan (2011), *Under a Bad Sign: Criminal Self-Representation in African American Popular Culture*, Chicago: The University of Chicago Press.

Nama, Adilifu (2011), *Super Black: American Pop Culture and Black Superheroes*, Austin: University of Texas Press.

O'Brien, Daniel (2017), *Black Masculinity on Film: Native Sons and White Lies*, London: Palgrave Macmillan.

Patches, Matt (2020), "Get Your First Look at Anthony Mackie's New Sci-Fi Thriller, Outside the Wire," *Polygon.com*, 11 December. Available online: https://www.polygon.com/2020/12/11/22169296/anthony-mackie-outside-the-wire-photos-preview-release (accessed 31 July 2021).

Purse, Lisa (2011), *Contemporary Action Cinema*, Edinburgh: Edinburgh University Press.

Reich, Elizabeth (2016), *Militant Visions: Black Soldiers, Internationalism, and the Transformation of American Cinema*, New Brunswick, NJ: Rutgers University Press.

Reid, Mark A. (2005), *Black Lenses, Black Voices: African American Film Now*, Lanham, MD: Rowman & Littlefield Publishers.

Romano, Nick (2021), "*Outside the Wire* and *Fate: The Winx Saga* Top Most-Watched Netflix Movies and TV Shows of the Year," *Entertainment Weekly*, 12 April. https://ew.com/movies/outside-the-wire-fate-the-winx-saga-most-watched-netflix-movies-tv-shows/ (accessed 31 July 2021).

Stuart, Cameron (2019), "8 Actors on Exploring Darkness by Playing Unlikeable Characters," *Backstage.com*, 19 June. https://www.backstage.com/magazine/article/playing-villains-natasha-lyonne-aaron-paul-uzo-aduba-68414/ (accessed 31 July 2021).

Tasker, Yvonne (2015), *Hollywood Action and Adventure Film*, Malden, MA: Wiley Blackwell.

Tucker, Patrick (2003), *Secrets of Screen Acting*, 2nd edn, New York: Routledge.

Chapter 7

Samuel L. Jackson in Geriaction: "Bad Ass" Black Screen Masculinity, Aging, and Redundancy

Glen Donnar

Early in the action comedy *The Hitman's Bodyguard* (Patrick Hughes, 2017), notorious hitman Darius Kincaid, played by Samuel L. Jackson, is brought before his Interpol captors. Offered clemency in return for testifying against a Belarussian dictator accused of war crimes, Kincaid replies, "That's mighty fuckin' white of you." Kincaid's derisive response not only reinforces how integral Jackson's profane diction is to his (action) star image, but also calls attention to race—and the continued predominance of whiteness—in Hollywood action cinema.

Since the mid-2000s, there has been a marked resurgence in Hollywood-style action films featuring older male heroes, showcasing stars ranging in age from their mid-50s to 70s. More unexpected was the global box office success of many of these films, such as *The Expendables* (Sylvester Stallone, 2010) and *Taken* (Pierre Morel, 2008), and the sequels and franchises they generated.[1] This "geriaction" cycle, a less-than-kind label that combines geriatric and action, revitalized or transformed the careers of aging stars, including Stallone, Arnold Schwarzenegger, and Liam Neeson. Despite the unanticipated global popularity of the Luc Besson-penned *Taken*, it was only with the collective appearances of aging action stars in films like *The Expendables*, featuring Stallone, Schwarzenegger, and others, and *RED* (standing for *Retired & Extremely Dangerous*; Robert Schwentke, 2010), starring Bruce Willis, that the cycle was mockingly coined in media coverage.[2]

Notable exceptions such as Denzel Washington, Jackie Chan, Jet Li, and Helen Mirren aside, the cycle quickly became identified with 1980s action film's white male "hard bodies." While scholarship has long critiqued narratives of decline or "successful aging," the initial associations of geriaction with the cultural iconicity and legacy of 1980s white male action stars have shaped scholarly analysis. This makes Jackson's prominence in the space of aging action particularly interesting. Jackson is more commonly associated with mid- to late-1990s and post-2000s action cinema than with the "pure" action film redolent of 1980s action. Accordingly, this essay examines how Jackson's geriaction roles complicate the presumed whiteness of the cycle—much as Chris Holmlund's essay here does for female stars—and thereby expands understanding of how action stars navigate aging.

In this period Jackson is prolific. In what follows I explore elements from recent films that are representative of his extensive geriaction oeuvre—*The Hitman's Bodyguard*, *Kong: Skull Island* (Jordan Vogt-Roberts, 2017), *The Incredibles 2* (Brad Bird, 2018), *Captain Marvel* (Anna Boden and Ryan Fleck, 2019), *Glass* (M. Night Shyamalan, 2019), and *Shaft* (Tim Story, 2019). I also consider why his action stardom has been underappreciated by scholars. Beyond the revivals of long-running franchises, "new" multi-generational ensembles, and late-career moves within action cinema, Jackson's roles permit fuller consideration of biracial buddy pairings, intergenerational dynamics, and the place of villainy in geriaction. I survey the interrelated reasons for Jackson's longevity as an action star, explore how his action stardom has changed since the mid-1990s, and discuss the ways he has successfully resisted the specter of professional redundancy as he ages—by turns embracing and complicating long-standing tropes of Black screen masculinity.

Geriaction: A Cycle Grounded in Redundancy

Geriaction satisfies Amanda Klein's characterization of an intrageneric film cycle: it is one of several smaller film cycles that exist within action as a cinematic mode. Less defined by key images and themes and more by how they are used, film cycles are subject to defined time constraints. Forming within a shorter period they are "poised either to become stable genres or disappear quickly." Though often neglected, as Klein argues, because of their transparent motive "to cater to audience desires in order to turn a profit," analysis of cycles within genres "can facilitate a more detailed, nuanced understanding of that genre." Attuned to one specific moment in time, cycles better reveal "the state of contemporary politics, prevalent social ideologies, aesthetic trends, and popular desires and anxieties" expressed by or associated with a genre (2011: 6, 9). The geriaction cycle is linked to broader production, exhibition, and film-going trends that continue to favor sequelization, franchises, and international presales, and now target aging theater audiences. Audience nostalgia—and stars' nostalgia for their earlier, ascendant stardom—appears to be a core reason for the success of the cycle as well, as Chris Holmlund (2014) notes. This nostalgia not only relates to previous action narratives, tropes, and characteristics, but also to "the phenomenological force of the star body's past performances in comparison to their present iteration" (Purse 2017: 164). Geriaction offers both nostalgic narratives of star identities that resist outward decline and stars/characters who reassert threatened cultural-professional worth.

Repetition is an oft-maligned feature of genre films, and perhaps particularly of action. It can be stylistic, evident, for example, in the employment of flashbacks from earlier installments in a series to signify a protagonist's suffering or trauma. Through hyperbolic spectacle and/or transformation of the body, the outsider figure hero may be seen as "used (up)" by anonymous, distant others or as a lone warrior battling, and besting, seemingly overwhelming numbers of foes. There are montages of the building and "suiting up" of his body, as well as sequences of wounding and self-repair. The geriaction cycle amplifies and ironically engages with those hypermasculine action star images, filmographies, and genre tropes that had assumed prominence by the late 1980s–early 1990s. Yet though a source of predictable pleasure for fans, such redundancies exemplify the repetition that critics often find tiresome.

More than a recent development associated with advanced aging and diminished physical capacity, anxieties about no longer being needed or useful, hence becoming redundant and being stripped of status and worth, were already central to 1980s action star images and characters. Relatedly, 1980s action has been consistently linked to changes in American culture and politics—and associated with a perceived desire to remasculinize the nation. Additionally, 1980s action stars have (in)famously been deemed to mark the vanguard of a violent cultural response against supposed threats to white male hegemony (Jeffords 1994; Tasker 1993). In these terms, the emergence of geriaction in the wake of the 2007–2008 global financial crisis invoked cultural nostalgia for a period of supposed American cultural and political certitude and ascendancy. At the same time an insistent desire in geriaction to remasculinize and reassert cultural-professional worth is evidence of those unremitting concerns that the hypermasculine 1980s action "hard body" sought to abolish. This is true of defining 1980s action characters—from John Rambo (Stallone) through to John McClane (Willis)—who violently embody and resist perceived cultural, economic, and professional redundancy in a world they perceive as no longer valuing or needing them.[3] More than the symbolic muscular embodiment of reinvigorated American neoliberal strength or the remasculinization of downtrodden working-class white masculinity, these 1980s characters are typically presented as victims of economic and cultural change. They exhibit a vulnerability that their idealized bodies and violent actions can never fully expunge.

Such vulnerability is redoubled in the figure of the aging action star. Reminiscent of the genre trope of being "used (up)" by anonymous, distant others, redundancy for aging action stars centers on perceptions of *being aged* or having passed their use-by date. The geriaction resurgence intriguingly resists *and* confirms its stars' redundancy as "hard-bodied" action stars, albeit differently than the 1980s films did. For example, the transition to multi-generational, multinational star ensembles not only accords with the ascendance of the multi-protagonist format in contemporary action cinema, but also signals deep-seated fears about aging stars' capacity to "perform," waning audience drawing power, and declining star value. Although geriaction extends star lives, it paradoxically admits these aged stars' redundancy *as* action "performers." Anxiously attempting to conceal their aging bodies, attenuated agility, and diminished physical capacities, hyperbolic spectacle is "displaced onto oversized guns, fetishized vehicles and younger action bodies," including digital recreations of their younger selves (Donnar 2016: 2).

Jackson's geriaction roles afford an opportunity to recast these assumptions since he was never an action performer in the same sense as Stallone or Schwarzenegger and never identified as a 'hard body' in the 1980s. Moreover, he has remained productive throughout the 2000s, tackling a range of action roles—from cameos and buddies through to baddies and leads.

A "Bad Ass," Not a "Hard Body": Introducing Jackson and Flexible (Action) Stardom

Age 75 in 2023, Jackson has been an action star since the mid-1990s. He achieved critical notice in dramas and other supporting roles early in his Hollywood career and was nominated for Best Supporting Actor for *Pulp Fiction* (Quentin Tarantino, 1994), a film and performance that came to define much of his action star text as hitman, biracial buddy, and "bad motherfucker." He has since appeared in an astonishing array of highly commercial action-oriented genre films, from crime, war, and spy films to superhero movies and sci-fi fantasies. Lisa Purse's understanding of the "difficulty demarcating action cinema's generic parameters" is equally applicable to Jackson's filmography (2011: 2). His work highlights the proliferation and multiplicity of action throughout contemporary cinema: action as mode rather than genre. Jackson's determined "genre mobility" has prolonged his action career and broadened his stardom, including with new generations of audiences. It also defers concerns about professional redundancy, about his having passed his "use-by date," *and* confounds the well-worn action trope of being "used (up)" by others.

Jackson's career exemplifies Paul McDonald's notion of flexible stardom, the creative and commercial mobility that sees "elite actors traversing multiple categories and conditions of production and distribution" (2017: 493). In Jackson's case, his "presence [is] flexibly dispersed across the film market"

(2017: 511), across major Hollywood corporate films and occasional independent productions. As for other aging action stars, sequelization and franchises are key in both reviving earlier films and exploiting the success of new ones. In recent years alone, Jackson has had roles in sequels—*The Incredibles 2*, *Glass*, and *The Hitman's Wife's Bodyguard* (Patrick Hughes, 2021), in franchise reboots— *xXx: The Return of Xander Cage* (D.J. Caruso, 2017), in reboots *of* reboots—the 2019 *Shaft* revives Jackson's 2000 version (directed by John Singleton) of the 1971 original (Gordon Parks), and in blockbuster franchise installments—most notably across the sprawling Marvel Cinematic Universe (MCU). Yet he is also a player in the films of Tarantino and Spike Lee, as well as in independent films and passion projects such as the race drama, *The Banker* (George Nolfi, 2020), for which he was an executive producer. His flexibility is more uniquely signaled by his renowned work ethic and the variety of roles he willingly accepts as an established star—from scene-chewing cameos to star turns. Jackson's flexible stardom enabled him to build his profile and status in the 1990s, and now allows him to persuasively maintain his action stardom into his seventies, without having to assume clearly *aged* roles.

Jackson's body has always constituted a minor element of his action star image relative to other geriaction stars. While tall and lean, as befits many an action or Western hero, Jackson is more associated with word and gunplay as well as cool swagger. There are three key factors here: Jackson's film career only takes off in his early 40s (that is, in the early 1990s); more specifically his action career begins in the mid-1990s, a period in which there was less emphasis on "hard bodies" in action film; and, perhaps most importantly, his voice and diction are distinctive. That is, more than physicality or embodied action, Jackson's screen image is anchored in his profane and expletive-riddled vocabulary, rhetorical questions, and occasional uproarious laugh. On screen and off, he is a self-styled "bad motherfucker," an association that begins with the moniker embroidered on the wallet of Jackson's Bible-quoting hitman, Jules Winnfield, in *Pulp Fiction*.

Samuel L. Jackson is a "bad ass," not a "hard body." His body is not constructed as spectacle in the manner Tasker (1993) notes was true of "hard body" action stars but is also not unimportant to his geriaction star image, as is evident in some of his onscreen introductions. As Paul McDonald observes, the "spectacularization of the star" is especially resonant in moments "staged precisely to display the star attraction," from advanced marketing through to the star's entrance in the narrative (2013: 184). Jackson's introductions often frame him as a star, regardless of the status or centrality of his character. In *Kong: Skull Island* and *The Hitman's Bodyguard* his characters are introduced from behind, the camera emphasizing the back of his head and then his height. (He is taller than 1980s action stars like Stallone and Schwarzenegger.) Each introduction ends with a front-on close-up of his downcast face, which he slowly raises to reveal to the camera/audience, accentuating his eyes.

Kong: Skull Island is a dizzyingly hybrid monster-action/adventure-war film. As Colonel Packard, a military hero cum maniacal bad guy, Jackson indulges his penchant for playing outsized villains—as in *Glass*, *Miss Peregrine's Home for Peculiar Children* (Tim Burton, 2016), and *Kingsman: The Secret Service* (Matthew Vaughn, 2014). On his character's first appearance, the camera tracks back from behind Packard as he looks down over his young unit. His soldiers are preparing to withdraw from Vietnam late in the war. Sparks appear to rain down on either side of the military paterfamilias. Jackson's star framing is emblematic of what Stella Bruzzi calls "men's cinema," where spectacle, visual style, and *mise en scène* serve to "convey masculinity, not merely to represent it" (2013: 5). However, the scene is also ambivalent: the equation of insufficient military might and manpower hint at the inadequacy, waning, and redundancy occasioned by aging: Packard wonders forlornly as he looks at his medals and honors, "All this, for what?"

Jackson's character in *The Hitman's Bodyguard*, albeit tonally quite different to his role as Packard, is introduced with a similar shot: Jackson's face is gradually revealed to the audience in a frontal close-up, another instance of "spectacularization." Head down, incarcerated hitman Darius Kincaid/Jackson slowly looks up when he is offered a deal (Figure 7.1). His smirk is menacing. Despite being introduced in chains and handcuffs, only he will be "brave enough to come forward" to testify against the former Belarusian dictator, Vladislav Dukhovich (Gary Oldman), on trial at The Hague for war crimes. Michael Bryce (Ryan Reynolds), an executive protection agent, is tasked with escorting Kincaid to The Hague. When Bryce declares that his job is to keep Kincaid out of harm's way, Kincaid dismissively replies, "Shit, motherfucker, I *am* harm's way." The construction of Jackson's action stardom, both films suggest, revolves not so much around what his body can do, but around *who he is*.

Figure 7.1 Jackson's introduction in *The Hitman's Bodyguard* refigures the Black man as criminal as (also) potential hero (© Summit Entertainment, 2017. All Rights Reserved).

Ageless, De-Aged, and "Fucking Unkillable"

A persistent discourse around Jackson's star persona since the 2010s is his perceived agelessness, which Manohla Dargis and A.O. Scott (2015) mention when discussing Jackson's undimmed star power. The perception of "agelessness" is key to prolonging his action career and forestalling redundancy. It is, moreover, tied not to Jackson's body but instead to his tireless output and the undiminished vigor of his speech in franchise extensions, documentaries, television shows, and games.[4]

Although there is a fourteen-year gap between the animated films *The Incredibles* (Brad Bird, 2004) and *The Incredibles 2*, the storyline of the sequel immediately succeeds the original's conclusion. Jackson's character, the superhero Frozone, enters wordlessly, surfing along a bed of ice he creates while gliding to the support of the Incredibles family as they combat a new supervillain. Thanks to Jackson's now more substantial action cinema pedigree, the character in the sequel is drawn more clearly in his likeness. We have the impression, supported by the undiminished dynamism of Jackson's laugh, not only that no time has passed in the story world, but also that Jackson himself has not aged.[5]

Further feeding the sense that Jackson is somehow defying aging, several recent live-action films de-age him, and this includes *Shaft* and *Captain Marvel*. The first female-led superhero movie in the MCU, a prequel set in 1995, *Captain Marvel* is primarily an origin story for Carol Danvers as Captain Marvel (Brie Larson). For much of the film, Danvers believes she is a Kree warrior named Vers (the Krees are engaged in intergalactic conflict with the shapeshifter Skrulls). Jackson's character, Nick Fury, is digitally de-aged by twenty-five years. He first appears after Vers crash lands outside a Blockbuster Video store in Los Angeles. Vers is filmed up close, inside a telephone booth, as she tries to contact her field leader. Suddenly Fury's hand appears in the background of the shot, rapping knuckles on the side of the booth to get her attention. Then the camera pans and tracks left to reveal a younger Fury than in previous films, and a younger Jackson than the actor appears now in real life. As Drew Ayers observes, facial de-aging "reveals the fractures in the composite body" produced by digital visual effects (2018: 174). In de-aging Jackson's face, the film invites us to compare his now older body, seen in other Marvel movies, with memories of his comparatively lithe 1990s body, invoked by this younger body's supposed reappearance in *Captain Marvel*. His weight is differently distributed now, and his de-aged face is less capable of exhibiting emotion. Such dramatic aging down potentially extends Jackson's action star life, his voice anchoring the uncanny visual representation, although his relative lack of facial movement is unsettling.

Since the 2010s, Jackson's characters have relied on vehicles. Younger performers run in his place, disguising the fact that he is older, slower, and stiffer.

Jackson's physical action performance in *Captain Marvel* is attenuated and occasional, including a car chase and a perfunctory fight with a Skrull commander (Ben Mendelsohn) in a records storage room. In each instance, his movements are supplemented using rapid editing, a stunt double shot either from behind or in extreme long shot, and abbreviated bursts of fighting choreographed in confined spaces (Donnar 2022).

In *The Hitman's Bodyguard* action is again displaced onto younger and more mobile action star bodies, while Jackson's character, Kincaid, moves about primarily in cars. Both strategies position Jackson's character—and by extension Jackson himself—as inexhaustible and indomitable. In the parallel action sequence that begins the final act, driving a small Ford hatchback that Bryce earlier chose to Kincaid's extreme displeasure, Kincaid eludes Belarussian henchmen. The sequence bears the hallmarks of a typical action car chase, with Kincaid traversing urban infrastructure and expertly dispatching multiple attackers while driving. Meanwhile, having been earlier unceremoniously ejected from the car when it crashed, Bryce travels on foot. As Vers does in *Captain Marvel*, Bryce defeats multiple attackers in brutal hand-to-hand combat, first in a restaurant kitchen and ultimately a hardware store.[6]

In one respect, *The Hitman's Bodyguard* is unusual within Jackson's geriaction roles, using film style to "speed" up his typical, unhurried swagger. In a short sequence in which Kincaid rescues Bryce from torture, stunt and fight coordination and rapid editing effectively make Jackson-as-Kincaid move faster and hit more powerfully. Kincaid, unlike Bryce, seems not only tireless, but also indomitable. Later, after finally killing the head Belarussian henchman in a hardware store, Bryce lies bloodied and exhausted on the floor. Kincaid arrives unscathed in the now near-destroyed hatchback and honks the horn. Expected shortly at The Hague, Kincaid points at his watch as the camera dolly zooms into a close-up: "Yo, you about done?! Tick tock, motherfucker!" The contrast between Kincaid and the younger Bryce is striking. Bryce crawls out of frame and towards the car, weakly muttering: "Shit, he's fucking unkillable." Kincaid compares his seemingly effortless killings to Bryce's exertions: "While all you guys are wasting your time planning and aiming and deducing, I just do my thing. And my thing has always been better than your fuckin' thing!" Much as the younger character cannot keep pace with the older, Kincaid's assertion perhaps extends to the respective stars. In (geri)action, Jackson's "thing" is better than Reynolds's.

Refiguring the Black Buddy and the Intergenerational Dynamic

Like *Captain Marvel* and *The Hitman's Bodyguard*, Jackson's foundational action roles feature a Black/white buddy dynamic. This dynamic is most famously evident in Jules Winnfield's "work friendship" with fellow hitman Vincent Vega (John Travolta) in *Pulp Fiction.* Two other highly successful buddy films followed. Jackson was paired with Willis's John McClane in *Die Hard with a Vengeance* (John McTiernan, 1995) where, as activist shopkeeper Zeus Carver, he reluctantly helps McClane thwart an elaborate foreign terrorist plot. A year later in *The Long Kiss Goodnight* (Renny Harlin, 1996), he plays low-life private detective, Mitch Hennessy, who helps amnesiac homemaker/lethal CIA assassin Samantha Caine/Charly (Geena Davis) rediscover her past and rescue her daughter.

Donald Bogle characterizes the biracial buddy films of the 1980s "as wish-fulfillment fantasies" that ignore America's complex and contradictory interracial dynamics, invariably position the white buddy as "in charge," and subordinate the Black man as helper (2016: 245). For Ed Guerrero, biracial buddy films work to contain "the socially charged and vexed issue of race relations on screen," while functioning to constrain Black talent (1993: 128). Yet, as Bogle notes, Jackson's early performances individualize and complicate characters that might otherwise be types, emphasizing their shrewd intelligence (2016: 377–81).

Jackson's canny embrace of a variety of (anti-)hero and villain, helper and sidekick, buddy, and (disabled) mentor roles both continues to extend his action stardom and complexly reinforces *and* transcends long-established constraints on Black screen masculinity. In *The Incredibles 2*, Frozone is a superhero and a helper-protector figure. He often swoops in, mid-battle, uncalled for and unannounced, to support the Incredible family's efforts. He uses his freezing and skating powers to lessen damage to civilian infrastructure and civilian lives, but leaves apprehending the supervillain to the family. Jackson's character's narrative sidelining is echoed in *Captain Marvel*. Though Fury will later become the feared Director of S.H.I.E.L.D., here he plays sidekick to Captain Marvel/Vers, and is often placed either at the edge of the frame or in the background when both are on-screen. He is marginalized and effectively redundant. After Vers learns that she is the superhero, Captain Marvel, she battles with the Kree in space and on Earth to halt their imperialistic ambitions and shepherd the remaining Skrull refugees to safety. Fury does little more than hold what he thinks is a house cat, Goose. He does not shoot, hit, or kick. Vers allows Fury to break a fingerprint lock before disclosing she can simply blast through locks: "I didn't want to steal your thunder." Fury is aggrieved when a Kree scan identifies Goose as "Species: Flerken. Threat: High," while Fury is "Species: Human male. Threat: Low to none." Later, Danvers' best friend, Maria Rambeau (Lashana Lynch) shoots several Kree soldiers before Goose reveals itself to be an alien Flerken and devours the rest with enormous tentacles that come out of its mouth. Ultimately, Fury settles in as a passenger on the spaceship that Rambeau pilots to safety, while Marvel defeats a fleet of Kree battleships.

In the film's epilogue, Fury founds the Avengers and begins wearing his famed eyepatch, which is revealed to be the consequence of a scratch from the cat/

Flerken. Because the film is a prequel for Fury as much as for Captain Marvel, he is not yet a "bad ass," although the audience will be aware of the subsequent development of the character and the distinctive tone of Jackson's performance.

A key shift in the buddy dynamic in Jackson's geriaction films is the increasingly prominent representation of generational difference. Geriaction certainly "represents a site of intense cultural negotiation over the lived experience of the aging male body" (Purse 2017: 163) but aging in geriaction is more often jokily dismissed by protagonists rather than genuinely confronted. In Jackson's films, aging and generational difference gain prominence by being located instead in references to "new" technologies, "old-fashioned" methods, "traditional" gender attitudes, and music tastes. Fury may be younger in *Captain Marvel* than in previous MCU films, but he is older than Captain Marvel. Generational difference—both with Danvers and most audience members—is signaled through Fury's pride in his "state-of-the-art two-way pager," which Marvel later upgrades for intergalactic use, and his soulful rendition at film's end of The Marvelettes' "Please Mr. Postman" for a puzzled Marvel.

Jackson's role in *The Hitman's Bodyguard* also complicates the politics of the 1980s biracial buddy films. Although his character is a criminal, the film arguably reverses the Black/white buddy dynamic by making Jackson the real star and central character. Reynolds's lovelorn, emotionally constipated character, Bryce, is contrasted with Jackson's passionate, alive Kincaid. The pair's different attitudes to life and love, and tastes in clothing and music are racially, gender-, and generationally coded. When Kincaid returns to consciousness after he is shot in the leg, he asks, horrified, about the origin of the "wack ass, hipster clothes" that Bryce has put on him. Later Bryce sings 1990s Swedish pop (Ace of Base's "The Sign") in counterpoint to Kincaid's blues. (Jackson wrote the song "Nobody Gets Out Alive" for the film.)

The trope of the Black helper as witness to white heroism, unmistakable in *Die Hard with a Vengeance* and *The Long Kiss Goodnight*, is significantly modified here. Kincaid is not only a skilled assassin, but a heroic figure. He fights off Dukhovich's men in an ambush, despite being in custody, and later rescues Bryce from torture. After escaping from Bryce's Amsterdam apartment, he buys flowers for his wife to see from her jail cell even though would-be attackers converge on him, desperate to prevent him testifying. Hobbled by his leg injury, Kincaid is seemingly oblivious as Bryce takes out multiple attackers on his behalf, now as Kincaid's "helper." Kincaid's obliviousness is only a pretense, however, and he subsequently describes each attacker and details the "help" Bryce provided in each instance. While Kincaid sees Bryce's heroism, his total awareness of the events that unfolded implies that it was never needed.

The intergenerational dynamic is most fully rendered in the Black father/son dynamic in the 2019 action-comedy reboot of *Shaft*. Here Jackson's Shaft partners with his estranged son, JJ (Jessie Usher), to investigate the killing of

JJ's best friend. A neighborhood drug cartel is responsible. A late cameo from the original Shaft, Richard Roundtree, as Jackson's character's father expands the intergenerational backstory, but given Roundtree is only four years older than Jackson, the effect is uncanny once more. Again, Jackson is aged down, but not digitally; coats conceal his paunch, and a beanie covers his frown lines. Riffing on an iconic Black character, directed by a Black filmmaker, and centered on a Black story, *Shaft* figures generational difference through racially inflected gender- and class-related formations related to clothing, home furnishing, employment, and music. Private detective Shaft is Black working class, while FBI cyber analyst JJ is a "buppie" (Black urban professional). Jackson's character considers a "buppie" to be inauthentically Black, sexually repressed, unmasculine, and, thanks to his mother's influence, almost "a bona fide white boy!" In contrast, Shaft considers his hypermasculine and hypersexual Black identity to be "authentic."

Shaft's age is jokily acknowledged through references to erectile cream, an aversion to computers, and requiring reading glasses. His "old-fashioned" methods, however, remain potent and are presented as necessary to bring down the cartel. Lennart Soberon observes that absent fathers in geriaction are typically restored through "the heroic violence that distanced him from his family in the first place" (2021: 164). This includes recourse to "the same tools, techniques, and violent practices" (164), or, in the words of Shaft's appalled son, "aggravated assault, illegal use of firearms . . . and torture!" By film's end, JJ becomes like his father, proudly adopting his name ("Shaft, John Shaft"), style (leather overcoat and sunglasses), speech, and violent practices (spitting "motherfucker" when he kills his final adversary). Before this, Shaft has shown he is capable of change as well. While his attitudes to women and sexuality remain retrograde, father becomes like son, adopting contemporary masculine norms to apologize to JJ's mother.

Immobility, Inaction, and Being Spectacular

An unconventional characteristic of Jackson's action star text is his relative *immobility*, a quality that he has transformed into a cinematic action virtue. Purse observes that "action cinema is defined by a persistent and detailed attention to the exerting body" (2011: 2). While Jackson is an action figure, his is rarely an "exerting" or laboring action body. As early as Singleton's 2000 *Shaft* — in a scene notably referenced in the 2019 film's opening titles montage — Shaft tells a young assailant who calls him "Pop-pop" that he is "going to fuck you up for making me run!" (He does.) Extending that in the 2019 geriaction sequel, Jackson-as-Shaft

Figure 7.2 Jackson, as John Shaft, "coolly" disregards generational change, swaggering back into center frame at the end of *Shaft* © (New Line Cinema, 2019. All Rights Reserved).

shoots out the windscreen of a passing truck to creatively halt the escape of a drug dealer rather than chase after him. In geriaction, Jackson has transformed not wanting—and no longer being able—to run into a marker of "cool." In contrast to innumerable white-led geriaction films, where guns are proxies for embodied action, for Jackson they are not oversized compensations for an aged "hard body," but instead are synonymous with an aesthetic of cool. For example, the "Shaft Theme" only begins when his character cocks a sawn-off shotgun and swaggers (wearing a long leather overcoat) towards the camera in extreme long shot. The swagger is as—if not more—important than the shotgun here. It reappears in the film's final scene as well, with father, son, and grandfather strutting across the street in matching calf-length suede overcoats (Figure 7.2). Although the father has learned from the son, his "thing" is still better: the older star returns to center frame—emphatically *not* running.

Immobility—and indeed, *not needing* to be mobile—is even more striking in *Glass*, the third film in M. Night Shyamalan's twenty-year superhero saga. In the final film, Jackson again plays comic book obsessive and Svengali mastermind Elijah Price/Mr. Glass, who, as we learned in the first film, *Unbreakable* (M. Night Shyamalan, 2000), has suffered from brittle bones syndrome (osteogenesis imperfecta) since childhood. Sitting in a wheelchair, detained in a psychiatric hospital in *Glass*, Glass's unresponsive immobility is occasioned more by disability, heavy sedation, and camera surveillance than by age. Jackson-as-Glass's introduction in the film diverges starkly from those examples discussed earlier. His inert hand is first presented from Glass's point of view, then he is shot from below in his wheelchair, his head downcast. This has the effect of making his limbs appear longer and thinner. Over successive appearances, Glass remains unresponsive, though occasional direct looks at the camera/audience convey Jackson's star power while progressively increasing facial twitches signal

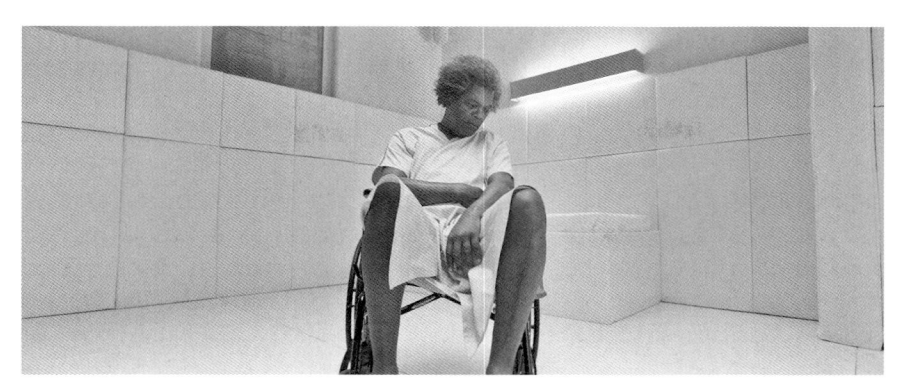

Figure 7.3 Jackson's introduction as Mr. Glass in *Glass* (© Universal Pictures, 2019. All Rights Reserved)—inert, expressionless, and wheelchair-bound—deviates from other geriaction roles.

the character's villainous potential. Glass's catatonic stasis is only a ruse, and it is no surprise to the audience when he adroitly moves around the hospital undetected since we know from the two previous films that he is a criminal genius (Figure 7.3).

To accomplish his escape and fulfil his masterplan, Glass incites the much younger Beast (James McAvoy) to execute the spectacular violence that Glass maniacally desires but *cannot* himself perform. In the film's final act, Glass sets up a "showdown." In comic book lore, superheroes and their abilities are revealed to the public in such combats. Here the "showdown" takes place in a parking lot rather than, as threatened, at the opening of a downtown skyscraper. The Beast, David Dunn/The Overseer (Bruce Willis), and Glass are all killed by an organization dedicated to keeping the existence of people with super abilities secret. Yet, it turns out, Glass has arranged for their sacrificial deaths to be recorded and posthumously released, disclosing the existence of people with super abilities via the Internet. Glass's purple suit and wig are flamboyant, but Glass does not need to be an action performer to produce action spectacle: as his mother tells him before his death, "You were spectacular."

Glass exemplifies the ways that, as he has aged and his action stardom has developed, Jackson has become integral to, even part of, the action by not moving, simply by being a "bad ass." Early in his action film career, Jackson's characters were often caught up beyond their skill set. In both *Die Hard with a Vengeance* and *The Long Kiss Goodnight*, Jackson's Black helper characters are seemingly out of their depth once the action begins; Zeus Carver is not an ex-cop and Mitch Hennessy is not a CIA assassin. In his geriaction roles, Jackson's characters again watch or are enveloped by violence. However, the older characters Jackson plays are increasingly at ease. In the final action sequence in *The Hitman's Bodyguard*, after Kincaid's damning testimony, Dukhovich makes an audacious last attempt to escape justice. He signals to a getaway helicopter, then watches in dismay as bullets riddle its cockpit and it crashes onto the rooftop of the International Criminal Court. Tracking the last moments of the helicopter's flight, the camera pans to reveal Kincaid, gun in hand, standing in front of the crestfallen dictator. Shot from Dukhovich/Oldman's perspective, Kincaid/Jackson's height is emphasized, as it was in his first appearance in the film. Although the helicopter violently explodes directly behind him, Kincaid is unmoved. He does not turn; he does not flinch. The framing conveys Jackson's stardom, both standing out from and a part of the inferno at his back.

A similar relationship to explosive action imagery is evident even when Jackson plays a villain marked for violent death. Over the course of *Kong: Skull Island*, Packard morphs from a revered, aging leader eager for one final redemptive mission into a Conradian monster obsessed with exacting revenge on Kong for killing his men after, on his order, they bomb the island that the giant ape stewards: "This is one war we're not going to lose." Several extreme close-ups of Packard's eyes mirror the presentation of Kong's eyes. Each is lit by flames but only Packard's are filled with hate. This effectively, and troublingly—given the racist imagery and colonial discourses associated with successive iterations of King Kong—confers monstrosity onto Packard instead.[7] As in *The Hitman's Bodyguard*, Jackson's height is emphasized through low-angle shots: he seems to tower in the frame. Accentuated by a belt slung low on his hips, Jackson's swagger recalls John Wayne's gait. In the final act, Packard sets napalm alight to burn Kong, a look of evil glee on his face. He watches the fiery conflagration in front of him, unmoving, remaining defiantly immobile even when the giant ape violently retaliates against his men and Kong collapses to the earth in Packard's midst. Revived, Kong eventually crushes Packard under his fist before the soldier can destroy him. Though Jackson's villainous characters in geriaction may die, they form part of the actor's prolific output suggesting that Jackson-as-action star is "unkillable."

The Positive Potential of "Bad Ass" Black Geriaction Masculinity

Jackson has been an established action star for over two decades, yet his longevity is not always centered in the critical reception to his films. Racquel Gates's concept of the "double negative" can help us understand the reasons for this frequent inattention to Jackson's action career *and* enables us to recognize its subversive, progressive potential.[8] Gates seeks to transcend binary categorizations of "positive" or "negative" representations to salute the "liberatory pleasures" of otherwise critically or scholarly ignored or disparaged Black media texts (2018: 27). She champions non-normative feminist, queer, and Black subjectivities and calls for greater attention to popular-though-derided commercial genres. The meanings invariably assigned to such texts are "primarily construed via their relations to other texts that occupy privileged [cultural, critical, and scholarly] positions" (2018: 16).[9] She argues that, despite often "troublesome" performances, cultural politics, and constructions of race, so-called "negative texts" hold subversive, progressive potential in the way that they privilege disreputable behavior, characters, and genres, and allow us to negotiate, complicate and trouble the "normative aesthetics of whiteness in cinema" (2018: 20).

Jackson's action films are arguably "disreputable," which accounts for scholarly underappreciation of him as an action performer. Although he is commonly considered to be better than his material, he appears without apology in highly commercial event or franchise films and critically panned reboots. Jackson's articulation of action stardom does not fit with the emphasis in much action scholarship on muscularity, bodily display, wisecracking Everyman ingenuity, or embodied action. Black scholars perhaps particularly object to the ways in which many of his characters liberally, even pointlessly, voice racial, homophobic, and sexist epithets and adopt retrograde attitudes. Perhaps most "disreputable," though, is Jackson's defiant defense, even celebration, of such roles. However, his unashamed embrace of his performances and films, no matter how problematic, commercial, or variable in "quality," also invokes the unapologetic, disruptive spirit of Gates's "double negative."

Samuel L. Jackson embodies a distinctive model of geriaction stardom. His leading, co-starring, and supporting presence interrogates the all-too-readily presumed whiteness of the cycle and variously navigates the challenges of aging action stardom. He resists the aged action star's redundancy, disrupting anxieties about having passed one's action "use-by date" in numerous ways: his unrepentant support of even his most "disreputable" representations; his stated pleasure in working in films he would like to see, irrespective of their "quality"; and his enthusiastic acceptance of a range of action cinema roles— from cameos and buddies through to baddies and leads. Jackson plays across action as hero, anti-hero, and villain, fragile, destructible, and invincible, an assortment finally recognized in an honorary Oscar in 2022.[10] Jackson's "spectacular" stillness, willing delegation, and invocation of the coolness of the "badass" offer a counterpoint to the way that a decrease in physical strength and agility is either masked or framed negatively in other geriaction stars' roles. Jackson's geriaction career, rather than "disreputable," may instead illustrate the positive potential of his "motherfuckin' badass," post-2000s Black action masculinity.

Notes

1   *Taken* (2008) earned US $226 million globally, *Taken 2* (Olivier Megaton, 2012) $376 million, *The Expendables 1* and *2* (Simon West, 2012) over $275 and $315 million in 2010 and 2012 respectively, and *A Good Day to Die Hard* (John Moore, 2013) $305 million.

2   Although recently coined, geriaction has historical precursors in British-American cinema. See Donnar (2016) and Purse (2017) for more on the cycle's cinematic lineage.

3   See O'Brien (2012) and Tasker (2016) for similar observations.

4   Jackson narrates both Spike Lee's *Chi-Raq* (2015) and the acclaimed documentary on writer James Baldwin, *I Am Not Your Negro* (Raoul Peck, 2016).

5   It is common for actors to voice significantly younger characters in animation. On the release of the sequel, Craig T. Nelson, who voices Mr. Incredible, was 74 years old and Holly Hunter, who voices Elastigirl, was 60. Because this is a family film, Frozone is less prone to profanity than Jackson's other characters.

6   This reverses a scene from *The Long Kiss Goodnight* in which Jackson's battered character is unceremoniously ejected from a vehicle by Geena Davis's character.

7   For more on the cultural history of representations of Kong on screen, see Erb (2009) and Roche Cárcel (2022).

8   In the context of Jackson's career, it is important to note Gates's interest "in the idea of 'black' as it comes to be defined in the process of circulation throughout pop culture," rather than in African American-produced media, *per se* (2018: 28). This supports the examination of even his supporting/minor roles in films made by white directors and/or for Hollywood studios.

9   Gates compares Melvin van Peebles's celebrated independent film *Sweet Sweetback's Baadasssss Song* (1971) with its "symbiotic 'other'" (2018: 23), the MGM-produced *Shaft* (Gordon Parks, 1971). Van Peebles's assertion that Parks's film lacks the cultural authenticity of his because it was (also) marketed to white audiences, is a criticism that can also be leveled at the two attempted reboots starring Jackson.

10 The Oscar also recognized Jackson's extensive philanthropic work. Jackson exploits his action film screen image as a "bad motherfucker" to support progressive cultural institutions, helping with the establishment of the National Museum of African American History and Culture, supporting Alzheimer's care and research, and participating in men's health and cancer awareness campaigns. As the spokesperson for the One for The Boys and #BadAssHealth campaigns since 2016, Jackson refigures his profane Black screen masculinity to advocate "speaking up," in contrast to the monosyllabism and stoic suffering idealized in "hard-bodied" action cinema: "If you're going to look like a man, then you better start acting like one, motherfucker."

Works Cited

Ayers, Drew (2018), "The Composite Body: Action Stars and Embodiment in the Digital Age," in James Kendrick (ed.), *A Companion to the Action Film*, 165–86, Hoboken, NJ: John Wiley & Sons.

Bogle, Donald (2016), *Toms, Coons, Mulattoes, Mammies, and Bucks: An Interpretive History of Blacks in American Films*, 5th edn, New York: Bloomsbury Academic.

Bruzzi, Stella (2013), *Men's Cinema: Masculinity and Mise-en-Scène in Hollywood*. Edinburgh: Edinburgh University Press.

Dargis, Manohla, and A.O. Scott (2015), "This Summer's Action Heroes Are Several Shades of Gray," *The New York Times*, 1 May. Available online: https://www.nytimes.com/2015/05/03/movies/this-summers-action-heroes-are-several-shades-of-gray.html (accessed 1 April 2019).

Donnar, Glen (2016), "Narratives of Cultural and Professional Redundancy: Aging Action Stardom and the 'Geri-Action' Film," *Communication, Politics & Culture*, 49 (1): 1–18.

Donnar, Glen (2022), "The Art of Making Do: Ageing Recent-to-Action Stars in Hollywood-Style French Action Cinema", in Steven Gerrard and Renée Middlemost (eds), *Gender and Action Films 2000 and Beyond: Transformations*, 21–33, Bingley: Emerald Publishing Limited.

Erb, Cynthia (2009), *Tracking King Kong: A Hollywood Icon in World Culture*, 2nd edn, Detroit, MI: Wayne State University Press.

Gates, Racquel (2018), *Double Negative: The Black Image and Popular Culture*, Durham, NC: Duke University Press.

Guerrero, Ed (1993), *Framing Blackness: The African American Image in Film*, Philadelphia: Temple University Press.

Holmlund, Chris, ed. (2014), *The Ultimate Stallone Reader: Sylvester Stallone as Star, Icon, Auteur*, New York: Columbia University Press.

Jeffords, Susan (1994). *Hard Bodies: Hollywood Masculinity in the Reagan Era*. New Brunswick, NJ: Rutgers University Press.

Klein, Amanda (2011), *American Film Cycles: Reframing Genres, Screening Social Problems, and Defining Subcultures*, Austin: University of Texas Press.

McDonald, Paul (2013), *Hollywood Stardom*, Malden, MA: Wiley-Blackwell.

McDonald, Paul (2017), "Flexible Stardom: Contemporary American Film and the Independent Mobility of Star Brands," in Geoff King (ed.), *A Companion to American Indie Film*, 493–520, Hoboken, NJ: John Wiley & Sons.

O'Brien, Harvey (2012), *Action Movies: The Cinema of Striking Back*, London: Wallflower.

Purse, Lisa (2011), *Contemporary Action Cinema*, Edinburgh: Edinburgh University Press.

Purse, Lisa (2017), "Confronting the Impossibility of Impossible Bodies: Tom Cruise and the Ageing Male Action Hero Movie," in Sabrina Qiong Yu and Guy Austin (eds), *Revisiting Star Studies: Cultures, Themes and Methods*, 162–86, Edinburgh: Edinburgh University Press.

Roche Cárcel, Juan A. (2022), "King Kong, the Black Gorilla," *Quarterly Review of Film and Video*, 39 (5): 1113–57.

Soberon, Lennart (2021), "TOO OLD FOR THIS SH*T: Aged Action Heroes, Affect, and 'the Economy of Exertion'," *Journal of Popular Film and Television*, 49 (3): 155–67.

Tasker, Yvonne (1993), *Spectacular Bodies: Gender, Genre and the Action Cinema*, London; New York: Routledge.

Tasker, Yvonne (2016), "Contested Masculinities: The Action Film, the War Film and the Western," in Kristin Lené Hole, Dijana Jelača, E. Ann Kaplan and Patrice Petro (eds), *The Routledge Companion to Cinema & Gender*, 111–20, London: Taylor & Francis.

Chapter 8
Action Latinas in an Era of Precarity

Mary Beltrán

Latina action heroines brave challenges in 2010s film narratives that are daunting, deadly, and often rooted in our current social history. A scene from the US remake of *Miss Bala*[1] (Catherine Hardwicke, 2019) provides a vivid snapshot of these trends. In a climactic moment in the film, the narrative transforms from a tense drama about a Mexican American woman abducted by a Mexican drug cartel into a traditional action film, as Gloria Fuentes (Puerto Rican actress Gina Rodriguez) extricates herself from her traumatic situation. Having been forced by Los Estrellas to commit crimes and finally to compete in the Miss Baja California beauty pageant as their rigged winner, she wears a glamorous red evening gown slit up the thigh at the after-party at a corrupt police chief's elegant resort property. Looking grim, Gloria incongruously wields an automatic rifle she took from a dying officer. She makes her way through the expansive compound as shots fly around her. Shooting the police chief (Damián Alcázar) and killing the cartel leader, the handsome but ruthless Lino (Ismael Cruz Córdova), she saves her friend and herself. Gloria's ultimate, Hollywood-style empowerment and subsequent job offer from the Central Intelligence Agency (CIA) are a far cry from how her counterpart fares in the original film and from the real-life drama on which both are based, raising ethical questions regarding recent action narratives based on real-life calamities experienced by Latinas and others in regions of Latin America and near the US–Mexico border.

Gloria's triumphant moments call to mind those of her Latina predecessors in 1990s and 2000s films, about which I wrote with optimism in 2004. Like the characters played by Jennifer Lopez and Michelle Rodriguez, of Puerto Rican and Puerto Rican and Dominican descent, respectively, in films like Lopez's *Anaconda* (Luis Llosa, 1997) and Rodriguez's *Resident Evil* (Paul W.S. Anderson, 2002), Gloria is a canny survivor, despite her traditionally feminine body type and appearance. Like Lopez and Rodriguez, she does not undergo a masculinizing transformation to gain the ability to protect herself and her loved ones, as was the case for some white female action heroines in the 1980s and 1990s, for example Sarah Connor (Linda Hamilton) in the first two *Terminator* films (James Cameron, 1984 and 1991), as Yvonne Tasker (1998) documented. As I theorized about those first Latina action protagonists, comparing them to their counterparts in Westerns and urban gang films of earlier eras and building on the work of Charles Ramírez Berg (2002) and Carlos E. Cortés (1997), US cinematic paradigms had established that Latinas could always "handle themselves," whether in a battle or, in later decades, confronting a people-eating anaconda. Linked to this, as I noted, depictions of Latinas as physically powerful entail a potential downside. When few other Latina images are found in popular culture, innately *macha* Latinas could be misconstrued as reinforcing negative associations. That the US was recently led by a president who described Mexicans and Latina/o immigrants as criminals and rapists in countless speeches and tweets adds fuel to the flames, so to speak: racism and hate crimes against Latina/os have risen with this rhetoric (Brooks 2019).

With this cinema and social history in mind, I update my previous study. I first survey US films of the 2010s that include Latina protagonists and feature sustained "action" elements. In doing so I define action broadly, as having to use one's body or skills in dangerous situations for self-protection, survival, to defend others, or in support of a cause. Latinas playing non-Latinas or non-human characters in superhero and fantasy films thus are not considered. In films that range from *Miss Bala* to *Zombieland: Double Tap* (Ruben Fleisher, 2019), I find a number of Latina protagonists who are intrepid in the face of threats. These heroines possess the *cojones* (the balls; arguably it should be the ovaries) to combat hostile forces that would destroy or exploit them or their communities, whether drug cartels, anti-immigration vigilantes, zombies, supernatural monsters, or sexist jerks who underestimate their abilities. Even so, this handful of Latina protagonists is depicted by an even smaller handful of actors. Most are played by Michelle Rodriguez and Gina Rodriguez (no relation), both of whom are cast in multiple films. The remaining roles are depicted by Mexican actress Eiza González, cast in a few films, and by Rosario Dawson (of Puerto Rican, Afro-Cuban, Irish and Indigenous ancestry), Jessica Alba (of Mexican and European American heritage), and Jennifer Lopez, in just one film each. While the longevity of Michelle Rodriguez's action star career is testimony to her ongoing appeal, the dearth of actresses in these roles underscores the stagnated progress of Latinas in the US film industry, as confirmed by the USC Annenberg Inclusion Institute's recent study (Smith, Choueti, and Peiper 2020). Meanwhile, only actresses with Hollywood's preferred "Latin look" (Rodriguez 1997) of light tan skin, long dark hair, and European facial features are cast in starring Latina roles (Beltrán 2009). These norms exclude many performers even before the audition process.

Additionally, Latinas are less often the primary protagonists in these films, in contrast to 1990s and early 2000s action narratives. Latina action roles of the 2010s include, for Michelle Rodriguez: Letty Ortiz in several *Fast and Furious* films

(Justin Lin, 2011, 2013; James Wan, 2015; F. Gary Gray, 2017), now a two-decade old franchise centered on car stunts and a multicultural ensemble; and immigrant rights activist Luz in *Machete* (Robert Rodriguez and Ethan Maniquis, 2010) and *Machete Kills* (Robert Rodriguez, 2013). Jessica Alba also stars as immigration enforcement agent Sartana Rivera in the *Machete* films. Gina Rodriguez and Eiza González are the popular newcomers. Gina Rodriguez's action roles include oil rig operator Andrea Fleytas in the disaster film *Deepwater Horizon* (Peter Berg, 2016), paramedic Anya Thorensen in the female-centric supernatural *Annihilation* (Alex Garland, 2018), and Gloria in *Miss Bala.* González plays Darling, the professional name of criminal Monica Costello, in *Baby Driver* (Edgar Wright, 2017), a role that arguably reads as Latina, and former Navy Seal KT in the superhero film *Bloodshot* (David S.F. Wilson, 2020). Finally, Rosario Dawson's one clear action role is that of saucy gunslinger and Elvis fan Nevada in the zombie action comedy *Zombieland: Double Tap*, and Jennifer Lopez's most relevant role is that of a grieving mother out for revenge in the urban crime film *Lila and Eve* (Charles Stone III, 2015).

These characters are rarer than might have been predicted a decade prior. This shift is linked in part to the waning of action-oriented crime films, as comic book and other fantasy-oriented films have come to eclipse them in quantity and popularity since the late 2000s. While a number of Latino and Latina super heroes and other protagonists have appeared in US comics since the post-World War II era, as Frederick Luis Aldama (2009) shows, these characters have seldom made the leap to film, even in this era of comic book movie franchises. Coinciding with these shifts in response to audience interests, action and crime films have evolved in tone and content. Action film trends in the post-9/11 era observed by Lisa Purse (2011a) and others include darker themes and a focus on global concerns.

Where Latina protagonists are most often found in 2010s films is in story worlds set against the backdrop of the global drug trade, or in relation to the sharp rise of individuals and families fleeing to the US from no-win situations as armed gangs have gained control in regions of Mexico and Central and South America. Similarly, in Spanish-language films and media targeting the Latin diaspora audience and other global viewers, Latinas are featured as protagonists in an ongoing cycle of "narco novelas," telenovelas focused on individuals working for, trying to stop, or victimized by drug cartels, and related films. The telenovela *La Reina del Sur* (2011, 2019, 2022–2023), about the female leader of a global drug cartel, and the original *Miss Bala* (Gerardo Naranjo, 2011), a Mexican film based on the 2008 abduction of a beauty pageant winner by a cartel, for instance, are well-known examples from the cycle. These films and series arguably reflect growing global concerns regarding the shifting status of Latin Americans in relation to the dismal conditions and lawlessness in afflicted regions of the world.[2] As a result, it is unsurprising that financial, social, and physical precarity is increasingly a theme of Latina and Latino-centric action narratives. Given that action films typically depict the protagonists soundly defeating villains and threats, how might we understand the significance of cinematic Latina empowerment in relation to these bleak circumstances?

Within this exploration, aesthetic and narrative distinctions among action films are useful to consider. The Hollywood action film's common usage of stunt doubles, pyrotechnics, and other special effects to heighten the excitement, glamor, and/or comedy of action sequences contributes to a bifurcation within the genre, with some films hewing to an aesthetic of realism and others embracing fantasy full tilt. This bifurcation can be found in the films I surveyed. Filmmakers' production choices in this regard can highlight or obscure the social history and broader social context linked to scenarios that form the backdrop of action narratives, as I note in my analysis.

To explore the impact of these aesthetic and narrative choices and the evolution of Latina action heroines in recent years, I examine two US films centered on Latina protagonists. The first is the aforementioned 2019 *Miss Bala*. I compare it with the 2011 Mexican film of the same name on which it was loosely based. Both crime dramas recall the vulnerability experienced by Mexican women and families in cities like Tijuana, where armed gangs have begun to operate unchecked. The 2019 adaptation combines a realist aesthetic and more far-fetched action conventions, resulting in a distorted picture of the region and its residents' experiences. While it centers Gloria's experience, it ultimately does little to relate the narrative from her perspective or to develop her inner world, as I expand on further below.

My second case study is Rodriguez and Maniquis's *Machete*. It features two Latina lead characters: Luz (Michelle Rodriguez) and Sartana (Jessica Alba). As a film that blends the action film, the labor rights film, and the Mexican-inflected exploitation film (Brayton 2011; Fojas 2016), *Machete* combines a fantastical narrative and gratuitous sex and violence with serious subject matter: the real-life violence, discrimination, and uncertainty experienced by undocumented border crossers and workers in the United States. Luz leads a covert advocacy organization, The Network, and is a guerrilla fighter known popularly as Shé (pronounced, not coincidentally, "she"). Sartana is a by-the-book enforcement agent tasked with arresting violators of US immigration law, before she comes to side with ex-Mexican Federale turned-protector of immigrants Machete (Danny Trejo) and with The Network.

To illuminate the significance of these films and of their protagonists, I engage in in-depth textual analyses of the two *Miss Bala* films and *Machete*, with particular attention to how their Latina protagonists contend with dangers and other challenges. My examination of these films' treatment of Latina/o precarity and empowerment also takes into consideration Hollywood industry culture and employment practices that have resulted in few Latina and Latino writers and directors working within the action genre.

Latina Action and Questions of Power, On- and Off-Screen

A poster and trailer for a film that was never made illustrates how Latina action heroines often embody a Hollywood-sanctioned version of Latina beauty intertwined with aggression and devoid of connection to Latina realities. "What Would You Xanadu?" is the tag line on a striking, sepia-toned film poster for the purported 2011 film *Citizen Jane*. Featuring a young Michelle Rodriguez in black pants and tank top, "Jane" holds a smoking bazooka and looks focused on her target. In chiaroscuro light and shadow, she looks angelic, gorgeous—and deadly. The tag line is not explained. The poster includes a link to a film trailer, now found only on YouTube, which features Rodriguez in the same outfit, on a large rock surrounded by hot lava, yelling in anger while decimating who-knows-what with a steady barrage of bullets. Finally satisfied, she turns to the camera and says quietly, "That's right, bitches." In other words, the footage of Rodriguez depicts a moment of nonsensical (but for action film nerds, joyful) action iconicity. Cult film news outlets breathlessly announced the new film after the poster appeared at Fantastic Fest on September 29, 2011. A *Citizen Jane* film did not actually exist; the footage instead appears in *Blacktino* (Aaron Burns, 2011), as a film watched by its mixed-race, teen "nerd" protagonist. That Charlotte Foster Jane (Rodriguez) is fighting to save her "Rosebud" is all that is ever revealed. The action film lovers who announced the film did not appear to need to know more about the character other than that she was beautiful and—given that she was played by Rodriguez—surely tough and indefatigable, too. This faux film and its reception raise the question of whether the fierce, and otherwise undeveloped Latina character with no connection to a cultural community has become a limitation or a trap—a stereotype expected of Rodriguez and other Latinas in Hollywood films. As Charles Ramírez Berg (2002) explains in his explication of the narrative function of stereotypical Latina and Latino characters in film, such roles are underdeveloped so that others can shine more brightly.

Similarly, with the power of film narratives to confer status and respect in mind, it is informative to look at the role played by US film production culture in supporting the evolution, and often, devolution of Latina protagonists. As noted earlier, most Latina action characters of recent years are not fully developed protagonists. This can be traced in part to who gets to conceive of the action films that reach global audiences. In this regard, among the almost exclusively white and male writers and directors of US action films, Robert Rodriguez, who is Mexican American, is an anomaly. He has included Latina lead roles in his story worlds throughout his career, in films such as *El Mariachi* (1992), *Spy Kids* (2001), and the more recent *Machete* and *Machete Kills*.[3] He has consistently featured Latina characters as worthy protagonists for whom audiences should cheer. On the other hand, these heroines often serve male-dominated narratives. The only other non-white male directors to include Latina protagonists in 2010s action films are Justin Lin, of Taiwanese American descent, director of many of the *Fast* films, and Catherine Hardwicke, the white female director of *Miss Bala*. We are still waiting to meet the formidable action women and girls who will be the brainchildren of future Latina writers and filmmakers.

Robert Rodriguez's *macha* Latinas raise questions of intent, character development, and impact. Strong Latinas have become trademarks of his films, alongside exploitation elements such as over-the-top, comedic violence and female characters in fetishized, sexy attire. Many of these characters at first glance could be mistaken for the *bandidas* and harlots of classical Hollywood Westerns and crime dramas, character types that Charles Ramírez Berg (2002) has detailed. On a deeper examination, Tasker's (1998) and Purse's (2011b) descriptions of "postfeminist" action heroines are apropos. The most extreme of these *bandida* characters are unscrupulous villains, among them Madame Desdemona (Colombian actress Sofia Vergara), who wears an outlandish bodice gun that shoots as if from her nipples, and Blanca Vasquez (non-Latina Amber Heard), a double-crossing agent, both in *Machete Kills*.[4] While most of his Latina protagonists are effective leaders with strong hearts and integrity, at times they are mere props to male heroes and fantasy. These trends are relevant to my examination of Luz and Sartana in *Machete*, below.

To begin, I study the US remake of *Miss Bala*, with focus in particular on its treatment of Mexican women and their restricted options and protections in regions where criminal gangs have gained control. A comparison with the more nuanced and somber original film reveals the consequence of the adaptation's reliance on Hollywood action conventions.

Latina Survival, Hollywood-Style: *Miss Bala* (2019)

Centered around one woman's story of survival after her abduction, Catherine Hardwicke's *Miss Bala* initially appears grounded in everyday realities. Like the original film, it relates a fictionalized version of what happened to Laura Zuñiga, a model and the Nuestra Belleza Sinaloa pageant winner, in 2008. When the beauty pageant winner, whose boyfriend was a member of the Juárez cartel, was arrested with several cartel members that year, she told journalists that she had been abducted and forced to take part in the group's crimes. Her story was a national and global sensation that prompted other news stories of beauty queens and other women abducted by cartels. As Elena Nicolaou (2019) comments, citing an interview that Gerardo Naranjo gave to *Indiewire,* he and his

Figure 8.1 Laura (Stephanie Sigman) realizes the hopelessness of her situation after her abduction by Lino (Noé Hernández), the leader of the Estrellas cartel, in the original *Miss Bala*, directed by Gerardo Naranjo (© 20th Century Fox, 2011. All Rights Reserved). Courtesy of Moviestore Collection Ltd./Alamy.

production team focused on the news media's retelling of the story after they interviewed Zuñiga and found her inconsistent; the truth of her experience was never clear. The original *Miss Bala* thus may also be largely fictional.

In the 2011 film, Mexican actress Stephanie Sigman, a pretty and light tan brunette, plays unlucky pageant contestant Laura Guerrero, who joins the pageant with a friend (Figure 8.1). We see her decrepit home and neighborhood in Tijuana; it is clear the pageant represents an escape from poverty. What transpires is instead a frightening ordeal. Quietly gripping, the film feels like a documentary in its focus on Laura's survival. She is abducted and held by a cartel. To stay alive she endures being groped by the group's leader, Lino, and later having sex with him. She is coerced into taking money taped to her body across the border and drawing out a Drug Enforcement Agency (DEA) agent who has infiltrated the group. He is murdered at Lino's order. Laura's desperation is palpable. She never registers as an action heroine: she never holds a gun and scarcely speaks. On the other hand, she is careful to survive. Pushed to rejoin the pageant, she becomes the de facto winner because the cartel has bribed the judges. Looking wan in a light peach evening gown that she lacks the curves to completely fill, she accepts the crown and flowers with zombie-like quietude in front of an excited audience, knowing the gang members' guns are never far away. Later clothed in an inelegant white minidress, she is expected to sleep with a corrupt general at the pageant after-party so that the cartel can take this moment to kill him. Instead, she tips off the general, leading to a massive gun battle between the cartel and law enforcement. Even so, Laura is later arrested and convicted for taking part in the gang's activities. She is anticlimactically freed by guards apparently paid off by the cartel, pushed out of a transport van onto a random city street. The camera pans to show her view of trash, graffiti, and people going about their days in the distance. Laura's reputation ruined and presumably her life's options with it, she begins to walk into an unknown future.

The narrative underscores the intense challenges that ordinary people face today in cities like Tijuana, where crushing poverty and criminal control have eradicated many legal opportunities. One scene drives this home early in the narrative, as Laura and her friend Suzu (Lakshmi Picazo) wait in line to audition for the pageant. The camera lingers on the long line of women vying to be contestants. The young women are of every possible appearance and body type, some dressed and groomed in middle-class fashion, others in clothes and shoes that signal a lack of financial means. An air of desperation permeates the scene; winning a beauty pageant clearly is one of the only ways a young woman without means could provide a better life for her family. But that kind of opportunity and visibility brings potential vulnerability. The film highlights the dynamic by which cartel leaders and corrupt law and military officers consider local beauty queens their spoils. Beginning with few options, after her abduction Laura can only hope, at best, to survive and protect her father and younger brother.

The US remake of *Miss Bala* revises the narrative in several striking ways. Laura is now Gloria, and is Mexican American rather than Mexican, a decision that creates a remove from the realities of Mexican citizens depicted in the narrative. Gloria is also more independent than Laura; she is an orphan and childless. A makeup artist living in Southern California who grew up in part in Tijuana, she returns to help her friend Suzu (Cristina Rodio), who is competing in the Miss Baja pageant. She hopes to protect Suzu and Suzu's younger brother. When members of Los Estrellas turn up at the nightclub where Gloria, Suzu, and other pageant contestants are dancing, a major shoot-out between the cartel and DEA officers ensues. Gloria and Suzu are separated. As in the original film, Gloria is abducted by the cartel when a police officer that she approaches for help instead hands her over to them. Her passport and phone taken, her privileges as a US citizen temporarily beyond reach, Gloria becomes as vulnerable as Laura in the original film.

That Gloria is played by Gina Rodriguez, a star from the US romantic comedy series *Jane the Virgin* (2014–2019, The CW), with presumably both adult and child fans, likely prompted additional changes.[5] Rodriguez's Gloria appears in beautiful but subtle makeup, in well-fitting and flattering apparel, and is well lit throughout her time as an abductee. The entire cast, both in Tijuana and the rural areas outside the city, oddly speak English. More importantly, the dangers associated with Gloria's abduction are depicted as abstract and minimal, even while individuals that she encounters are killed by the cartel at Lino's order. Her time in captivity with the cartel is spent at their inexplicably luxurious safe house, with huge walls of windows overlooking the remote and hilly countryside. Dangerous but handsome, Lino also surprisingly does not rape Gloria. There are hints that he might have a heart beneath his intimidating cartel persona and romantic feelings toward her. Indeed, he risks his life and is shot while rescuing her from a later gunfight.

Nonetheless, the narrative focuses on Gloria's dire situation as a captive. She initially attempts to flee but is thwarted. She is forced to partake in criminal activities such as a bombing that kills several DEA agents, with Lino's promise to help her find Suzu her only consolation. Soon Gloria is covertly pulled aside by an American DEA agent and also forced to spy on the cartel. To her chagrin, she is provided next to nothing in the way of protection after doing so. Her expendability in the DEA's eyes, of all of the details in the narrative, realistically hints at the insecure status of Mexican citizens in narco-controlled regions. Gloria later witnesses the shooting of a woman who has been kept and routinely forced to have sex with members of the group, when she is suspected of what Gloria is actually doing—spying on the cartel.

As was the case in the original film, Gloria is forced to participate in the Miss Baja pageant and named the winner because of the cartel's pressure on the organizers. In the final, climactic scene, at a party at one of the police chief's properties, Gloria shows her mettle. Lino has insisted that she lure Chief Saucedo into his bedroom; Lino wants a good shot at the man. Saucedo's stylish compound is off the beach, with plenty of room for partygoers and privacy for those who want it. Gloria is surprised to learn that Suzu is there; Lino had sold her into prostitution. Realizing she has been lied to, Gloria gives Saucedo a note warning him of Lino's plan, and Saucedo devises a trap for Lino. As bullets fly and many of Lino's men and Saucedo's officers are gunned down, Gloria makes her escape after taking an automatic rifle from a dying man (Figure 8.2). She is clear eyed and resolute. Gunshots ring out, and parts of the compound are on fire. Gloria makes her way through smoke in the large main house, and finally locates Suzu.

The two women rush outside, where cars are parked, but find themselves in the midst of a shoot-out between the police and Estrellas members. In the confusion, Saucedo manages to grab Suzu. Gloria shoots him in the leg to save her friend. Lino emerges from the shadows. "You've got to finish the job, Chula," he says, shooting Saucedo a few more times. Instead she raises her gun and points it directly at Lino; an extreme close-up frames her face behind the barrel

Figure 8.2 Gloria (Gina Rodriguez) looks both classy and deadly as she prepares to shoot her way out of captivity in Catherine Hardwicke's *Miss Bala* (© Sony Pictures Releasing, 2019. All Rights Reserved). Courtesy of Alamy.

of the rifle. Lino tries to defend what he did to Suzu; Gloria is not won over. "Both eyes open," she responds, repeating what Lino said while teaching her how to shoot while she was in captivity. She fires three times, killing him. Police arrive as Gloria and Suzu are making their way to leave. The camera captures them in a long shot, their hands up, Gloria in her long evening gown and Suzu in a sparkly minidress, dead bodies all around them. They are survivors. While Suzu returns to her family, Gloria returns to the US with a possible job with the CIA on the horizon.

Comparisons to the original *Miss Bala* and the real-life scenario on which the films were based are revelatory with respect to how recent action narratives can sanitize real life. Ultimately, the 2019 *Miss Bala* relies on Hollywood action conventions that privilege fantasy and sensationalism and position US law enforcement as honest and effective and Mexican forces as corrupt beyond hope. In the 2011 *Miss Bala*, Laura quietly endures her difficult situation, which prevents her death and that of her father and brother at the hands of the cartel. Considering the violence and killings enacted by armed gangs in Mexico, Laura's tactics are shrewd.[6] In the 2019 adaptation, in contrast, Gloria is never forced to engage in sex, and the man in charge of her destiny, the gang's leader, is softened into a potential romantic figure. The risks and ramifications of directly fighting armed cartel members and corrupt police officers also are not fully acknowledged. When Gloria picks up a weapon and makes her way to Suzu and out of Saucedo's home, the production elements of the scene, including the camera work, lighting, and sound mix, only heighten our sense of her efficacy. Gloria is cool, collected, and deadly when she needs to be, in other words, a Hollywood action heroine. While she is a capable Latina heroine, she is a flimsy stand-in for the Mexican women who are exploited and discarded with no safety net in these scenarios in real life.

Finally, the 2019 *Miss Bala* supports US fantasies about US innocence and distance from the global drug trade. Mexican law enforcement's complicity with the cartel is emphasized, while the US DEA and CIA are shown thwarting drug cartel activities and killings. When Gloria returns to the US unscathed, to a presumably well-paying job and to the possibility of another life, a kind of adventure tourism has been substituted for Laura Zuñiga and other Mexican women's traumatic and life-threatening experiences.

Fantasy Heroines and Real Battles at the Border: *Machete*

In contrast to the *Miss Bala* films, which purport to a stylized realism, Rodriguez and Maniquis's *Machete* presents fetishized, comic book-style Latina heroines. The film's generic trappings bring both progressive activist and retrograde heterosexual male fantasy perspectives to the action film. The details of the narrative include a corrupt senator (Robert De Niro), an evil, white Mexican drug lord, and multiple arsenals of weapons. But these are not as important as Machete's fight, with Luz and Sartana's support, to protect undocumented immigrants and the film's broader plea for integrity and compassion versus corruption and xenophobia. Meanwhile, as Russell Meeuf notes, the actions of Senator McLaughlin and his compatriot, Von Jackson (Don Johnson), the racist leader of a group of violent anti-immigrant vigilantes, showcase the dangerous excesses of "hyperwhiteness."[7] Throughout, *Machete* critiques hyperwhite rhetoric and violence through comedy and satire.

Of *Machete*'s two heroines, Luz is the greater renegade from the onset. Tough and kind-hearted, she sells food to Latino day laborers from a taco truck in an unnamed Texas border city. "I just make tacos, and I sell them to the workers of the world. It fills their bellies with something other than hate," she says sardonically to Sartana, when asked whether she is doing something illegal. Her day job is in fact a cover for her role as the leader of The Network, which helps undocumented immigrants get jobs and seeks justice for those who died or were killed crossing the border. As mentioned earlier, Luz is also a revolutionary leader. Her name, Shé, clearly is meant to call to mind the legendary Che Guevara, the Argentine revolutionary leader whose image is often used to symbolize rebellion, while the name also calls to mind the impact of strong women everywhere. As Shé, she famously fought for justice and inspired others in her Central or South American home country, although she never admits this even to Machete.[8] When he notices newspaper clippings and photos featuring Shé and other women and girls in various rebellions and strikes in Luz's humble but cozy home, she claims that Shé is just a symbol that she made up. "Shé brings hope. Shé rights the wrongs," she tells him. Machete does not press her, responding only that the people need hope.

Meanwhile, Von Jackson's thugs target The Network and the immigrants they have helped, wanting to destroy both. It becomes known over time that Jackson has forged a partnership with Senator McLaughlin and the Mexican drug lord, Rogelio Torrez (Steven Seagal), who earlier murdered Machete's wife. Shot in the eye and left for dead by Jackson, Luz surprises everyone when she returns as Shé the next day to carry on in the struggle. In *Machete*'s final battle scene, Shé, now wearing an eye patch, black leather bra, and black gunfighter pants, a bandolier around one leg, is an impressive and effective combatant (Figure 8.3). While her character is not developed beyond these broad strokes, she is shown to be a community organizer and leader, a far cry from the classic Western's *cantineras* (saloon waitresses) or the harlots of early urban crime dramas. They were all guts and nothing more.

Jessica Alba's Sartana, in contrast to Luz, initially is not an activist nor (we are meant to think at first) a fighter. Although presumably Mexican American, she

Figure 8.3 Luz (Michelle Rodriguez), as her alter-ego Shé, fights for the just treatment of immigrants in *Machete* (© 20th Century Fox and Sony Pictures Releasing, 2010. All Rights Reserved).

cares more about immigration law and fulfilling the expectations of her job than about the injustices that have led individuals to risk their lives to cross the border illegally. Shown proof by Luz, in the form of photographs and other evidence collected by The Network, that immigrants are being killed indiscriminately by Jackson's men while attempting to reach the United States, she quickly changes sides.

Despite her slight build and the high-heeled shoes that she wears more often than not, Sartana proves to be a proficient fighter. When men in *luchador* (Mexican *lucha libre* wrestler) and other leather masks come to her house to kill her and Machete, she, like Machete, handily defends herself. To an exciting rock music soundtrack with a driving guitar riff, she manages to locate and use ordinary household objects and finally her own stiletto heels as weapons. She, like Machete, is skilled in hand-to-hand combat, knocking out one man with her elbow and kicking a knife out of the hand of another. She finally vanquishes a man in a *luchador* mask by felling him with a heel through the eye. Even though her character, like Luz, is minimally developed and primarily serves Machete's story, she too demonstrates that Latinas can fight, and that they will staunchly follow their moral compass when they learn of injustice.

Nonetheless, in line with exploitation film conventions, both women sleep with Machete when alone with him, despite his age, rough visage, and full set of prison tattoos.[9] Perhaps in keeping with a desire to present Luz and Sartana as feminist characters, the women initiate the encounters; sex occurs on their terms. Luz is not ultimately interested in a long-term relationship, but the romantically inclined Sartana has fallen for Machete. In both cases the vast age difference between the characters, or at least the actors who depict them—Trejo was 66, Rodriguez 32, and Alba 29 when *Machete* was released—is glossed over. As Meeuf remarks, Machete's allure is linked to nostalgia "for an uncomplicated, violent manhood of the past" (2017: 119). In other words, aging male heroes improbably bed younger women in this fantasy world, as was the case in earlier exploitation films.

It is Luz, or rather Shé, who fights alongside Machete in the final battle against Jackson's thugs and Torrez's minions. Not coincidentally, Shé and Machete are joined in this fight by dozens of marginalized, too-often-unseen Latina and Latino laborers who presumably had been helped by The Network: domestic workers, restaurant staff, nurses (in minidresses; this is still exploitation), urban *cholos* (young men in urban garb associated with gangs), and gardeners. In keeping with their jobs, they wield machetes, guns, shovels, mallets, a toilet plunger, a frying pan, a pickaxe, even a notepad and pen as weapons. Machete, no surprise, wields a huge machete; he uses it to slice, jab, and topple immigrant-hating enemies. As throughout every action sequence in this film, the violence is over-the-top, often comedic, and ultra gory (but not realistically bloody), accompanied by loud, gratuitous sound effects and vibrant nondiegetic rock music. Shé joins the battle, stepping out of an emergency medical vehicle that had transported the nurses. The camera takes in her black eye patch, taut body, and black leather bra. She is fierce. "How's the eye?" is heard coming from the crowd. "What eye?" she responds with a snarl. Seeing that Machete has been surrounded by Jackson's men, Shé calmly and slowly holds up an automatic machine gun and fires. Bullets tear through The Network's opponents. Some are killed, the rest scatter. Later in the battle she demonstrates her proficiency with firearms, shooting pistols with both hands, then one holstered to her leg, and finally a much larger and more lethal double-barreled gun. Compared to the chaos around her, she is poised, deliberate, efficient.

Sartana, for her part, is kept out of the melee, having been abducted by Torrez. He later frees her, presumably so she can watch him kill Machete, whom he has trapped without a weapon. All of the fighting stops; it appears Machete has no hope of survival. But Sartana knows better. "He's Machete," she says matter-of-factly to Luz. And Machete in fact manages instead to impale Torrez with his machete. "Good point," Luz responds. Torrez dies, and the struggle is over. Machete climbs on top of a car, and holds his machete high. The men with machetes and other tools do the same, as do the women and the diverse young people led by Luz's lieutenants of The Network; the entire group shouts in victory. Luz and Sartana stand on cars, Luz in her combat boots and Sartana in her high heels. They hold their arms high in solidarity with Machete and the rest of the group. Together they have defeated the bigoted thugs who aimed to keep them powerless and afraid. Despite the fantastical and farcical elements of the battle, their triumph calls to mind the all-too-real struggles of immigrant workers and asylum seekers off screen, in 2010 and since. Their humble weapons are reminders that Latina/os in various situations, whether gardeners with machetes or screenwriters with notepads, are able to resist with what they have on hand, especially when they unite. Rodriguez and Maniquis's film salutes the stamina and smarts of Latina/o laborers and citizens, "with papers" and without.

Conclusions

As embodied by Gloria, Luz, and Sartana, Latina action heroines of the 2010s are survivors who remain unfazed by past traumas and intense present-day challenges. These capable heroines' victories are especially appealing in recent years, as destructive forces and corruption seemingly run rampant in global contexts, particularly in Central and South America and at the US–Mexico border.

While the two films draw on news reports and mythology about hyperwhite vigilantism and the global drug trade, Hollywood production elements add tension and excitement. The physical capabilities and bravery of Shé, Sartana, and Gloria are accentuated for instance through expensive camera work, lighting, and editing, and the work of talented stunt people.[10] While both films' budgets are minute in comparison to that of a tentpole action film such as *No Time to Die* (Cary Joji Fukunaga, 2021), with its staggering $250 million budget, they likely are massive compared to that of the 2011 *Miss Bala*, with an unknown budget but which garnered only $1.5 million in worldwide box office.

While the original *Miss Bala* is the most realistic of the three films—Laura does not wield a weapon, and her future is uncertain at the narrative's end—it should be noted that she too survives, in keeping with action cinema tradition. The casting of Stephanie Sigman, a lithe, light-skinned actress, repeats another pattern of Mexican and US film. Shifts are on the horizon, however. Some other recent Latina protagonists possess greater nuance and character development than those in the films examined here. Examples include Gina Rodriguez's role in *Deepwater Horizon* as Andrea Fleytas, a warm and stalwart computer expert whose bravery is put to the test when the oil rig where she works blows out, and Isabela Merced as the sweet, dorky, and capable teenaged Dora in the children's action caper *Dora and the Lost City of Gold* (James Bobin, 2019). Their characters experience moments of doubt as well as moments of delight, and their relationships are depicted with dramatic and comedic nuance.

The creators of these films are key to whether they repeat or challenge patterns that have marginalized Latinas and that efface or reveal the complicated web of global politics that undergirds levels of violence experienced in various regions of the world. The lack of Latina creators of action narratives ultimately dims Latina voices within the genre. The 2019 *Miss Bala* was directed by Catherine Hardwicke, a white woman, but the film does not escape Hollywood tradition, particularly regarding how Latinas are depicted. That *Machete* was directed by Robert Rodriguez and Ethan Maniquis and written by Rodriguez and his cousin Álvaro Rodriguez, both Latinos, as an exploitation send-up, was not enough to sidestep the film's centering of nostalgic, macho, heterosexual fantasies.

The fantastical aspects of Luz, Sartana, and Gloria's roles also do not fully save them from the double-edged nature of stereotypes. As noted earlier, a faultline runs from these gun-wielding roles back to US stereotypes of Latinas as naturally criminal and aggressive. Perhaps unsurprisingly, then, when Michelle Rodriguez agreed to reprise her role as Letty, a bold and capable car racer, criminal, and now mother, in *F9* (Justin Lin, 2021), a recent film in the *Fast* franchise, she insisted that at least one female writer be added to the creative team to better develop her role and those of the other female characters. Having the star power to make such a demand is rare among female and particularly Latina performers, however, and underscores what is too often missing in current action narratives, namely Latina perspectives, realities, and dreams.

Notes

1   In English, this translates to "Miss Bullet."

2   As armed gangs have affiliated with international crime syndicates and systems of law enforcement have failed to protect communities, women, men, and children face a loss of livelihood, potential violence, kidnapping, and other dangers with few or no resources. Individuals who choose to flee meet dangers as well on their journey, as well as uncertain job prospects and possible deportation at the journey's end.

3   Robert Rodriguez's centering of powerful female film protagonists began with *Bedhead* (1991), a film short starring his sister (Rebecca Rodriguez) as Rebecca, a girl who discovers she has magical powers and uses them to school her unruly and obnoxious brother.

4   *Machete Kills*'s focus on these anti-heroines rather than on Sartana and Luz resulted in the film's elimination as a case study in this research.

5   *Jane the Virgin* is an adaptation of the popular Venezuelan telenovela *Juana La Virgen* (2002).

6   Cartels and armed criminal gangs, estimated in 2021 to control 20 percent of Mexico, have engaged in countless kidnappings and over 35,000 murders annually in recent years, including the killings and disappearances of journalists, politicians, and law enforcement officers (Sheridan 2020).

7   As Russell Meeuf (2017) notes, the term "hyperwhiteness" was coined by Gretchen Bakke to describe the depiction of evil white excess in relation to greed, corruption, and villainy.

8   Luz's home country is never specified, likely to keep the narrative at arm's reach from reality and to broaden audience appeal.

9   The tattoos are Danny Trejo's own, acquired in and out of prison, before he became an actor.

10   The female stunt workers who performed in *Machete,* presumably doubling for Michelle Rodriguez and Jessica Alba in action scenes, included Desireé Avalos and Cheryl Wheeler Duncan. Gina Rodriguez's stunt double in *Miss Bala* was Ellette Craddock. Mónica López also performed as part of the film's 12-person stunt crew. As Lauren Steimer illuminates in this volume, the work of stunt doubles too often goes unnoticed by viewers, even while their physical labor contributes significantly to the dramatic and emotional pleasure of action narratives.

Works Cited

Aldama, Frederick Luis (2009), *Your Brain on Latino Comics*, Austin: University of Texas Press.

Beltrán, Mary (2004), "Más Macha: The New Latina Action Hero," in Yvonne Tasker (ed.), *Action and Adventure Cinema*, 186–200, London: Routledge.

Beltrán, Mary (2009), *Latina/o Stars in U.S. Eyes: The Making and Meanings of Film and TV Stardom*, Champaign: University of Illinois Press.

Berg, Charles Ramírez (2002), *Latino Images in Film: Stereotype, Subversion, and Resistance*, Austin: University of Texas Press.

Brayton, Sean (2011), "Razing Arizona: Migrant Labour and the 'Mexican Avenger' of *Machete*," *International Journal of Media and Politics*, 7 (3): 275–92.

Brooks, Brad (2019), "Victims of Anti-Latino Hate Crimes Soar: FBI Report," *Reuters* (12 November), Available online: https://www.reuters.com/article/us-hatecrimes-report/victims-of-anti-latino-hate-crimes-soar-in-u-s-fbi-report-idUSKBN1XM2OQ (accessed 14 August, 2020).

Citizen Jane trailer (2011), FilmIsNow Movie Trailers, *YouTube*. Available online: https://www.youtube.com/watch?v=jH16B29Hv4U (accessed 24 April 2021).

Cortés, Carlos E. (1997), "Chicanas in Film: History of an Image," in Clara E. Rodríguez (ed.), *Latin Looks: Images of Latinas and Latinos in the U.S. Media*, 121–41, New York: Routledge.

Fojas, Camilla (2016), "Latino Film in the End Times," in Frederick Luis Aldama (ed.), *The Routledge Companion to Latina/o Popular Culture*, 34–42, New York: Routledge.

Meeuf, Russell (2017), *Rebellious Bodies: Stardom, Citizenship, and the New Body Politics*, Austin: University of Texas Press.

Nicolaou, Elena (2019), "*Miss Bala* is Inspired by the Long History of Mexican Pageant Queens and Drug Lords," *Refinery 29* (29 January), Available online: https://www.refinery29.com/en-us/2019/01/222904/miss-bala-true-story-real-person-laura-elena-zuniga (accessed 13 May 2021).

Purse, Lisa (2011a), *Contemporary Action Cinema*, Edinburgh: Edinburgh University Press.

Purse, Lisa (2011b), "Return of the 'Angry Woman': Authenticating Female Physical Action in Contemporary Cinema," in Melanie Waters (ed.), *Women on Screen: Feminism and Femininity in Visual Culture*, 185–98, Basingstoke: Palgrave Macmillan.

Rodriguez, Clara E. (1997), "Introduction," in Clara E. Rodriguez (ed.), *Latin Looks: Images of Latinas and Latinos in the U.S. Media*, 1–12, New York: Routledge.

Sheridan, Mary Beth (2020), "Losing Control: Violent Criminal Groups are Claiming More Territory, *The Washington Post* (29 October), Available online: https://www.washingtonpost.com/graphics/2020/world/mexico-losing-control/mexico-violence-drug-cartels-zacatecas/ (accessed 30 October 2021).

Smith, Stacy, Marc Choueti, and Katherine Pieper (2020), *Inequality in 1,300 Popular Films: Examining Portrayals of Gender, Race/Ethnicity, LGBTQ and Disability from 2007 to 2019*, Los Angeles: USC Annenberg Inclusion Initiative.

Tasker, Yvonne (1998), *Working Girls: Gender and Sexuality in Popular Cinema*, London: Routledge.

Chapter 9

Bollywood's New Action Cinema: The Woman-led Action Film and the Nation

Krupa Shandilya

The action film has long been a staple of Bollywood cinema. First popularized in the 1970s with Angry Young Man films such as *Zanjeer* (*Shackles*, Prakash Mehra, 1973) and *Deewaar* (*The Wall*, Yash Chopra, 1975), these films usually featured a working-class male protagonist who used violence to redress class injustices (Rai 2006; Sinha 2013).[1] While the Angry Young Man film marked the onset of action as a distinct cycle in Bollywood, action sequences—battles with swords and javelins, gun fights, fistfights—were part and parcel of Bollywood cinema from its very inception. Drawing on two films, this essay will examine a more recent iteration of this mode, in which women figure as action protagonists. As Lalitha Gopalan (2002) argues, Bollywood cinema's appeal to audiences of different social and economic classes necessarily entails an intermixing of different genre elements, thus earning the nickname of the *masala* (spice) film. Thus, the films that I discuss here prominently feature action but equally important are romance, historical saga, and thriller elements, exemplifying the generic intermixing characteristic of Bollywood cinema. The action sequences are, however, central to the plots and key to explicating their ideological tenor—whether a rejection of state institutions, a fight against patriarchy, or an embrace of secessionist nationalisms.

Since the 1970s, action has evolved into distinct cycles, which can be understood as responding to political moments. In the 1980s and 1990s, a new cycle became popular, the Avenging Woman film, which focused on a female protagonist seeking justice for a rape victim through violence. Like the Angry Young Man film before it, the Avenging Woman film reflects on "the class—and gender—inflected social crises" of the time (Dayal 2015: 68). While the former reflected the urban Indian working class's frustration with corruption in business and government, the latter represented anger at the patriarchal structures of society and was fueled by the burgeoning Indian feminist movement of the period. Both cycles were premised on the failure of state and legal institutions to address systemic inequality, and both foregrounded the hero/heroine's ability to take the law into his/her own hands to fight injustice.

The liberalization of the Indian economy in the 1990s and the increasing power of the urban middle classes were registered in the 2000s as a populist transformation of the 1970s Angry Young Man films. In this new manifestation, settings typically shift from urban centers to small-town India with feudalism serving as a sort of shorthand for capitalist exploitation. Although in action films such as *Dabangg* (*Fearless*, Abhinav Kashyap, 2010) and *Singham* (Rohit Shetty, 2011) the hero fights for the poor and the working class of small-town India, the fight sequences are inflected with humor, self-consciously mocking the genre conventions of the earlier films. Arguably, this new populist cycle works to shore up the very systems it sets out to critique, such as patriarchal feudalism and police corruption, thus reflecting the contradictions inherent in pushing for the rights of the oppressed without disturbing the status quo.

The Avenging Woman film too has morphed in this period, but in a more progressive vein, re-inscribing familiar action tropes to reflect the gains of the feminist movement, the increased presence of women in the workforce, and their active participation in the political sphere in the 2000s. Thus, the heroine of these new films is, as Benazir Manzar and Aju Aravind argue, "strong enough to resist and negate . . . patriarchal influences," openly "confront[ing] the social conditions that confine women in the name of family, marriage and domestic households" (2019: 3). For Sukanya Gupta, this figure is less a victim and more "an agent of her fate" (2015: 108). We see this new feminist figure in films like *Kahaani* (*Story*, Sujoy Ghosh, 2012) and *Gulaab Gang* (*The Pink Gang*, Soumik Sen, 2014). In both, women commit violent acts that shatter the patriarchal status quo. This was concomitant with the rise of another woman-centric action cycle, namely the woman-led "terrorist film" (Kabir 2010).

The Indian terrorist film was a reaction to the growing power of Hindu nationalism, much as the new and old Angry Young Man and Avenging Woman cycles evolved in reaction to different political crises in the nation, in the 1990s and 2000s. Reflecting the political situation of the mid-1990s, when Kashmir with its majority Muslim population became the flashpoint for tensions between India and Pakistan, these films are focused on the figure of the Muslim terrorist in Kashmir. This cycle of terrorist films "recod[ed] [Kashmir] in terms of the discourse of Islamicization" (Devdas 2013: 225) and popularized the stereotypical characterization of the Kashmiri Muslim male as a terrorist who is vanquished by the good Indian (read: Hindu) male.[2]

Typically, in these films, a Kashmiri Muslim terrorist initiates acts of violence (bombing, kidnapping, gunfire), is intercepted by the Hindu Indian male hero, and is ultimately vanquished. For example, in Mani Ratnam's *Roja* (*The Rose*, 1992), Rishi, an Indian computer scientist, is kidnapped by Wasim Khan, a Kashmiri Muslim terrorist, and eventually vanquishes the terrorist by appealing to his humanity. Rishi's intervention saves the Indian nation from an overpowering Muslim threat, exemplified in an iconic scene, where Rishi throws his body onto a burning Indian flag, thus literally showing his willingness to sacrifice himself for the nation.

The late 1990s also saw the emergence of the woman-led terrorist film, which melded together the conventions of the terrorist film and the Avenging Woman films to show women picking up arms to defend an alternative vision of the nation. Significantly, unlike the Kashmiri terrorist films, in which the Hindu nation is saved by the valor of a Hindu man, in these films, a woman picks up arms to defend a secessionist movement—whether for an independent Northeastern state in India in *Dil Se* (*From the Heart*, Mani Ratnam, 1998) or for the Tamil Elam in Sri Lanka in *Theeviravaathi* (*The Terrorist*, Santosh Sivan, 1998). These female protagonists, doubly estranged from the nation through their gender and their affiliation to a secessionist movement, usually meet their deaths at the end of the film, suggesting the tensions inherent between women's agency and the nationalist project.

Women-led Action Cinema Since 2010

My essay focuses on the intersection of gender and nationalism and its implication for women's agency. I have chosen two recent women-led films that bring together the Avenging Woman film and the woman-led terrorist film in distinct ways, namely *Raazi* (Meghna Gulzar, 2018) and *Bajirao Mastani* (Sanjay Leela Bhansali, 2015). Although these films draw on historical fictional texts,[3] and are set in disparate time periods (*Raazi* in the 1970s during the Third Indo-Pakistan war in East Pakistan [now Bangladesh], and *Bajirao Mastani* in the 1700s), I read them as a reaction to the current political moment, much as *Dil Se* and *The Terrorist* are reactions to the political upheaval of the 1990s. Significantly, unlike previous women-led terrorist films, the woman protagonists of these films are Muslim, thus drawing attention to the tensions between Hindu right-wing ideology, gender, religion, and nationalism. By comparing them to each other we see how each film's action sequences index its ideological tenor and its gender politics; in other words, how its woman action figure's violence is a symbolic reaction that either reinforces or deconstructs Hindu nationalism.

Bajirao Mastani deploys its female protagonist to consolidate Hindu nationalism's use of hypermasculine violence to secure the nation. In contrast, the woman-directed action film, *Raazi*, questions warfare in the service of the nation, and presents an alternative, Gandhian,[4] and feminist vision of the nation, premised on the "de-masculinisation of the public sphere" (Nandy 2007: 175). Additionally, *Raazi* embraces Muslim femininity as a source of power and moral strength. Through the actions of their lead characters, both films depart from the Bollywood woman-led action film's usual distance from mainstream nationalism. While terrorist films and Avenging Woman films celebrate women's violence as a necessary antidote to state terror or state corruption, respectively, they do not reflect on nationalism as an ideology. In contrast, the two films I examine either critique the patriarchal ideology of Hindu nationalism (*Raazi*) or endorse it (*Bajirao Mastani*) by depicting Muslim women as warriors.

Bajirao Mastani is a love story set in the context of the Maratha kingdom and the Mughal empire of the eighteenth century. The film recreates the war as a fight between the Hindu Marathas and the Muslim Mughals and complicates it by introducing a largely fictional love story between the Hindu king Bajirao Peshwa (Ranveer Singh) and the Muslim Mastani (Deepika Padukone), the illegitimate daughter of the Hindu king of Bundelkhand, Maharaja Chhatrasal (Benjamin Gilani). Mastani, a warrior princess, enlists Bajirao to help her fight against the Muslims who have attacked Bundelkhand. When he saves her life on the battlefield, she falls in love with him. She follows him to his home and is rejected by Bajirao's mother (Tanvi Azmi), wife (Priyanka Chopra), and the Hindu ministers. Bajirao nevertheless accepts her as a second wife and establishes her in a lavish separate home. His family makes several attempts to get rid of Mastani, but all fail because Mastani is a warrior and fights back both tactically and physically. When Bajirao leaves for battle against the Muslim ruler Nasir Jung (Kaartik Ahuja), however, Bajirao's mother imprisons Mastani. The film ends with Bajirao's death on the battlefield and Mastani's death in prison. A final title card celebrates the lovers who could not be united in life but are united in death, a common trope in several South Asian folk love stories and the films derived from them.

Raazi tells the story of a Kashmiri Muslim woman, Sehmat (Alia Bhatt), who is manipulated by her father into becoming a spy for India by marrying into a Pakistani military family. Sehmat spies on this family to gain military secrets that will help India win the war: her husband Iqbal (Vicky Kaushal), father-in-law (Shishir Sharma), and brother-in-law (Ashwath Bhatt) are all high-ranking Pakistani military officers. When the family begins to suspect her, she kills them — first an old retainer, Abdul *chacha* (uncle) (Arif Zakaria) who suspects her, and then her brother-in-law who is about to find her out. However, when her husband learns that she is a spy, she is unable to pull the trigger on him and flees the house. In the ensuing shootout between Indian and Pakistani forces, her husband is murdered. On discovering his death, Sehmat rejects the violence of warfare and returns to India. The film concludes with an older Sehmat sitting alone in a room and reflecting on her past, while her son (Sanjay Suri), an officer in the Indian navy, listens to his commanding officer tell the story of his mother's life as an example of patriotic nationalism.

Unlike the more straightforward action drama of the Avenging Woman films, in both *Bajirao Mastani* and *Raazi*, action is woven into a complex love story, which allows the films to contrast the female action figures' gendering in the romantic sequences with what happens in the action sequences. That both Sehmat and Mastani are Muslim places them outside a right-wing conceptualization of the Hindu nation. In what follows, I focus specifically on how their femininity is visually encoded through Bollywood's shorthand for Muslim femininity, then show how it coheres or conflicts with a Hindu right-wing notion of Muslim women's agency in the nation. I contrast the ideologies of gender and nation each film presents by looking at the ways in which the female lead negotiates violence. Specifically, *Bajirao Mastani* embraces Hindu nationalism through combining violence in defense of the Hindu nation with a visually encoded Muslim femininity: because she is so enticing, Bajirao marries Mastani, incorporating her into the Hindu nation. *Raazi*, on the other hand, presents a more nuanced picture of women's relation to violence. Sehmat's Muslim identity is enfolded into her Kashmiri identity, and her initial agreement to spy for India stems from her willingness to identify as an Indian citizen, which is in concert with the right-wing vision of Kashmir as Indian territory.[5] As a spy in service of India, she wields a gun, chases down a man, and kills her brother-in-law by poking him with the tip of a poisoned umbrella, but ultimately rejects the Hindu nationalist vision of India. In both films, the representation of violence in the context of the female action figure is crucial to the film's political message and to how we read these films as feminist political texts.

Women and Violence in Bollywood Cinema

The female action figure is a politically mobile symbol that can be deployed to ideological ends in a variety of ways. In the Avenging Woman films, femininity is associated with weakness; thus, the female protagonist's physical shedding of all signs of "female-ness" is crucial for her psychic shedding of feminine "weakness." This is often shown through a scene in which the protagonist exchanges her traditional clothes for modern Western clothing, a process which then allows her to pick up a gun. Gopalan describes the Avenging Women of the rape and revenge films of the 1980s and 1990s as "hardened, cynical, vengeful creatures" (2002: 77). Although the post-2010 feminist Avenging Woman films do not rely on the same correlation of modernity and violence—in *Kahaani* and *Gulaab Gang* the lead women (both Hindu) wear traditional clothes—these films too are at pains to dissociate femininity from weakness. In *Kahaani*, for example, the protagonist's pregnant belly, hidden behind a sari, is in fact a plastic prosthetic that she uses as a weapon to beat the villain in the final scenes of the film. As Gupta notes, "the female characters seem passive and helpless [because of their traditional femininity], but as the plots unfold their actions reveal their strengths. . . . It shocks the audience and forces us to face some of our inherent assumptions about women, while also allowing us to understand how misleading these assumptions can be" (2015: 114). The post-2010 Avenging Woman films draw on tropes of the dangerously sexual femme fatale from film noir because they deploy femininity (though not necessarily sexuality) as a hidden weapon of warfare.

Unlike these films, however, in *Raazi* and *Bajirao Mastani*, the female lead is both a Muslim woman and an action hero, a combination hitherto unseen in Bollywood cinema. In previous terrorist films that feature Muslim women, they are marked as passive victims in need of saving by the Hindu male, thus enabling their unproblematic inclusion in the Indian (read: Hindu) nation.[6] In contrast, in *Raazi* and *Bajirao Mastani* the fact that a Muslim woman is the protagonist leads to a more ideologically complex portrait of women's relation to the nation. Following a trend established by the Avenging Woman films, *Bajirao Mastani* dresses Mastani in male clothing and thereby associates her violence with masculinity. Indeed, the first time she is seen it is unclear whether she is a man or a woman. Dressed in a chain-link suit of armor she forces her way into Bajirao's camp and jousts with soldiers who are intent on denying her entry (Figure 9.1). She is finally subdued by Bajirao and falls to the ground. Her helmet comes loose and her long hair cascades onto the floor. The film thus links femininity to defeat, as is common in the Avenging Woman cycle. Following her defeat, Mastani demands that Bajirao's army help her family's Hindu kingdom of Bundelkhand fight Muslim invaders, telling him that her father, Maharaja Chhatrasaal, the Hindu king who rules over the Marathas, will be happy to know that one Hindu king is going to help another.[7] With this, Mastani squarely places herself in the Hindu camp, thus erasing the "difference" of her Muslim body and locating it within the rhetoric of muscular Hindu nationalism. Mastani is introduced as

Figure 9.1 Mastani (Deepika Padukone) wears armor and is associated with war in *Bajirao Mastani* (© Eros International, 2015. All Rights Reserved).

ambiguously gendered, then feminized in defeat before being masculinized by her call for violence against invading Muslims; in doing so, the film depicts Mastani's violence as in accordance with Hindu nationalism's hypermasculine codes of warfare.

In *Raazi*, Sehmat's first experience with warfare is shown via a rapidly edited training sequence in which she is introduced to traditional techniques of espionage, such as planting listening devices, using poison, practicing self-defense in hand-to-hand combat, and shooting guns. At no point in this sequence can we mistake Sehmat for a man; not only is she traditionally attired in women's clothes, but she also trembles when wielding a gun and is told by her handler to "man up." Her first murder forms a stark contrast to the scene of violent combat in *Bajirao Mastani* described above. Sehmat is caught by an old family retainer Abdul *chacha* (uncle) stealing military files from her father-in-law's study room. Abdul *chacha* confronts Sehmat before rushing out of the house to inform the family. Having chased Abdul in a car, Sehmat repeatedly runs him over. The scene combines action and thriller elements, popularized in films such as *Deewaar* and *Don* (Chandra Barot, 1978). The mise-en-scène shows a dark night with the adversary on the loose, while the music crescendos to mounting suspense. Sehmat's chase of Abdul *chacha* is—similar to *Bajirao Mastani*—conveyed through rapid cuts: he is on foot; she pursues in a jeep. But when she runs him over repeatedly, crushing him, her face streams with tears. After confirming he is dead, she collapses on the steering wheel in grief.

Her character's breakdown is a striking departure from the conventions of the Avenging Woman film, and contrasts with Mastani's brazen attack on Bajirao and his soldiers. Mastani and Sehmat thus represent two extremes of how films frame the violent Muslim woman. As in newer, more feminist Avenging Woman films, Sehmat's visual markers of femininity—long hair, traditional clothes—do not prevent her from taking up arms and accomplishing her mission. She wears the beautiful, flowing clothes of a wealthy homemaker even when she is at war, associating her violence with Bollywood norms of visual Muslim femininity. However, unlike the post-2010 Avenging Woman films, Sehmat's femininity is her strength—not because she uses it as a weapon, as in *Kahaani*—but because it leads her to the more traditionally feminine emotions of remorse and guilt. Her femininity, indicated visually through her tears in this scene and the remorse she later shows when the family mourns Abdul *chacha*'s death, makes her question the norms of violence that underlie nationalism. We see her struggle to overcome her doubts with each subsequent mission.[8]

Sehmat and Mastani's bodies must also be read in the context of Bollywood conventions that depict Muslim women as "figures of difference." As Shoba Sharad Rajgopal points out, the Muslim woman typically appears burqa-clad to mark her otherness, while the Muslim man is marked as different "through elimination/erasure on the one hand, or totally [*sic*] demonizing on the other. The principal characters are all Hindu, and if there are other communities represented, they are usually the enemies, representing Pakistan" (Vishwanath 2013: 243). The figure of the burqa-clad Muslim woman, unlike "the vilified bad Muslim man, father, brother, lover, the separatist-terrorist," is usually shown as "the good Muslim woman, mother, sister, daughter, or lover, who gently prods her man into the nationalist fold and away from doomed political adventure" (Virdi 2017: 9). She is also usually either a passive victim in need of rescue by India or a threatening other whose body is, in Vijay Devdas's terms, "doubly marked by the history of Partition and a post-9/11 world (2013: 223). Indeed, Devdas notes that "Bollywood cinema has a tendency to demonize, exoticize and marginalize Muslim identities to consolidate and solidify a secular Indian (Hindu) nationalism" (ibid.).[9] So how do these two films fit into this wider set of conventions?

When at war, Mastani and Sehmat's costuming conforms to a gendered binary code—Mastani's suit of armor is male, Sehmat's traditional clothes are female. However, things change when violence occurs in domestic settings. In *Bajirao Mastani*, we never see Mastani dressed in anything but drab clothes or suits of armor when she is fighting. This underlines her adherence to the hypermasculine codes of warfare endorsed by the Hindu state. Yet in more overtly romantic scenes, Mastani's clothing, dancing, and mannerisms suggest a Muslim hyper-femininity. The spaces of violence and action are consistently opposed to spaces of intimacy and eroticism. In her first love scene with Bajirao she is dressed in a light cream-colored, gauze and chiffon outfit. Her hair is loose. She wears a nose ring, and her many scarves fall in luxurious folds around her, a portrayal reminiscent of the famous Muslim courtesan of *Umrao Jaan* (Muzaffar Ali, 1981). Unlike the close-ups of Mastani's blood-stained face in the action sequence described above, the camera circles around her, allowing the viewer to linger and see her body at various angles, making it more obviously a sexual object. As Rachel Dwyer notes, Bollywood stereotypes Muslim women as "veiled beauties" (2013: 247, cited in Umar 2020: 3). We see this most explicitly later in the film where, as Baijyanti Roy notes, Mastani's dance performance explicitly evokes the Muslim courtesan of innumerable Bollywood films (2018: 254). In this first erotic encounter, Mastani's Muslim hyper-femininity is clearly on display. However, the dialogue reinforces her identity as a (putatively Hindu) Rajput,[10] in keeping with the film's politics. When Bajirao asks her to reveal the wound she suffered at war, she replies that Rajputs never show their wounds. Nonetheless Bajirao lifts her scarves with his dagger and looks at the wound. He plunges the dagger in a flame and places the burning hot metal on the wound, making her flinch and hold on to him, as if she were "weaker." He then gives her his dagger, unwittingly marrying her by a custom common among Hindu Rajputs. That this is a Hindu custom implies that the Muslim

Figure 9.2 Mastani (Deepika Padukone) in her boudoir is framed through codes of hyper-femininity in *Bajirao Mastani* (© Eros International, 2015. All Rights Reserved).

woman can be enfolded in the Hindu nation only through symbolic violence: the dagger is simultaneously a weapon of violence, of erotic play, and of marriage (Figure 9.2).

Contrastingly, eroticism disrupts the muscular nationalist ideology of Hindu nationalism in *Raazi*. While Mastani's violence is staged explicitly in terms that mark her as a warrior, equivalent to any man, Sehmat's more furtive espionage and covert acts of violence position the action—and its relationship to eroticism and domestic spaces—in different ways. Mastani's defense of the Hindu nation and her Hindu husband justifies her violence. Sehmat, however, increasingly finds little justification for her own acts of violence. When Sehmat realizes that her husband, Iqbal, knows she is a spy, she points a gun at him. Again, tears stream down her face.

The dialogue overtly opposes intimacy and love to nationalism, unlike the seamless connections presented in *Bajirao Mastani*. Iqbal asks Sehmat if she ever loved him; her reply reveals the war within her. She says, "Even if I were to tell you the truth, would you believe me? But perhaps the greatest truth is that

Figure 9.3 An emotional Sehmat (Alia Bhatt) points a gun at Iqbal (Vicky Kaushal) in *Raazi* (© AA Films and Zee Studios International, 2018. All Rights Reserved).

nothing trumps my love for India." Unlike the scene from *Bajirao Mastani* described above, Sehmat, not Iqbal, holds the weapon. Her hand shakes, making the gun she holds wobble. (In contrast, Mastani's sword is always unswerving.) Although Sehmat clearly articulates her allegiance to India and this allegiance might imply her adherence to nationalism, the mise-en-scène of the bedroom and her tears invite us to consider a more nuanced reading (Figure 9.3).

Reading the conflict between Iqbal and Sehmat metonymically as that between India and Pakistan or as Kashmir at war with itself (both Sehmat and Iqbal are Kashmiris), the film suggests that love triumphs over nationalism for both Iqbal and Sehmat, reinforcing a Gandhian ethos. Sehmat does not pull the trigger and Iqbal does not overpower Sehmat. (Indeed, he explicitly states that he will not overpower her.) One cannot help but notice the film's departure from the usual ideology underpinning Bollywood terrorist films, in which the "bad Muslim" is forever at war with India and must be tamed by the good Hindu hero. Sehmat's hesitation and tears and Iqbal's refusal to overpower her critique the parochial patriotisms of India and Pakistan. Each film's view of violence is, then, intimately linked to its female figure and her erotic attachments, in depictions that ultimately perpetuate or question the muscular nationalism at the heart of the Hindu nation. Her erotic attachments are, in turn, also connected to the home, which plays a central role in defining her agency in the films.

The Authority of the State and the Home

Both Sehmat and Mastani are primarily seen in spaces that are either in or proximate to the home, making home a battleground (and metonym) for the nation. The trope of home as nation was popularized in post-1990s Bollywood films, functioning to consolidate an aggressively Hindu nationalist ideology through the figure of the patriarch.[11] In those films, the values of the Hindu nation aligned explicitly with the Hindu home, such that dissension and betrayal in the home became a metonym for the undisciplined citizen more broadly. Thus, the location of violence in the domestic is particularly significant for the female-led action film.

In *Bajirao Mastani*, although Mastani is not accepted by Bajirao's family as his legitimate wife, and her second home as Bajirao's wife is saturated with signs of her Muslim-ness (such as the celebration of Eid, her clothing, the home's Indo-Saracenic architectural adornments), her willingness to be incorporated in the Hindu fold is repeatedly stressed. She names the son she bears to Bajirao Krishna after the Hindu god, pays tribute to his Hindu first wife according to Hindu custom, and so on. Mastani's putative incorporation into the Hindu home is evident in the scene where she defends herself and her son against the assassins sent by Bajirao's mother to kill her, while Bajirao is distracted by the *puja* (Hindu prayer ceremony) in his home. The scene intercuts between closeups of Mastani fighting and Bajirao's immersion in the *puja*, thus joining Mastani visually to the Hindu home.[12] Mastani ably fights off all the assassins, deftly parrying their attacks with her superior sword play. However, just as we think she has triumphed, a swordsman attacks her from behind. As he is about to strike the fatal blow, Bajirao kills the assassin, saving his beloved. His intervention implies that her defeat at the hands of "bad Hindus" is countered by the "good Hindu," reinforcing Hindu nationalist ideas of Muslim women's willingness to embrace Hindus (especially Hindu men) as their protectors. This moment thus functions as a double move in gendered terms, showcasing both Mastani's martial abilities and her reliance on male assistance.

Yet in *Raazi* Sehmat ultimately rejects the Hindu nationalist ideology that structures the relationship between home and nation. She manages to escape Pakistani forces and to arrive at the Indian camp. Until this point in the film she has been a willing tool of the state. Having ended her mission as a spy but failed to kill her husband, she is finally able to question the ideology of violence that underlies state power. Confronting Khalid Mir (Jaideep Ahlawat), her Indian, Muslim handler, she criticizes Pakistan and India's meaningless massacre of many innocent people, including an Indian woman who was deployed as a decoy for Sehmat. Mir was even willing to abandon Sehmat herself to Pakistani gunfire in the final shootout. "I gave up my conscience, my life's desires for you, and you didn't even spare my life?" she asks. Sehmat's distrust and condemnation align *Raazi* with other action films, which similarly manifest a "lack of faith . . . in figures of authority—the government and the police" (Gupta 2015: 118). However, unlike the protagonists of those films, Sehmat starts by believing in the infallibility of the nation, and only gradually begins to mistrust the state.

Since both Mir and Sehmat are Muslim, Sehmat's rejection of Mir's vision of state-sponsored violence cannot be read as a mere retreat into feminine passivity but rather demands a rethinking of state ideology itself. Her rejection of Mir is a conscious rejection of a militarized worldview, evident in her uses of *zameer* to indict Mir. *Zameer* means conscience, but also refers more broadly to mind, heart, and way of being. The linkage is crucial to dismantling the masculinist rhetoric of war that Mir promotes, whereas in *Bajirao Mastani* Mastani accepts, even embraces violence. Sehmat's insistence on *zameer* and on relationships and lives explicitly embeds her in a Gandhian moral matrix at odds with the violence of the state.[13] Vamsee Juluri argues for reading "the familiar terrorist" film through a framework of "Gandhian nonviolence" because the "ethical choices made by the main characters occur within an emotional-relational matrix" (2008: 118 and 122). This is in keeping with Gandhi's idea that it is the relations between people that structure and maintain society, rather than the abstract forces of the nation state. In the woman-led terrorist film, in *Dil Se* for example, Meghna/Moina (Manisha Koirala) avenges her rape by an Indian army officer by becoming a suicide bomber. Juluri suggests that rape has permanently damaged her relational structures, such that the Hindu male protagonist of the film, Amar (Shah Rukh Khan) who offers her love, domesticity, and family through marriage, proves unable to change her; revenge and death are her only solution.[14]

Sehmat's display of femininity and her rejection of violence can be read as a source of power and moral strength (Nandy 2007: 54–6). We see Sehmat's display of femininity and an illustration of Gandhian *satyagraha* (moral force) in which the exertion or the insistence on non-violence is an indication of "soul force." Further, we can read this femininity as a feminist gesture because it undoes the correlation of femininity with weakness and reminds the viewer of the feminist reinforcement of relational structures and specifically social and ethical relations as necessary antidotes to the patriarchal underpinning of state and legal institutions.

In *Bajirao Mastani*, Mastani's affective relationships structure her relationship to violence and thus to action; that is, she resorts to violence to defend her Hindu father, her Hindu husband, and her putatively Hindu child. Her violence in defense of the Hindu family erases her Muslim "difference" and reinforces the film's Hindu nationalist ideology. In *Raazi*, on the other hand, Sehmat's affective relationships consistently interrupt a Hindu nationalist ideology, and this is especially evident in the scenes described above. Unlike *Dil Se* or *Theeviravaathi*, Sehmat's conflict is explicitly shown at several different moments, preparing the viewer for her ultimate rejection of Mir and the Hindu state.

Raazi can critique Hindu nationalism because the metonymic representation of the nation is the Kashmiri Muslim home rather than the Hindu home, a pointed departure from *Bajirao Mastani*, in which the "Muslim-ness" of Mastani's home is neutralized by Bajirao's presence as a Hindu man who has brought Mastani into the Hindu fold through marriage. *Raazi*, too, departs from the terrorist film where Muslim home (especially the Kashmiri Muslim home) is the enemy of the nation. The devastation of the Kashmiri Muslim home indicates that India and Pakistan's muscular nationalism, especially when it concerns Kashmir, threatens to tear apart the nations from within.

Bajirao Mastani, Raazi, and the Reproductive Politics of the State

Both films analyzed in this chapter link violence and nationalism to reproduction. Sehmat and Mastani each give birth to sons. That they do so is in fact common in women-led terrorist films as well: there women's violent acts are often in tension with their female bodies—witness Meghna/Moina's rape in *Dil Se* or Malli (Ayesha Darker)'s pregnancy in *Theeviravaathi*. The female protagonist must choose between two competing discourses—sacrifice to the terrorists' idea of nation or service to the normative ideals of marriage and motherhood, respectively, that condition womanhood and would lead to reincorporation into the dominant national imaginary.[15] In *Dil Se*, Meghna/Moina seems to choose to be a suicide bomber, but dies accidentally when the Indian radio announcer who loves her, Amar (Shah Rukh Khan), embraces her, causing her suicide vest to explode, killing them both. Her death nonetheless reunites her with her group's vision of the nation; consistently she rejects Amar's offers of marriage. With *Theeviravaathi* Malli's pregnancy gives her an increased appreciation for life, yet—as with the assassination of Rajiv Gandhi, the incident on which this film is based—Malli probably kills herself, her unborn baby, and her target. (That film ends ambivalently, on a blank black screen.) In *Raazi*, Sehmat's pregnancy does not result in her domestication and reincorporation into the nation. After her pregnancy is revealed, the film cuts to the present day. An Indian naval officer, Sehmat's son stands at attention while his commander narrates his mother's story. In this account, Sehmat's journey is obliterated, remade into a narrative of patriotic nationalism. If the film ended here, we would be compelled to read Sehmat as reincorporated into the Indian nation through motherhood: her past with and love for Iqbal have been erased. However, the film continues. The camera cuts to an older Sehmat sitting in a bare room looking out of a window over untrammeled valleys and fields. The nameless space that she occupies, and the sparse conditions of her existence, suggest that she is literally and figuratively in a no-man's land. Rather than being reincorporated into the nation through motherhood and marriage as Mastani was, Sehmat's rejection of muscular nationalism has estranged her from the nation. We can read her isolation as a feminist act: she insists on her own inner moral vision, at whatever cost, rather than giving in to the forces of patriarchal nationalism. We can also read her estrangement as a political allegory: Sehmat, like Kashmir, is caught between the war of India and Pakistan, and cannot swear allegiance to either nation. Much like Kashmir, she insists on her own "sovereignty." The starkness of her home is a deliberate reminder of the no-man's land that Kashmir has become, and her estrangement shows the impossible existence of Kashmiri subjects.

Unlike other recent female-led action films such as *Kahaani* or *Gulab Gang*, in which women are rewarded for their violent actions, *Raazi*'s conclusion proposes that patriarchal structures of society create violence. Sehmat opts for a moral sphere removed from violence. In contrast, Mastani and Bajirao die at the end of *Bajirao Mastani*. Neither film looks to the next generation to resolve the problem of Hindu-Muslim relations. Yet *Bajirao Mastani*'s ultimate message is that a successful Hindu-Muslim marriage based on love is not only possible, but that the memory of it transcends time. In these feminist action-romance-drama *masala* films, neither simplistic victory nor final defeat are possible.

Notes

1 Original release titles are given first throughout this chapter, followed by English translations in parentheses. (Proper names stand alone.) Bollywood films are known, including in Anglophone countries, by their original titles.

2 Ajay Gehlawat argues that the past becomes a "metatextual critique of such [Hindu nationalist] activism and intolerance" by relying on the audience's ability to parse the semiotic system of the film in the context of contemporary political events and of the nation's past as rendered through Bombay cinema (2017: 338–9).

3 *Bajirao Mastani* is adapted from N.S. Imandar's Marathi novel *Rau* (1972) and *Raazi* from Harinder Sikka's English novel, *Calling Sehmat* (2008).

4 By Gandhian I mean a more pacifist and non-violent approach to nationalism and nation-formation.

5 Indian imperialism in Kashmir is based on a Hindu right-wing ideology of "sacred geography." According to this, India is a Hindu nation and needs to preserve its territorial integrity by "recuperating" Kashmir within its national body. To preserve the unity of India as a Hindu nation, Kashmir must be cleansed of Kashmiri Muslims and all visible signs of Islam in the Valley must be destroyed.

6 See for example *Roja* and *Mission Kashmir* (Vidhu Vinod Chopra, 2000).

7 Roy argues that *Bajirao Mastani*'s Hindutva (Hindu right-wing) film is drawn from Hindu nationalist leader V.D. Savarkar's *Hindu pad-padshahi* account of Bajirao's conquest: "Bajirao after the conquest and settlement of Gujarat, Malva and Bundelkhand [. . .] was not likely to cry halt there forever. His aim was a consolidated Hindu Empire that should embrace all *Hindustan* in its sweep" (Savarkar 124, cited in Roy 2018: 252).

8 As Meheli Sen argues, since the rise of Hindu nationalism in the 1990s, the political climate in India has reflected "a certain aggressive militant Hindutva gathers within itself other resonances that can be characterized as 'male'" (2010: 150). Bollywood films depict this climate in terms of an aggressive, Hindu, male-dominated and patriarchal order.

9 See also Hirji (2008) and Kabir (2010).

10 Rajputs regarded themselves as part of a warrior caste.

11 Sen argues that the patriarchal structure of this feudal Hindu home was used towards "romancing authoritarian power . . . and a triumphant symbolic Father" (2010: 150).

12 For Gehlawat, the scene functions as a critique of Hindu nationalism and references the large-scale massacre of Muslims in the 2004 Godhra riots (2017: 343).

13 As Nandy puts it, Gandhi "refuses to give centrality to the modern nation-state in human affairs," emphasizing instead the relations between people that structure and maintain society (2007: 170).

14 Kachawala argues that in the woman-led terrorist film, whether *Theeviravaathi* or *Dil Se*, the woman action figure is represented only through her "gender, grief, and personal histories to the point that their political beliefs and ideologies are sidelined" (cited in Mezey 2018: 38).

15 As Dayal suggests, "[Malli's] reclamation involves soliciting spectatorial sympathy in a discourse simultaneously of liberalism and normative femininity that reinscribes the ethical borders around an idealized woman" (2015: 111–12).

Works Cited

Dayal, Samir (2015), *Dream Machine: Realism and Fantasy in Hindi Cinema*, Philadelphia: Temple University Press.

Devdas, Vijay (2013), "The Shifting Terrains of Nationalism and Patriotism in Indian Cinemas," in K. Moti Gokulsing and Wimal Dissanayake (eds), *The Routledge Handbook of Indian Cinemas*, 218–45, Oxford: Routledge.

Dwyer, Rachel (2013), "The List—Top Ten Muslim Characters in Bollywood," in Robin Yassin-Kassab and Ziauddin Sardar (eds), *Critical Muslim 5: Love and Death*, 247–53, London: Oxford University Press.

Gehlawat, Ajay (2017), "The Metatext of *Bajirao Mastani*: Intolerance in the Time of Modi," *South Asian History and Culture*, 8 (3): 338–48.

Gopalan, Lalitha (2002), *Cinema of Interruptions: Action Genres in Contemporary Indian Cinema*, London: British Film Institute.

Gupta, Sukanya (2015), "*Kahaani, Roja Gang* and *Queen*: Remaking the Queens of Bollywood," *South Asian Popular Culture*, 13 (2): 107–23.

Hirji, Faiza (2008), "Change of Pace? Islam and Tradition in Popular Indian Cinema," *South Asian Popular Culture*, 6 (1): 57–69.

Imandar, N.S. (1972), *Rau*, Pune: Continental Publications.

Juluri, Vamsee (2008), "Our Violence, Their Violence: Exploring the Emotional and Relational Matrix of Terrorist Cinema," in Anandam P. Kavoori and Aswin Punathambekar (eds), *Global Bollywood*, 117–30, New York: New York University Press.

Kabir, Ananya Jahanara (2010), "The Kashmiri as Muslim in Bollywood's 'New Kashmir Films,'" *Contemporary South Asia*, 18 (4): 373–85.

Manzar, Benazir, and Aju Aravind (2019), "(Re) Thinking Women in Cinema: The Changing Narrative Structure in Bollywood," *South Asian Popular Culture*, 17 (1): 1–13.

Mezey, Jason H. (2018), "The Pyrotechnics of Gender and Terrorism in Mani Ratnam's *Dil Se*," *South Asian Popular Culture*, 16 (1): 29–49.

Nandy, Ashis (2007), "The Lure of 'Normal' Politics," *South Asian Popular Culture*, 5 (2): 167–78.

Rai, Amit S. (2006), "'Every Citizen Is a Cop Without the Uniform' The Populist Outsider in Bollywood's New Angry Young Man Genre," *Interventions*, 8 (2): 193–227.

Rajgopal, Shoba Sharad (2013), "Bollywood and Neonationalism: The Emergence of Nativism as the Norm in Indian Conventional Cinema," *South Asian Popular Culture*, 9 (3): 237–46.

Roy, Baijayanti (2018), "Visual Grandeur, Imagined Glory: Identity Politics and Hindu Nationalism in Bajirao Mastani and Padmaavat," *Journal of Religion and Film* [Special Issue: 2018 International Conference on Religion and Film, Toronto; Omaha], 22 (3): 1–33.

Sen, Meheli (2010), "'It's All About Loving Your Parents': Liberalization, Hindutva and Bollywood's New Fathers," in Rini Bhattacharya Mehta and Rajeshwari V. Pandharipande (eds), Bollywood and Globalization: Indian Popular Cinema, Nation, and Diaspora, 145–68, London: Anthem Press.

Sikka, Harinder (2008), *Calling Sehmat*, India: Penguin Random House.

Sinha, Suvadip (2013), "Vernacular Masculinity and Politics of Space in Contemporary Bollywood Cinema," *Studies in South Asian Film & Media*, 5 (2): 131–45.

Umar, Lubna (2020), "Bollywood and the Re-Orientalization of India: The Making of the Muslim 'Other' in Bhansali's *Bajirao Mastani* (2015) and *Padmaavat* (2018)," *Film Matters*, 11 (1): 126–37.

Virdi, Jyotika (2017), "A National Cinema's Transnational Aspirations? Considerations on 'Bollywood,'" *South Asian Popular Culture*, 15 (1): 1–22.

Chapter 10

Anxiety in Action: Jackie Chan, COVID-19, and Brexit along the Belt and Road

Gina Marchetti

Jackie Chan remains one of the few globally recognized Asian stars in contemporary action cinema. He now serves less as a Hong Kong hero and more as a soft-power ambassador for mainland China. The years 2017–2020 illustrate the complexities of Chan's stardom. Acrobatic ideological gyrations keep him and his starring vehicles afloat on world screens. He appeared in four feature films released in 2017, and they testify to his global reach. *Namiya* (*Jie you za huo dian*), directed by Han Jie, is based on the Japanese novel by Keigo Higashino. *Kung Fu Yoga* (*Gong fu yu jia*), written and directed by Stanley Tong, is set in India, Tibet, Dubai, Beijing, and Xi'an. *The Foreigner*, directed by Martin Campbell, is based on the 1992 novel, *The Chinaman*, by Stephen Leather, and is set primarily in the United Kingdom. *Bleeding Steel* (*Ji qi zhi xue*), directed by Leo Zhang, is set in Australia. In addition, Chan did voice work on several animated films and appeared in other projects as well, including *Vanguard* (*Ji xian feng*, Stanley Tong, 2020). While these films vary tremendously in budget, location, theme, tone, box office earnings, and critical and audience reception, they have two things in common: they are co-productions with mainland Chinese companies, and they star Jackie Chan.

This chapter focuses on two of these features. Both highlight Chan's star image as a site of geopolitical anxiety. *The Foreigner* obliquely references the disquiet surrounding Brexit, immigration, national borders, and the economic rise of China, while relying on the box-office value of the film's aging stars, Pierce Brosnan and Chan. In sharp contrast, *Kung Fu Yoga* adopts a comedic approach to China's relationship to India. This takes on added significance because of continuing tensions between the two countries that erupted in border clashes in 2020 and 2021.

Though very different, both star vehicles combat cross-border anxiety by imaginatively smoothing over geopolitical stumbling blocks along China's "belt and road" linking Europe and the rest of Asia to China. China's current leader, Xi Jinping, who came to power in 2012, quickly became associated with the Belt and Road Initiative (BRI), and Chan followed with vocal support for the regime in Beijing and its BRI policies. The locations covered by *The Foreigner* and *Kung Fu Yoga* allow Chan to traverse China's Eurasian Belt and Road through Western China into South, Southeast, and Central Asia, the Middle East, and Europe. Chan's pro-People's Republic of China (PRC) political sympathies thereby keep pace with the changing global market for action cinema. Yet there are explosive contradictions at the root of the star's mercurial screen image, as I now show.

The Geopolitics of Action

In "Action-Adventure as Ideology" (1989), I wrote about the ways in which action-adventure films take up political events to express and imaginatively resolve ideological contradictions through fiction. Influenced by Fredric Jameson's notions of how ideology operates in narratives, that essay drew on what he terms the "political unconscious" (1982) to look specifically at action-adventure plots within a Cold War geopolitical framework. Action films speak to global anxieties and attempt to reconcile contradictions through fiction. New global configurations map reinvigorated nationalisms, populisms, and authoritarian regimes in Brazil, Russia, India, and China (the BRICs) with China's "rise" disturbing the complacency of the rest.[1] Beyond the power of mainland China's box office, its aspirations to soft power on global screens have also put it on the cultural map in potent ways.

Paola Voci and Luo Hui (2017) connect Joseph Nye's 1990 formulation of "soft power" as the assertion of global influence through non-military means with William A. Callahan's 2013 conceptualization of the "China dream." The authors probe Xi Jinping's rhetorical connection of the two terms to highlight ways in which his dream of soft power undergirds his ostensible geopolitical ambitions and is characterized by an "ambivalent . . . and unpredictable relationship with the officially articulated vision" (2017: 7). This ambivalence can also be keenly felt in various ways in the transnational Chinese action film as Hong Kong talent becomes an increasingly central component of PRC blockbusters.[2] Although the "China dream" predates Xi's rise, the push to consolidate China's soft power has intensified since he took command, and the action spectacular provides a fitting example. Referencing Chris Berry's 2003 discussion of the "de-Westernization" of the blockbuster film in China, Aynne Kokas observes:

> The political pressure to advance local films also underscores the reality that if Chinese movies become more appealing to international audiences, Hollywood productions may become less relevant on a global scale, because

some filmmakers and policymakers in the Chinese film market seek to limit collaboration with foreign partners.

2017: 64–5

More recently, Berry notes the increasing pressures placed on filmmakers working between mainland China and the global film market: "we now live in a 'Two Globalizations' world of competing transnational trade policies anchored in the United States and the PRC, as well as various reactions against globalization in its two major forms" (2021: 2). Berry observes that the overlap of cinematic centers of influence moves the PRC beyond the Chinese language into transnational, multilingual co-productions, with global stars such as Jackie Chan given top billing. However, because of the pressures of domestic censorship and inability to appeal to broader audiences, these films underperform outside of mainland China.

Jackie Chan's reinvention of himself as a mainland Chinese star illustrates this dilemma. While still recognized in Hollywood because of the lingering success of the *Rush Hour* series (Brett Ratner, 1998, 2001, 2007), his luster has faded in Taiwan, South Korea, Japan, India, and in his hometown, Hong Kong, primarily because of his decision to dedicate himself to the mainland Chinese market. However, as his honorary Oscar indicates, Chan still has some credibility as a global celebrity, and his films travel with less effort than most Chinese domestic blockbusters do.[3]

Chan's films, however, do not follow Hollywood's major franchises with Chinese ornamentation, among them *Iron Man 3* (Shane Black, 2013) and *Transformers: Age of Extinction* (Michael Bay, 2014). *The Foreigner* and *Kung Fu Yoga* instead exploit the profitable periphery of James Bond-imitation spy actioners and Bollywood spectaculars with shades of Steven Spielberg's 1981 *Raiders of the Lost Ark*'s archeological action, respectively. Both films also wed Chan's star appeal to current Chinese soft-power ambitions.

The Foreigner delivers on visual, visceral, as well as ideological levels in a post-Cold War environment roiled by Brexit and the rise of nationalism in Europe. Brosnan and Chan play against type under the direction of Martin Campbell.[4] *Kung Fu Yoga*'s director, Stanley Tong, is Chan's frequent collaborator. To ensure consistency for fans drawn nostalgically to a Chan vehicle, Tong not only directed, but also wrote the screenplay on one of Chan's favorite topics: looted antiquities. Chan imaginatively maps out Chinese power and influence through his star charisma and inimitable stunts. In his wake, the star trails anxieties associated with an increasingly powerful China.

The Foreigner Blasts into Action

The Foreigner opens with a blast from what should be the past. Chan, playing Quan Ngoc Minh, a Chinese refugee from Vietnam, witnesses the death of his daughter in a bombing in London's Knightsbridge shopping district. In the opening sequence, Quan drops his daughter Fan (Katie Leung) at a shop and lovingly looks on through his car's windshield as she enters the store. An explosion shatters the auto's glass and transforms Quan from a spectator of British commercial prosperity into a victim of its colonial legacy, specifically here the Troubles in Northern Ireland.

The fatal blast propels Quan into the action. The film's double plotting weaves together Quan's quest to avenge the death of his daughter with Northern Irish politician Liam Hennessy's (Brosnan) attempts to rein in rogue militants through his own paramilitary operation and, later, to prevent the militants' bombing of a commercial airliner. The two stories intertwine as Quan relentlessly pursues Hennessy as key to uncovering the identities of the bombers responsible for his daughter's death.

The Foreigner updates Leather's 1992 novel about the Irish Republican Army (IRA)'s London bombing campaigns in the 1970s and 1980s. Although screenwriter David Marconi provides copious references to the Troubles before and after 1998's Good Friday Agreement, the finished film speaks most directly to Northern Ireland in the shadow of Brexit. Production on *The Foreigner* was announced in June 2015 at the height of the debates surrounding the promised referendum on whether the United Kingdom (including Northern Ireland) should remain in the European Union (EU) or (Br)exit it. Although the film does not reference Brexit directly, it does dramatize the possible violence to come due to unresolved tensions involving the status of Northern Ireland.

Changing the title from the racially charged *The Chinaman* to *The Foreigner* speaks to the sensitivities of the project's Chinese partners and to the anxieties at the heart of the Brexit debates. Concern over immigration and limitations on national sovereignty fueled the push to leave the European Union. Brexiteer anxiety about the identity of the United Kingdom (UK) viewed everyone—from Eastern and Southern European immigrants to refugees from Africa and the Middle East—as "foreigners" who too easily funneled into Britain thanks to Europe's porous borders.

Fearing the destabilization of the border it shares with the Republic of Ireland, Northern Ireland voted to remain in the EU in the 2016 referendum held before *The Foreigner*'s 2017 release.[5] The film contains several oblique references to Brexit anxiety. For example, after the initial Knightsbridge bombing in which Quan's daughter dies, a journalist exclaims: "There goes the peace accord back into shit." An IRA leader turned Sinn Fein politician with links to the UK government, Hennessy embodies the political anxieties at the heart of Brexit. He masterminds the clandestine bombing campaign but nevertheless plans to take credit for stopping it. He aims to parlay his supposed peacekeeping into official pardons for his IRA comrades from his British government contact, Cabinet Minister Katherine Davies (Lia Williams).

The IRA had officially ceased active hostilities against the British in 2005 as a confirmation of the 1998 Good Friday Agreement, so Hennessy has clearly gone rogue. Now he loses control of the bombing operation he planned, and the "authentic IRA" targets civilians in shops, on public buses, and commercial airplanes. Moving from Belfast to the Irish countryside to London, Hennessy gets pushed around by everyone. The women in his life betray him, from his political extremist/terrorist mistress Maggie aka Sara McKay (Charlie Murphy) to his wife Mary (Orla Brady), who is out to avenge the death of her brother at the hands of the paramilitary Ulster Volunteer Force. Hennessy's comrade Hugh McGrath (Dermot Crowley) undermines his authority to keep the factions fighting for his own profit. Hennessy's nephew Sean (Rory Fleck Byrne) betrays sensitive secrets to his mistress, Mary—who is, yes, his aunt. By the film's conclusion, even if Quan had not forced Hennessy to publicize his affair with a dead bomber, his political and personal future would be bleak. Cabinet Minister Katherine Davies says in no uncertain terms: "make no mistake, Deputy Minister, you are ours now." Mary exhibits only contempt for her husband when she says to her lover/his nephew, Sean: "He's just a washed-up old man trying to hold on to whatever he can."

In contrast, the other "old man" in the film, Quan (Chan), remains a potent figure. As such, Chan's character addresses the film's Chinese stakeholders' and the global audience's desire for action. Yet Quan's story resembles Hennessy's in several ways: both characters end up suffering in political conflicts as a consequence of the geopolitical maneuverings of China, Britain, and the United States. Quan notes the irony of the use of the plastic explosive Semtex II in the London bombing that kills his daughter, since the same explosive saw routine use in Vietnam.

In my 1989 essay, I asked, "Why Vietnam?" The same question can be posed of *The Foreigner*. The irony behind Stephen Leather's 1992 novel, *The Chinaman,* comes from the fact that Nguyen Ngoc Minh is not a "Chinaman" but a former North Vietnamese Army (NVA) operative who went south to aid the Viet Cong (VC) but switched sides to fight with the Army of the Republic of Vietnam (ARVN) and US forces. A Chinese co-production, *The Foreigner*, in contrast, insists Quan is Chinese, not Vietnamese, changes the character's surname from Nguyen to Quan, and erases the character's connections to the NVA and VC. All these changes accommodate the film's financial backers and anticipated audience in mainland China.

At one point Quan tries to offer a reward for the capture of the bombers responsible for his daughter's death. British Commander Richard Bromley (Ray Fearon) reads aloud from a file on the restauranteur's background. Quan comes from Guangxi province in mainland China and became a British citizen in 1984. Later Hennessy uncovers other details about Quan's past. Documents confirm his association with the US military and show he was one of the "boat people" who fled the new regime at the end of the war. A flashback sequence involves a Thai pirate attack on the refugee boat in the South China Sea. Quan's two elder daughters are captured, raped, and murdered, and he and his wife are thrown off the boat.

The flashback sequence reinforces the Chinese propaganda push that accompanies its current military buildup in the contested waters of the South China Sea. The lawlessness at sea in the 1970s and 1980s that threatens innocent Chinese lives in the film imaginatively justifies the twenty-first century show of naval power now routinely touted in the PRC media. Moreover, Quan's ordeal contributes to the PRC's version of the 1979 Sino-Vietnamese war as a badge of patriotism, linking the character's past to current territorial claims. *The Foreigner* thereby addresses Chinese viewers who may not be familiar with the Troubles, but who have seen films about the Sino-Vietnamese war, such as Xie Jin's *Garlands at the Foot of the Mountain* (*Gao shan xia de hua huan*, 1984) or, more recently, Feng Xiaogang's *Youth* (*Fang hua*, 2017).

Actions Speak Louder than Words

Since *The Foreigner* privileges action, it comes as no surprise that Quan, the consummate man of action, should come off better in the end than Hennessy, the man of words. When Hennessy suggests they share a common bond because both have seen combat, Quan pistol whips him and counters angrily: "We are nothing alike. You're nothing! You kill women and children." Linked to a dead terrorist mistress and responsible for the political assassination of his wife as well as the victims of the bombings—including Quan's daughter Fan—Hennessy has blood on his hands, if indirectly so.

Most of the action leading up to the thwarted bombing of the commercial flight in the film involves suspense sequences surrounding explosives associated with the espionage plotting. That Quan seeks revenge allows the film to invoke Chan's martial arts skills and stunt-based choreography. Quan, a guerrilla fighter in the Vietnam war, connects both the revenge and the espionage subplots: he is an expert in demolitions as well as an accomplished hand-to-hand combatant.

The spectacle of Jackie Chan's body in action tells another story that belies the dialogue in which others repeatedly refer to Quan as an "old man." In effect, Chan the star recapitulates the narrative of his rise to global stardom by returning to specific stunts, situations, and standard choreography from his action archive. As he ages, Chan relies on these intertextual references to solidify ties with nostalgic older supporters as well as educate newer fans about his achievements. Thus, even though Chan ostensibly acts against type in this film, eschewing his substantial comedic talents, he still manages to channel significant elements of his personal combat style and to refer to other key action classics. This assures his action fans that *The Foreigner* is more than a political thriller.

I'm wearing a bomb.

Figure 10.1 The two "old men": Jackie Chan as Quan has Pierce Brosnan as Hennessy at an apparent disadvantage in *The Foreigner* (© Intercontinental Video Ltd., 2018. All Rights Reserved).

Arguably, the film voices and reconciles the cross-cultural contradictions of the narrative more through its action sequences than its plot. The performance set pieces recall Chan's vertiginous stunts and falls. The hybrid martial arts choreography references Bruce Lee's gestures, Wing Chun punches, Brazilian Jujitsu traps, judo throws, and stylized Chinese opera acrobatics. As Chris Holmlund points out, this strategy of returning to previous successful properties in "success with sequels" became a key part of Chan's career circa 2010 at middle age (2010: 96–112). As he ages and plays older characters, these references to earlier successes multiply.

The Foreigner shows Jackie Chan sliding down from a height as he does most famously in the shopping mall scene in *Police Story* (Jackie Chan, 1985). Now he wears a bomb vest, as in *Police Story 2* (*Ging chaat goo si juk jaap*, Jackie Chan, 1988) (Figure 10.1). He dukes it out in a rooftop fight that resembles many earlier vertiginous antics, including the climactic combat scene in Rotterdam in *Who Am I?* (*Ngo si seoi*, Benny Chan and Jackie Chan, 1998). He makes use of ambient materials and quotidian objects in his fights and in the scenes featuring his conditioning for combat, much as Bruce Lee did. *The Foreigner* additionally recalls Rambo's guerilla tactics and Rocky's training techniques. Like fellow Vietnam veteran Rambo (Sylvester Stallone), Quan filches combat techniques perfected by the Viet Cong, notably, the trip wire and the punji stick. He exploits the quiet subtlety of the knife attack and uses the blade to cauterize his wound in a scene reminiscent of Rambo stitching up his own flesh in *First Blood* (Ted Kotcheff, 1982). Like Rambo as well, Quan emerges from the forest as if out of nowhere—invisible until he strikes.

Quan's fight with Hennessy's underling and nephew, Sean, which takes place in Irish woodland, stands out because of this intertextual intensity. The film

Figure 10.2 Jackie Chan as Quan employs a chokehold that displays his skill against his younger opponent in *The Foreigner* (© Intercontinental Video Ltd., 2018. All Rights Reserved).

presents the younger and older men as evenly matched with Quan's wounds giving Sean a slight edge in the combat. At one point, Sean goes on the offensive with a knife attack. Quan rolls away as Sean stabs. This echoes ground movements characteristic of the martial artistry associated with Peking Opera, which Chan learned as a child. Quan kicks out with both legs from the ground then leaps up to stand. Later, he takes two sticks out from one of his traps, much as Bruce Lee used Philippine arnis/kali/escrima sticks in *Enter the Dragon* (Robert Clouse, 1973). Quan disarms Sean using the sticks and then places his opponent in a chokehold (Figure 10.2).[6] Quan applies pressure but lets Sean go before he loses consciousness. Quan ends the fight by kicking Sean away.

A long shot of the two sitting by a campfire at night changes the mood. Sean opens up to Quan, telling him about the renegade IRA operative behind the fatal bombings, and says he fought in Iraq with the Royal Irish Regiment, serving two tours with Special Forces. Quan questions him: "You're Catholic, but you fought for the British?" Sean replies, "I fought for the regiment. Out there, religion didn't matter. We were all the same." Quan asks about his family—moving from the political to the personal. Sean says he has a brother, but neglects to mention that Hennessy is his uncle. Quan cuts Sean's restraints after this exchange: brotherhood extends to fellow soldiers, who respect the discipline and skill needed for unarmed combat. Quan, the former Chinese fighter in Vietnam and Sean, the former Northern Irish Catholic soldier in Iraq, both navigate politically complex identities through apparently flexible loyalties. However, unlike Quan, Sean's loyalty to his family has limits. His betrayal of his uncle is ultimately more personal than political: he is involved with Hennessy's wife.

Quan and Sean's fights in *The Foreigner* pale in comparison with Chan's earlier action sequences. Nevertheless, the aging star manages to maintain his role as a martial arts master.[7] The climactic fight inside the terrorist cell's apartment, for example, exhibits Chan's considerable skill in using materials Quan finds at hand in close quarters. The choreography is exquisitely timed and crisply executed. The handpicked martial arts performers of Chan's stunt team allow him to compose action sequences that show his skills to best advantage and exert his star power.

Ultimately, Quan helps to thwart the airplane bombing plot and forces Hennessy to expose his ties to terrorism. By *The Foreigner*'s conclusion, Hennessy has been ruined by the women in his life, while Quan ends up in the arms of Lam, played by Liu Tao, a popular television actress in mainland China. Although world screens continue to be dominated by American action heroes, *The Foreigner* has a Chinese refugee from Vietnam who has become a British immigrant save the day. This places the film firmly in the Chinese market as a Jackie Chan (not a Pierce Brosnan) vehicle. Accordingly, Chan, not former-James Bond Brosnan, "gets the girl" at the end. Unlike the novel, which kills its titular "Chinaman" off, the film allows Chan, battered and bruised, to triumph and, presumably, to return to his takeout restaurant and simmering romance. The film concludes with Commander Bromley acknowledging Quan's success and challenging a directive to eliminate him: "I believe we owe this chap something. This Chinese man won't give up. Keep back for now. No point in waking the dragon."

At the end of *The Foreigner*, Brexit anxieties intersect with the specter of the rise of the PRC and renewed fears of its economic muscle and racial, political, and cultural alterity. Though Quan has been a British citizen for decades, he remains forever foreign, much like others within the Asian diaspora who confront racist exclusionism in Europe and the US. For Chinese viewers, however, this confirms that those born or descended from Han Chinese parents will remain forever part of the Chinese nation as defined by Beijing. Bromley's reference to "waking the dragon" also serves as a pun on Chan's Chinese stage name, "Cheng Lung," which means "Becoming the Dragon." In this phase of Chan's career, the mainland Chinese "dragon" and the Hong Kong star have merged into one.

Hunting for Treasure on the Belt and Road in *Kung Fu Yoga*

With comedy rather than the political thriller among its core genres, *Kung Fu Yoga* nevertheless has more in common with *The Foreigner* than first may appear. Both films draw on nostalgic references to Jackie Chan's star oeuvre, use expert choreography to highlight Chan's martial arts prowess within a carefully selected supporting cast, and interweave mainland Chinese political propaganda into the workings of the plot. The soft power mix also differed, moreover, and this had a noticeable impact on the box office and critical reception. *Kung Fu Yoga* was a box office success in mainland China but a notorious flop in India.[8]

Directed by Chan's frequent collaborator Stanley Tong, the film opened as a much-anticipated, star-studded feature inaugurating India's 2014 co-production agreement with the PRC.[9] Produced primarily in Mandarin, with some English and even less Hindi woven into the script, the film principally addresses the Chinese-speaking audience. The plot follows a typical action-adventure thread involving a valuable artifact that the protagonist Jack (Chan) must rescue with the help of Ashmita (Disha Patani), a descendent of Indian royalty. As I point out in my 1989 essay, these sorts of treasure-hunting plots highlight the apparent rights of the representatives of imperial powers (such as the United States and Britain) to determine the ownership of precious cultural artifacts. The Indiana Jones series comes immediately to mind as an example, and Chan's character refers directly to the Harrison Ford franchise in *Kung Fu Yoga*.[10] Here, however, *Kung Fu Yoga* inserts China in place of America as the rightful guardian of the world's cultural heritage.

Jackie Chan has made several treasure-hunt films, including the *Armour of God* series (*Armour of God*, *Lung hing foo dai*, Jackie Chan and Eric Tsang, 1986, and *Armour of God II: Operation Condor*, *Fei ying gai wak*, Jackie Chan, 1991), as well as later films that provide a nostalgic nod to past successes such as *CZ12* (aka *Chinese Zodiac*, Jackie Chan, 2012) and *The Myth* (*San wa*, Stanley Tong, 2005). *Kung Fu Yoga* complicates the anti-colonial nationalism at the heart of that narrative since it involves a tributary gift between imperial powers—the Tang court and the Magadha Kingdom—and not modern nation-states.

The film opens with a map that visualizes Asia from a distinctly Chinese perspective, if one from the Tang Dynasty (618–907 CE). India appears as "Tianzhu," the ancient Chinese name for the territory, and Tibet as "Tubo." *Kung Fu Yoga* uses CGI, stylistically reminiscent of *300* (Zack Snyder, 2006), to recreate an episode from history featuring Chan as General Wang Xuance battling Arunasva, rebel leader of the Magadha Kingdom (Figure 10.3).[11] As Wang somersaults into action, spear in hand, against a legion led by huge, bejeweled war elephants, General Bhima, sent by Princess Gitanjali, arrives to help Wang fight their common enemy. Gitanjali dispatches Wang and Bhima, with tribute treasures, to request military assistance from the Tang court. However, a blizzard engulfs Bhima and the treasure. When Wang emerges from the whiteout, his escort has disappeared.

The blizzard sets the stage for the treasure hunt that drives the narrative; however, it also presages the 2020 border clash that propelled the disputed Sino-Indian border to world news headlines. Just as Thai pirates in *The Foreigner* excuse the PRC presence in the South China Sea, ancient tributary hierarchies

Figure 10.3 Jackie Chan as a CGI version of Wang Xuance in *Kung Fu Yoga* (© Edko Films Ltd., 2017. All Rights Reserved).

in Central Asia legitimize Han Chinese domination. The disputed treasure symbolizes tensions that have been brewing for centuries in and around Kashmir, Tibet, and Xinjiang, tensions that were exacerbated by Russian, British, and Chinese imperial maneuvering in the nineteenth century. Mainland Chinese ambitions in the region, crystallized in the Belt and Road Initiative, provide a foundation for the extension of PRC military and economic interests. Yet as Antonina Łuszczykiewicz and Krzysztof Iwanek note in their review of the film:

> No historical or current Sino-Indian antagonism is ever mentioned. Just like a holy man, the movie pretends to levitate in a blissful state of eternal friendship between civilizations, high above the ground reality of present Beijing-New Delhi tensions. These, let us remember, include a long, disputed border; the issue of Indians sheltering Tibetans and the Chinese helping Pakistan; the race for supremacy in the Indian Ocean; the struggle for influence in Nepal; and many other aspects.
>
> 2017: 4

After the initial credit sequence, the Sinocentric narrative picks up in modern-day Xi'an, the ancient capital of the Tang Dynasty. Jack lectures to students in an auditorium about Wang Xuance and his memoir, *Journey to Central Asia*. In the next sequence, Xi'an's Army Museum director Liu (Gao Ming) hurriedly ushers Jack away to meet Ashmita of the Palace Museum Research Institute in Rajasthan. A stunning beauty, she has come to see if his new technology could help decipher an ancient map. Later, in Jaipur, the film reveals that Ashmita is not an archeology expert but the descendent of Princess Gitanjali of Magadha. When she welcomes Jack and his team to her palace, she wears a traditional outfit and gold ornaments and appears with antiques associated with India, including elephants and a multi-armed Hindu goddess.

Visually linked to the ancient world in both Xi'an and Jaipur, by embodying a perennially pacific historical relationship between India and China, Ashmita symbolically acquiesces and approves China's claims to disputed territories at its western frontier.[12] In Xi'an, Ashmita cites the Belt and Road Initiative directly to solicit Jack's help: "We could increase the cooperation in archaeological research between China and India. It would be in line with the 'One Belt, One Road' policy." Director Liu responds with enthusiasm: "Ashmita, your tremendous political awareness surprises me." Jack and the Communist establishment, represented by the museum director, grant her request, and the treasure hunt begins for Bhima's lost bounty.

Casting the Belt and Road

The casting furthers *Kung Fu Yoga*'s transnational and multicultural credentials. Moreover, the multiethnic cast lends credence to the soft power underpinnings of the film's narrative. Jackie Chan, born in Hong Kong, of course, brings the sometimes-troublesome territory on board by playing the hero. Lay Zhang, who plays Xiaoguang, one of Jack's teaching assistants, is a member of the popular Sino-Korean boy band Exo and appeals to K-pop fans. He is, like Chan, of Han Chinese descent with cosmopolitan connections. Miya Muqi, who plays another teaching assistant, is a celebrated yoga instructor who also teaches the Korean martial art of Taekwondo. She is part of Yunnan's ethnic Yi minority. Aarif Lee Rahman, born in Hong Kong of Arab, Malay, and Chinese descent, plays Jones, a professional treasure hunter conversant with high-tech robotics. Another supposedly Mandarin-speaking Bollywood actress, Amyra Dastur, accompanies the Indian princess. When they arrive in the Kunlun Mountains to excavate Bhima's treasure, Hong Kong celebrity Eric Tsang turns up.[13] As an engineer involved in advanced drilling techniques, he brings equipment to bore a hole to access the buried treasure. Astonished by the wonders of Chinese engineering and implicitly legitimizing the BRI's promise to bring modernity and prosperity through economic development to the lands along the ancient trade routes, Jack exclaims: "Modern technology really rocks."

Randall (Sonu Sood) is the principal villain. As another Indian actor in a key supporting role, Sood, too, implicitly legitimizes China's claims to a regional leadership with India as an enthusiastic supporter of PRC ambitions. As a descendent of Arunasva, he claims Bhima's treasure. Ashmita also insists on ownership in the name of the Gitanjali family. Jones asserts the rights of the treasure hunter to a valuable find. Jack insists the treasure belongs to the "government" without feeling any compulsion to clarify this claim: "Everything here, according to the law, belongs to the government." No one bothers to ask which government in this disputed border region.

In the film's first fight scene, Randall and his underlings try to steal the Magadha diamond from the ice cave. Randall tells his underlings to put away their guns because Jack is not a threat but "just a professor." However, the film has established Jack's kung fu credentials in earlier training scenes. Now his martial arts prowess surprises only the heavies. While Quan acts alone in *The Foreigner*, Jack fights with a team in *Kung Fu Yoga* (though in both films, Chan relies on his own stunt performers to create ensemble action that shows the star to best advantage). Including younger action players also serves the interests of the plot. In this case, after the brawl, Jones escapes with the "Eye of Shiva" diamond, leaving Jack and Ashmita behind, cut off in the cave. An expert in yoga breath control, Ashmita saves Jack's life by helping him navigate an underwater passage to freedom. Her act confirms the need for both kung fu and yoga, as the film's title suggests.

The action-adventure genre promises exotic locales and *Kung Fu Yoga* delivers these with remote-controlled rider-less camel races, undercover bathing beauties, and a car chase through Dubai, where the diamond is to be auctioned off.[14] Dubai, part of the United Arab Emirates (UAE), situated between the Persian Gulf and the Gulf of Oman, has its own Silk Road strategy and certainly provides a valuable strategic spot on mainland China's geopolitical map of the BRI.[15] A wealthy Chinese businessman (Zhang Guoli) assists Jack in Dubai, signaling the transnational reach and financial influence of overseas Chinese. Another Chinese character (Jiang Wen), who turns up in Dubai, testifies to the fact that the overseas Chinese are ready to step up to assist their compatriots all along the Belt and Road.

Back in Jaipur, the urban market includes all the exotica expected of a cinematic fantasy of India, including a rope trick, a gulal-colored powder vendor, a snake charmer, a fire-eater, a sword swallower, and a levitating holy man. All provide props for the fight choreography. Randall's gang kidnaps Jones and Kyra to pressure Jack to use the diamond to uncover the Magadha trove that is buried below the Thuban temple. Jack reluctantly agrees. Meanwhile, however, with Xiaoguang's assistance, Jones and Kyra escape from the hyena enclosure in which they had been imprisoned, giving the younger generation of action performers an opportunity to display their skills without Chan on screen.

At the temple, Jack breaks the secret code, falling into a hidden chamber leading to the buried treasure. The underground complex is riddled with booby-traps and cobras and resembles the Indian Kali temple set in *Indiana Jones and the Temple of Doom* (Steven Spielberg, 1984). The final martial arts standoff between Jack and Randall pales, of course, in comparison to the fight scenes with South Asian contortionist Dupar Singh in the classic Hong Kong comedy, *Kung Fu vs. Yoga* (*Lao shu la gui*, Chan Chuen, 1979).[16] Pacing and choreography in this scene resemble that earlier film with exchanges of blows, blocks, locks, grabs, and takedowns interspersed with running commentary on the names of his kung fu moves. References to animals and monks remind viewers of the putative links between India and China's Shaolin Temple and recall Chan's Hong Kong kung fu classics. When Jack takes up a crane stance, balancing on one leg with arms extended, before delivering "mystical kicks in succession," he triumphantly proclaims, "Chinese Kung Fu!"[17] Jack manages to free Ashmita from a machete held to her throat, and the two confront Randall. In a move reminiscent of Chinese opera acrobatic combat and Chan's use of such choreography in his screen combat repertoire, Ashmita flips over Jack's back in order to kick Randall. Sino-Indian teamwork thus saves the day.

Randall prefers gold to cultural heritage. However, Jack touts the importance of the ancient medicinal and Buddhist scriptures, scolding his opponent by saying: "The modern world was built by these ideas." This seems to link China with a morally superior modernity legitimized by historical precedent to which Randall/India is blind. As the fight winds down, a holy man and some pilgrims arrive. Jack reverts to his role as professorial sage and says: "I told you the treasure doesn't belong to you; it belongs to the whole world; it belongs to the people." A Chinese national, he validates the importance of India's heritage, rationalizing the need for closer ties between the two countries. The film ends with all, including Randall, bowing to the statue of the Hindu god Shiva. The entire cast assembles to sing and dance in a closing Bollywood number choreographed by the renowned Farah Khan.

Jackie Chan as Pedagogue and Pedant

As Meaghan Morris points out in her seminal essay, "Learning from Bruce Lee: Pedagogy and Political Correctness in Martial Arts Cinema," teaching, learning, and training from the most banal level of "self-help" platitudes to more profound understandings of identity, culture, and society form a fundamental part of the kung fu genre (2001: 171–86). In fact, through the course of his career, Jackie Chan has evolved from recalcitrant pupil to avuncular *sifu* and now to even more authoritative master. Although the title of Chan's memoir, *Never Grow Up*, seems to argue against this, Chan has evolved as he ages on screen.

In earlier starring vehicles, Chan assumes, as Mark Gallagher argues, feminized "submissive, masochistic positions, destabilizing his characters' control over the films' humor, if not their action" (1997: 25).[18] Yvonne Tasker notes, however: "Chan's 'softness' does not consist in a lack of masculinity or an inability to fight, but more in a refusal either to take the male body too seriously or to play the part of Oriental other" (1997: 334). The transformation from his *Never Grow Up* boyishness to his assumption of the role of stern moralist has never been clear-cut or complete. In fact, Chan's performance of masculinity varies enormously as he transitions from middle-aged to senior action star. This can perhaps best be seen in the way Steve Fore characterizes the star in *Rumble in the Bronx* (Stanley Tong, 1995). Fore describes the conclusion of a scene in which Chan defeats a biker gang in their own hangout as follows:

> Chan lectures the beaten bikers about their socially irresponsible behavior and departs with the words (preserved in Cantonese in the US release), "I hope that the next time we meet we can sit down and have tea together." After getting a translation from a gang member who conveniently knows Cantonese, the leader of the bikers is so impressed that he decides on the spot to change his and the gang's ways.
>
> 1997: 255

As in *Kung Fu Yoga*, Chan lectures his opponents on their moral failings. Pedagogy and pedantry are central to the star's twenty-first century persona and link to his jingoistic off-screen proclamations.

In *The Foreigner*, although Quan uses the Socratic method with Sean to probe his ethics, he prefers to lecture Hennessy on his moral failings. At one point, he proclaims: "Politics and terrorism are different ends of the same snake." In *Kung Fu Yoga*, too, Jack takes every opportunity offered to deliver a disquisition on one topic or another. In the Kunlun Mountains, for example, Jack reminds Jones to "Let your body and environment be one . . . Chinese kung fu has its roots deep in the Chinese culture. There's a lot you have to learn." The references to Chinese nationalism underscore the fact that *Kung Fu Yoga* must deliver on its chauvinistic message even in an ostensibly transnational co-production. The direct link between specific PRC initiatives such as the BRI and the assertion of Chinese cultural superiority through history, tradition, and the martial arts help to fuel the growth of the mainland Chinese film market as well as specific policies such as the Closer Economic Partnership Arrangement (CEPA) that have made it more lucrative for Hong Kong creative talents to work across the border.[19]

That Indian critics find *Kung Fu Yoga*'s patronizing attitude offensive comes as little surprise. However, Chan has also rubbed the Hong Kong public the wrong way. Laikwan Pang, for example, argues that Hong Kong audiences find the doctrinaire Chan offensive:

> Hong Kong viewers . . . are . . . repelled by his increasingly didactic attitude to the Hong Kong people. . . . Chan is prone to give lectures. . . . He assumes a heavy, Chinese paternal voice when he speaks to Hong Kong's media. . . . There is also a strong nationalist dimension to Chan's lectures, particularly after the 1997 reunification.
>
> 2007: 207

Beyond the patriotism expressed indirectly and overtly in films such as *The Foreigner* and *Kung Fu Yoga*, Chan misses few opportunities to express his loyalty to the authorities in Beijing at the expense of popular sentiment in his native Hong Kong. In her article, "Here's Why Jackie Chan Is Really Unpopular in Hong Kong," Heather Chen (2020) notes that Chan has been critical of the electoral process in Taiwan as well as calls for democracy in Hong Kong. Saying the Chinese need to "be controlled," Chan has come out publicly in favor of harsher measures for protesters desecrating the PRC flag and for the police crackdown during the 2019 anti-Extradition Bill (anti-ELAB) movement. In 2020 he supported implementation of the controversial National Security Law. His characters in *The Foreigner* and *Kung Fu Yoga* have no Hong Kong connections, and he no longer plays a local Hong Kong hero on- or off-screen.

While it may be easy to dismiss Chan's jingoism as an economic move to secure his success in a growing mainland market, that may not take the entire picture into account. Embracing Communist Party rule in Beijing has cost Chan fans in Taiwan, South Korea, India, the Philippines, and other regions where the People's Republic has flexed its muscle territorially, militarily, politically, or economically. As Pang (2007) rightly points out, Jackie Chan does not enjoy the same level of stardom and artistic autonomy as an action lead in Hollywood as he did earlier in Hong Kong. The racism that pushed Bruce Lee to Hong Kong still propels talents as diverse as Donnie Yen, Wong Kar-wai, Andrew Lau and John Woo to work in mainland China after forays into filmmaking in the United States. Jackie Chan has followed suit. Until the Sino-US Trade War and the 2020 COVID-19 crisis, Jackie Chan's pivot from Hong Kong to China even helped him in Hollywood. Arguably, his popularity in mainland China made him attractive as a co-star in co-productions such as *The Karate Kid* (Harald Zwart, 2010) and *The Foreigner*. Revisiting his past glory through intertextual allusions while appealing to the mainland market keeps Jackie Chan relevant.

Geopolitical maneuvering is at the core of global action, and both *The Foreigner* and *Kung Fu Yoga* provide wish-fulfillment and physical heroism for the mainland Chinese market. *The Foreigner* paints a picture of a divided United Kingdom, threatened with renewed violence in the run-up to Brexit thanks to the UK's unresolved (post)colonial relationship with Ireland. The hero, Quan/Jackie Chan, however, remains a "foreigner." *Kung Fu Yoga* argues for China's rights to the Western territories it claims, particularly along the Indian border. India and the United Arab Emirates need to get on the Belt and Road with the assurance that China, through its principal global ambassador, Jackie Chan, respects their religious differences and cultural heritage. Concerns involving Tibetan Buddhists and Uighur Muslims are allayed imaginatively through a Bollywood dance at a sacred site and a joyride through Muslim-majority Dubai. Both *The Foreigner* and *Kung Fu Yoga* thus keep Xi Jinping's China dream alive in Belt and Road soft power productions. As he ages and falls out of favor with audiences elsewhere,

Jackie Chan's star today shines primarily in mainland China. The box office statistics highlight this fact. *The Foreigner* did exponentially better in the PRC than in other markets, and, although the United Arab Emirates warmed to the Dubai-set *Kung Fu Yoga*, the overwhelming bulk of its profits came from the mainland Chinese box office.[20]

A COVID-19 Coda

When the novel coronavirus hit China in 2020, Jackie Chan sprang into action. Treating the race for an effective vaccine like a treasure hunt, he offered a cash reward.[21] Having no sense of the way medical research and the pharmaceutical industry operate, Chan's gesture, of course, proves meaningless. The star also stepped up during the Lunar New Year when Wuhan remained the epicenter of the outbreak to record a Mandopop song to support those affected.[22] As the virus took hold outside of China, Chan encountered criticism of his efforts to back the PRC's position on the pandemic.[23] As the virus spread to India, Chan sent a message on the Internet:

> Namaste and Hello. I am Jackie Chan. I would like to send my love and wishes to everyone in India. I know we are all facing a very difficult time right now. We should stay positive and follow the advice of your country. Protecting yourself is protecting your family.[24]

Needless to say, many Indian netizens did not appreciate Chan's efforts.[25] In fact, as Dorothy Wai Sim Lau points out in *Chinese Stardom in Participatory Cyberculture*, Chan had made more than one online gaffe before the COVID-19 crisis (2018: 82).

In the wake of the pandemic, Chan continues to be a productive fixture in mainland Chinese popular cinema.[26] Given the vitriol leveled against mainland China globally because of its handling of the virus, treatment of the Uighurs, Inner Mongolians, and Tibetans, crackdown in Hong Kong,[27] increasingly bellicose attitude toward Taiwan, and military maneuvering in the South China Sea, it remains to be seen whether Chan's star appeal can save mainland China's soft power initiatives or whether the aging star will fade with China's international ambitions.

As PRC cinema digs even deeper into jingoistic narratives that have little appeal outside of the mainland, Hong Kong action filmmakers bank on mainland China for their career ambitions. Hollywood's reluctance to go beyond racial tokenism in front of as well as behind the camera can be seen in its inability to accommodate Hong Kong action superstars such as Jet Li, Donnie Yen, John Woo, Tsui Hark, Andrew Lau, and the late Ringo Lam, among many others, more adequately. As the PRC eclipses domestic Hong Kong production, these transnational action filmmakers gravitate toward an expanding market that provides more opportunities for Chinese-speaking talent. Jackie Chan serves as simply one example among many.

In this way, Hong Kong action talent moves into the ideological service of mainstream PRC cinema. Sidelining soft power, *The Battle at Lake Changjin* (*Chang jin hu*, 2021), directed by Hong Kong action stalwarts Tsui Hark and Dante Lam, along with Fifth Generation American-based director Chen Kaige, for example, reimagines the Korean war, from the Chinese point of view, as an epic anti-imperial struggle against the United States (rather than the United Nations) that conveniently leaves out Koreans (both North and South). Sidelining India on the Belt and Road as well as Korea in its unresolved civil conflict makes films such as *Kung Fu Yoga* and *The Battle at Lake Changjin* less about soft-power persuasion and more about solidifying the Party's standing through the appeal of action on screen.[28]

Acknowledgments

Many thanks to Georgina Challen for her assistance with this article as well as the editors of this volume for their support, encouragement, and perceptive suggestions.

Notes

1   See further Laukkanen (2016).

2   Meaghan Morris (2005) captures the triangular tensions at the heart of transnational action involving Hong Kong, the PRC, and Hollywood at an earlier historical moment.

3   Examples include films such as *Wolf Warrior 2* (*Zhan lang II*, Wu Jing, 2017), *Operation Mekong* (*Gong he xing dong*, Dante Lam, 2016), *Operation Red Sea* (*Hong hai xing dong*, Dante Lam, 2018), and *The Wandering Earth* (*Liu lang di qiu*, Frant Guo, 2019).

4   Campbell had worked previously with Brosnan on the James Bond franchise in *GoldenEye* (1995).

5   Nonetheless, Northern Ireland was bound by the result of the overall vote across the UK to leave the EU, with the consequences for the border continuing to play out politically as of this writing.

6   The chokehold has been in the news because of its frequent misuse by the police in the United States, notably in the deaths of George Floyd and Eric Garner. However, it remains part of the standard repertoire of combat choreographers with many variations across the martial arts.

7   For glimpses of Jackie Chan choreographing the fight scenes see "'The Foreigner' Behind the Scenes with Jackie Chan" (2017).

8   See further Bhushan (2017).

9   The Indian partner in the co-production, Viacom 18, pulled out before shooting ended.

10 The Indiana Jones series includes *Raiders of the Lost Ark* (1981), *Indiana Jones and the Temple of Doom* (1984), *Indiana Jones and the Last Crusade* (1989), *Indiana Jones and the Kingdom of the Crystal Skull* (2008), and *Indiana Jones and the Dial of Destiny* (2023). The first four films are directed by Steven Spielberg. The last is directed by James Mangold.

11 See further Singh (2009). Only Chan is clearly identifiable as Wang Xuance, though Arunasva and Princess Gitanjali do bear a resemblance to Sonu Sood and Disha Patani, respectively. Both Sood's and Patani's modern-day characters in the film are introduced as descendants of those portrayed in the opening CGI sequence. It is unclear whether General Bhima is meant to resemble another character in the production.

12 In both scenes, Ashmita addresses Jack in fluent Mandarin, obviously dubbed and an octave above Patani's natural speaking voice that can be heard in scenes in which Ashmita speaks English.

13 *Kung Fu Yoga* was filmed in Iceland rather than Tibet.

14 The "Eye of Shiva" jewel is, in fact, a product placement for Swarovski. See Chan (2017).

15 The connection between China and Dubai has been reinforced by Dubai's ruling royals as recently as 2019. "The Silk Road: Dubai's Green Gateway to the World" (2019).

16 *Kung Fu vs. Yoga* does not star Jackie Chan.

17 The crane stance here alludes to the importance of that technique in both the original *The Karate Kid* (John G. Avildsen, 1984) and the remake with Jackie Chan (Harald Zwart, 2010).

18 K.C. Lo points out, however, that Chan provides a hard-bodied view of his performance in the outtakes that accompany many of his features, which show the danger and injuries he endures to execute the action on screen (1996: 105–25).

19 See further Szeto and Chen (2013).

20 Box Office Mojo, no date, "*The Foreigner* (2017)" and Box Office Mojo, no date, "*Kung Fu Yoga*."

21 "Jackie Chan Offers $140,000 Reward for Coronavirus Vaccine" (2020).

22 "Jackie Chan and other Mandopop Artistes Sing Songs to Show Solidarity with China Amidst Coronavirus Outbreak" (2020).

23 Lin (2020).

24 See "Covid-19: Hollywood Ace Jackie Chan Has this Message for India" (2020).

25 See "China Uses Jackie Chan's Star Power to Woo Indians amid COVID-19" (2020).

26 See Davis (2021).

27 In conjunction with the imposition of the National Security Law in 2020, Hong Kong has enacted strict censorship regulations targeting the film industry in 2021. See Cheung (2021).

28 See further Chu (2022) on Hong Kong filmmakers' contributions to PRC propaganda.

Works Cited

Berry, Chris (2003), "What's Big about the Big Film? 'De-Westernizing' the Blockbuster in Korea and China," in Julian Stringer (ed.), *Movie Blockbusters*, 217–29, London: Routledge.

Berry, Chris (2021), "What Is Transnational Chinese Cinema Today? Or, Welcome to the Sinosphere," *Transnational Screens*, 12 (3): 1–16.

Bhushan, Nyay (2017), "Jackie Chan's 'Kung-Fu Yoga' Slammed by Indian Critics for Perpetuating Stereotypes," *The Hollywood Reporter*, 5 February. Available online: https://www.hollywoodreporter.com/news/jackie-chans-kung-fu-yoga-slammed-by-indian-critics-perpetuating-stereotypes-972335 (accessed 28 October 2020).

Box Office Mojo (no date), for *Kung Fu Yoga*: https://www.boxofficemojo.com/releasegroup/gr1152078341/ (accessed 13 December 2021).

Box Office Mojo (no date), for *The Foreigner* (2017): https://www.boxofficemojo.com/title/tt1615160/ (accessed 13 December 2021).

Callahan, William A. (2013), *China Dreams: 20 Visions of the Future*, Oxford: Oxford University Press.

Chan, Jackie, with Zhu Mo (2018), *Never Grow Up*, trans. Jeremy Tiang, New York: Gallery Books.

Chan, Rachel (2017), "What's Real and What's Not in *Kung Fu Yoga*?," *The Popping Post*, 26 January. Available online: https://sg.style.yahoo.com/real-not-kung-fu-yoga-182413189.html#:–:text=Swarovski%20crystal%20with%2028%20facets,of%20Vintage%20Rose%20and%20Siam (accessed 12 October 2023).

Chen, Heather (2020), "Here's Why Jackie Chan Is Really Unpopular in Hong Kong," *Vice*, 20 August. Available online: https://www.vice.com/en/article/wxqkn5/heres-why-jackie-chan-is-really-unpopular-in-hong-kong (accessed 28 October 2020).

Cheung, Tony (2021), "Hong Kong Passes Bill to Ban Films Deemed Threats to National Security, Increase Penalty for Unauthorized Screenings," *South China Morning Post*, 27 October. Available online: https://www.scmp.com/news/hong-kong/politics/article/3153857/hong-kong-passes-bill-ban-films-deemed-threats-national (accessed 13 December 2021).

"China Uses Jackie Chan's Star Power to Woo Indians amid COVID-19" (2020), *Big News Network*, 20 May. Available online: https://www.bignewsnetwork.com/news/265145217/china-uses-jackie-chan-star-power-to-woo-indians-amid-covid-19 (accessed 28 October 2020).

Chu, Stephen Yiu-Wai (2022), *Main Melody Films: Hong Kong Film Directors in China*, Edinburgh: Edinburgh University Press.

"Covid-19: Hollywood Ace Jackie Chan Has this Message for India" (2020), *The Times of India*, 3 September. Available online: https://timesofindia.indiatimes.com/videos/news/covid-19-hollywood-ace-jackie-chan-has-this-message-for-india/videoshow/75822345.cms (accessed 28 October 2020).

Davis, Rebecca (2021), "Jackie Chan's Latest Comedy 'Ride On' Wraps Production," *Variety*, 11 November. Available online: https://variety.com/2021/film/news/jackie-chan-ride-on-wraps-production-1235110321/ (accessed 13 December 2021).

Fore, Steve (1997), "Jackie Chan and the Cultural Dynamics of Global Entertainment," in Sheldon Hsiao-peng Lu (ed.), *Transnational Chinese Cinemas: Identity, Nationhood, Gender*, 239–62, Honolulu: University of Hawaii Press.

Gallagher, Mark (1997), "Masculinity in Translation: Jackie Chan's Transcultural Star Text," *The Velvet Light Trap*, 39: 23–41.

Holmlund, Chris (2010), "Celebrity, Ageing and Jackie Chan: Middle-aged Asian in Transnational Action," *Celebrity Studies*, 1 (1): 96–112.

"Jackie Chan and Other Mandopop Artistes Sing Songs to Show Solidarity with China Amidst Coronavirus Outbreak" (2020), *DimSum Daily*, 7 February. Available online: https://www.dimsumdaily.hk/jackie-chan-and-other-mandopop-singers-sing-songs-to-show-solidarity-with-china-amidst-coronavirus-outbreak/ (accessed 28 October 2020).

"Jackie Chan Offers $140,000 Reward for Coronavirus Vaccine" (2020), *The Roanoke Times*, 12 February. Available online: https://roanoke.com/video/news/jackie-chan-offers-reward-for-coronavirus-vaccine/video_10d0c83c-56c6-5b32-99c1-528462bd9584.html (accessed 28 October 2020).

Jameson, Fredric (1982), *The Political Unconscious: Narrative as a Socially Symbolic Act*, New York: Cornell University Press.

Kokas, Aynne (2017), *Hollywood Made in China*, Berkeley: University of California Press.

Lau, Dorothy Wai Sim (2018), *Chinese Stardom in Participatory Cyberculture*, Edinburgh: Edinburgh University Press.

Laukkanen, Tatu (2016), "The Contemporary Cinema of the BRIC Countries and the Politics of Change," PhD Thesis, The University of Hong Kong.

Lin, Laura (2020), "Jackie Chan Helps Lead China's COVID-19 Propaganda War," *Worldcrunch*, 16 April. Available online: https://worldcrunch.com/coronavirus/jackie-chan-helps-lead-china39s-covid-19-propaganda-war (accessed 28 October 2020).

Lo, Kwai-Cheung (1996), "Muscles and Subjectivity: A Short History of the Masculine Body in Hong Kong Popular Culture," *Camera Obscura*, 13 (3): 104–25.

Łuszczykiewicz, Antonina, and Krzysztof Iwanek (2017), "*Kung Fu Yoga*: A Chinese-Indian Soft Power Romance," *The Diplomat*, 1 June. Available online: https://thediplomat.com/2017/06/kung-fu-yoga-a-chinese-indian-soft-power-romance/ (accessed 28 October 2020).

Marchetti, Gina (1989), "Action-Adventure as Ideology," in Ian Angus and Sut Jhally (eds), *Cultural Politics in Contemporary America*, 182–97, London: Routledge.

Morris, Meaghan (2001), "Learning from Bruce Lee: Pedagogy and Political Correctness in Martial Arts Cinema," in Matthew Tinkcom and Amy Villarejo (eds), *Keyframes: Popular Cinema and Cultural Studies*, 171–86, London: Routledge.

Morris, Meaghan (2005), "Introduction: Hong Kong Connections," in Meaghan Morris, Siu Leung Li and Stephen Chan Ching-kiu (eds), *Hong Kong Connections: Transnational Imagination in Action Cinema*, 1–18, Hong Kong: Hong Kong University Press.

Nye, Joseph S., Jr. (1990), "Soft Power," *Foreign Policy*, 80: 153–71.

Pang, Laikwan (2007), "Jackie Chan, Tourism, and the Performing Agency," in Gina Marchetti and Tan See Kam (eds), *Hong Kong Film, Hollywood and the New Global Cinema: No Film Is an Island*, 206–18, London: Routledge.

Singh, Upinder (2009), *A History of Ancient and Early Medieval India: From the Stone Age to the 12th Century*, New York: Pearson Education.

Szeto, Mirana M., and Yun-chung Chen (2013), "Mainlandization and Neoliberalism with Post-colonial and Chinese Characteristics: Challenges for the Hong Kong Film Industry," in Jyotsna Kapur and Keith B. Wagner (eds), *Neoliberalism and Global Cinema: Capital, Culture, and Marxist Critique*, 239–60, London: Routledge.

Tasker, Yvonne (1997), "Fists of Fury: Discourses of Race and Masculinity in the Martial Arts Cinema," in Harry Stecopoulos and Michael Uebel (eds), *Race and the Subject of Masculinities*, 315–36, Durham, NC: Duke University Press.

"'The Foreigner' Behind the Scenes with Jackie Chan" (2017), YouTube, 5 October. Available online: https://www.youtube.com/watch?v=0ys9reoYXlo (accessed 28 October 2020).

"The Silk Road: Dubai's Green Gateway to the World" (2019), *The Sustainabilist*, 7 March. Available online: https://thesustainabilist.ae/the-silk-road-dubais-green-gateway-to-the-world/ (accessed 28 October 2020).

Voci, Paola, and Luo Hui (2017), *Screening China's Soft Power*, London: Routledge.

Chapter 11

Aging, Disability, Acting: Pam Grier and Sigourney Weaver

Chris Holmlund

Actors, Movement, Action

Do women star in geriaction films? "Geriaction" originally referred to keeping female patients in nursing homes active and, to the extent possible, able-bodied.[1] In 2013 *Guardian* critic Charlie Lyne applied the label to action films with aging male stars, among them Sylvester Stallone, Arnold Schwarzenegger, and Bruce Willis.[2] But are older women actors today confined to supporting roles and bit parts or cast as villains, as Black, Latino, and Asian male players are?[3] The list of women aged 60+ in Anglo action is not long, but it *is* growing, and includes Judi Dench (88), Charlotte Rampling (77), Susan Sarandon and Glenn Close (both 76), Pam Grier and Sigourney Weaver (both 73), Linda Hamilton and Cynthia Rothrock (both 66), Angela Bassett and Jamie Lee Curtis (both 64), and Demi Moore and Michelle Yeoh (both 60).[4]

So far only Helen Mirren (78) has co-starred in geriaction, in *RED* (Robert Schwentke, 2010) and *RED 2* (Dean Parisot, 2013). "RED" stands for "retired and extremely dangerous." Sexy and svelte, Mirren's Victoria is gun-savvy and energetic, fully the equal of male lead Bruce Willis and co-stars John Malkovich and Brian Cox. She runs, limps, shoots, burns, and banters *while* wearing furs, gowns, and combat boots. No wonder Sadie Wearing (2012) describes her as both exemplary and exceptional. Is she a model for other older actresses?

Lisa Purse argues that action cinema is "defined by its persistent and detailed attention to the exerting body, a focus which shapes its audio-visual aesthetics as much as its characterization and narrative design" (2011: 2). Discussing male actors, Purse charts the "consequences of real-world ageing—visible or simply known—on the construction of the ageing action star." With "normative presumptions of ageing as an inevitable slowing or stiffening of movement," how long, she speculates, will the middle-aged Tom Cruise and others continue to enjoy success (2017: 163, 162)?

How does age affect or alter the way older female characters are written and rendered? What does the nigh compulsory requirement that action leads be able-bodied—certain war films and science fiction movies notwithstanding—mean for older actresses? Will older female protagonists need to demonstrate physical strength and agility in action to the same extent geriaction's older male characters do? Or might know-how and skill, spirit, and spunk, compensate for decreased speed and wider waistlines? How do race and reputation impact casting, shape spectacle, and influence narrative?

Film performances figure amid the cultural road maps for "successful" aging that we in the contemporary neoliberal West encounter. Watching and listening to older actors in action affects us viscerally and emotionally as well as intellectually. Explosions, chases, and gunfire enhance—or attenuate—our responses to their gestures, poses, stances, delivery. In most Western societies women live longer than men do, yet aging often brings disability. Most action films encourage us to push anxieties about aging into the future: 60 is the new 40, 70 the new 50. Seeing older stars move freely and look ever youthful we ponder "how to age without becoming old?" (Gilleard and Higgs 2013: 13). *How* we age is left to us; the state assumes little responsibility. Most action films sidestep disability, especially in tandem with old age.[5] That severe disease, hospitalization, and death in real life occur mainly among people over 65 exacerbates the quandary most people face, because requiring assistance for any reason, at any age, is touted as threatening the economic well-being of the majority.[6] What we fear most is "the loss of independence, of autonomy, of control; in other words, subjection to fate" (Longmore and Umansky 2001: 7).

In search of cinematic paradigms and alternative options, I turn to two of the very first female action stars, Pam Grier and Sigourney Weaver, both born in 1949. Both have become icons. Grier made her name in 1970s women-in-prison films, action horror movies, and urban revenge pictures, among them *Women in Cages* (Gerardo de Leon, 1971), *Black Mama White Mama* (Eddie Romero, 1973), *Coffy* (Jack Hill, 1973), *Scream Blacula Scream* (Bob Kelljan, 1973), and *Foxy Brown* (Jack Hill, 1974). Part Native American, part Black, part white, part Asian—with an aquiline nose, high cheekbones, and bounteous breasts—she was beautiful, for some exotically so. Never afraid to get dirty, she epitomized daring, especially in her early films: "I rode horses and motorcycles and jumped off of buildings into nets. If you needed a woman of color to handle a gun, do a wheelie on a chopper, or fall off a cliff into a rice paddy, I was the one to call" (Grier 2010: 129).[7]

Tall and imposing, Sigourney Weaver has left an indelible imprint on science fiction action thanks to the four *Alien* films she starred in and—in 1992 and 1997—helped produce. Who can ever forget her in *Aliens* (James Cameron,

1986)? She *is* "Rambolina" thanks to her loader-suit, more muscular, more powerful, than even Stallone as Rambo! From the 1980s on, she stars or co-stars in crime dramas, war romances, action comedies, and adventure biopics, most of them, like the *Alien* franchise, with bigger budgets than Grier's. *Eyewitness* (Peter Yates, 1981), *The Year of Living Dangerously* (Peter Weir, 1982), *Ghostbusters* (Ivan Reitman, 1984), and *Gorillas in the Mist* (Michael Apted, 1988) constitute examples of her action-affiliated range in the 1980s alone.[8]

In 1997, Grier and Weaver turned 48. Grier's down-on-her-luck airline stewardess outmaneuvered everyone in *Jackie Brown* (Quentin Tarantino). Part-human, part-alien, a clone, Weaver's 200-year-old Ripley triumphed over United Military scientists and alien Xenomorphs in *Alien: Resurrection* (Jean-Pierre Jeunet). Global box office figures testify to the pleasures audiences found watching them in middle-age: according to The Numbers (n.d.), *Jackie Brown* has now earned nearly $75 million worldwide; *Alien: Resurrection* has grossed more than $160 million. Since 2000, moreover, Grier and Weaver have continued to play characters written as middle-aged or older. Sometimes they embody types; sometimes they create rounded, naturalistic characters; sometimes they send up cliché and type. Audiences have been able to observe them age on and offscreen.

Comparing the opportunities Grier and Weaver have had and the acting choices they have made, aged 51–73, in action hybrids released between 2000 and 2023 helps account for some of the blind spots in current research: those studies of female aging and disability that exist focus on horror films, melodramas, and dramas, not action.[9] I concentrate on six action hybrids that feature Grier and Weaver, aged 50 to late 60. Two were blockbusters, one went straight to streaming, and three had small theatrical runs. I ask whether the stars' renowned talents—here in action-inflected thrillers, action adventure, horror, science fiction, comedy, and noir—stake out strategies of embodiment that question the rote equation of older age with enfeeblement and deterioration. My hope is that thinking about Grier and Weaver's performances will suggest to other actresses, and to viewers as well, ways to envision, treat, and live aging and disability differently. I return to these themes in conclusion.

Sidestepping Age in Action and Action Adventure: *Slow Burn* (a.k.a. *Wilder*) (Rodney Gibbons, 2000) and *Holes* (Andrew Davis, 2003)

Grier was the principal character in *Jackie Brown*; Tarantino wrote the film with her in mind. Yet after *Jackie Brown* she was not offered another starring role until

2000, at age 51, when she was cast in Gibbons's crime thriller, *Slow Burn*. Although Gibbons's film clearly tries to capitalize on *Jackie Brown*'s success, it was nonetheless released straight-to-DVD and only then in 2003. No box office or budget information is available.

The detective Grier plays is, like Jackie, indebted to her Blaxploitation heroines. Detective Della Wilder (Grier) is single, self-reliant, kick-ass, down-home, and righteously feminist. Where *Jackie Brown* had Max Cherry (Robert Forster, then 56) slowly, sweetly court Jackie, *Slow Burn* has Dr. Sam Charney (Rutger Hauer, then 56) woo Wilder. A womanizing gynecologist, Charney is initially Wilder's prime suspect, but ultimately—as the tag line rather misleadingly puts it—"her only hope for survival."

Wilder mistrusts Charney's motives, as Grier's half smiles and ironic delivery indicate. The two actors are never given a chance to explore whether their characters have real chemistry, however, because *Slow Burn* is more interested in action than in romance. As one of several cops Grier has incarnated over the course of her career, and like most of her 1980s and 1990s characters, Wilder carries a gun.[10] She also kicks, punches, and kills, much as Grier's Blaxploitation avenging angels did, and found objects again work as weapons. One example: with Wilder assisting, Charney performs an illegal autopsy on the victim of a serial killer. Suddenly an assassin attacks them. Thinking quickly, Wilder pushes the man onto his own knife, then with Charney's assistance dumps him in a freezer. Her partner (Romano Orzari) upbraids her the next day: "Della! . . . You can't go around killing fools and not tell anyone. . . . You gotta get control of your emotions!" His sexist paternalism enrages Wilder: "Don't give me that PMS shit!" "I didn't say anything about PMS." "You don't have to. I know how men think. A woman gets a little pissed off, a little out of control, and automatically men think, 'oh, here comes five more days of PMS.'"

The autopsy uncovers radiation poisoning. Wilder and Charney interview another woman, also suffering from radiation poisoning and largely confined to a wheelchair. A multinational pharmaceutical corporation knowingly marketed the deadly drug prescribed to her. In the final action sequence, the firm's lawyer (Eugene Clark) tries to kill Wilder, knocking her down, kicking her, then flinging her across the room. She remains defiant. Charney enters just in time to give Wilder time to struggle to her feet, seize a metal rod, and clobber her adversary. Costuming and editing make it look like Grier is doing her own stunts. Her movements elsewhere have been smooth and unhampered but uncredited Charlene Francique probably doubled Grier.[11]

Wilder's age is never an issue. Yes, she is the mother of two preteens, but as in *Mars Attacks!* (Tim Burton, 1996), she is attractive, with sculpted cheekbones and lively eyes (Figure 11.1). Grier inserts energy and intensity into the expressive moments that interrupt and pace action sequences, delivering lines rapidly, often adding emphatic head nods and forceful gestures. She ensures that Wilder seems both sassy and angry. No surprise, then, when Wilder's captain (John

Figure 11.1 The 51-year-old Pam Grier gets the glamor treatment: as Detective Della Wilder in *Slow Burn* lighting highlights Grier's sculpted cheekbones, full lips, and aquiline nose (© MTI Home Video, 2003. All Rights Reserved).

Dunn-Hill) tells her: "The precinct is full of guys who think you're a hotheaded, big-mouthed, man-hating bitch."

Sigourney Weaver creates a different kind of "man-hating bitch" in her first action film of the decade, *Holes*. Made and released theatrically the same year that *Slow Burn* went straight-to-DVD, based on Louis Sachar's Newberry- and National Book Award-winning story, *Holes* cost $20 million and grossed $71.5 million world-wide.[12] Weaver was cast for her ability "to combine femininity and toughness [and] . . . give the character her edge" ("*Holes*" 2003). As she had recently done in *Alien: Resurrection* and *Galaxy Quest* (Dean Parisot, 1999), Weaver modulates her delivery to suit the circumstances in which her character finds herself. The Warden is, by turns, deceptively sympathetic, quietly commanding, fetchingly maleficent, and falsely contrite. Make-up artist Linda DeVetta and hair stylist Lyndell Quiyou guarantee that Weaver looks enticing, pulling her hair into a loose braid or letting it loose in come-hither tendrils, highlighting her cheeks, and painting her lips and nails bright red.

The film's three storylines cover different time periods; in conclusion, they interweave. The Warden is part of the main, present-tense, story. She has turned her parched ranch into a camp for delinquent boys like Stanley Yelnats (Shia LaBoeuf). She forces the boys to dig holes for buried treasure in the hot sun. A second plot revolves around a fortune-telling crone's (Eartha Kitt) curse; a third is set further in the past. Together with a friend (Khleo Thomas), Stanley undoes the curse and finds the treasure. The two boys engage in most of the action and enjoy most of the adventures. Ultimately, they and the other boys go free. The Warden and her two evil employees, Mr. Sir (Jon Voigt) and Dr. Pendanski (Tim Blake Nelson), are arrested.

Weaver's Warden does not appear until 40 minutes into the main story. Emerging from a huge Cadillac, wearing boots, tight jeans, a cowboy hat, and the first of many pretty blouses, she looks lovely (Figure 11.2). With Voigt chewing scenery beside her, Weaver does not need to raise her voice: her politely ominous repetition of "Excuse me?" is enough. Weaver pitches her words higher, emphasizing her character's youthfulness. Faintly she/the Warden hints at a past dalliance with the flirtatiously obsequious Voigt/Mr. Sir, cooing "I liked you better when you smoked," then slashing him across the face with rattle-snake-venom painted nails. He screams and writhes in agony.

Unlike Grier/Wilder's tussles in *Slow Burn*, this is the most "action" we see Weaver/The Warden engage in, though Weaver does frequently adopt a classic hands-on-hips action stance, signifying — depending on context — impatience, readiness, or resolve. Fleetingly she gives a doubled performance: her insincere delivery of "Thank God, you're OK!" when the young heroes return to the ranch says much about the Warden's selfishness and greed.

Both Grier and Weaver's movements are free-flowing, unconstrained. In their early 50s, both are credible as vibrantly active, attractive adults of no specific age; they could even be in their 30s. Grier is still a physical performer. As in most

Figure 11.2 Friendly smiles hide deadly designs as, aged 53, Sigourney Weaver plays the duplicitous Warden in *Holes* (© Disney DVD, 2003. All Rights Reserved).

of the Blaxploitation films she—i.e., she and her stunt double—are fully a match for every male attacker. For the first time since *Working Girl* (Mike Nichols, 1988) Weaver embodies a composite villain/vamp, albeit now in a PG-rated Disney film rather than an R-rated one. Crucially, almost no one saw or sees the low-budget *Slow Burn*. Children, teens, and adults are still watching *Holes*.

Circumventing Senescence in Action Horror and Science Fiction: *Bones* (Ernest R. Dickerson, 2001) and *Avatar* (James Cameron, 2009)

Unlike *Slow Burn*, *Bones* was given a theatrical release and also lost money at the box office. Made for roughly $16 million, released by independent studio New Line, *Bones* grossed $8 million in US theaters. Action elements pace the narrative: the sustained backstory is full of violence, pimps, drug dealers, and dirty cops. Using color filters, black and white, double exposures, jump cuts, canted angles, smoke, eerie music, and creaking steps, Dickerson makes maggots, goo, blood, and vomit look arty. Events unfold non-sequentially: *Bones* jumps from 1979 to the end 1990s/early 2000s and back again. Age and aging would seem to be necessary to the plot but are not: the senescence that attends older age is utterly absent.

A devotee of Grier's 1970s work, rapper-star Snoop Dogg wanted then 52-year-old Grier to be his character's girlfriend, Pearl. She was 22 years his senior. At points in the 1970s sequences Grier/Pearl rests her head lovingly on Snoop Dogg/Jimmy Bones's shoulder. Aged down via hairstyling and costuming, Grier sports an Afro and a boa. Speaking in a higher register, she makes Pearl a seductive if less intrepid composite of the "buxom bad-bitch" Blaxploitation characters she created in *Coffy*, *Foxy Brown*, *Friday Foster* (Arthur Marks, 1975), and *Sheba, Baby* (William Girdler, 1975), and other 1970s films, too (Means Coleman 2011: 203). Pimp-stylish in a long flowing coat, pinstripe suit, and large hat, a numbers runner, Snoop Dogg cuts a dashing figure at her side. He is good at posing; Grier is the better actor. She gives her performance an arc; Snoop Dogg's younger and older Bones are indistinguishable, even though Bones transforms from gentleman gangster to fiendish ghoul.

As the older Pearl, Grier lowers the pitch of her voice and moves deliberately. Pearl has become a grey-haired, dreadlocked seer who reads tarot cards and lives next to her former lover's dilapidated, rat-infested mansion. Calling themselves the "Resurrection Brothers"—the signposting is not subtle—Bones's former partner's son (Khalil Kain) and friends buy the abandoned estate and turn it into a hip-hop club. Pearl tries to warn them that danger lurks inside, without success.

The narrative and visuals pivot from crime to horror with Bones's murder. A corrupt white cop and a bad-ass Black drug dealer try to convince 1970s Bones to sell crack. Bones refuses. They shoot him, then at gunpoint force his associates, including Pearl, to knife him. Handed the switchblade last, Grier/Pearl screams, sobs, pleads, and moans. Technically she deals Bones the final deadly blow, but Pearl is as much victim as action agent. Nowhere is a demonstration of physical stamina or strength required of Grier. In the second half of *Bones* all hell literally breaks loose when 1970s-Bones returns as a ghost intent on payback. No one escapes his wrath, not even Pearl or their 20-something daughter (Bianca Lawson).

Released eight years later, *Avatar* reunites the 60-year-old Weaver with writer-director Cameron. Nominated for nine Academy Awards, *Avatar* won Oscars for Best Art Direction, Best Production Design, and Best Special Effects. One of the most expensive films ever made, with a production and advertising budget of $425 million, it was the world's highest earning film as of January 2023, having raked in $2.92 billion since its release (Box Office Mojo 2023).

Weaver's supporting character, biologist/xeno-anthropologist Dr. Grace Augustine, seen in both live-action and animation, is a courageous, capable professional with a penchant for "mothering" characters who are not family members. In this she is much like Ripley in *Aliens* and Diane Fossey in *Gorillas in the Mist*. But when the military-industrial complex stymies her study of the indigenous, blue-skinned, humanoid Na'vi's effortless communications on the planet Pandora, Grace becomes angry. She values science over financial gain and military might.

Live-action-Grace is the oldest of the film's humans. Her face is wrinkled, but no one mentions her age, let alone thinks about the physical challenges that attend most aging. To play the researcher Weaver presses her thin lips together disapprovingly and sometimes cusses mildly (*Avatar* was rated PG-13.) She employs commanding gestures and hands-on-hips poses, strides rather than walks, and stands ramrod-straight. In pants and white lab coat she looks relatively genderless. At 6'1" she towers over the 5'7" Giovanni Ribisi/her corporate boss.[13]

Because Pandora's atmosphere is toxic to humans, Grace and her team inhabit Na'vi-like avatars to carry out their research. Depicted through animation derived from motion capture and a head-mounted facial performance capture camera, Grace's avatar is female, no question: she wears khaki shorts and a short crimson Stanford University T-shirt that shows off her bare midriff and wasp-waist. As avatar-Grace, Weaver moves more freely, swinging her arms loosely and swaying her hips. Unlike live-action-Grace, she smiles frequently. Per Weaver, live-action Grace was "bristling, impatient"; her avatar was "so much more joyous" (in Kaplan 2009: 4).

But neither live-action-Grace nor avatar-Grace fight or engage in spectacular feats. Combat is for younger humans—the Marines and fighter pilot Trudi Chacon (Michelle Rodriguez)—and for younger Na'vi led by Jake Sully's (Sam Worthington) heroic and able-bodied avatar. As in most war films, *Avatar* explicitly considers disability only in relation to live-action-Jake's combat injuries; he is a paraplegic Marine.[14] In contrast, death looms large: many Na'vi perish, as do many of the marauding Marines, and Grace, too. Avatar-Jake places her failing real body next to her avatar's shell, near the sacred Tree of Souls. He and the Na'vi implore the goddess Eywa to accept her spirit. Weaver gives a muted performance. "I'm with her, Jake," she whispers. Then her voice trails off: "She's . . . ." Strands of light envelop her avatar- and live-action bodies.

Unlike her doubled performance in *Holes*, Weaver's twinned live-action and animated performances in *Avatar* point toward what Christopher Faircloth calls the "paradox of aging": the "gap between the physical presentation of aging on the external body and the subjective experience of aging that lies beneath" (2003: 18). Decline and degeneration are, as in *Bones*, not at issue: the transitions from human to avatar bodies are largely painless, always swift. Through acting, however, Weaver—and Worthington, too—imply their live-action characters remember and find joy in being able to move about freely as avatars unimpacted by the physical deteriorations occasioned by older age and/or disability. The décalage between their differently performed, differently embodied states rejects the linkage of youthfulness and able-bodied-ness on which action films rely.

But Weaver's performance—like that of every actor—went unnoticed. Attention focused instead on the film's technological innovations and imprecise politics.[15] Grier's acting in *Bones* also received no comment, even though costuming, makeup, and movement distinguish the younger and older Pearls. Pearl-the-performed-character experiences no temporal paradox, no contradiction between outer and inner selves.

Avatar's scope and reach surpassed anything Pam Grier has ever been involved with. *Bones*'s audience was considerably smaller, though Snoop Dogg's fame and Grier's iconicity ensure the film is still available on DVD and streamed. Importantly for Grier, Dickerson's film afforded her a chance to work again, as she did in *Foxy Brown*, *Posse,* and *Mars Attacks!*, with talented Black actors and artists.

Combatting Redundance in Action Comedy and Thriller Pastiche: *Bad Grandmas* (Srikant Chellappa, 2017) and *The Assignment* (Walter Hill, 2016)

The performances Grier and Weaver give in *Bad Grandmas* and *The Assignment* differ markedly. Now age 67 and 68, their movements are no longer youthful.

Grier is heavier. Weaver's face is creased, with many wrinkles.[16] Yet their signature tics and characteristic traits remain in evidence, even playing grotesques who occasionally protest the notion that older and/or disabled women are used up, good-for-nothing.

A paean to elderly female solidarity, the action-comedy *Bad Grandmas* could well be one of the least expensive geriaction films made. Preoccupied with the ways older people are treated and how they respond, aging and criminal action are front and center. Shot in three and a half weeks, first-time director Chellappa raised $20,000 for post-production through crowd sourcing. His low-budget independent grossed a mere $16,000 in domestic release, then disappeared to DVD and streaming.[17]

As the film begins four friends aged 60+ to 80+ gather to play cards and swap gossip. All are retired and live independently. One is about to lose her home to a sleazy banker. Eager to help her, Mimi (Florence Henderson) threatens the man with a gun. When it goes off accidentally he collapses. The friends transport his body to Mimi's house. Suddenly he regains consciousness. Mimi finishes him off as Grier's character, Coralee, summarizes the nonsensical plot—"A dead man is a good man." In solidarity the women carve up the body and hide it in Mimi's freezer chest.

Grier and Henderson are the best-known actors. The 81-year-old Henderson serves as group leader; Grier is her best friend. Everyone makes fun of Grier/ Coralee's girth—"Coralee, is your butt gonna fit through that door?"—but everyone relies on her strength and "can do" attitude.

Grier's performance consists mostly of non-verbal reactions and the occasional smart-ass one-liner. Her trademark moues figure prominently. Sometimes Coralee pretends to be doddery and feeble using stereotypes about the elderly as "harmless" and "accident-prone" to advantage. The other women also play-act but Grier/Coralee's masquerades are more overblown, more histrionic, quite unlike the naturalist performances Grier gives in Blaxploitation, *Fort Apache, the Bronx* (Daniel Petrie, 1981), and TV's *The L-Word* (2004–2009): here she practices actorly incoherence to comic *and* critical effect. At one point she bashes a bad guy with a frying pan, then sits on him and clocks him to death (Figure 11.3). The pacing of her performance and the rhythm and register of her voicing change abruptly. "Help me get up!" she asks the others, her voice unexpectedly weak, her movements awkward. Much as Bette Davis uses arrestingly wide-eyed expressions and unhurriedly pantomimed gestures as Baby Jane, Grier stretches "the temporal economy of spectacle, charging the image with a kind of rage" (Brooks 1999: 234–5).

Coralee and Mimi scoff at the idea that elderly women do not enjoy porn or sex. Having asked Mimi's teenage neighbor to help them access a flash drive, Grier/Coralee purses her mouth, leaving it to Mimi/Henderson to prevent him from exploring its contents. "It's elderly porn. Made *by* the elderly, *for* the elderly,

Figure 11.3 Grier's heroines are ever resourceful: in *Bad Grandmas* the 68-year-old Grier/Coralee fells an adversary using a frying pan and her own weight (© WOWNOW Entertainment, 2018. All Rights Reserved).

with those elderly actors," says Mimi. Disgusted, the boy rushes off: "a pervasive, residual horror and anxiety surround breaches to the taboos attached to older bodies and sexuality" (Wearing 2012: 149). The film ends happily: "Us girls can take care of ourselves," Mimi proclaims as Coralee goes to the freezer for ice cream. Inside is a man's head, mouth open in a frozen scream.

Crafting an insane surgeon in *The Assignment*, Sigourney Weaver is less active but more of a fury-filled force. With origins in a 1978 script about "transsexuals," in this film retribution and redundance due to disability rule. Likely Weaver's least successful appearance, the $5 million movie grossed less than $390,000, then went to DVD and streaming. Thanks to director Walter Hill's action credentials and to Weaver and Michelle Rodriguez's contrastive performances and action-based fame, *The Assignment* has nonetheless acquired a cult following. The two actresses ensure that the film taps, then saps, gendered expectations about action bodies, sending up the "anxiety over the existence and definition of masculinity and normality," ability and disability, that typifies noir (Dyer 1978: 91) and, arguably, action in general. A "bad trans(gender) object," *The Assignment* is full of instructive flaws and illuminating virtues (Keegan 2022).

The movie begins as younger hitman-for-hire Frank Kitchen (Rodriguez) is recovering from an unwanted sexual reassignment operation. The arrogant Dr. Rachel Jane (Weaver) has operated on him against his will because Kitchen killed her brother. Subsequently barred from practicing medicine, she is now in a psychiatric hospital and, for much of the film, a straitjacket. Weaver's/Dr. Jane's movements are thus limited. To convey her character's hauteur Weaver can use only voice, diction, and posture. At two points Dr. Jane becomes violent, attacking the psychiatrist (Tony Shalhoub) who questions her, and, in flashback, trying to defend herself using a scalpel against a gun-wielding, female-presenting Kitchen. Kitchen-the-"woman" stomps about searching for the person who changed his sex. Dead bodies pile up in his gender dysphoric wake.

Rodriguez plays both Kitchen-the-man and Kitchen-the-"woman." Each embodiment comes with corresponding genital display. For added camp oomph Kitchen-the-"woman" dresses as a blonde hooker when he attacks Dr. Jane. She manifests a certain gender dysphoria, too: at work she wears suits, ties, and vests, no make-up; for good measure she slicks back her short hair (Figure 11.4). She deserves, she believes, to wear the pants, literally and figuratively: "My manner has always caused me problems with those less equipped to keep up. I was a better surgeon than any of them. They hated that. And I was a woman. That made it worse." Her genitalia are not shown; instead, we see her climb atop her male assistant to gratify herself sexually.

Both Weaver and Rodriguez ham it up, exploring the hubris that underpins noir masculinity. Weaver draws on her experience with villainous and comic two-faced characters.[18] Rodriguez ridicules working class macho, slurring her words, speaking crudely, gesturing brusquely. The final physical and psychic vengeance Kitchen wreaks on Dr. Jane corresponds to what she has done to him, albeit with the proverbial eye for an eye replaced by (her) hands for (his) cock. In the last scene, Dr. Jane raises arms that end in bandaged stumps: she is permanently disabled, robbed of her work as she robbed Kitchen of his, redundant.

Figure 11.4 In *The Assignment* male attire, prominent wrinkles, and pronounced neck cords betray Dr. Rachel Jane's gender dysphoria and the 67-year-old Sigourney Weaver's aging (© Lionsgate, 2016. All Rights Reserved).

Weaver and Rodriguez's co-starring performances toy with upended genre conventions, detonate gender stability, play with masculinity, and question macho "ability" in *The Assignment*. Grier is a likeable supporting character in *Bad Grandmas*. Though slower, she still *werqs* it,[19] fueling the film with feminist rage and "claiming an enthusiasm in the expansive capacity of fleshiness to . . . make it happen"—together with her "sisters" (Bey 2019: 142).

Recognition, Resistance, Rage

Grier feels she gave her best performance in *Jackie Brown*. Co-star Samuel L. Jackson was confident that after this film Grier would "soar," enjoying the kind of box office success he had known starting with *Pulp Fiction* (Quentin Tarantino, 1994) ("Pam Grier" 2020). But a top PR person warned her *Jackie Brown* was not going to revitalize her career the way *Pulp Fiction* had revitalized John Travolta's: "You're not going to sell to the masses. You're not going to appeal to the little farm girl in Idaho" (Sternbergh 2006). Grier agreed: she knew that, as an older, mixed-race Black woman, she would be triply challenged. She was right. Today she works primarily in television and the occasional independent film. Infrequently she pops up in TV guest spots and documentaries.[20]

Weaver, in contrast, is globally recognized, both in and out of action. "The idiosyncratic nature of her career has made aging easier . . . [Her] parts never depended on dewiness" (Bruni 2020). With the *Alien* action franchise to her name, she could have fronted a geriaction prequel or sequel, but she does not appear in Ridley Scott's *Prometheus* (2012) or *Alien: Covenant* (2017). She graces magazine covers and makes cameo appearances in, for example, the all-female *Ghostbusters* (Paul Feig, 2016). Playing a version of her aging star self in 2020, in an episode of France's popular TV series "Call My Agent" ("10 Pour Cent"), her character demands that a 20-year-younger male actor be cast as her lover. Fair is fair, reasons "la belle Sigourney": older male stars are routinely paired with ingenues.

Both Grier and Weaver are interested in acting as a craft. Both have often worked in theater. Grier has tried to stay true to her 1975 goals: "no mindless women, no dumb situations" (Salvo 1976: 53), but Weaver nets more roles that allow her to grow. *Avatar: The Way of Water* (James Cameron, 2022) is the latest. Again, she portrays two characters: the part-Na'vi/part-human 14-year-old daughter, Kiri, of Dr. Grace Augustine, and Grace herself. For Kiri, Weaver studied high schoolers and became adept at holding her breath like a free diver—for over six minutes![21]

Neither Grier nor Weaver is, like now-geriaction-star Sylvester Stallone, linked to a limited set of genres and dependent on a stable star image. Both are, instead, what Christine Geraghty calls "stars-as-performers." As she explains, "this emphasis on performance works well . . . for the ageing star since it has the added merit of valuing experience and allowing a career to continue well beyond the pin-up stage" (2000: 193). Happily, neither actress attempts to mask her aging through plastic surgery, hormones, Botox, or skin peels, which means that neither can be taken to task for aging "badly," as are other action stars—Stallone, Mickey Rourke, and Pamela Anderson among them. Her face unlined, Grier is no longer as thin as she was in her early 50s, let alone her 20s. Still trim, Weaver is sinewy. Without careful make-up her face shows wrinkles.[22] Those of us who remember and/or compare Grier and Weaver's past and current action output easily identify signature physical traits: Grier's crooked smiles, feisty phrasing, and sexy voicing; Weaver's thin mouth, strong jaw, and authoritative poses. In interviews, each maintains she is OK with getting older. Grier wants to be remembered for being "real," not "perfect." A rape and cancer survivor, she has been through a lot, but men in their 40s continue to court her, she reports happily (Kugel 2019). Weaver is similarly upbeat. "I see actresses who I know are much older than I am, who now say they're 60. It's like—whatever, you know? I just can't be bothered. People are going to hire me because I'm Sigourney Weaver, not because I'm five years older or younger" (Kaplan 2009: 6). "My hope is that what I receive from the universe is even more outrageous than anything I can think of. I don't really say to myself, 'Well, you can't do this.' Or 'You can't do that.' Let me at it! And we'll see" (Bruni 2020).

For all their optimism, however, "the space in which one can age 'well' is severely delimited" (Jermyn and Holmes 2005: 19). Make-up, hairstyling, framing, prosthetics, lighting, editing, and camera angles cannot disguise very old age; CGI "de-aging" is often implausible.[23] As we age fatty tissue just below the skin decreases and wrinkles appear. Muscles lose strength, endurance, and flexibility. Bones become more susceptible to fracture. Cartilage in knees, hips, and lower backs shrinks, making it harder to run, jump, walk. The upper thoracic spine curves, pulling shoulders forward. Foot structure changes, altering gait. Calf and glute muscles atrophy, shortening stride. Coordination, stability, and balance are all affected. Women as well as men gain or lose weight; weight is redistributed. Some men acquire love handles and a gut; some develop breasts. Women's breasts sag. Secondary gender characteristics such as body hair and vocal pitch blur.[24] Hearing declines; arthritis, hypertension, arrythmias, and dementias reduce mobility. Eye problems like glaucoma, macular degeneration, and cataracts are common.

All this means that, while old age can sometimes be credibly performed, it cannot convincingly be "unperformed." Older male stars avoid bodily display for good reason. Their geriaction characters drive speeding vehicles and heft guns— the bigger the better—in compensation for decreased mobility and strength. Flashbacks, nostalgic taglines, and training montages recall more fit, more youthful times, substituting past for present. Younger, usually male, characters become real or surrogate progeny fighting alongside—or in place of—their fathers/mentors.

True, the supporting characters and villains Grier and Weaver play since 2000 perform in action hybrids, not in geriaction. Yet their action scenes, too, are diminished, with running, jumping, and kicking kept to a minimum. Weaver's characters avoid guns, and in the most recent films, so do Grier's. Although Grier clearly enjoys strutting her tightly clad zaftig stuff in the action-comedy *Poms* (Zara Hayes, 2019), in all other films she wears figure-masking garb like turtlenecks, coats, and shawls. Though *Avatar* and *Avatar 2* "rejuvenate" Grace's avatar and Kiri through motion capture, Weaver's other characters work in business suits and/or lab coats. Only the youngest, the Warden, wears tight-fitting jeans.

Importantly, in *Bad Grandmas* and *The Assignment* Grier and Weaver give performances that exceed narrative constraints and mock derogatory associations of older age with infirmity, disability, and/or insanity. Grier shifts the pacing of her movements and the delivery of her lines to caricature assumptions that aging automatically equals decrepitude and older people's sexuality is monstrous. Weaver's over-the-top acting renders toxic "masculinity" risible. So much for Freud's portrayal of post-menopausal women as "quarrelsome, vexatious, and overbearing" (1958 [1913]: 323); so much for penis envy.

Films help shape how we view and treat aging and disability. Surely cinema can imagine things otherwise! After all, "cinema *is* cosmetic surgery," as Vivian Sobchack maintains (1999: 208). We should be able to see new lines or wrinkles or graying hair not so much as aging, but rather as always becoming. We should be able to think of identity as changeable and changing. Widening who we regard as action's "exerting bodies" may provide insights for other actors and for us (Purse 2011: 2).

To recap key take-aways from "my" six films: in *Slow Burn* and *Holes*, Grier and Weaver's characters are unmarked by disability and untouched by aging. Indeed, they seem even more beautiful, agile, and limber because minor characters are visibly infirm or ancient and because, in *Slow Burn*, Grier has a stunt double. In *Bones* and *Avatar*, the older Pearl and real-life-Grace also move without difficulty. The films' narratives make little of either aging or disability; killing and death alone are what counts. At best the younger Pearl and avatar-Grace may remind us that, as Kathleen Woodward says, "if we are old, we carry youth with us; we identify in part with the young. . . ." This may, she posits, help explain our resistance to old age: it "may be *unconscious*" (1991: 156); analogously, perhaps it helps elucidate society's eschewal of disability.

Because none of these four narratives overtly address age or disability, however, we fail to recognize the actors' performances: youth and agility are so synonymous with action that acting drops out. This is not the case with *Bad Grandmas* or *The Assignment*. Grier and Weaver's performances, and the storylines too, articulate resistance and express rage. There *are* ways, these two actresses suggest, to act, to age, to live with congenital, disease, accident, or age-related disability, in action.

Notes

1   "Geriaction" was first used in the early 1970s. The Australian Association for Geriatric Nursing Care published a journal entitled *Geriaction* from 1970–2009.

2   See also, for example, Donnar (2016 and Chapter 7, this volume), Lennard (2014), and Soberon (2021).

3   Samuel L. Jackson and Danny Trejo are the only stars of color to play leading roles in geriaction. On Jackson, see Donnar Chapter 7, this volume; on Trejo, see Jimenez-Murguia (2015) and Meeuf (2017).

4   All ages as of early March 2023. A fair amount has been written about the older Dench and Mirren, but only Cook Overton et al. (2015) briefly discuss Mirren in action.

5   Disability in older age is rarely explored in academic literature. On older disabled men in action, see however Holmlund (2010a) on Jackie Chan in *Forbidden Kingdom* (Rob Minkoff, 2008), Tasker (2019) on Professor X (Patrick Stewart) in *X-Men* (Bryan Singer, 2000) and *Logan* (James Mangold, 2017), and Donnar (Chapter 7, this volume) on *Glass* (M. Night Shyamalan, 2019).

6   Over 30% of Americans over age 65 have a disability of some kind; the percentage rises to 50% for those age 75 and up; "Aging and the ADA" (2018). See also Faircloth (2003). On the linkage between disability, age, and class for white Britons and Americans see Zaninotto et al. (2020).

7   Like many stuntwomen Grier was a gymnast growing up and a skier and runner. See Kugel (2019). Jadie Hill performed most of Grier's stunts starting with *Coffy* (Jack Hill, 1973). See Gregory (2015: 80–1).

8   See Holmlund (2010b) on Weaver in the 1980s.

9   See, e.g., Brooks (1999) on *Whatever Happened to Baby Jane* (Robert Aldrich, 1962) and *Sunset Boulevard* (Billy Wilder, 1950); Chivers (2011) on *Iris* (Richard Eyre, 2001) and *Away from Her* (Sara Polley, 2006); and Gravagne (2013) on *Strangers in Good Company* (Cynthia Scott, 1990), *Iris*, *Away from Her*, and *The Notebook* (Nick Cassavetes, 2004).

10   Grier plays cops in *Above the Law* (Andrew Davis, 1988), *In Too Deep* (Michael Rymer, 1999), *Love the Hard Way* (Peter Sehr, 2001), and *Mafia* (Ryan Combs, 2012). In *Posse* (Mario van Peebles, 1993), *Escape from L.A.* (John Carpenter, 1996), *Original Gangstas* (Larry Cohen, 1996), and *Ghosts of Mars* (John Carpenter, 2001) her characters carry guns. See Holmlund (2005: 103–6).

11   Credits list Francique as both a stunt performer and an actor. Designated stunt doubles are not common on low-budget movies.

12   Unless otherwise indicated, all domestic and global box office statistics come from the Internet Movie Database (IMDb).

13   Weaver plays strong women in *Vantage Point* (Pete Travis, 2008) and *Chappie* (Neill Blomkamp, 2015), too.

14 On disability in *Avatar* see Nesbitt (2016: 27) and Smock (2014).

15 *Avatar* was read as pro-environment, pro-smoking, anti-military, anti-capitalist, anti-American, and as racist. See e.g., Itzkoff (2010) and Travers (2010).

16 Grier had no make-up artist in *Bad Grandmas*. Vanessa Giles did make-up and Jessica Rains did hair for Weaver in *The Assignment*.

17 Production costs are not available.

18 In *Ghostbusters* Dana Barrett (Weaver) is possessed by a demon dog. In *Working Girl* Katharine Parker (Weaver) is a treacherous professional. In *Alien Resurrection*, Ripley's clone (Weaver) sends up the cultural norms of white beauty through "self-conscious play with the performance of passing" (Stacey 2003: 252).

19 "Werq" is Black queer slang, used for example by drag queens on "RuPaul's Drag Race." It means to act with attitude, to work something or someone out or over.

20 Grier played the know-it-all sheriff of a small Nebraska town in ABC's short-lived "Bless This Mess" (2019). The sequel to *Original Gangstas* (Larry Cohen, 1996) featuring Grier, Fred Williamson, Jim Brown, Paul Winfield, Richard Roundtree, and Ron O'Neal never got off the ground.

21 Cameron used motion capture to film Weaver's expressions and gestures on land and under water, then transformed them, as in *Avatar*, into animation. Released in December 2022, in early 2023 *Avatar 2* already ranks among the highest ever global box office successes.

22 Weaver has been nominated twice for American Association of Retired People (AARP) awards, first in 2003, again in 2017. Like Helen Mirren, she has the kind of fit body and manicured good looks the AARP relishes. Grier has never been nominated.

23 Uncanny fractures are often visible in joins between the elements of composite bodies. Even limiting de-aging to the face has its problems. See Ayers (2019).

24 See further Holmlund (2002) and Purse (2017). Dr. Ryan Dulling provided additional observations.

Works Cited

"Aging and the ADA" (2018). Available online: https://adata.org/factsheet/aging-and-ada (accessed 17 April 2022).

Ayers, Drew (2019), "The Composite Body: Action Stars and Embodiment in the Digital Age," in James Kendrick (ed.), *A Companion to the Action Film*, 165–86, Hoboken, NJ: John Wiley & Sons.

Bey, Marquis (2019), *Them Goon Rules: Fugitive Essays on Radical Black Feminism*, Tucson: University of Arizona Press.

Box Office Mojo (2023), "Top Lifetime Grosses," 16 January. Available online: https://www.boxofficemojo.com/chart/top_lifetime_gross/?area=XWW (accessed 15 January 2023).

Brooks, Jodi (1999), "Performing Aging/Performance Crisis (for Norma Desmond, Baby Jane, Margo Channing, Sister George—and Myrtle)," in Kathleen Woodward (ed.), *Figuring Age*, 232–47, Bloomington: Indiana University Press.

Bruni, Frank (2020), "Sigourney Weaver Goes Her Own Way," *New York Times Style Magazine,* 19 October. Available online: https://www.nytimes.com/interactive/2020/10/19/t-magazine/sigourney-weaver.html (accessed 24 May 2022).

Chivers, Sally (2011), *The Silvering Screen: Old Age and Disability in Cinema*, Toronto: University of Toronto Press.

Cook Overton, Barbara, Athena du Pré, and Loretta L. Pecchioni (2015), "Helen Mirren and the Media Portrayals of Aging," in Norma Jones and Bob Batchelor (eds), *Aging Heroes: Growing Old in Popular Culture*, 181–97, Lanham, MD: Rowman & Littlefield.

Donnar, Glen (2016), "Narratives of Cultural and Professional Redundancy: Ageing Action Stardom and the 'Geri-Action' Film," *Communication, Politics and Culture*, 49 (1): 1–18.

Dyer, Richard (1978, "Resistance through Charisma: Rita Hayworth and *Gilda*, in E. Ann Kaplan (ed.), *Women and Film Noir*, 91–9, London: British Film Institute.

Faircloth, Christopher A. (2003), "Introduction: Different Bodies and the Paradox of Aging: Locating Aging Bodies in Images and Everyday Experience," in Christopher A. Faircloth (ed.), *Aging Bodies: Images and Everyday Experience*, 1–26, Lanham, MD: AltaMira Press.

Freud, Sigmund (1958 [1913]), "The Disposition to Obsessional Neurosis," in James Strachey (ed.), *The Standard Edition of the Complete Psychological Works of Sigmund Freud*, volume 12, 312–26, London: Hogarth Press.

Geraghty, Christine (2000), "Re-examining Stardom: Questions of Texts, Bodies and Performance," in Christine Gledhill and Linda Williams (eds), *Reinventing Film Studies*, 183–201, London: Arnold.

Gilleard, Chris and Paul Higgs (2013), *Ageing, Corporeality and Embodiment*, London: Anthem Press.

Gravagne, Pamela (2013), *The Becoming of Age: Cinematic Visions of Mind, Body and Identity in Later Life*, Jefferson, NC: McFarland.

Gregory, Mollie (2015), *Stuntwomen: The Untold Hollywood Story*, Lexington: University Press of Kentucky.

Grier, Pam with Andrea Cagan (2010), *Foxy: My Life in Three Acts*, New York: Grand Central Publishing.

"*Holes* Production Notes" (2003), Buena Vista.

Holmlund, Chris (2002), "The Aging Clint," in *Impossible Bodies: Femininity and Masculinity at the Movies*, 141–57, London: Routledge.

Holmlund, Chris (2005), "Wham! Bam! Pam! Pam Grier as Hot Action Babe and Cool Action Mama," *Quarterly Review of Film Studies*, 22 (2) (April/June): 97–112.

Holmlund, Chris (2010a), "Celebrity, Ageing, and Jackie Chan: Middle-aged Asian in Transnational Action," *Celebrity Studies*, 1 (1) (March): 96–112.

Holmlund, Chris (2010b), "Sigourney Weaver: Woman Warrior, Working Girl," in Robert Eberwein (ed.), *Acting for America: Movie Stars of the 1980s*, 139–59, New Brunswick, NJ: Rutgers University Press.

Internet Movie Database (IMDb) (n.d.). Available online: https://www.imdb.com (accessed 15 January 2023).

Itzkoff, David (2010), "You Saw What in *Avatar*? Pass Those Glasses!," *New York Times*, 20 January. Available online: https://archive.nytimes.com/www.nytimes.com/2010/01/20/movies/20avatar.html (accessed 9 April 2022).

Jermyn, Deborah and Su Holmes (2005), "Introduction: A Timely Intervention – Unravelling the Gender/Age/Celebrity Matrix," in Deborah Jermyn and Su Holmes (eds), *Women, Celebrity and Cultures of Ageing*, 1–11, New York: Palgrave Macmillan.

Jimenez-Murguia, Salvador (2015), "The Recharacterization of Age and the Aging *Bricoleur*: Danny Trejo's Reinvention of Aging in Acting," in Norma Jones and Bob Batchelor (eds), *Aging Heroes: Growing Old in Popular Culture*, 223–32, Lanham, MD: Rowman & Littlefield.

Kaplan, James (2009), "A Force of Nature," *Parade*, 29 November: 4, 6.

Keegan, Cáel (2022), "On the Necessity of Bad Trans Objects," *Film Quarterly*, 75 (3): 26–37.

Kugel, Allison (2019), "Pam Grier on Her New Movie *Poms* and Sitcom 'Bless This Mess,'" tribute.ca, 8 May. Available online: https://www.tribute.ca/news/pam-grier-on-her-new-movie-poms-and-sitcom-bless-this-mess/2019/05/08/ (accessed 5 December 2021).

Lennard, Dominic (2014), "Too Old for This Shit?: On Ageing Tough Guys," in Imelda Whelehan and Joel Gwynne (eds), *Ageing, Pop Culture and Contemporary Feminisms: Harleys and Hormones*, 93–107, London: Palgrave Macmillan.

Longmore, Paul K. and Lauri Umansky (2001), "Introduction: Disability History: From the Margins to the Mainstream," in Paul K. Longmore and Lauri Umansky (eds), *The New Disability History: American Perspectives*, 1–29, New York: New York University Press.

Lyne, Charlie (2013), "Geriaction Heroes and the Age of Aged Movie Stars," *Guardian*, 30 March. Available online: https://www.theguardian.com/film/2013/mar/30/geriaction-heroes-age-of-aged-stars (accessed 6 January 2023).

Means Coleman, Robin R. (2011), *Horror Noire: Blacks in American Horror Films from the 1890s to Present*, New York: Routledge.

Meeuf, Russell (2017), *Rebellious Bodies: Stardom, Citizenship, and the New Body Politics*, Austin: University of Texas Press.

Nesbitt, Jennifer P. (2016), "Deactivating Feminism: Sigourney Weaver, James Cameron, and *Avatar*," *Film & History*, 46 (1) (Summer): 21–32.

Numbers, The (n.d.), "*Alien Resurrection* (1997)—Financial Information," Available online: https://www.the-numbers.com/custom-search?searchterm=alien+resurrection (accessed 15 January 2023).

Numbers, The (n.d.), "*Jackie Brown* (1997)—Financial Information." Available online: https://www.the-numbers.com/movie/Jackie-Brown#tab=summary (accessed 15 January 2023).

"Pam Grier: Lifetime Achievement Award Interview and Q&A" (2020) Cine-Excess Conference, Birmingham City University, UK, 6 November.

Purse, Lisa (2011), *Contemporary Action Cinema*, Edinburgh: Edinburgh University Press.

Purse, Lisa (2017), "Confronting the Impossibility of Impossible Bodies: Tom Cruise and the Ageing Male Action Hero Movie," in Sabrina Qiong Yu (ed.), *Revisiting Star Studies: Cultures, Themes and Methods*, 162–86, Edinburgh: Edinburgh University Press.

Salvo, Patrick (1976), "Pam Grier: The Movie Super-Sex Goddess Who's Fed Up with Sex and Violence," *Sepia*, 25 (2) (19 February): 48–54.

Smock, Ryan (2014), "'I Got This': Disability, Stigma, and Jake Sully's Rejected Body," in George A. Dunn (ed.), *Avatar and Philosophy: Learning to See*, 139–50, Chichester: Wiley Blackwell.

Sobchack, Vivian (1999), "Scary Women: Cinema, Surgery, and Special Effects," in Kathleen Woodward (ed.), *Figuring Age: Women, Bodies, Generations*, 200–11, Bloomington: Indiana University Press.

Soberon, Lennart (2021), "'Too Old for This Sh*t': Aged Action Heroes, Affect, and 'the Economy of Exertion,'" *Journal of Popular Film and Television*, 49 (3): 155–67.

Available online: https://doi.org/10.1080/01956051.2021.1957336 (accessed 20 November 2021).

Stacey, Jackie (2003), "She Is Not Herself: The Deviant Relations of *Alien Resurrection*," *Screen*, 44 (3) (Autumn): 251–76. Available online: https://doi.org/10.1093/screen/44.3.251 (accessed 24 April 2022).

Sternbergh, Adam (2006), "The Education of Pam Grier," *New York Magazine*, 28 December. Available online: https://nymag.com/arts/tv/features/26028 (accessed 19 January 2022).

Tasker, Yvonne (2019), "X-Men/Action Men: Performing Masculinities in Superhero and Science-Fiction Cinema," in James Kendrick (ed.), *A Companion to the Action Film*, 381–97, Hoboken, NJ: Wiley Blackwell.

Travers, Peter (2010), "*Avatar*: A Closer Look at a Megahit," *Rolling Stone*, 10 February: n.p.

Wearing, Sadie (2012), "Exemplary or Exceptional Embodiment? Discourses of Aging in the Case of Helen Mirren and *Calendar Girls*," in Josephine Dolan and Estella Tincknell (eds), *Ageing Femininities: Troubling Representations*, 145–57, Newcastle upon Tyne: Cambridge Scholars Publishing.

Woodward, Kathleen (1991), *Aging and Its Discontents: Freud and Other Fictions*, Bloomington: Indiana University Press.

Zaninotto, Paola, George David Batty, Sari Stenholm, et al. (2020), "Socioeconomic Inequalities in Disability-free Life Expectancy in Older People from England and the United States: A Cross-national Population-Based Study," *Journal of Gerontology: Series A*, 75 (5) (May): 906–13. Available at https://doi.org/10.1093 (accessed 14 January 2023).

Chapter 12

What Does Power Look Like? Women Heroes in Digital Action Cinema

Lisa Purse

Introduction

The US action cinema of the 2000s often ostentatiously showcases a digitally enabled mode of action, and a digitally enhanced or extended action body. Such spectacles are central to big-budget franchises such as the Marvel and DC cinematic universes, as well as to tentpole homages celebrating visual effects films or past franchises.[1] This digital action cinema re-opens a space for the female action hero as part of the major studios' push to reach previously neglected audience demographics with their franchises. Digitally enabled action sequences are not bound by the demands for credibility that clustered around earlier action heroines and lower budget, more prosaically profilmic, action movies. Yet digital action cinema remains a site where studios and misogynous fans believe it is risky or wrong to feature anyone other than a white, straight, cis male hero.[2]

This chapter will argue that when a woman becomes the primary protagonist of the digital action blockbuster the audiovisual forms that her power takes are nonetheless bounded by normative ideas of power circulating in US culture. Female leads remain marked, in other words, by the "continuing cultural uncertainty around female action" that Yvonne Tasker noted (2015: 189). A corollary axiom is, moreover, that these women heroes be white. That has only begun to change from the very late 2010s on.

Taking DC and Marvel's first two solo female superhero movies as my focus, I will first situate *Wonder Woman* (Patty Jenkins, 2017) and *Captain Marvel* (Anna Boden and Ryan Fleck, 2019) in the longer recent history of the female action hero, exploring the nature of the digital spectacle that framed women in the first decade of the twenty-first century. I will then turn to my two case studies, interrogating their nature and significance as digital spectacles of white female power in established franchise cinematic universes. They are connected to a broader late-2010s increase in Black and white women protagonists in such franchises. I argue that turning to solo woman-led narratives so late in the current superhero franchise era—what I call the *logic of deferral*—creates consequences for the visualization of female power and its narrative framing. The second half of this chapter thus examines the films' over-arching storylines, and the articulation of their heroines' evolving powers. I then analyze the formal design of the respective final battle sequences: this is where their powers are most emphatically asserted. Throughout I ask, what *does* female physical power look like, and why?

Women in Digital Action Cinema: A Brief History from 1999 to 2023

A turn-of-the-millennium film heralded the digital shift in what the female action hero's power looked like. *The Matrix* (Lilly and Lana Wachowski, 1999) envisions female empowerment as both spatial mastery *and* digital spectacle. The opening action sequence shows Trinity (Carrie-Anne Moss) skillfully mastering space. Discovered by police at a computer in a small room, she escapes by killing multiple law enforcement officers in seconds with a combination of high-speed martial arts-inspired kicks, blocks, and gravity-defying leaps across walls. The culminating fight beat of the sequence is staged as a then-novel "bullet-time" digital effect, in which a virtual camera circles around her body as she rises into the air in slow motion to deliver a final decisive kick.[3] Trinity arrives fully formed as an expert action body. Her bullet-time introduction contrasts with the mode of action that 1990s women were generally permitted. In films like *G.I. Jane* (Ridley Scott, 1997), *Anaconda* (Luis Llosa, 1997), and *Jurassic Park* (Steven Spielberg, 1993), action sequences involving women kept relatively close to real world physics—hand-to-hand combat, gunplay, or vehicular action. *The Matrix* contrastingly locates its female hero in a science-fiction fantasy space and gifts her science-fictional abilities to control aspects of her environment, presented celebratorily with state-of-the-art digital visual effects.

Yet Trinity's fighting style, tight costume, and their digital presentation also reinforce normative notions of gendered physicality and display that we can detect elsewhere in the first decade of the 2000s. *The Matrix* evidences and further precipitates the transnational circulation of Hong Kong wire-work- and martial arts-influenced action design and stunt performance practices (Steimer 2021a), drawing on Chinese and Hong Kong swordplay films and Hong Kong action traditions in which women fighters were commonplace (Teo 1997; Lo

2007). In US digital action cinema this intensifies an emphasis on grace and decorum when the action hero is a woman. From *Charlie's Angels* (McG, 2000) to *Catwoman* (Pitof, 2004) and *Elektra* (Rob Bowman, 2005), female action heroes spin, kick, and leap in graceful arcs while sporting figure-hugging clothing, reflecting binary conceptions of gendered behavior found in other cultural arenas, not least sports culture, which situates non-contact forms of female athleticism (figure-skating, synchronized swimming, gymnastics) as more gender-appropriate than contact sports (like football, boxing) (Lindner 2011). This preference for non-contact modes of female physical action is also evident in big-budget ensemble superhero franchises of the 2000s. In films like *X-Men* (Bryan Singer, 2000) female heroes are often integral components of the melodramatic logic of the narrative but tend to be visually decentered within the ensemble in the action sequences. Their powers (e.g., telepathy, telekinesis, weather control) manifest through—or imply—a lack of physical contact or involve "graceful" martial arts-based fighting skills, in keeping with normative logics of gender appropriateness. They are also often depicted rising slowly into the air as a shorthand for their powers manifesting; they are not dynamically propulsive action bodies.

In this first decade of the 2000s, women do, however, find a space as solo action heroes in modestly budgeted digital action-horror franchises, as well as in non-digital action cinema.[4] The zombie videogame adaptions of the *Resident Evil* series (Paul W.S. Anderson, 2002–) and the vampire/werewolf action-fantasy of the *Underworld* films (Len Wiseman, 2003–) have become long-running franchises. They draw on exploitation and horror traditions in which women can be physically violent, and their smaller budgets protect studio coffers if they fail to find a sympathetic audience. They feature action women already expert in gunplay and martial arts skills locked in a battle for survival. Both *Resident Evil* and *Underworld* franchises are indebted to *The Matrix* in their emphasis on wire-work action (accentuating female poise and grace), and in their insistence on leather- or PVC-clad bodies in slow motion. As in "digital backlot" films like *Sin City* (Frank Miller and Robert Rodriguez, 2005) and *300* (Zack Snyder, 2006), here digital speed ramping, digital compositing, and digital alterations of color, greyscale, and surface reflectance, insistently display the female form.

What these lower budget digital action films share with the ensemble superhero movies of the early 2000s is a spatially and durationally bounded form of female action. The action heroines of these franchises assert their physical power in short bursts, echoing the "alternation of swift attack and abrupt rest" in Hong Kong action design that produces "an overall flow that harbors a percussive rhythm" (Bordwell 2000: 224, 221). However, their swift attacks are often contained in small spaces (labs, offices, corridors, allies, subways), and are durationally attenuated by scene changes, diminishing the sense of an expansive overall flow. Such bounded forms of female action are at odds with the move in the 2010s towards more extensive bodily trajectories in the big-budget action sequence.

The affordances of the virtual camera and the digital body or environment have made highly mobile, extended, digital long takes—*or* an edited sequence that emphasizes the continuity of an elongated flow of action—commonplace elements (Purse 2019). Such sequences provide not only the traditional action fantasy of transcending the spatial, economic, and social strictures of urban space but also a utopian mastery of digital flows and structures. Nevertheless, female characters such as Black Widow (Scarlett Johansson) in *The Avengers* (Joss Whedon, 2012) tend to be marginalized, visible for only short moments as part of the overall collaborative team flow. This moves Tasker to note that "Strong women are present yet oddly peripheral to superhero cinema" (2015: 189). So: what happens when they move from the periphery to the center?

The Logic of Deferral and Its Consequences

By the early 2010s, feminist fan sites such as *The Mary Sue* and *DC Women Kicking Ass* were increasingly derisory about DC and Warner Bros' hesitation to bring Wonder Woman to the screen, blaming sexist industry conceptions of target audiences (Howell 2015). Here in microcosm is the logic of deferral that delays the white male hero's "others" from taking up the centerground of a franchise. Studios commonly cite audience demographics, fan service, or challenges around the right script or creative team as reasons to postpone the arrival of female and non-white principles. But as the history of Hollywood representation proves, such claims too often obscure institutional racism, sexism, or unconscious biases that exclude and marginalize certain groups. The two major superhero franchises of the 2000s only permit women and people of color to be main characters in the later 2010s. *Wonder Woman* (2017) in the DC Cinematic Universe and *Captain Marvel* (2019) in the Marvel Cinematic Universe are the first films to feature white female protagonists. The first superhero leads of color arrive in 2018, with Marvel's *Black Panther* (Ryan Coogler) and DC's *Aquaman* (James Wan). *Black Panther* forcefully foregrounds Black female action characters alongside its male lead. That *Wonder Woman* and *Black Panther* alike are celebrated as milestones of cultural representation makes clear, moreover, their ongoing status as exceptions.[5]

This tardy timing is as much about economics as answering calls for inclusion. In the mid-to-late 2000s DC Entertainment was facing declining comic book sales, despite the critical and commercial success of 2008's *The Dark Knight* (Christopher Nolan). Attempting to optimize its comic book and film revenues, in 2011 DC Entertainment relaunched its monthly superhero comics as "The New 52," while its parent company started production on Superman reboot *Man of Steel* (Zack Snyder, 2013), conceived as the first of a new DC Extended

Universe. Superman and Wonder Woman were key triumphs of the New 52 comics relaunch. Wonder Woman appeared as a member of the Justice League in DC's *Batman v Superman: Dawn of Justice* (Zack Snyder, 2016). In the same period, Marvel Studios sought to reinvigorate engagement in their Marvel Cinematic Universe through the transition from "phase three"—completing character arcs for Iron Man, Captain America, and Black Widow—to "phase four"—adding and diversifying characters to expand audience share.

The logic of deferral that produced genuine diversification a long 17 years into the 2000s superhero franchise boom does not simply withhold and delay representation. It also has consequences for the ways in which power is depicted once access to the centerground is granted. The first consequence is that *Wonder Woman* and *Captain Marvel* must be origin stories.

All action films feature the becoming-powerful of the hero as a process mapped across the action sequences: early sequences show potential; middle sequences prove specific skills; end sequences offer a culminating mastery as proven skills are combined to secure victory. This also happens in origin stories, but the becoming-powerful has a different shape and emphasis. The central character's powers are only uncertainly taken up for much of each film's running time before mastery is briefly expressed near the end. As a result, the female possession of power is framed as preliminary, unstable, or precarious in both *Wonder Woman* and *Captain Marvel*. Even unwittingly, longstanding misogynist cultural ideas about women being too emotional or weak to handle great power are evoked as a result. As we will see later, the end battle sequences offer a spectacle of culminating female mastery whose form may nonetheless qualify this moment of achievement. First, let us look at how the films negotiate this tension between great power and uncertainty in the introduction of their powered heroines.

Wonder Woman (Gal Gadot) and Captain Marvel (Brie Larson) are initially encountered at a moment of significant lack of self-knowledge. While they are each shown to have (or to be developing) proficient fighting skills, they do not yet know the extent of their superhuman powers. *Wonder Woman* charts Diana's rise from plucky child to the discovery of her powers as an adult, when she journeys into the "world of men" during World War I and uses her newfound powers to vanquish the returning God of War, Ares (David Thewlis). Her mother Queen Hippolyta (Connie Nielsen) had told her as a child about the "god-killer" weapon that Zeus forged with the last of his powers to combat Ares but failed to mention that Wonder Woman herself *is* the weapon. In *Captain Marvel* the audience encounters an adult protagonist with powers at the outset, but the extent of her powers and their origin are unclear. Vers (Larson) cannot remember her past, and unbeknown to her, the alien Kree community with whom she lives are hiding it from her in a bid to benefit from her powers. Vers (a Kree derivation of her real name, Carol Danvers) fights and trains with the Kree military. They are engaged in a war with another alien race, the shapeshifting Skrulls. When Vers/Danvers accesses her suppressed memories and understands her real past lies on Earth where she was a military fighter pilot subjected to an alien energy core explosion, her full power emerges and she, too, becomes a weapon: the titular Captain Marvel.

Both films stress their feminist credentials while framing their origin stories through postfeminist media discourse. A white, affluent heroine frees herself from constraining narratives about who she is and asserts herself as an individual outside of the group within which we first encounter her. She then discovers and chooses to become her "authentic" empowered self (Tasker and Negra 2007). Both films feature a man who advises the heroine during her period of incomplete knowledge but becomes superfluous when the heroine acquires the full extent of her power: Allied spy and pilot Steve (Chris Pine) in *Wonder Woman*, Kree military mentor Yon-Rogg (Jude Law) in *Captain Marvel*. Both films also poke fun at social edicts around female attire and behavior, using their settings in the past (1910s and 1990s respectively) to assure audiences that the contemporary moment is more progressively feminist. These postfeminist elements sit alongside a questioning about what happens when women possess outsized physical power. Like several other 2000s superhero films featuring women, moreover, both films point to "the supposed destructive nature of emotions" for the female hero—particularly when that emotion is anger—"while also positioning emotions as a (feminine) weakness" (Kent 2021: 83) although they refract this in distinctly different ways.

Wonder Woman thematizes but remains ambivalent about the relationship of emotion to women's possession and control of superpowers. Early in the film a naive Wonder Woman-in-training is told by General Antiope (Robin Wright) to "let go" of her restraint in combat to fully access her power. When she follows this advice and inadvertently unleashes a powerful bolt of energy from her bracelets, there are consequences. She brings Ares' human war to Themiscyra, and in the Amazons' defense of their island General Antiope dies by gunfire. Wonder Woman leaves her community against her mother's wishes, teaming up with Steve to try to stop World War I. The scale of her ambition signals her naivety and her emotion-driven resistance to the dictates of others, although this refusal will subsequently prove a crucial element of her success. Later she defies Steve to go over the top into No Man's Land, saving an entire village from German attack. Later still, when Steve sacrifices himself for the greater good, she resists Ares' encouragement to unleash her rage and despair at the humans around her, growing fully into her own power as a result. Wonder Woman's self-realization as an empowered being rests on an emotion (grief) that binds her to Steve and the heterosexual contract their pairing implies. This (re)centers Wonder Woman as a hero who is aligned with normative cultural expectations of feminine behavior—heterosexual, emotional, and angry enough to act, but not *too* angry at the moment of her total mastery. Similarly, her short skirt, low cut corset, bare shoulders, arms and thighs, and long hair, also position her normatively, as a woman to be looked at.

Captain Marvel offers a more self-aware critique of female representation than *Wonder Woman* does. Pointedly, this female superhero is not fully on display: her costume eschews bare skin, instead covering Larson's body from boots to neck. In the film's opening scenes Vers/Danvers trains with mentor Yon-Rogg, who paternalistically insists that her superpowers *and* her emotions need controlling. He consistently conflates emotions and self-knowledge with combat weakness: "There's nothing more dangerous to a warrior than emotion"; "Let go of the past. It's causing you doubt, and doubt makes you vulnerable." Vers/Danvers fires bolts of energy from her arms that floor Yon-Rogg: she is less vulnerable than he implies. This scene is part of a wider pattern of gaslighting, denigration, and coercive control by Yon-Rogg and the Kree that seeks to prevent Vers/Danvers from recovering her memory and realizing her true identity. This is further underscored by the montage of childhood and army training memories shown when Vers/Danvers has her brain scanned by Skrulls early in the film, and later as her memories resurface on their own. In each recollection, Vers/Danvers attempts a physical feat (go-karting, rope-climbing, military flight) and is reprimanded by a male figure: "You need to go slow!" "You don't belong out here!" "They'll never let you fly," "You're a decent pilot but you're too emotional." Such montages have real-world resonances for female-identifying audience members with lived experience of gendered policing by men, giving these sequences an affective power that encourages the audience to view Yon-Rogg's edicts negatively and to respond positively to Vers's growing assertions of her power.

Outsize female power is articulated through conventional cultural reference points using an audio-visual shorthand that explains why and how these women can wield power without unsettling established ideas about where power resides. Strikingly, *Wonder Woman* and *Captain Marvel* stage the evolution of their heroines from a lack of self-knowledge to full empowerment in a manner deeply marked by military iconography. Both films embed their protagonists into military contexts, Wonder Woman in the Amazon training camp, and Captain Marvel in the Kree military. Both are dropped into military power struggles, Wonder Woman into World War I, and Captain Marvel into the Kree/Skrull war. By the end, they literally become weapons to overcome their foes. As Tasker has noted: "That the masculinity and misogyny of military culture is in many ways officially sanctioned renders the incorporation of military women into that culture, and the narratives that represent or valorize it, a particularly acute site of contest over gender and power" (2011: 17).

Wonder Woman: Power and Ambivalence

After its prologue in the present, *Wonder Woman* relocates its narrative to the past, to Themiscyra, the Amazon island hidden from the human world. Wonder Woman is seen first as the child Diana (Lilly Aspell). She has escaped her school tutor

(Josette Simon) to watch the Amazons in training. This is one of the few sequences in the film where women are depicted as fighting and moving under their own real-world physical power (Figure 12.1). The stunt performers who play the Amazons bring an affective thickness to the action. They wield swords, shields, arrows, and spears in gracefully pivoting motion. They spin, catapult, or jump into the air, enact sharp changes of direction, perform feints and counter attacks, leap on and off horseback. They are versatile, strong, and their agility is seemingly omnidirectional. An occasionally mobile camera and speed-ramped slow motion capture the gymnastic work in short phrases of physical action. We see little Diana watch and mimic them, which implies that as an adult Wonder Woman will similarly combine graceful, pivoting fight elements. Instead, however, the adult Wonder Woman's actions solidify into a reduced "palette" for physical action that is visually linked to the differently articulated and more prominently male vision of power depicted in the storybook her mother reads to the child Diana. The storybook tells of Amazons, human wars, Zeus and Ares, and the creation of the god-killer weapon. Tableaux of bodies caught mid-gesture punch, push, stab, or flail backwards in defeat to illustrate the tale. These depictions persistently foreground the notions of resistance, propulsion, and penetration that are central to the militarized human evil Wonder Woman will oppose when she evolves into the god-killer. Indeed, the image of Zeus' subduing of Ares that ends the storybook sequence foreshadows Wonder Woman's final battle. Via an homage to Michelangelo's *Creation of Adam* (1512), Zeus repels Ares with a streaming bolt of energy. His superhuman marshalling of power symbolizes his status as a god and visually invokes religious depictions of divine power and the development of propulsive war technologies. Both will be in evidence in the final stages of Wonder Woman's own journey.

When Wonder Woman travels to the human world of World War I, the repelling power of her fighting technologies is initially emphasized. Her bracelets deflect

Figure 12.1 Stuntwoman Georgina Armstrong completes a backwards somersault off a horse as an Amazon archer in *Wonder Woman* (© Warner Bros. Pictures, 2017. All Rights Reserved).

bullets during an early side street ambush. In the much celebrated No Man's Land sequence, in which Wonder Woman goes "over the top" and uses her shield to draw German artillery fire away from British forces, her shield becomes an overdetermined emblem of pacifist choice: she defends rather than attacks. General Antiope's death by gunfire has already underscored the advantage that propulsive, penetrative forms of fighting represent, however. Even as the film invites the audience to view the Germans' deployment of bullets and canisters of chemical weapons as immoral, Wonder Woman's own growing power takes the shape and the destructive force of the ballistic weapons she opposes. Clearing a village of German soldiers, Wonder Woman smashes her body through a window to surprise troops inside, then throws herself against a tank with enough force to disable its gun, and finally hurls her body into a clock tower, annihilating the sniper inside and the clock tower, too. Herein lies the paradox of *Wonder Woman*'s anti-war sentiment and its militarized depiction of female heroism: she saves and destroys at the same time.

The film seeks to thematize this in Wonder Woman's final confrontation with Ares himself, as they face off on a military airfield. They throw progressively larger objects at each other—wooden planks, metal airfield lights, concrete slabs, explosive missiles—but Ares' telekinetic powers exceed Wonder Woman's efforts to subdue him. Steve's self-sacrifice, blowing himself up to destroy an arsenal of chemical weapons, drives Wonder Woman into a rage against the German soldiers closest to her. Ares seeks to encourage this vengeful and destructive impulse. The airfield, in the darkness of night, becomes a landscape of fire, and Wonder Woman herself risks descending into hell. Just in time she remembers the human qualities that she prizes most: love, bravery, solidarity, and compassion. The realization gives her pause. The film thereby suggests that her subsequent renewed commitment only to "just" forms of destruction precipitates her transformation into the fully-powered god-killer.

In the last act of the battle with Ares Wonder Woman no longer needs her shield to deflect his attacks—she can generate her own forcefield to do so. Ares escalates the fight by throwing bolts of energy, but Wonder Woman can now absorb them. She accumulates such a large store of energy that when she chooses to redirect it at Ares it destroys him. Christian imagery shapes her moment of triumph, as does imagery of post-apocalyptic destruction. Wonder Woman rises into the air, arms outstretched sideways, like Jesus on the cross, and closes her eyes before unleashing the killing bolt of energy as if in prayer (Figure 12.2). Ares disintegrates in a flash of blinding light that recalls a nuclear explosion. The landscape is lit by the first beams of dawn—a Christian trope of rebirth and renewal—but resembles nothing less than an atomic wasteland. A huge bomb crater is visible, with flattened debris as far as the eye can see, and ash falls from the sky. Thankful soldiers remove their gas masks and emerge literally and metaphorically into the light: one sinks to his knees, as if in worship of Wonder Woman herself, who stands in wide shot in front of the rising sun.

Figure 12.2 Wonder Woman (Gal Gadot) and her glowing "god-killer" powers are digitally composited into a featureless night sky in *Wonder Woman* (© Warner Bros. Pictures, 2017. All Rights Reserved).

Wonder Woman thus offers an overt rejection of male warmongering, but its antiwar narrative belies the extent to which the visual articulation of Wonder Woman's power is couched in traditional concepts of military might. Wonder Woman's divergent roles—as innocent abroad, witness to the horrors of war, and fighter who avenges the fallen—are linked by her capacity for emotion and empathy. All this reads not as a total rejection of war, but as a reassurance that those fighting on the "right side" can be trusted with extensive military might. What results is a deeply ambivalent image of female empowerment, endorsed by Christian imagery as much as by a narrative of overcoming war. We are offered an image of soldiers kneeling before an almighty power capable of razing all human structures to the ground. Visually spare even if more "populated," lacking the detail and movement that characterized the film's earlier Amazon action sequences, *Wonder Woman*'s ending is, paradoxically enough, less able to affectively convey the force of an empowered female body. The film seeks to smooth over these contradictions by cutting to flag-waving victory day celebrations in London, turning to a simpler—but thicker, more "peopled"—evocation of communal joy over the win and sadness over the fallen.

Captain Marvel: Power and Petro-Nostalgia

Captain Marvel shares with *Wonder Woman* an evolution from early "practice" action scenes to the portrayal of the body itself as a weapon in a militarized milieu. It also shares a visual emphasis on power as glowing, directable energy. The first shot is of soil rising in slow motion, driven upwards by glowing flames.

It seems a dream. Vers/Danvers lies dazed on the ground after an explosion. An older woman stands nearby, gun in hand. An indistinct man approaches through smoke, raising his gun to fire. Vers/Danvers wakes confused. A closeup reveals her fist glowing with flame-like energy. She suppresses the flame, looking somber. The problem of memory is paired immediately with the problem of the power she possesses. The motif of power as fiery glow is symptomatic of Anglophone cultures' racist idealization of the ethereal glow of the angelic white woman.[6] *Captain Marvel* is more persistently visually preoccupied with this glow than *Wonder Woman* is, not just with glow-as-energy but also with Vers/Danvers's sunlit blonde hair, whether worn down or seen flaming out the top of her/Captain Marvel's battle helmet. Given this, the intersectional female solidarity symbolized by her close friendship with African American fellow pilot Rambeau (Lashana Lynch) and her daughter (Akira Akbar)—as well as her team-up with Nick Fury (Samuel L. Jackson)—reads rather differently. As Miriam Kent (2021) argues, Vers/Danvers's white femininity is not coincidentally positioned as central.

The film's introduction of its heroine in the grip of a dream that she cannot understand, and in possession of powers she does not yet fully comprehend or control, is significant because it invites uncertainty about the female action hero's capacity for command. Later we learn of the moment Vers/Danvers acquired her powers while on a secret mission on Earth, on a test flight of an experimental plane with a light-speed engine powered by an alien fuel source. The craft is shot down by the Kree, and Vers/Danvers destroys the engine before the Kree can acquire it. In doing so, she accidentally suffuses herself with alien energy. As in *Wonder Woman*, the narrative and visual focus becomes the unanticipated ability of a woman to absorb more power than should be possible, and the unpredictable outcomes that power promises. In *Wonder Woman*, unpredictability is experienced late in the narrative when Ares, who underestimates Wonder Woman, is destroyed when she redirects his power back at him. In *Captain Marvel*, in contrast, unpredictability pervades the diegetic world for much of the time. The central mystery for Vers/Danvers, her friends, and her foes is how she, as an emerging and initially amnesiac action heroine, will shape the outcome of the longstanding Kree/Skrull war. Alongside her precarious, unstable power, the audience also witnesses her wise-cracking, unflappable demeanor in the face of uncertainty, challenge, and attempted coercion. Faced with and already containing powers of unknown extent, Vers/Danvers's training as a fighter pilot and her ability to acquire expertise and access to military air power despite male disparagement convinces us that she will ultimately control the alien power she has been gifted.

Military iconography consequently reassures the audience that this female action hero "has what it takes," while also shaping what power looks like. The film's recurrent glow motif visually evokes the fiery afterburn of the jet engine and recalls the histories of military and vehicular power that prioritized and valorized the propulsion of white, male, bodies. Vers/Danvers's wise-cracking, Ray-Bans, flight suits, and pilot banter purposefully reference the military-sanctioned spectacle of *Top Gun* (Tony Scott, 1986). Larson's square-jawed grin offers a compelling gender reversal of the preceding film's masculinist and misogynist elaboration of military power, critiquing real-world histories of military and space flight that have until recently actively excluded women and people of color.[7] Yet the culmination of Vers/Danvers's journey of self-discovery and her transformation into the fully powered-up Captain Marvel is steeped in the very imagery of explosive, high-speed, responsive, jet propulsion.

Vers/Danvers's ability to generate energy on command, and eventually to fly huge distances, connects a traditionally masculinist fantasy of possession of state-of-the-art military power—jet power, surveillance power, and ballistic power—to a fantasy of endless power generation in and of itself. At a sociocultural moment at which climate crisis is driving calls for the abandonment of fossil fuels, this film's fantasy of endlessly generated energy and momentum together with its overt embrace of nostalgic imagery of 1980s and 1990s military jet engines makes it an example of "petro-nostalgia" (Daggett, 2018: 32).[8] In Cara Daggett's feminist analysis of masculine identities whose power and agency are founded on the intensive exploitation of fossil fuels—what she calls "petro-masculinity"— she calls attention to the "historic relationship between fossil fuels and white patriarchal rule" (2018: 29). Reliance on—and nostalgia for—fossil fuels is secured through military, corporate, and government structures as much as through social patterns of behavior, consumption, and fossil-fuel-enabled freedom of movement. US digital action cinema's preoccupation with energy, fantasies of endless motion, fondness for digital long takes, and fascination with multi-dimensional movement all speak to this same petro-nostalgia. All are most emphatically present in *Captain Marvel*'s final battle scene.

The scene is constructed around three aerial "dogfights." Vers/Danvers, Fury, and Rambeau need to deliver the alien energy source to Skrull refugees currently in Earth orbit, so they can escape the Kree's attacks. Rambeau, Fury, and the refugees depart for Earth, pursued by female Kree pilot Minn-Erva (Gemma Chan). The two crafts swing and twirl, exchanging fire along deep crevasses in a rocky terrain, recalling similar dogfights in war films, as well as in science fiction films like *Star Wars* (George Lucas, 1977). With some brilliant evasive maneuvering, Rambeau eliminates her pursuer. Meanwhile Vers/Danvers hitches a ride on the outside of Yon-Rogg's escape jet which is also heading for Earth. In a mid-air face-off, Yon-Rogg loosens Vers/Danvers's grip on his jet and knocks her into an out-of-control freefall. She composes herself, and with this composure—her arms outstretched like Wonder Woman—acquires the epitome of her powers: flight. Hair, hands, and eyes ablaze, she smoothly swoops through Earth's atmosphere, a trail of energy left in her wake, as if from a jet engine's afterburn. Leaving Yon-Rogg in the dirt on Earth, she moves onto another

Figure 12.3 Captain Marvel (Brie Larson) epitomizes the white woman's glow (Dyer 1997) and the destructive force of jet-powered ballistic weaponry at the end of *Captain Marvel* (© Marvel Studios, 2019. All Rights Reserved).

dogfight, this time in space, neutralizing an array of military craft and ballistic missiles unleashed by Yon-Rogg's superior, Ronan the Accuser (Lee Pace), by smashing her body into—and through—them (Figure 12.3). Hovering Wonder Woman-like again, this time in front of Ronan's ship, Vers prepares her energy field to deal a final blow. Ronan retreats.

Vers has completed the arc from the newly-powered being-without-a-clear-sense-of-herself to a fully-powered body-as-weapon. Now her possession and control of energy are literally cosmic in scale. Yet in the final dogfight this cosmic scale is accompanied by a clear reduction in the thickness of visual texture. Mostly in extreme long shots, Captain Marvel repels Kree warheads, fighter planes, and warships, with her own body the projectile of choice. She has become a superhero envisioned in the familiar masculinist terms of jet-fueled, ballistic-supported, military destruction, but using the sparest of visual detail. On the rare occasion the sequence provides a closer view, visual performance cues are almost entirely absent due to the flaming battle helmet which masks Larson's face and eyes. Furthermore, Captain Marvel is framed persistently against the featureless expanse of space, sweeping through the environment with a smoothness and ease that undercuts any sense of the necessary friction of multidirectional combat. She has become so powerful that all sense of dramatic tension falls away: her combat skills have solidified into a single trope of never-ending propulsion.

Conclusion

The logic of deferral in digital action franchises does not simply decide *when* the space of action opens up, but also determines *how* the resulting visions of action heroism are depicted, and their relationship to wider cultural discourses on gender, race, and power. *Wonder Woman* and *Captain Marvel* were marketed to build anticipation and awareness of their status as solo female "firsts" in their respective cinematic universes. For fans, they had been a long time coming. The thrill embedded in their early action sequences, in which stunt performers lend an affectively thick materiality to expansive, multi-directional, physical action, corresponds to the thrill of finally seeing central female protagonists embodying expansive forms of empowerment previously only available to white male principles in each franchise universe. Yet that thick materiality of action gives way to a less visually rich and less affectively dense image of female empowerment in each film's latter stages. Larson and Gadot's facial and physical expressiveness are constrained in service of their characters' transformation into glowing bodies-as-weapons. The paucity of visual interest in the end battle sequences exacerbates the denuded narrative stakes, as women with god-like powers overcome all before them. In the context of the recent reluctance to even represent a central female protagonist in these extensive comic-book cinematic universes, is it a coincidence that these first solo women are manifested in such digitally, visually, and narratively lackluster ways at the moment of their greatest power?

Both *Wonder Woman* and *Captain Marvel* offer highly militarized visions of the solo female action hero, recuperating conventional notions of military power through their visual emphasis on ballistic weapons and jet flight, even as they signal their progressive anti-war and feminist credentials. Digital action cinema's ability to visualize its heroines in innovative ways is here constrained by the longstanding cultural ambivalence about women in possession of great power. Unwittingly but conspicuously, both films eschew alternatives and reach for conventionally masculinist tropes of military might, and of the fantasy of endless propulsion on which our patriarchal petro-culture has historically been founded.

These are also depictions that locate whiteness as the seat of unimaginably extensive powers, shoring up their fictions through recourse to Christian imagery of divinity and its human manifestation. The foregrounding of white superheroine protagonists appears to have been a necessary "gateway" for the studios to move into a more diverse range of Marvel and DC female superheroes—testing the market appeal of a solo woman superhero clearly means testing a white woman's appeal first. Released only slightly later, *Black Panther* and its sequel, *Black Panther: Wakanda Forever* (Ryan Coogler, 2022), have unapologetically offered forms of digitally enabled visual empowerment for women of color that are not so closely tied to the intersection of white military and petro-cultures that continues to shape much of the imagery of power in the Marvel and DC Cinematic Universes.[9] Their narrativizing of the challenges of retaining access to power and energy at least encourages a more critical stance on such issues.

While the comparative rise in the numbers of action women at the center of these expansive cinematic universes is to be celebrated, it is important to remain alert to the creative choices that shape the digital articulation of female power, and the industrial, cultural and social contexts that underpin them. So let us continue as scholars and viewers of action cinema to ask: what does power look like, and why? These are vital questions not only for action cinema but ultimately for our world.

Notes

1 *Tron: Legacy* (Joseph Kosinski, 2010) and *Blade Runner 2049* (Denis Villeneuve, 2017) are examples.

2 See further Brannon Donoghue (2022) and Banet-Weiser (2018).

3 The effect is created by digitally combining footage from a line of cameras that simulate a virtual camera's path around the action, creating a heightened sense of depth in the image.

4 Examples include female spy films like *Salt* (Phillip Noyce, 2010), *Colombiana* (Oliver Megaton, 2011), *Atomic Blonde* (David Leitch, 2017), and *Red Sparrow* (Francis Lawrence, 2018), or female avenger films such as *The Brave One* (Neil Jordan, 2007), *Proud Mary* (Babak Najafi, 2018), and *Kate* (Cedric Nicolas-Troyan, 2021).

5 Queer erasure and other forms of erasure are ongoing issues in these franchises. See Tuoriniemi (2018).

6 See for example Dyer (1997).

7 The US Air Force admitted women into its fighter pilot program in 1991. *Captain Marvel* is set in 1993. Just like the American frontier before it, US military prowess and space exploration have been historically understood as the purview of white men. See further Palmer and Purse (2019).

8 Building on Boyer et al. (2017), Daggett describes petro-nostalgia as a contemporary nostalgia for the "American way of life [that was] centered around a version of white, patriarchal rule in which the achievement of hegemonic masculinity required intensive fossil fuel consumption and, for the working or middle-class, jobs within or reliant upon fossil fuel systems" (2018: 32).

9 At the same time, *Black Panther*'s expansion of the pool of stunt people of color is making big-budget films featuring women of color without an overtly digital approach possible, among them *The Woman King* (Gina Prince-Bythewood, 2022). See further Steimer (2021b).

Works Cited

Banet-Weiser, Sarah (2018), *Empowered: Popular Feminism and Popular Misogyny*, Durham, NC: Duke University Press.

Bordwell, David (2000), *Planet Hong Kong: Popular Cinema and the Art of Entertainment*, Cambridge, MA: Harvard University Press.

Boyer, Dominic, Cymene Howe, and Timothy Mitchell (2017), *Cultures of Energy: The Energy Humanities Podcast*, 57 (16 February). Audio podcast episode available at https://podcasts.apple.com/gb/podcast/ep-57-timothy-mitchell/id1073817284?i=1000381322323 [accessed 28 March, 2023].

Brannon Donoghue, Courtney (2022), "Gendered Expectations for Female-Driven Films: Risk and Rescue Narratives Around Warner Bros.' *Wonder Woman*," *Feminist Media Studies*, 22 (3): 485–501.

Daggett, Cara (2018), "Petro-masculinity: Fossil Fuels and Authoritarian Desire," *Millennium: Journal of International Studies*, 47 (1): 25–44.

Dyer, Richard (1997), *White*, London: Routledge.

Howell, Charlotte E. (2015), "'Tricky' Connotations: Wonder Woman as DC's Brand Disruptor," *Cinema Journal*, 55 (1) Fall: 141–50.

Kent, Miriam (2021), *Women in Marvel Films*, Edinburgh: Edinburgh University Press.

Lindner, Katharina (2011), "Bodies in Action: Female Athleticism on the Cinema Screen," *Feminist Media Studies*, 11 (3): 321–45.

Lo, Kwai-Cheung (2007), "Copies of Copies in Hollywood and Hong Kong Cinemas: Rethinking the Woman-Warrior Figures," in Gina Marchetti and Tan See Kam (eds), *Hong Kong Film, Hollywood and the New Global Cinema: No Film is an Island*, 126–36, London: Routledge.

Palmer, Lorrie and Lisa Purse (2019), "When the Astronaut Is a Woman," *Science Fiction Film and Television*, 12 (1): 1–7.

Purse, Lisa (2019), "The New Dominance: Action-Fantasy Hybrids and the New Superhero in 2000s Action Cinema," in James Kendrick (ed.), *A Companion to the Action Film*, 55–73, Chichester: Wiley Blackwell.

Steimer, Lauren (2021a), *Experts in Action: Transnational Hong Kong-Style Stunt Work and Performance*, Durham, NC: Duke University Press.

Steimer, Lauren (2021b), "The Power in Numbers: Ensemble Stunt Performance in *Black Panther* and Histories of Practice," in Renée T. White and Karen A. Ritzenhoff (eds), *Afrofuturism in* Black Panther*: Gender, Identity, and the Re-Making of Blackness*, Lanham, MD: Lexington Books, 33–52.

Tasker, Yvonne and Diane Negra (2007), *Interrogating Postfeminism: Gender and the Politics of Popular Culture*, Durham, NC: Duke University Press.

Tasker, Yvonne (2011), *Soldiers' Stories: Military Women in Cinema and Television Since WWII*, Durham, NC: Duke University Press.

Tasker, Yvonne (2015), *The Hollywood Action and Adventure Film*, Chichester: Wiley Blackwell.

Teo, Stephen (1997), *Hong Kong Cinema: The Extra Dimensions*, London: BFI Publishing.

Tuoriniemi, Frances (2018), "Elisions & Illusions of Queerness: What Sacrifices Are Made in Appeals to a Mass Audience?" *[sic] Journal of Literature, Culture and Literary Translation*, 9 (1): 1–22.

Chapter 13

Beyond the Dark Moment: Seriality and Heroic Failure in Contemporary Action Cinema

Scott Higgins

The action film thrives on tension between what Linda Williams identifies as "in the nick of time" and "too late" (2001: 25). The greater the threat of catastrophic failure, the thinner the margin for success, the stronger an action film's corporeal, emotional, and cognitive attraction. Melodramatic dramaturgy depends on reversal; heroes must fall before they rise. But there are at least two complications to the equation. First, familiarity robs the device of power. As Linda Williams notes with regard to cross-cut races to the rescue, "paradoxically, it is as if the more the temporal prolongation of suspense builds, the surer we can be that this investment of time will have a successful outcome" (2001: 34). Genre viewers know that few things guarantee a last-minute success like the apparent inevitability of failure. Second, the pressure and adversity that precondition melodramatic transcendence can also be spectacularly pleasurable in themselves. A fall is more than just the prelude to a rise. These factors cooperate to make the depiction of a hero's defeat prime for elaboration: a storytelling device with which filmmakers can experiment and in which viewers can indulge. By breaking continuity between cliffhanger episodes, film serials promoted scenes of failure as a defining pleasure. This spirit lingers on in features, though the cliffhanger's radical potential is qualified by narrative closure. Recent action films, notably those in the Marvel Cinematic Universe, return the thrill of catastrophe to near serial heights. This chapter explores the spectacular appeal of heroic failure in twenty-first-century action films.

Catastrophe and Reversal in the Sound Serial

Depictions of the worst possible outcome form a little-remarked generic potential played out in late-twentieth-century action exemplars like *Superman* (Richard Donner, 1978) and *The Matrix* (Lana and Lilly Wachowski, 1999). In the former, Lex Luthor's (Gene Hackman) plan to decimate the American West Coast with earthquakes works, and Lois Lane (Margot Kidder) is crushed beneath a fallen utility pole. Superman (Christopher Reeve) is too late. Nonetheless, our hero restores the nick of time by spectacularly flying rings around the earth, reversing its spin and rolling back history. Two decades later, Neo (Keanu Reeves) loses his race to escape the matrix and is mercilessly gunned down by agents before he can reach a landline. Beyond the last minute, Trinity's (Carrie-Anne Moss) reviving kiss to his lifeless body grants Neo the power to physically master his world and surmount death itself. Both films are as remarkable for the extremity of their fairy-tale logic as for their influence on the genre. But neither invented the dramatic device. Rather, they make salient an impulse with deep historical roots in action cinema. This pattern of catastrophe and reversal made its way into popular American cinema through film serials, particularly sound-era chapterplays produced between 1930 and 1956. Weekly episodes promoted heroic calamity to the status of a routine event. Where feature films tend toward the continuity of the hero's fall and rise to a conclusive victory, the sound serial's inherent discontinuity encouraged regular and vivid depictions of failure.

Cliffhanger endings commonly carry hopeless situations well past the point of return. At the conclusion of chapter nine of *Undersea Kingdom* (B. Reeves Eason and Joseph Kane, 1936), Crash Corrigan (Ray Corrigan), is strapped to the front of a battle tank and slammed into an iron gate. The event comes complete with a plume of debris and horrified reactions from onlookers. Likewise, in chapter nine of *The Tiger Woman* (Wallace Grissell and Spencer Gordon Bennet, 1944) Rita Arnold (Linda Stirling) pilots her speedboat directly into a passing river ferry, which bursts into the fiery explosion promised by the episode's title "Cruise to Cremation." Mortal failure is common in the serial world. Wagonloads of innocents go over the cliff and heroes succumb to firing squads, bombings, plane crashes, electrocutions, and all manner of inescapable peril. Of course, the cliffhanger formula almost inevitably guarantees that the situation will be reversed either through clever contrivance or outright contradiction at the start of the next chapter. Despite all previous evidence, in episode ten of *Undersea Kingdom* and *The Tiger Woman* respectively, Crash Corrigan passes unharmed through the gate, and Tiger Woman finds time to abandon her vessel before collision. One of the serial form's unique appeals is that it allows viewers to indulge in disasters that would end continuous narratives, because we know that the cataclysm will eventually be neutralized. Sound serials deliver both tragedy and fortune at regular intervals, and engaging with a cliffhanger entails recognition, even expectation, of this reversibility.

Presentation of disaster in the sound serial also entails an odd balance of prominence and disposability. By classical standards, a cliffhanger's intensity is out of proportion with its effect on the causal chain. One moment our hero faces certain death; the next moment all is more or less forgotten. Chapter ten of *The Tiger Woman* does not miss a beat and we follow along, never giving the conflagration of ferry passengers a second thought. Instead, we plunge forward into another round of exposition, action, and the setup for the next cliffhanger. But perils are dropped only after dwelling on them. The production process encouraged emphasis on short-term intensity over long-term consequence. Serial screenwriters were assigned cliffhangers and had the task of building chapters around them. These hazards and traps received more budget, screen time, and attention to craft than the rest of the chapter. They dominate the viewing experience with vividness, clarity, and suspense. All the serial's cinematic resources are brought to bear on enthralling viewers in the terrible moment. If this low-budget and formulaic mode of filmmaking is ever captivating, it is during the cliffhanger.

In interrupting the story at the point of failure, serials shift the nature of our relationship to narrative. The episode's end, and the week-long break between chapters, converts spectacular destruction into a puzzle. With each chapter's closing command that we "return next week," often accompanied by footage of heroes continuing their adventures, our in-the-moment concern for the protagonist is transformed into a riddle about how reversal can be possible. We are left to speculate how the trap might be escaped, how the bullet might be dodged, how the clutches of death could once again be slipped. For young viewers, this question was charged with ludic potential. Cliffhanger situations provided rules for play and re-enactment, a phenomenon that Alice Miller Mitchell identified in 1929 as "playing movies" (75–6). For a surprisingly large audience of adults, cliffhangers posed an occasion for speculation or even debate (Barefoot 2011: 167–90; Vela 2000). Any viewer could purchase the puzzle's solution in the form of next week's admission, but the answer would always pale compared to the upcoming depiction of another "too late."

From Cliffhanger to Dark Moment

Connections between the sound serial and the contemporary action film are not difficult to trace. Albert Broccoli and Harry Saltzman's James Bond series was launched just six years after the last American sound-era serial and found an audience familiar with expectations, conventions, and viewing strategies planted by the chapterplay. For the *Film Bulletin* reviewer who called *Dr. No* (Terence Young, 1962) a "super-duper cliffhanger," the serial lineage was plain ("Review of

Dr. No" 1963: 18). George Lucas and Steven Spielberg paid explicit homage to the form in *Star Wars* (1977) and *Raiders of the Lost Ark* (1981) while also laying the groundwork for the mainstream action franchise as we know it.[1]

However, the continuities between serials and action films are probably less a matter of direct influence than shared melodramatic roots. In their races-to-the-rescue, outlandish contrivances, and down-to-the-wire reversals, both forms resort to situational dramaturgy, a mode of plotting founded in blood-and-thunder theatrical melodrama. The concept was brought to film studies by Ben Brewster and Lea Jacobs in their study of pre-classical filmmaking in the 1910s, *Theater to Cinema* (1997). Situational dramaturgy was a critically disreputable but popular and practical way of building plots from stock elements.[2]

The practice in nineteenth-century stage melodrama, the early feature film, and the sound serial is characterized by implicit discontinuity stemming from the combination of pre-existing modules in contrast to the imputed Aristotelian dramatic unity of the studio-era feature. Situations are ready-made states of affair strung together, nested, and repeated to deliver regular measures of sensation and excitement. Sound serials refine and repeat a narrow set of melodramatic possibilities, most of them based on fundamental structures that were already well developed in the one-reel era. The chief serial situations include the taking and freeing of hostages, the standoff, the chase, and the race to the rescue. These, in turn, are filled in from a menu of concrete options: the time bombs, car chases, sieges, and gunfights that populate the serial world. The combinatory logic of situational melodrama helped producers churn out vivid thrills on a tight schedule. Where classical feature films appear to subordinate events to unified psychologies and goals, Brewster and Jacobs point out that "situations can be thought of independently of the particular plots and characters which motivate them. . . . A weakening or even disregard of narrative continuity and logic is thus implicit" (1997: 24). The hero's extravagant demise or magnificent failure need not derail a story that prizes thrilling interruption over absorbing continuity.

Ties between action and melodrama are well recognized. Yvonne Tasker, Jennifer Bean, and Steve Neale have pointed out continuities between silent-film melodrama and the action film, signaling serial production in the 1910s as a predecessor to classical and contemporary trends.[3] In her seminal work, Linda Williams observes that pathos and action typify the melodramatic mode, with sentimental dramas and action films constituting two paths to "the staging of virtue through adversity and suffering" (2001: 15). Elsewhere, I have explored how melodramatic forms across cinema retain the vestiges of situational dramaturgy built into unifying schemes like the three-act structure.[4] The action film, at least since the advent of the Bond franchise, has kept melodramatic plotting alive within the apparently causal and continuous framework of feature-film storytelling.

Contemporary screenwriting parlance variously refers to situations of heroic failure as "dark moments," "black moments," or "the dark night of the soul," but they maintain much of the cliffhanger's structure and appeal. Screenwriting manuals usually suggest placing them at the end of a feature's second act where they set up the third-act climax. Linda Aronson's *Screenwriting Updated* describes the hero's "second-act turning point" as the "closest that they come to death and despair . . . designed to pump up suspense and the audience's anxiety. After the second-act turning point, the protagonist rallies for act three, which is the final battle towards the goal" (2001: 77). H.R. D'Costa, on her website *Scribe Meets World* and in her book *The Trough of Hell*, recommends creating what she calls the "all is lost moment" that combines physical pain and emotional loss, with the apparent paradox that only by losing everything can the hero gain the resources to win (2014). William C. Martell describes the "Popeye Point," a life threatening action sequence where "he's had alls he can stands and he can't stands no more" (2000). Dark moments are the essence of melodrama, a welding of pathos and spectacle that triggers the emotional recognition of virtue. They function as embedded cliffhangers, perilous situations that, even as they crystalize, signal the likelihood of spectacular reversal.

Feature-film continuity and the requirement of immediate resolution tends to tame the cliffhanger, to blunt the scale of heroic failure. Luke Skywalker (Mark Hamill) loses his mentor who becomes a wise ghost, Han Solo (Harrison Ford) is frozen in carbonite but not quite dead, John McClane (Bruce Willis) pulls glass from his bloody bare feet and says goodbye to his wife, but he doesn't literally lose her and he only limps slightly. All is only *seemingly* lost, if that. Perhaps spurred on by the success of *The Matrix*, some twenty-first-century action films heighten the dark moment's importance and take it as an occasion to innovate. One method is to deny reversal. The Bond franchise, recalling the abortive commercial experiment of *On Her Majesty's Secret Service* (Peter R. Hunt, 1969), was successfully rebooted in 2006 with *Casino Royale* (Martin Campbell), which climaxes with Daniel Craig's 007 failing to save Eva Green's Vesper Lynd from drowning beneath a collapsed Venetian palazzo. Two years later, Christopher Nolan's *The Dark Knight* (2008) varied the game by allowing Rachel Dawes (Maggie Gyllenhaal) to die in a hostage situation without the requisite reversal. In this case, Batman's (Christian Bale) failure becomes an occasion for pathos and a lengthy pause in the action. Subverting melodramatic convention helped Bond and Batman court critical acclaim – these were "serious" blockbuster action films. Neither movie avoids melodramatic dramaturgy, but they vary it for effect: they are exceptions that prove the rule. The trend may well have culminated in *No Time to Die* (Cary Joji Fukunaga, 2021), which stages a fiery heroic sacrifice unimaginable in a Bond film before the era of the Cinematic Universe and the reboot.

Closer to the serial model are the invariably situational plots of the *Mission Impossible* series. *Mission: Impossible—Fallout* (Christopher McQuarrie, 2018) flirts no less than three times with the spectacle of too late. The bombings of major cities at the start of the movie are quickly revealed to be a ruse staged in the interrogation of a suspect. Ethan Hunt's (Tom Cruise) failure to protect innocents during a heist turns out to be his mental projection of what "might" happen. Finally, the climactic cross-cut race to disarm nuclear devices appears to fail when Hunt, hanging from a cliff, faces a blinding flash of white light. This last apparent failure is short lived, revealed to be the cinematographer's (Rob Hardy) stylistic flourish rather than a diegetic event. Few films are so devoted to teasing viewers with catastrophic failure.

Marvel and Melodrama

The depth and range of contemporary action's situational lineage is on proud display in films of the Marvel Cinematic Universe. At the very least the films merit study as the dominant version of American popular action cinema in the early twenty-first-century. *Forbes* columnist Mark Hughes's (2019) claim that "the fanbase for the MCU is the biggest fanbase for any franchise of films in the world, in the history of cinema" may sound hyperbolic, but it is supported by cumulative world-wide box-office north of $22 billion ($12 billion more than the *Star Wars* franchise) ("Movie Franchises" 2020). Commercial success aside, the MCU's thirty-three feature films (to date) represent an extraordinary experiment in cinematic seriality, and one that marshals dark moments with originality and brio. Superhero films may well be today's most vital brand of cinematic melodrama. As the genre's founding blockbuster *Superman* illustrates, they can return the intense pleasures of total failure, albeit momentarily. The Marvel films innovate by intermixing and varying the placement of conventional blood-and-thunder situations.

Ryan Coogler's *Black Panther* (2018) offers a standout example of how heroic failure can be creatively rearranged and recalibrated to complicate a story's cultural dynamics. The dark moment involves a play on the state of affairs described by Georges Polti in his 1895 playwriting handbook *The Thirty-Six Dramatic Situations* as the "Loss of Loved Ones" variation "A1: The Slaying of Kinsmen While Powerless to Prevent It" (1977 [1895]: 121). In this, *Black Panther* recalls a host of familial losses that motivate and define Marvel heroes, including the killing of Thor's (Chris Hemsworth) mother Frigga (Rene Russo), stabbed just before Thor and Odin (Anthony Hopkins) arrive on the scene in *Thor: The Dark World* (Alan Taylor, 2013) and Black Panther's (Chadwick Boseman) father T'Chaka (John Kani), struck by an explosion even as his son attempts to warn him in *Captain America: Civil War* (Joe and Anthony Russo, 2016) (Figure 13.1). In a universe of reversible losses, these are moments of pathetic recognition. Generally, such situations are handled as they were in sound-era serials; they are opportunities to launch concrete action.[5] Superhero films, like their serial forebearers, capitalize on situational plotting in the name of adventurous but reassuring fantasy. The death of a loved one demonstrates the hero's virtue,

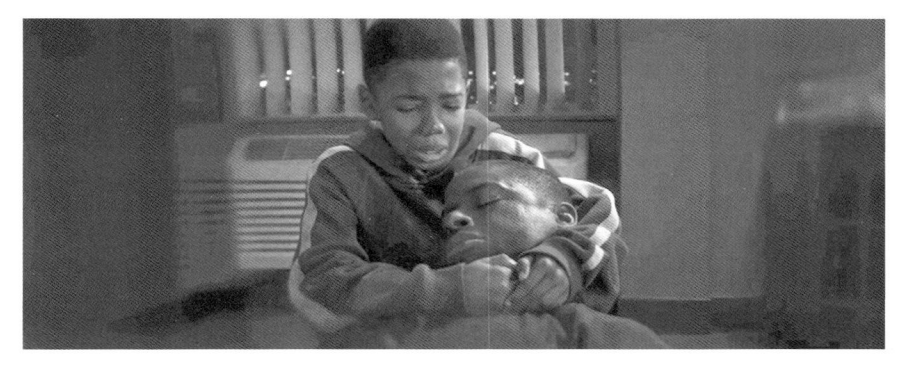

Figure 13.1 Young Killmonger (Seth Carr) discovers his dead father (Sterling K. Brown) in *Black Panther* (© Marvel Studios, 2018. All Rights Reserved).

emotionally implicates viewers, underlines moral opposition, and provokes physical pursuit. It is precisely this reassurance that Coogler disrupts.

Black Panther's dark moment crystallizes when T'Challa (Chadwick Boseman) apparently falls to his death as Killmonger (Michael B. Jordan) defeats him in ritual combat. Then, in a break with norms, Coogler and Joe Robert Cole's screenplay apportions the scene of pathetic loss not to the hero or his people, but to the movie's villain. As the new king, Killmonger receives the heart-shaped herb which both imparts the powers of the Black Panther and stimulates a visit to the Ancestral Plane. Where T'Challa's spirit walk consists of abstract conversations with his dead father set in a mystical savannah, Killmonger's is specific and tactile. In it, he returns to his childhood apartment in an Oakland California housing project. The sequence begins as a flashback that continues the opening scene as young Killmonger (Seth Carr) returns home to discover and then cradle his father's lifeless body. This poignant and visceral image lingers over the adult villain's hallucination as he re-enters the apartment to find an empty floor where his father had lain and an other-worldly purple sky beyond the window. When Killmonger's father, N'Jobu (Sterling K. Brown) appears, Coogler handles the conversation in shot-reverse-shot, exchanging child and adult versions of the villain between cuts. N'Jobu asks his son "no tears for me?" and the young boy glances coolly toward the camera: "everybody dies, that's just life around here." In reverse shot, N'Jobu, beginning to cry, replies "well look at what I've done," and Coogler returns to the now grown Killmonger, tears streaming down his face (Figure 13.2).

The scene is *Black Panther*'s emotional peak; loss of innocence is grounded in the social reality of violence experienced in Black communities. Coogler's handling of the moment recalls his depiction of Oscar Grant's (Michael B. Jordan) death in *Fruitvale Station* (2013), which flashes to the dying man's memory of his young daughter, and *Creed*'s (2015) introduction of the young Adonis Johnson (Alex Henderson) locked up in a juvenile detention facility which is indistinguishable

Figure 13.2 Adult Killmonger's (Michael B. Jordan) pathos dominates *Black Panther*'s dark moment (© Marvel Studios, 2018. All Rights Reserved).

from prison. In each case, Coogler realizes scenarios of racial injustice through the pathos-laden imagery of children deprived of parents. It is a melodramatic touch that serves him well in both critical independent and mainstream studio production.

In four minutes of screen time, Coogler delivers the tragic pietà, the boy's inability to process trauma, and the grown-man's grief. The scene also reveals that the ruthless Killmonger is the child glimpsed playing basketball in the movie's prologue, something the plot had thus far obscured. Intercutting the child and man at a moment of abject despair, Coogler invests the villain with unexpected and unrivaled pathos. After this scene, Killmonger must be viewed as the outward manifestation of a poor Black child who lost his father to violence in America. The melodrama of purity's violation challenges the melodrama of irredeemable supervillainy. True to form, the death of a loved one accelerates the plot. Though hateful, Killmonger's incineration of the heart-shaped herbs and seizure of the throne is also charged with an air of righteousness: of pathos answered by action.

Black Panther juggles elements of the dark moment, making Killmonger the center of emotion while T'Challa suffers a turnaround in the plot. In distinction to the sound serial, the hero must rise and rectify things in continuity. T'Challa's reversal of fortune comes courtesy of Nakia (Lupita Nyong'o), Shuri (Letitia Wright), and Ramonda (Angela Bassett), Wakandan women who revive him to fighting strength with one last heart-shaped herb. As antagonist, Killmonger must fail, but as the figure of pathos he is given a noble end, watching the Wakandan sunrise that his father described to him and choosing to die free rather than live as a prisoner.

It is well known that *Black Panther* attained unusually high critical regard for a Marvel blockbuster, in part because of some perceived moral ambiguity around Killmonger, which was thought to harbor critical potential rarely entertained by the genre. Manohla Dargis, for one, credited Killmonger's "emotional, fraught backstory" with providing "the movie more heft and real-world friction than any of Marvel's other superhero blowouts" (2018). This friction emanates not from a rejection but a reworking of melodramatic building blocks, a case of creativity through recombination. Coogler cannily engages in the melodramatic mode, which, as Williams (2001) demonstrates, remains a prism for making sense of race in America. The film as an entirety cannot be credited with revolutionary intent. If anything, the epilogue in which T'Challa unites Wakanda with the global economy and opens an outreach center in Killmonger's Oakland neighborhood mirrors the very kind of soft power that Disney exercises by producing and releasing a film like *Black Panther*. Nonetheless, melodramatic scenes of pathetic failure and loss are designed to resonate beyond the moment—to launch a rise, that in this case is not exhausted by the putative hero's story.

Super Heroic Failure in *Infinity War*

This kind of innovation sets the context for the climax of *Avengers: Infinity War* (Joe and Anthony Russo, 2018), easily contemporary cinema's most audacious heroic failure and a case study of its generic pleasures. In contrast to *Black Panther*, the film courts neither critical praise nor the coherence of closure. As A.O. Scott somewhat cynically points out, Coogler's film may be one of Marvel's "carefully planned exceptions that uphold a rule (meaning a regime as well as a norm) of passive acceptance disguised as enthusiasm. . . . Above all, the Disney-Marvel combination is a giant machine that manufactures maximum consent" (2018). *Infinity War* makes few appeals to refined cultures of taste, but it has the burden of satisfying fans' expectations wrought by eighteen prior movies and focusing viewer desire on the next Avengers release, *Avengers: Endgame* (Joe and Anthony Russo, 2019). These are demands well answered by the logic of the serial cliffhanger which arrives with a vengeance when Thanos (Josh Brolin) completes his quest and snuffs out half the population of the universe with a snap of his fingers. *Infinity War*'s climax stages pathetic loss on a scale rarely afforded the action film. Placing the dark moment at the end of the third act revives serial tradition, but in a framework that emphasizes the last-minute conversion of action to pathos, switching between Williams's terms for melodrama's dialectic.

In pressing the cliffhanger into high-profile service, Marvel cites and transforms the sound serial formula. Thanos's Infinity Gauntlet borrows its logic from the serial convention in which hero and villain struggle over control of a prized object. The Marvel franchise recalls the very first superhero serial, *Adventures of Captain Marvel* (John English and William Witney, 1941), in which the masked villain progressively gathers lenses that fit into a golden scorpion statue.[6] Once assembled, rearranging the lenses held in the statue's pincers produces a ray that either explodes objects by smashing their atoms or turns any metal into gold. As in *Adventures of Captain Marvel*, the Infinity Gauntlet grants the episodic plot an itinerary and identifies narrative progress with the construction of a machine. Also, as in the serial, the contest for the prized object (or "weenie" in industry parlance) and its assembly confer a game-like logic on the proceedings which engages viewers in the chain of problem solving and builds a ready bridge between spectatorship and play, between the multiplex and the toy store. The Avengers' ultimate failure caps a series of struggles to prevent the villain from assembling the weenie.

Unlike a serial chapter, though, the feature film experience is not weighted with the expectation of failure. Instead, a villain's progress usually points to a victorious reversal. *Infinity War* elaborates on this condition by turning to the final act a full forty-eight minutes before the film's end. Thanos receives the soul stone and our heroes gather in Wakanda to face a final onslaught as he attacks for the sixth and final gem. Elongated buildup and repeated near-misses conspire, cueing viewers to yearn for (and hypothesize) victory. True to form, the worse things get, the more likely they will turn out all right. At first *Infinity War* accedes to expectations. Our heroes foil Thanos by destroying the final stone before he can reach it. It is a winning move colored by pathetic sacrifice because a character's life depends on this particular piece of the weenie; Vision (Paul Bettany) is an artificial intelligence powered by the mind stone. Then, in a nod to *Superman*, Thanos snatches this pyrrhic victory by rewinding time, stealing the stone, and killing Vision a second time.

The turnaround primes hope for a last-minute save. When Thor arrives to face the villain, the odds are with him because he appears so late and because he is completing his own hero's journey having lost everything only to gain new power in the form of Stormbreaker, an enchanted battle axe forged by the heat of a sun. Despite this doubling of conventional cues for heroic success, he too fails to stop Thanos's finger snap. The film plays a far more sophisticated game of successively raising and disappointing expectations than the most accomplished sound serial, and it does so by expanding the race against time within a three-act structure.

A more fundamental elaboration of the cliffhanger, however, appears after the point of failure when narration extends and iterates scenes of pathetic loss. After the blinding white light that accompanies the big snap, our heroes begin to fall. The deaths are ordered for emotional impact. First Bucky Barnes (Sebastian Stan) and various Wakandans turn to dust, establishing the principle of disintegration. Black Panther is the first top-line hero to die, followed by teenage Groot (voiced by Vin Diesel) whose slower fading gives Rocket (voiced by Bradley Cooper) time to react. The disappearances of Scarlet Witch (Elizabeth Olsen), Falcon (Anthony Mackie), Mantis (Pom Klementieff), and Drax (Dave

Figure 13.3 Spider-Man (Tom Holland) dies tragically in Iron Man's (Robert Downey Jr.) embrace in *Avengers: Infinity War* (© Marvel Studios, 2018. All Rights Reserved).

Bautista) lead up to more prominent Avengers like Star Lord (Chris Pratt) and Doctor Strange (Benedict Cumberbatch) vanishing from view. But the final dusting is the most painful. Figured as the death of a son before his father, Peter Parker/Spider-Man (Tom Holland) protests his demise and embraces Tony Stark/Iron Man (Robert Downey Jr.) even as he evaporates: "I don't want to go, please." The sequence revels in suffering innocence and recognition of loss, melodrama's trademark emotional cocktail. In giving itself over to pathos, the moment reminds us that action films and tear jerkers share a common origin (Figure 13.3).

To fully account for how the film revisits and revises action melodrama, we cannot dwell within the confines of a single film. The engine that drives Marvel to pathos is seriality. For even as the heroes die, viewers know that they will revive to fight another day. The contemporary precedent for splitting a single adventure narrative into two feature-length parts is likely *The Empire Strikes Back* (Irvin Kershner, 1980), but the practice has been cemented over the past decade and a half by *Harry Potter and the Deathly Hallows: Part 1* and *Part 2* (David Yates, 2010, 2011), and *The Hunger Games: Mockingjay - Part 1* and *Part 2* (Francis Lawrence, 2014, 2015). In this, Marvel develops expectations and marketing practices forged by some of the highest profile blockbuster franchises in a generation. *Infinity War* refines the game by pushing beyond the dark moment and framing that catastrophe against at least six intertwined sub-franchises. As in a sound serial, where narrative sprawl can obliterate coherence, the cliffhanger's vivid simplicity, the razor-sharp pictorial and moral clarity of a melodramatic situation, provides indispensable balance. The same sort of logic has long informed television serials, with season breaks in *Game of Thrones* (David Benioff and D.B. Weiss, 2011–2019) and series 5–10 of *Doctor Who* (Steven Moffat, 2010–2017) giving the practice new prominence. Seriality integrates story into the consumer's lived experience, and this shapes our engagement both during and between episodes.

The final act of *Infinity War* calls up associations developed within the eighteen previous MCU movies as well as popular knowledge generated by franchise paratexts. Spider-Man's death, for instance, gains emotional resonance from the immediately depicted situation (death of a son before his adoptive father, death of an innocent, failure of the hero), and from the long-term relationships built between viewer and character across the Iron Man films and in *Spider-Man: Homecoming* (Jon Watts, 2017). But this is bracketed by extra-textual knowledge of Marvel's well publicized plans for the release of *Spider-Man: Far from Home* (Jon Watts, 2019), the following summer and of Robert Downey Jr.'s widely reported contract negotiations. The moment does not require all sets of knowledge to be dramatically effective, but as in the sound serial, it benefits from a kind of dual apprehension: knowing that this is not really the end allows us to bask in the depiction of that end. The order of the disintegrations is quite canny. Bucky Barnes and several Wakandan warriors may well be gone forever.[7] In 2018, however, Black Panther was simply too beloved and financially valuable to actually die. This effectively frames the subsequent disappearances as reversible, even as the pathos escalates. Audiences could luxuriate in the "too lates" because of their faith that the "nick of time" would return. Boseman's death in 2020 added another layer of poignance to his character's fall because the extra-textual reassurance of 2018 was so tragically reversed.

One final comparison to the sound serial illuminates Marvel's achievement here. From the 1930s to the early 1950s cliffhangers extended engagement with the serial world beyond the cinema into backyards, playgrounds, and daydreams (Higgins 2016). In depicting the graphic and logical outcomes of intractable dilemmas, sound serials gained vividness and amplified problem spaces that would linger until the next matinee. The week-long break between chapters severed narrational control and granted spectators the room to become the storyteller, to inhabit the game world. Marvel exploits this dynamic with unparalleled sophistication. It has, of course, dug into the tried and true markets for games and toys, which mesh particularly well with the ludic potential of a quest narrative. But the studio also feeds a much broader fan culture devoted to the constant and continual interaction with the story. The franchise nurtures the kind of "forensic fandom" that Jason Mittell (2009) identified with television shows like *Lost* (J.J. Abrams, 2004–2010), in which followers parse minutia for clues and insights to the ongoing story enigmas. As in the serial, interruption converts story to game. When the credits for *Infinity War* begin to roll, viewers are primed to move from scenes of hyperbolic emotion to longer-term puzzle solving. Nick Fury's (Samuel L. Jackson) post-credits disintegration acts less as a pathetic beat than a teaser as he sends a pager message to Captain Marvel and activates a specific field of narrative possibilities for fans to fill.

Paratexts and Pathos

Paratexts, Jonathan Gray's (2010) term for sources of peripheral information about a popular narrative, are especially salient to Marvel's strategy. Each new trailer, interview, toy release, and publicity image becomes fodder for fan speculation, conjecture, and play. Marvel's paratextual game is masterful. The studio famously plants misleading and digitally altered images in film trailers to feed the conversation. Fan sites compared the *Infinity War* trailer and film to reveal the removal of stones from Thanos's gauntlet and the appearance of the Hulk who is mostly absent from the film.[8] Each successive trailer for *Avengers: Endgame* was immediately subjected to frame-by-frame scrutiny.[9] When the 3-D trailer appeared in theaters, fans seized on visual effects elements omitted from a background explosion in the 2-D version as evidence that Hawkeye (Jeremy Renner) would be chased by Thanos's alien attack dogs, and, based on a leaked Lego playset, that the scene would take place at Avengers headquarters (Anderton 2019). Theories of how Thanos would be ultimately defeated spawned memes involving Ant Man shrinking down and attacking the villain from behind. What began as a text that fueled endless gifs, cartoons and visual puns, culminated in an official recognition by the film's directors, who adopted a suggestive Venn diagram as their Instagram Icon, and an unofficial erotic fantasy novel published on Amazon, *Antguy Gets Small to Go Into Thanos' Butt And Then Gets Big and Hard* by Chuck Tingle ("Ant-Man Will Defeat Thanos" 2019).

More prosaic entertainment industry news also helped structure speculation and engagement between the films. Leaks about stars who were leaving the franchise prepared the audience for an exercise in pathos. Based on star interviews and trade-press reports about actor contracts, sites predicted that Iron Man, Thor, and Captain America would perish or retire at the end of *Endgame*.[10] Taking stock of the MCU, *Hollywood Reporter* reflected common opinion that the film would end with "a glorious death" for Iron Man, and that "it's likely to be something that will have to be followed in the theater by a pause for audience mourning cries" (McMillan 2019). Indeed, the film follows Iron Man's ultimate heroic sacrifice with several scenes of mourning, including a funeral that reunites thirty-eight characters from across all the franchise films. Glorious death, that particular mixture of loss and victory, is a rarity in both sound serials and in contemporary action franchises because its emotional punch relies on irreversibility. Black Widow's demise in the same film is more typical. Despite her long-term membership in the Avenger's team, the narrative rushes past her death to continue the chase, perhaps a reflection of women's marginal placement in the MCU.[11] Beyond the dark moment lies the death of the story. The killing of the MCU's premiere hero may be emblematic of the way action melodrama in the twenty-first-century pushes the boundaries of heroic failure. At the same time, the event is only made possible by the serial sprawl, extra-textual engagement, and the seemingly endless propagation of heroes that mark contemporary cinema's most popular action franchise.

Avengers: Endgame replaced *Infinity War*'s tragic outcome with a more unifying heroic sacrifice, but Marvel's exercise in pathos reached beyond these two films. Mourning, usually confined to a few scenes that motivate vengeance, feeds the whole narrative of *Spider-Man: Far from Home*. Personal loss is built into Spider-Man's origin story through the death of his Uncle Ben, a first-act *Hurricane Express*-fashioned event that spurs action in the previous two cinematic incarnations (*The Hurricane Express*, Armand Schaeffer and J.P. McGowan, 1932). The current Spider-Man series does not depict Uncle Ben's death but amplifies grief by transposing the tragedy to the loss of Iron Man after three films that build a quasi-parental relationship. Peter Parker (aka Spider-Man) spends almost the entirety of *Far from Home* working through his anguish. His attempts to escape trauma on a school trip are repeatedly foiled by memorials to Tony Stark (aka Iron Man) that pop up in each city he visits. Left for dead by the villain, Spider-Man climbs from his dark moment when he is rescued by Tony Stark's driver, Happy Hogan (John Favreau). The two bond over their shared sadness and resolve to honor Iron Man by resuming the fight.

Loss echoed outside the cinema two months after *Homecoming*'s release when Disney and Sony reportedly severed the agreement to integrate Spider-Man into the MCU. Fans who rallied behind Marvel by calling for boycotts of Sony and reposting memes of tear-filled Tik Tok dancers also drew on cinematic pathos to express their dismay (Weiss 2019). On Twitter, protest took the form of repurposed images of Spider-Man embracing Iron Man as he disintegrates in *Infinity War*, Tony Stark announcing "I lost the kid" in *Endgame*, and the proclamation "Iron Man did not die for this" ("20 Marvel Fans" 2019; Gramuglia 2019). This outcry was eclipsed in December 2020 when Chadwick Boseman unexpectedly died of cancer. In a sincerely touching vein, fans processed the event through the Marvel lens, quoting T'Challa's comment about his father that "death is not the end" from *Captain America: Civil War* and excerpting the scene of Black Panther's return from the dead in the climax of *Endgame* (Sharma 2020). The fictional framing of death's impermanence helped soften grief over the star while also memorializing him through his character. Marvel's subsequent decision to retire T'Challa from the cinematic franchise reflects melodrama's intertextual complexities. Black Panther's ability to triumph over heroic failure reassured some fans, but real loss also forced the fiction to acknowledge the weight of death. The melodramatic mode as embodied by Marvel's dark moment overreaches the bounds of any single text.

Georges Polti's declaration that dramaturgy is the "Art of Combination," could well apply to Marvel's entire cinematic universe (1977 [1895]: 123). In addition to mixing characters from film to film, the franchise cycles and rejuvenates vivid and powerful moments drawn from the melodramatic lexicon. At base, the cliffhanger's commercial purpose is to monetize narrative suspense, ensuring admissions for subsequent episodes. Marvel's blockbuster seriality provides a much larger gap for fans and promotional material to fill while mining the aesthetic and experiential power of showing the worst outcome. Placing contemporary franchise action in the context of studio-era seriality reveals continuity and difference. On the one hand, these films offer a reassuring experience of spatial and temporal mastery (Purse 2011). On the other hand, big-budget contemporary variants indulge in the emotional recognition of suffering virtue in a way nearly absent in serials and rare in previous action films. Where cliffhangers were quickly revised and disposed of in the onward rush of chapterplay plotting, recent heroic failures can occasion sincere and elaborated pathos. The twenty-first-century action film continues to evolve on many fronts, as evidenced in this book. Marvel's Cinematic Universe obviously illustrates contemporary action's outward expansion, but it also points toward the deepening exploration of its melodramatic foundation.

Notes

1   For a fuller discussion of the relationship between the action film and the serial, see Higgins (2016) and (2017).

2   For a fuller discussion of situational plotting in contemporary action films, see Higgins (2008). Theatrical melodrama appears to be the most proximate point of influence for cinematic storytelling, but nineteenth-century serialized print media shared many of the same contrivances and undoubtedly served as a reference point as well (Barefoot 2017). Both kinds of melodrama also informed radio drama, though that format generally took the form of episodic series without cliffhangers rather than continuing serials.

3   Yvonne Tasker's important anthology *Action and Adventure Cinema* (2004) collects essays on early film melodrama by Jennifer Bean and Ben Singer, along with Steve Neale's useful overview of the action-adventure genre. In her introduction, Yvonne Tasker notes that action films "are typically melodramatic" (2004: 5). Though none of this work dwells on connections between contemporary action films and the nineteenth-century theatrical tradition, it very much affirms the need for further investigation.

4   See Higgins (2017) and (2016). The three-act structure is only the most prominent of myriad formulae proposed by screenwriting gurus and identified by commentators. Kristin Thompson (1999), for instance, persuasively argues that popular Hollywood cinema tends to employ a five-part structure. I do not intend to reify the three-act structure by referring to it here. In fact, I suspect that situational dramaturgy undergirds most of the unifying structures employed to explain popular film narrative.

5   For example, *The Hurricane Express* (Armand Schaeffer and J.P. McGowan, 1932) begins when Aviator Larry Baker (John Wayne) fails to prevent a train collision that kills his father (J. Farrell MacDonald), an engineer. Witnessing the cataclysm, Larry pulls his father's body from the wreckage, learns of foul play, and tearfully declares: "My father was murdered, and I'll bring that murderer to justice if it takes the rest of my life."

6 *Adventures of Captain Marvel* is based on the Fawcett Comics character that debuted in 1940 and is now known as Shazam. Marvel's *Captain Marvel* (Anna Boden and Ryan Fleck, 2019) is based on a character created by Stan Lee in 1967.

7 At this point Barnes is a relatively minor Avenger. Marvel subsequently expanded and promoted the character in the Disney+ series *Falcon and the Winter Soldier* (Malcolm Spellman, 2021). The emotional impact of his death in *Infinity War* might play differently for viewers of the show, though those viewers will also recognize his death as impermanent.

8 See for instance Zhiying Di (2018).

9 See for instance Antonia Haynes (2019).

10 See for example Childs (2018).

11 Thanks to Lisa Purse for pointing this out.

Works Cited

"20 Marvel Fans' Reactions to Sony and Disney's Spider-Man Fallout," 9GAG.com, 20 August 2019. Available online: https://9gag.com/gag/awobBWx (accessed 20 October 2019).

Anderton, Ethan (2019), "*Avengers Endgame* 3D Trailer Reveals Villains Removed from Key Sequence," SlashFilm.com. Available online: https://www.slashfilm.com/avengers-endgame-3d-trailer-secrets/ (accessed 8 January 2020).

"Ant-Man Will Defeat Thanos by Crawling Up His Butt and Expanding" (2019), KnowYourMeme.com. Available online: https://knowyourmeme.com/memes/ant-man-will-defeat-thanos-by-crawling-up-his-butt-and-expanding (accessed 9 January 2020).

Aronson, Linda (2001), *Screenwriting Updated*, Los Angeles: Silman-James Press.

Barefoot, Guy (2011), "Who Watched That Masked Man! Hollywood's Serial Audiences in the 1930s," *Historical Journal of Film, Radio, & Television*, 1 (2): 167–90.

Barefoot, Guy (2017), *The Lost Jungle*, Exeter: Exeter University Press.

Brewster, Ben, and Lea Jacobs (1997), *Theater to Cinema: Stage Pictorialism and the Early Feature Film*, Oxford: Oxford University Press.

Childs, Kevin (2018) "10 Actors Leaving the MCU (And 10 Who Will Stay) After Avengers 4," CBR.com. Available online: https://www.cbr.com/mcu-actors-leaving-staying-after-avengers-4/ (accessed 7 February 2019).

Dargis, Manohla (2018), "*Black Panther* Shakes Up the Marvel Universe," *The New York Times*, 6 February.

D'Costa, H.R. (2014), "How to End Act Two: 3 Essentials to Crafting an All Is Lost Moment Like a Boss" *Scribe Meets World*, Available online: http://scribemeetsworld.com/2014/screenplay-writing/all-is-lost/ (accessed 24 April 2019).

Gramuglia, Anthony (2019), "The Best Fan Reactions to the End of the Sony/Marvel Spider- Man Deal," CBR.com 21 August. Available online: https://www.cbr.com/sony-marvel-spider-man-fans-react/ (accessed 20 October 2019).

Gray, Jonathan (2010), *Show Sold Separately: Promos, Spoilers, and Other Media Paratexts*, New York: New York University Press.

Haynes, Antonia (2019), "Avengers End-Game Movie Trailer: A Shot-by-Shot Analysis," Goombastomp.com. Available online: https://goombastomp.com/avengers-endgame-trailer-analysis/ (accessed 8 January 2020).

Higgins, Scott (2008),"Suspenseful Situations: Melodramatic Narrative and the Contemporary Action Film," *Cinema Journal* 47 (2), Winter: 74–96.

Higgins, Scott (2016), *Matinee Melodrama: Playing with Formula in the Sound Serial*, New Brunswick, NJ: Rutgers University Press.

Higgins, Scott (2017), "Saturday Afternoon Blockbuster: James Bond's Serial Heritage," *Film Studies*, 17 (1), Fall: 73–91.

Hughes, Mark (2019), "How the Marvel-Sony 'Spider-Man' Dispute Will Be Solved One Way or Another [Updated]," *Forbes*, 21 August. Available online: https://www.forbes.com/sites/markhughes/2019/08/21/how-the-marvel-sony-spider-man-dispute-will-be-solved-one-way-or-another/?sh=bec5e1c6b501 (accessed 18 September 2019).

Martell, William C. (2000), *The Secrets of Action Screenwriting*, Los Angeles: First Strike Productions.

McMillan, Graeme (2019), "*Avengers Endgame*—Who Will Die?" *The Hollywood Reporter*, 22 April. Available online: https://www.hollywoodreporter.com/heat-vision/avengersendgame-deaths-who-will-die-1203776 (accessed 15 October 2019).

Mitchell, Alice Miller (1929), *Children and Movies*, Chicago: University of Chicago Press.

Mittell, Jason (2009), "*Lost* in a Great Story: Evaluation in Narrative Television (and Television Studies)," in Roberta Pearson (ed.), *Reading Lost*, 119–38, London: I.B. Tauris.

"Movie Franchises," (2020), The Numbers.com. Available online: https://www.thenumbers.com/movies/franchises/sort/World (accessed 28 December 2020).

Polti, George (1977 [1895]), *The Thirty-Six Dramatic Situations*, Boston: The Writer Inc.

Purse, Lisa (2011), *Contemporary Action Cinema*, Edinburgh: Edinburgh University Press.

"Review of *Dr. No* (1963)," *Film Bulletin*, 6 March: 18.

Scott, A.O. (2018), "*Avengers: Infinity War:* It's Marvel's Universe. We Just Live in It," *The New York Times*, 24 April. Available online: https://www.nytimes.com/2018/04/24/movies/avengers-infinity-war-review.html (accessed 28 December 2020).

Sharma, Aditi (2020), "Chadwick Boseman's Death: #WakandaForever Takes over Twitter as 'Black Panther' Fans Mourn," Republicworld.com, 29 August 2020.

Tasker, Yvonne (2004), *Action and Adventure Cinema*, New York: Routledge.

Thompson, Kristin (1999), *Storytelling in the New Hollywood: Understanding Classical Narrative Technique*, Cambridge, MA: Harvard University Press.

Vela, Rafael (2000), "With Parent's Consent: Film Serials, Consumerism, and the Creation of a Youth Audience, 1913–1938," PhD dissertation, University of Wisconsin, Madison.

Weiss, Josh (2019), "Jeremy Renner Asks Sony to Return Spider-Man to Marvel as Fans React to Disney Dispute," SyFy.com, 22 August 2019. Available online: https://www.syfy.com/syfywire/spider-man-disney-sony-twitter-reactions (accessed 15 October 2019).

Williams, Linda (2001), *Playing the Race Card*, Princeton, NJ: Princeton University Press.

Zhiying Di (2018), "Avengers Infinity War: Trailer vs. Movie Comparison," YouTube. Available online: https://www.youtube.com/watch?v=6OqXq69vEsk (accessed 7 February 2019).

Filmography

Non-Anglophone films are first listed by their English titles. The original titles are given in parentheses, except in the case of Bollywood films. They are known—including in Anglophone countries—by the Hindi titles. (N.B. *Bajirao Mastani*, *Don*, etc., are proper names.)

In most cases, Korean and Chinese family names are placed first. The original Korean and Chinese titles have been Romanized.

2001: A Space Odyssey (1968), Stanley Kubrick, UK/USA.
300 (2006), Zack Snyder, USA/Canada/Bulgaria.
36th Chamber of Shaolin, The (*Shao Lin sans shi liu fang*, 1978), Liu Chia-Liang, Hong Kong/China.
A Bittersweet Life (*Dalkomhan insaeng*, 2005), Kim Jee-woon, South Korea.
Above the Law (1988), Andrew Davis, USA.
Abyss, The (1989), James Cameron, USA.
Adventures of Captain Marvel (1941), John English and William Witney, USA.
A Good Day to Die Hard (2013), John Moore, USA/UK/Hungary.
Alibi.com (2017), Philippe Lacheau, France.
Alien (1979), Ridley Scott, UK/USA.
Alien: Covenant (2017), Ridley Scott, UK/USA.
Alien Resurrection (1997), Jean-Pierre Jeunet, USA.
Aliens (1986), James Cameron, UK/USA.
All the Way (2016), Jay Roach, USA.
Along with the Gods: The Two Worlds (*Sin gwa hamkke*, 2017), Kim Yong-hwa, South Korea.
Altered Carbon (2018–2020), [TV series], USA.
Anaconda (1997), Luis Llosa, USA/Brazil/Peru.
Annihilation (2018), Alex Garland, UK/USA.
Anything for Her (*Pour Elle*, 2008), Fred Cavayé, France/Spain.
Aquaman (2018) James Wan, USA/Australia.
Arès (2016), Jean-Patrick Bènes, France.
Armour of God (*Lung hing foo dai*, 1986), Jackie Chan and Eric Tsang, Hong Kong/Yugoslavia.
Armour of God II: Operation Condor (*Fei ying gai wak*, 1991), Jackie Chan, Hong Kong.
Assignment, The (aka *Tomboy*, 2016), Walter Hill, France/Canada/USA.
Atanarjuat: The Fast Runner (2001), Zacharias Kunuk, Canada.
Atomic Blonde (2017), David Leitch, USA/Germany/Sweden.
Avatar (2009), James Cameron, USA.

Avatar: The Way of Water (2022), James Cameron, USA.
Avengers, The (2012), Joss Whedon, USA.
Avengers: Endgame (2019), Anthony and Joe Russo, USA.
Avengers: Infinity War (2018), Anthony and Joe Russo, USA.
Away from Her (2006), Sarah Polley, Canada/UK/USA.
Baby Driver (2017), Edgar Wright, UK/USA.
Bad Grandmas (2017), Srikant Chellappa, USA.
Bajirao Mastani (2015), Sanjay Leela Bhansali, India.
Banker, The (2020), George Nolfi, USA.
Batman v Superman: Dawn of Justice (2016), Zack Snyder, USA.
Battle at Lake Changjin, The (*Chang jin hu*, 2021), Chen Kaige, Dante Lam, and Tsui
    Hark, PRC.
Bedhead (1991), Robert Rodriguez, USA.
Birth of a Nation, The (1915), D.W. Griffith, USA.
Black Hand, The (1906), Wallace McCutcheon, USA.
Black Mama White Mama (1973), Eddie Romero, Philippines/USA.
Black Mirror (2011–2019), [TV series], UK.
Black Panther (2018), Ryan Coogler, USA.
Black Panther: Wakanda Forever (2022), Ryan Coogler, USA.
Blacktino (2011), Aaron Burns, USA.
Blade (1998), Stephen Norrington, USA.
Blade Runner (1982), Ridley Scott, USA.
Blade Runner 2049 (2017), Denis Villeneuve, USA/UK/Canada.
Bleeding Steel (*Ji qi zhi xue*, 2017), Leo Zhang, PRC/Hong Kong.
Bless This Mess (2019–2020) [TV Series], USA.
Blood and Bone (2009), Ben Ramsey, USA.
Bloodshot (2020), David S.F. Wilson, USA.
Bloodsport (1988), Newt Arnold, USA.
Bones (2001), Ernest R. Dickerson, USA.
Bourne Identity (2002), Doug Liman, USA/Germany/Czech Republic.
Bourne Ultimatum, The (2007), Paul Greengrass, USA/Germany/France.
Boys in Company C, The (1978), Sidney J. Furie, Hong Kong/USA.
Brave One, The (2007), Neil Jordan, USA/Australia.
Brotherhood of the Wolf (*Le Pacte des loups*, 2001), Christophe Gans, France.
Buffy the Vampire Slayer (1997–2003), [TV Series], USA.
Call My Agent! (*Dix pour cent*, 2015–2020), [TV Series], France.
Captain America: Civil War (2016), Anthony and Joe Russo, USA.
Captain America: The Winter Soldier (2014), Anthony and Joe Russo, USA.
Captain Marvel (2019), Anna Boden and Ryan Fleck, USA/Australia.
Carbon Copy (1981), Michael Schultz, USA/UK.
Casino Royale (2006), Martin Campbell, UK/USA/Czech Republic/Germany.
Cast Away (2000), Robert Zemeckis, USA.
Catwoman (2004), Pitof, USA.
Chappie (2015), Neill Blomkamp, USA.
Charlie's Angels (2000), McG, USA/Germany.
Chi-Raq (2015), Spike Lee, USA.
Chronicles of Narnia: The Lion, the Witch, and the Wardrobe, The (2005), Andrew
    Adamson, USA.
Cleopatra Jones (1973), Jack Starrett, USA.
Coffy (1973), Jack Hill, USA.

Colombiana (2011), Olivier Megaton, France/USA/UK.

Creed (2015), Ryan Coogler, USA.

Crimson Tide (1995), Tony Scott, USA.

Crouching Tiger, Hidden Dragon (2000), Ang Lee, China, Taiwan/Hong Kong/USA.

Crying Fist (*Jumeoki unda*, 2005), Ryoo Seung-wan, South Korea.

CZ12 (aka *Chinese Zodiac*, aka *Armour of God III: Chinese Zodiac*, 2012), Jackie Chan, Hong Kong/PRC.

Da 5 Bloods (2020), Spike Lee, USA.

Dabangg (*Fearless*, 2010), Abhinav Kashyap, India.

Dark Knight, The (2008), Christopher Nolan, USA/UK.

Dark Manhattan (1937), Harry L. Fraser and Ralph Cooper, USA.

Deadpool (2016), Tim Miller, USA.

Dead Presidents (1995), Albert and Allen Hughes, USA.

Deepwater Horizon (2016), Peter Berg, USA/Hong Kong/PRC.

Deewaar (*The Wall*, 1975), Yash Chopra, India.

Departed, The (2006), Martin Scorsese, USA/Hong Kong.

Derailed (*Du namja*, 2016), Lee Seong-Tae, South Korea.

Die Another Day (2002), Lee Tamahori, UK/USA.

Die Hard (1988), John McTiernan, USA.

Die Hard with a Vengeance (1995), John McTiernan, USA.

Dil Se (*From the Heart*, 1998), Mani Ratnam, India.

Dirty Dozen, The (1967), Robert Aldrich, UK/USA.

District B-13 (*Banlieue 13*, 2004), Pierre Morel, France.

District B-13: Ultimatum (*B13-Ultimatum*,(2009), Patrick Alessandrin, France.

Doctor Who (1963–1989; 2005–present), [TV Series], UK.

Don (1978) Chandra Barot, India.

Dora and the Lost City of Gold (2019), James Bobin, USA/Australia.

Dr. No (1962), Terence Young, UK.

Duelist (*Hyeongsa*, 2005), Lee Myung-se, South Korea.

Easy Money (*Snabba Cash*, 2010), Daniel Espinosa, Sweden.

Eight Hundred, The (2020), Hu Guan, China.

Elektra (2005), Rob Bowman, Switzerland/Canada/USA.

Empire Strikes Back, The (1980), Irvin Kirshner, USA.

Enter the Dragon (1973), Robert Clouse, Hong Kong/USA.

Escape from L.A. (1996), John Carpenter, USA.

Everything Everywhere All at Once (2022), Dan Kwan and Daniel Scheinert, USA.

Exit (*Eksiteu*, 2019), Lee Sang-geun, South Korea.

Expendables 2, The (2012), Simon West, USA/Germany/PRC.

Expendables, The (2010), Sylvester Stallone, USA/Bulgaria/Spain.

Extreme Job (*Geunkhan jigeop*, 2019), Lee Byeong-hyeon, South Korea.

Eyewitness (1981), Peter Yates, USA.

F9 (2021), Justin Lin, USA.

Fabricated City (*Jojakdoen dosi*, 2017), Park Kwang-hyun, South Korea.

Falcon and the Winter Soldier, The (2021), [TV series], USA.

Fast & Furious 6 (2013), Justin Lin, USA/Japan/Spain.

Fast Five (2011), Justin Lin, USA.

Fatal Beauty (1987), Tom Holland, USA/Japan.

Fate of the Furious, The (2017), F. Gary Gray, USA/PRC/Japan.

First Blood (1982), Ted Kotcheff, USA.

Fifth Element, The (1997), Luc Besson, France/UK.

Forbidden Kingdom, The (2008), Rob Minkoff, USA/PRC.

Foreigner, The (2017), Martin Campbell, PRC/USA.

Fort Apache (1948), John Ford, USA.

Fort Apache, The Bronx (1981), Daniel Petrie, USA.

Foxy Brown (1974), Jack Hill, USA.

Friday Foster (1975), Arthur Marks, USA.

Fruitvale Station (2013), Ryan Coogler, USA.

Full Metal Jacket (1987), Stanley Kubrick, UK/USA.

Furious 7 (2015), James Wan, USA/PRC/Japan.

Galaxy Quest (1999), Dean Parisot, US.

Game of Thrones (2011–2019), [TV series], USA.

Garlands at the Foot of the Mountain (*Gao shan xia de hua huan*, 1984), Xie Jin, PRC.

Ghostbusters (1984), Ivan Reitman, USA.

Ghostbusters (2016), Paul Feig, USA/Australia.

Ghosts of Mars (2001), John Carpenter, USA.

G.I. Jane (1997), Ridley Scott, USA/UK.

Glass (2019), M. Night Shyamalan, USA/China.

Glory (1989), Edward Zwick, USA.

GoldenEye (1995), Martin Campbell, UK/USA.

Gorillas in the Mist (1988), Michael Apted, USA.

Gulaab Gang (*The Pink Gang*, 2014), Soumik Sen, India.

Hang 'Em High (1968), Ted Post, USA.

Harry Potter and the Deathly Hallows: Part 1 (2010), David Yates, UK/USA.

Harry Potter and the Deathly Hallows: Part 2 (2011), David Yates, UK/USA.

Harry Potter and the Sorcerer's Stone (aka *Philosophers Stone*, 2001), Chris Columbus, UK/USA.

Heat, The (2013), Paul Feig, USA.

Heroic Negro Soldiers of the World War (1919), William S. Smith, USA.

Hitman's Bodyguard, The (2017), Patrick Hughes, USA/Hong Kong/Bulgaria.

Hitman's Wife's Bodyguard, The (2021), Patrick Hughes, UK/USA/Sweden.

Holes (2003), Andrew Davis, USA.

Host, The (*Gwoemul*, 2006), Bong Joon-ho, South Korea.

Hunger Games: Mockingjay—Part 1 (2014), Francis Lawrence, USA/Canada/France.

Hunger Games: Mockingjay—Part 2 (2015), Frances Lawrence, USA/Germany/Canada.

Hurricane Express, The (1932), Armand Schaeffer and J.P. McGowan, USA.

Hurricane, The (1999), Norman Jewison, USA.

Hurt Locker, The (2008), Kathryn Bigelow, USA.

I Am Not Your Negro (2016), Raoul Peck, France/USA/Belgium.

Incredibles 2, The (2018), Brad Bird, USA.

Incredibles, The (2004), Brad Bird, USA.

Independence Day (1996), Roland Emmerich, USA.

Indiana Jones and the Kingdom of the Crystal Skull (2008), Steven Spielberg, USA.

Indiana Jones and the Last Crusade (1989), Steven Spielberg, USA.

Indiana Jones and the Temple of Doom (1984), Steven Spielberg, USA.

Indiana Jones and the Dial of Destiny (2023), James Mangold, USA.

In Too Deep (1999), Michael Rymer, USA.

IO (2019), Jonathan Helpert, USA.

Iris (2001), Richard Eyre, UK/USA.

I, Robot (2004), Alex Proyas, USA/Germany.

Iron Man (2008), Jon Favreau, USA/Canada.

Iron Man 3 (2013), Shane Black, USA.

Jackie Brown (1997), Quentin Tarantino, USA.

Jane the Virgin (2014–2019), [TV series], USA.

John Wick (2014), Chad Stahelski, USA/UK/PRC.

John Wick: Chapter 3—Parabellum (2019), Chad Stahelski, USA.

JSA: Joint Security Area (*Gondonggeonygbi guyeok*, 2000), Park Chan-wook, South Korea.

Juana la Virgen (2002), [TV series], Venezuela.

Jurassic Park (1993), Steven Spielberg, USA.

Kahaani (*Story*, 2012), Sujoy Ghosh, India.

Karate Kid, The (1984), John G. Avildsen, USA.

Karate Kid, The (2010), Harald Zwart, USA/PRC.

Kate (2021), Cedric Nicolas-Troyan, USA.

Kingsman: The Secret Service (2014), Matthew Vaughn, UK/USA.

Kiss of the Dragon (*Le Baiser mortel du dragon*, 2001), Chris Nahon, France/USA.

Kong: Skull Island (2017), Jordan Vogt-Roberts, USA/PRC.

Kung Fu Hustle (*Kung Fu*, 2004), Stephen Chow, Hong Kong/China.

Kung Fu vs. Yoga (*Lao shu la gui*, 1979), Chan Chuen, Hong Kong.

Kung Fu Yoga (*Gong fu yu jia*, 2017), Stanley Tong, PRC/India/Hong Kong.

Lady Vengeance (*Chinjeolhan Geumja-ssi*, 2005), Park Chan-wook, South Korea.

Last Metro, The (*Le dernier métro*, 1980), François Truffaut, France.

Lila & Eve (2015), Charles Stone III, USA.

Little Caesar (1931), Merlyn LeRoy, USA.

Logan (2017), James Mangold, USA.

Lola (1961), Jacques Demy, France/Italy.

Long Kiss Goodnight, The (1996), Renny Harlin, USA.

Lost (2004–2010), [TV series], USA.

Lost Bullet (*Balle Perdue*), (2020), Guillaume Pierret, France.

Love the Hard Way (2001), Peter Sehr, Germany/USA.

Lucy (2014), Luc Besson, France/Germany/Taiwan.

L Word, The (2004–2009), [TV Series], USA/Canada.

Machete (2010), Ethan Maniquis and Robert Rodriguez, USA.

Machete Kills (2013), Robert Rodriguez, USA/Russia.

Mafia (2012), Ryan Combs, USA.

Man and a Woman, A (*Un Homme et Une Femme*, 1966), Claude Lelouch, France.

Manchurian Candidate, The (2004), Jonathan Demme, USA.

Man of Steel (2013), Zack Snyder, USA/UK.

Man Who Knew Too Much, The (1956), Alfred Hitchcock, USA.

Malcolm X (1992), Spike Lee, USA/Japan.

Mariachi, El (1992), Robert Rodriguez, Mexico/USA.

Marrying the Mafia (*Gamunui yeonggwang*, 2002), Jeong Heung-sun, South Korea.

Mars Attacks! (1996), Tim Burton, USA.

Matrix, The (1999), Lana and Lilly Wachowski, USA/Australia.

Mea Culpa (2014), Fred Cavayé, France/Belgium/USA.

Mighty Morphin Power Rangers (1993–1996), [TV program], USA/Japan.

Milk (2008), Gus Van Sant, USA.

Miracle at St. Anna (2008), Spike Lee, Italy/USA.

Mirageman (2007), Ernesto Díaz Espinoza, Chile.

Miss Bala (2011), Gerardo Naranjo, Mexico.

Miss Bala (2019), Catherine Hardwicke, Mexico/USA.

Mission: Impossible—Fallout (2018), Christopher McQuarrie, USA/PRC/France.
Mission Impossible—Ghost Protocol (2011), Brad Bird, USA.
Mission Impossible—Rogue Nation (2015), Christopher McQuarrie, USA/PRC.
Mission Kashmir (2000), Vidhu Vinod Chopra, India.
Mississippi Masala (1991), Mira Nair, USA/UK.
Miss Peregrine's Home for Peculiar Children (2016), Tim Burton, USA/UK/Belgium.
Mulan (1998), Tony Bancroft and Barry Cook, USA.
Mulan (2020), Niki Caro, USA.
Myth, The (*San wa*, 2005), Stanley Tong, Hong Kong/PRC.
My Wife Is a Gangster (*Jopok manura*, 2001), Jo Jin-kyu, South Korea.
Namiya (*Jie you za huo dian*, 2017), Han Jie, PRC/Hong Kong.
Narc (2002), Joe Carnahan, Germany/Canada/USA.
Negro Soldier, The (1944), Stuart Heisler, USA.
Nest, The (*Nid de guêpes*, 2002), Florent-Emilio Siri, France.
New Jack City (1991), Mario Van Peebles, USA.
Night Catches Us (2010), Tanya Hamilton, USA.
Notebook, The (2004), Nick Cassavetes, USA.
No Time to Die (2021), Cary Joji Fukunaga, UK/USA.
Old Guard, The (2020), Gina Prince-Bythewood, USA.
On Her Majesty's Secret Service (1969), Peter R. Hunt, UK.
Operation Mekong (*Gong he xing dong*, 2016), Dante Lam, PRC/Hong Kong.
Operation Red Sea (*Hong hai xing dong*, 2018), Dante Lam, PRC/Morocco/Hong Kong.
Original Gangstas (1996), Larry Cohen, USA.
OSS 117: Lost in Rio (*OSS 177—Rio ne répond plus*, 2009), Michel Hazanavicius, France.
Outside the Wire (2021), Mikael Håfström, Hungary/USA.
Paddington (2014), Paul King, UK/France/USA.
Paddington 2 (2017), Paul King, UK/France/USA.
Pandora (2016), Park Jung-woo, South Korea.
Parasite (2019), Bong Joon-ho, South Korea.
Planet of the Apes (1968), Franklin J. Schaffner, USA.
Point Blank (*A Bout Portant*, 2010), Fred Cavayé, France.
Point Blank (2019), Joe Lynch, France/USA.
Police Story (*Ging chaat goo si*, 1985), Jackie Chan, Hong Kong.
Police Story 2 (*Ging chaat goo si juk jaap*, 1988), Jackie Chan, Hong Kong.
Polite Society (2023), Nida Manzoor, UK.
Poms (2019), Zara Hayes, UK/USA.
Posse (1993), Mario van Peebles, UK/USA/Netherlands.
Prey, The (*La Proie*, 2011), Eric Valette, France.
Prometheus (2012), Ridley Scott, UK/USA.
Proud Mary (2018), Babak Najafi, USA.
Public Enemy, The (1931), William A. Wellman, USA.
Pulp Fiction (1994), Quentin Tarantino, USA.
Quantum of Solace (2008), Marc Forster, UK/USA.
Raazi (2018), Meghna Gulzar, India.
Raging Fire (2021), Benny Chan, Hong Kong/China.
Raid 2, The (2014), Gareth Evans, Indonesia/USA.
RAID Special Unit (*RAID Dingue*, 2016), Dany Boon, France/Belgium.
Raiders of the Lost Ark (1981), Steven Spielberg, USA.
Rampart (2011), Oren Moverman, USA.

Ratatouille (2007), Brad Bird, Jan Pinkava, USA.
RED (2010), Robert Schwentke, USA/China.
RED 2 (2013), Dean Parisot, USA/France/Canada.
Red Sparrow (2018), Francis Lawrence, USA.
Red Tails (2012), Anthony Hemingway, USA.
Regeneration, The (1915), Raoul Walsh, USA.
Reina del Sur, La (2011, 2019, 2022–2023), [TV series], Mexico/USA/Spain.
Resident Evil (2002), Paul W.S. Anderson, UK/Germany.
Robocop (1987), Paul Verhoeven, USA.
Roja (*The Rose*, 1992), Mani Ratnam, India.
RRR (*Rise Roar Revolt*, 2022), S.S. Rajamouli, India.
Rumble in the Bronx (*Hung fan kui*, 1995), Stanley Tong, Hong Kong.
Rush Hour (1998), Brett Ratner, USA.
Rush Hour 2 (2001), Brett Ratner, Hong Kong/USA.
Rush Hour 3 (2007), Brett Ratner, USA/Germany.
Saloum (2021), Jean Luc Herbulot, Senegal/France.
Salt (2010), Phillip Noyce, USA.
Samouraï, Le (1967), Jean-Pierre Melville, France/Italy.
Scarface (1932), Howard Hawks, USA.
Scream Blacula Scream (1973), Bob Kelljan, USA.
Seberg (2019), Benedict Andrews, UK, USA.
Secret Reunion (*Uihyeongje*, 2010), Jang Hoon, South Korea.
Set It Off (1996), F. Gary Gray, USA.
Shaft (1971), Gordon Parks, USA.
Shaft (2000), John Singleton, Germany/USA.
Shaft (2019), Tim Story, USA.
Shaolin Temple (1982), Hsin-Yen Chang, Hong Kong/China.
Sheba, Baby (1975), William Girdler, USA.
She Hate Me (2004), Spike Lee, USA.
Shiri (*Swiri*, 1999), Kang Je-gyu, South Korea.
Silmido (2003), Kang Woo-suk, South Korea.
Sin City (2005), Frank Miller and Robert Rodriguez, USA.
Singham (2011), Rohit Shetty, India.
Skyfall (2012), Sam Mendes, UK/USA/Turkey.
Sleepless Night (*Nuit Blanche*, 2011), Frédéric Jardin, France/Belgium/Luxemburg.
Slow Burn (aka *Wilder*,(2000), Rodney Gibbons, Canada.
Son of Rambow (2012), Garth Jennings, UK.
Spider-Man 2 (2004), Sam Raimi, USA.
Spider-Man: Far from Home (2019), Jon Watts, USA.
Spider-Man: Homecoming (2017), Jon Watts, USA.
Spook Who Sat by the Door, The (1973), Ivan Dixon, USA.
Spy Kids (2001), Robert Rodriguez, USA.
Star Wars (1977), George Lucas, USA.
Star Trek: Deep Space Nine (1993–1999), [TV series], USA.
State Affairs (*Une affaire d'état*, 2009), Eric Valette, France.
Strangers in Good Company (1990), Cynthia Scott, Canada.
Subway (1985), Luc Besson, France.
Sucker Free City (2004), Spike Lee, USA.
Sunset Boulevard (1950), Billy Wilder, USA.
Superman (1978), Richard Donner, USA/UK/Canada.

Sweet Sweetback's Baadasssss Song (1971), Melvin Van Peebles, USA.
Synchronic (2019), Justin Benson and Aaron Moorhead, USA.
Tae Guk Gi: The Brotherhood of War (*Taegeukgi hwinallimyeo*,(2004), Kang Je-gyu, South Korea.
Taken (2008), Pierre Morel, UK/France/USA.
Taken 2 (2012), Olivier Megaton, France/USA/Turkey.
Taken 3 (2015), Olivier Megaton, France/Spain/USA.
Tango and Cash (1989), Andrey Konchalovskiy and Albert Magnoli, USA.
Taxi (1998), Gérard Pirès, France.
Taxi 2 (2000), Gérard Krawczyk, France.
Taxi 3 (2003), Gérard Krawczyk, France.
Taxi 4 (2007), Gérard Krawczyk, France.
Taxi 5 (2018), Franck Gastambide, France.
Terminator 2: Judgment Day (1991), James Cameron, USA.
Terminator, The (1984), James Cameron, UK/USA.
Theeviravaathi (*The Terrorist*, 1998), Santosh Sivan, India.
Thor (2011), Kenneth Branagh, USA.
Thor: The Dark World (2013), Alan Taylor, USA.
Tiger Woman, The (1944), Wallace Grissell and Spencer Gordon Bennet, USA.
Top Gun (1986), Tony Scott, USA.
Tower, The (*Tawo*, 2012), Kim Ji-hoon, South Korea.
Training Day (2001), Antoine Fuqua, USA.
Train to Busan (*Busanhaeng*, 2016), Yeon Sang-ho, South Korea.
Transformers (2007), Michael Bay, USA.
Transformers: Age of Extinction (2014), Michael Bay, USA/PRC/Hong Kong.
Transporter, The (2002), Louis Leterrier and Corey Yuen, France/USA.
Transporter 2, The (2005), Louis Leterrier, France/Germany/USA.
Transporter 3 (2008), Olivier Megaton, France/USA/UK.
Transporter Refueled, The (2015), Camille Delamarre, France/China.
Tron Legacy (2010), Joseph Kosinski, USA.
Trooper of Troop K, The (1917), Harry A. Grant, USA.
True Lies (1994), James Cameron, USA.
Tunnel (*Teoneol*, 2016), Kim Seong-hun, South Korea.
Typhoon (*Taepung*, 2005), Kwak Kyung-taek, South Korea.
Umrao Jaan (1981), Muzaffar Ali, India.
Unbreakable (2000), M. Night Shyamalan, USA.
Undersea Kingdom (1936), B. Reeves Eason and Joseph Kane, USA.
Underworld (1937), Oscar Micheaux, USA.
Underworld (2003), Len Wiseman, USA/UK/Germany.
Unleashed (*Danny the Dog*, 2005), Louis Leterrier, UK/France/USA.
Valerian and the City of a Thousand Planets (*Valérian et la Cité des mille planètes*, 2017), Luc Besson, France/PRC/Belgium.
Vanguard (*Ji xian feng*, 2020), Stanley Tong, PRC.
Vantage Point (2008), Pete Travis, USA/Mexico.
Veteran (*Beterang*, 2015), Ryoo Seung-wan, South Korea.
Waiting to Exhale (1995), Forest Whitaker, USA.
Wandering Earth, The (*Liu lang di qiu*, 2019), Frant Guo, PRC.
Warriors, The (1979), Walter Hill, USA.
Welcome to Dongmakgol (*Welkeom tu dongmakgol*, 2005), Park Kwang-hyun, South Korea.

Welcome to the Sticks (*Bienvenue chez les Ch'tis*, 2008), Dany Boon, France.
Whale Rider (2002), Niki Caro, New Zealand/Germany.
Whatever Happened to Baby Jane? (1962), Robert Aldrich, USA.
When Harry Met Sally (1989), Rob Reiner, USA.
Who Am I? (*Ngo si seoi*, 1998), Benny Chan and Jackie Chan, Hong Kong.
Who Killed Captain Alex? (2010), Nabwana I.G.G., Uganda.
Within Our Gates (1920), Oscar Micheaux, USA.
Wolf's Call, The (*Le chant du loup*, 2019), Antonin Baudry, France.
Wolf Warrior 2 (*Zhan lang II*, 2017), Wu Jing, PRC.
Woman King, The (2022), Gina Prince-Bythewood, USA.
Women in Cages (1971), Gerardo de Leon, Philippines/USA.
Wonder Woman (2017), Patty Jenkins, USA/PRC.
Working Girl (1988), Mike Nichols, USA.
X-Men (2000), Bryan Singer, USA.
xXx: Return of Xander Cage (2017), D.J. Caruso, PRC/Canada/USA.
Year of Living Dangerously, The (1982), Peter Weir, Australia/USA.
Youth (*Fang hua*, 2017), Feng Xiaogang, PRC.
Zanjeer (*Shackles*, 1973), Prakash Mehra, India.
Zazie in the Metro (*Zazie dans le métro*, 1960), Louis Malle, France.
Ziegfeld Follies (1945), Lemuel Ayers, Roy Del Ruth, Robert Lewis, Vincente Minnelli, and
    George Sidney, USA.
Zombieland: Double Tap (2019), Ruben Fleisher, USA.
Zookeeper's Wife, The (2017), USA/UK/Czech Republic.

Index